1998
Happy Birthday, dear friend.

Love, Bob

Sleeping *with* Literary Lions

The Booklover's Guide to Bed and Breakfasts

Peggy van Hulsteyn

FULCRUM PUBLISHING
GOLDEN, COLORADO

Book design by Bill Spahr

Book cover, inset photograph: The Archbishop's Mansion, San Francisco, California. Photo by Russell Abraham.
Book cover, background photograph: Courtesy of The Huntington Library, San Marino, California (digitally altered using Adobe PhotoShop).
Photograph page 19: The original Carter House, Eureka, California. Photo by Ridgeway.
Photograph page 48: The Archbishop's Mansion, San Francisco, California. Photo by Russell Abraham.
Photograph page 205: The birthplace of Walt Whitman. Photo by Knute Mohlman, courtesy of Walt Whitman Birthplace Association.

Library of Congress Cataloging-in-Publication Data

Van Hulsteyn, Peggy.
    Sleeping with literary lions : the booklover's guide to bed and
breakfasts / Peggy van Hulsteyn.
        p.   cm.
    Includes bibliographical references and index.
    ISBN 1-55591-319-9 (pbk.)
        1. Bed and breakfast accommodations—United States—Guidebooks.
    2. Literary landmarks—United States—Guidebooks.   I. Title.
    TX907.2.V36 1997
    647.9473'03—dc21   97-25068
                                                                                   CIP

Printed in Canada

0 9 8 7 6 5 4 3 2 1

Fulcrum Publishing
350 Indiana Street, Suite 350
Golden, Colorado 80401-5093
(800) 992-2908 • (303) 277-1623

To David, my favorite character, literary or otherwise

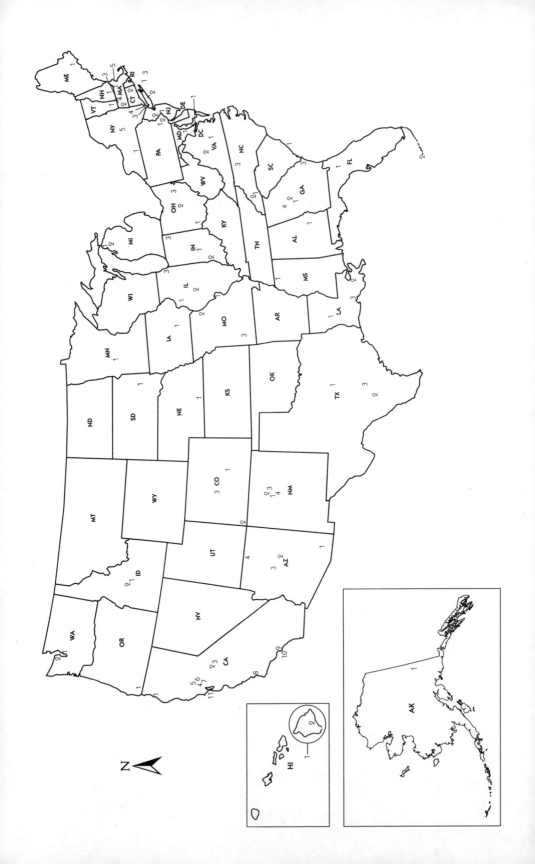

LIST OF LITERARY SITES

Alabama
1 The Oaks: Home of B. T. Washington

Alaska and the Yukon
1 J. London in Klondike; J. London's Cabin

Arizona
1 Tombstone National Historic Site
2 Z. Grey Museum
3 Z. Grey in Sedona
4 J. W. Powell Memorial Museum

California
1 B. Harte in Arcata
2 Angels Camp; Jumping Frog Jubilee
3 M. Twain Cabin
4 Sharpsteen Museum
5 R. L. Stevenson State Park
6 Silverado Museum
7 J. London State Historic Park
8 J. Steinbeck Library; National Steinbeck Center; Steinbeck Festival; Steinbeck House
9 Huntington Library
10 W. Rogers State Historic Park
11 Literary San Francisco

Colorado
1 H. H. Jackson: Colorado Springs Pioneer Museum
2 W. Cather: Mesa Verde National Park
3 O. Wilde and W. Stegner in Leadville

Connecticut
1 H. B. Stowe Center; M. Twain's House
2 E. O'Neill: Monte Cristo Cottage
3 E. O'Neill Theater Center

District of Columbia
1 Literary Washington, D.C.; Folger Shakespeare Library; Library of Congress

Florida
1 M. K. Rawlings and Dudley Farm
2 E. Hemingway Home and Museum

Georgia
1 S. Lanier Cottage
2 I. D. Russell Library: F. O'Connor Collection
3 F. O'Connor Childhood Home
4 Atlanta-Fulton Public Library: M. Mitchell Display Collection; Atlanta Historical Society Library and Archives; Emory University: R. W. Woodruff Library; M. Mitchell House

Hawaii
1 J. London's Island of Hawaii
2 M. Twain at Hawaii Volcanoes National Park

Idaho
1 E. Hemingway's Sun Valley
2 Hemingway House; Hemingway's Grave; Hemingway Memorial

Illinois
1 C. Sandburg State Historic Site
2 E. L. Masters: Oak Hill Cemetery
3 E. Hemingway Foundation

Indiana
1 J. W. Riley Museum Home
2 Lilly Library
3 Limberlost North: G. S. Porter State Historic Site

Iowa
1 M. Twain: Keokuk Public Library; Keokuk River Museum

Louisiana
1 K. Chopin's Cloutierville; K. Chopin Home and Bayou Folk Museum
2 Literary New Orleans
3 Longfellow Evengeline State Park

Maine
1 E. St. Vincent Millay: Whitehall Inn

Maryland
1 Westminster Hall and Burying Ground: E. A. Poe Monument and Grave

Massachusetts
1 Emerson House; Orchard House: Home of Alcotts; Wayside: Home of N. Hawthorne
2 The Mount: Home of E. Wharton
3 Arrowhead: Home of H. Melville
4 E. Dickinson Homestead
5 House of Seven Gables

Michigan
1 E. Hemingway in N. Michigan
2 Hemingway's Boarding House; Petoskey Public Library; Park Garden Cafe; Stafford's Perry Hotel; Hemingway Festival; Little Traverse Historical Society; Petoskey Chamber of Commerce

Minnesota
1 S. Lewis Foundation

Mississippi
1 Rowan Oak: Home of W. Faulkner

Missouri
1 E. Field House and Toy Museum
2 M. Twain Boyhood Home and Museum
3 L. I. Wilder–R. W. Lane Museum and Home

Nebraska
1 W. Cather State Historic Site; W. Cather Memorial Foundation

New Hampshire
1 R. Frost Farm

New Jersey
1 J. F. Cooper House
2 F. S. Fitzgerald's Princeton

New Mexico
1 W. Cather's New Mexico; L. Wallace in Santa Fe; Palace of Governors
2 D. H. Lawrence Ranch
3 La Fonda Hotel
4 E. Pyle Branch Library

New York
1 Elmira College: M. Twain Study and Exhibit
2 W. Whitman Birthplace
3 Literary New York City
4 Sunnyside: Home of W. Irving
5 Fenimore House Museum

North Carolina
1 C. Sandburg Home
2 T. Wolfe Memorial
3 Greensboro Historical Museum

Ohio
1 H. B. Stowe House
2 J. Thurber House
3 National Road/Z. Grey Museum

Oregon
1 Oregon Shakespeare Festival

Pennsylvania
1 Green Hills Farm: Home of P. S. Buck
2 E. A. Poe National Historic Site

South Carolina
1 Fort Sumter National Monument

South Dakota
1 L. I. Wilder Memorial Society

Texas
1 Baylor University: A. Browning Library
2 O. Henry's House: Lone Star Brewery
3 University of Texas: H. Ransom Center; O. Henry Museum

Vermont
1 Naulakha: Home of R. Kipling

Virginia
1 Poe Museum
2 University of Virginia: E. A. Poe's Room

Washington
1 Chief Seattle's Seattle
2 Squamish Museum

CONTENTS

Colorado   50

Connecticut   61

District of Columbia   68

Florida   75

Georgia   83

Hawaii   95

Idaho 99

Illinois 104

Indiana 112

Iowa 121

Louisiana 124

Maine 134

Maryland 137

Massachusetts 141

Michigan   157

Minnesota   164

Mississippi   166

Missouri   169

Nebraska   176

New Hampshire   180

New Jersey   183

New Mexico   188

New York 201

North Carolina 216

Ohio 223

Oregon 229

Pennsylvania 235

South Carolina 240

South Dakota 243

Texas 245

Vermont 256

Virginia 257

Washington 260

Wisconsin 262

ACKNOWLEDGMENTS

My deepest thanks, as always, go to my husband, David, who served as my editor, my driver, and my friend.

To Ruth Holmes, my special assistant, and Gene Delgado, literary sleuth and computer whiz.

To Carolyn Stupin and Lynn Cline, researchers extraordinaire.

To P. J. Liebson for her excellent editing.

To Richard Mahler, Sarah Lovett, Jeanie Fleming, and Reina Attias for their sage advice.

To Susan Hazen-Hammond, David Donoho, and John Sherman, good photographers and good friends.

To Valerie Brooker, my favorite librarian.

To Layne Vickers Smith for her organizational skills.

To Vanity, Bosque, and Apache, my three literary cats who help warm up my laser printer and my heart.

To Carmel Huestis, my kind and understanding editor at Fulcrum.

Thanks to Sara Hanson for thoughtful editing, to Bill Spahr for a beautiful cover, to the marketing department for their promotional know-how, and to all the folks at Fulcrum for making this an enjoyable experience.

INTRODUCTION

All literature is gossip.

—Truman Capote

Medicine is my lawful wife. Literature is my mistress.

—Anton Chekhov

A book ought to be an icepick to break up the frozen sea within us.

—Franz Kafka

A writer lives in awe of words for they can be cruel or kind, and they can change their meanings right in front of you. They pick up flavors and odors like butter in a refrigerator.

—John Steinbeck

The tools I need for my work are paper, tobacco, food and a little whiskey.

—William Faulkner

The difference between the right word and the almost right word is the difference between lightning and the lightning bug.

—Mark Twain

Writing this book, *Sleeping with Literary Lions: The Booklover's Guide to Bed and Breakfasts*, has been an incredible learning experience, a journey I have entitled "my own private graduate school." The literary sites I visited were magical and transported me to the pages of the novels I was writing about. For example:

- At Laura Ingalls Wilder's house in Mansfield, Missouri, I was once again an excited nine year old listening to the thrilling tales of *Little House on the Prairie.*
- In Salinas, California, I found myself playing in my mind scenes from *East of Eden* and reading aloud Steinbeck's description of the land, which remains unchanged.
- In Rome City, Indiana, I was reacquainted with one of my childhood heroines, Gene Stratton Porter, an early feminist and naturalist.
- In Calaveras County, California, I laughed at the wit and wisdom of Mark Twain while watching the town of Angels Camp get ready for the annual Calaveras Jumping Frog Contest.
- In Cross Creek, Florida, I read Marjorie Rawlings's scrapbook and learned that like all writers, including me, she felt "doomed to write."
- In Petoskey, Michigan, I interviewed Ernest Hemingway's 97-year-old former girlfriend and heard firsthand of their tennis matches, fishing expeditions, and parties.
- At The Huntington Library in Pasadena, California, I got goose bumps looking at the earliest editions of Chaucer's *Canterbury Tales* and Shakespeare's *Hamlet.*
- At the University of Texas in Austin, I read Dashiell Hammett's love letters to Lillian Hellman.
- At Indiana University in Bloomington, I read Sylvia Plath's surprisingly cheerful childhood letters.

- In Ashland, Oregon, I was enchanted to see an entire community revolve around William Shakespeare.

Many of the bed and breakfasts proved to be wonderful literary excursions as well. I have tried to augment your literary experience by finding interesting bookish (or at least conveniently located) B&Bs in each locale. Literary sites and bed and breakfasts prove to be a natural marriage that combines comfort with intellectual pursuits. For example, in Taos, New Mexico, I stayed at Hacienda del Sol, a B&B where D. H. Lawrence once lived.

- On the big island of Hawaii I read letters from the innkeeper's grandfather announcing the arrival of Jack London. Charmian and Jack London were honored guests for many weeks at this historic inn, the Shipman House.
- In South Bend, Indiana, fulfilling every bibliophile's dream, I stayed in The Book Inn, a B&B that is also a bookstore.
- In Camden, Maine, I take you to Whitehall Inn, where a young and very nervous Edna St. Vincent Millay once recited her now-famous poem, *Renascence.* Today in this historic B&B you'll find a parlor dedicated to Millay, along with an unpublished manuscript and a reproduction of the first draft of *Renascence.*
- In Lenox, Massachusetts, I introduce you to the Brook Farm Inn, named after the famous literary commune that attracted many of your literary favorites, including Nathaniel Hawthorne. This enchanting B&B is located below the very hill that Edith Wharton used as a setting for the final pages of *Ethan Frome.* If you are there on a weekend, you'll be treated to a formal poetry reading.
- In Sudbury, Massachusetts, I describe Longfellow's Wayside Inn, where the poet wrote *Tales of a Wayside Inn.* Today you can still stay at this historic hostelry.
- In Concord, Massachusetts, I bring you the Hawthorne Inn, a house on the property that once belonged to Ralph Waldo Emerson and Nathaniel Hawthorne. You can stay in the Emerson Room, the Alcott Room, or the Sleepy Hollow Room and walk around the property, which has an orchard planted by Bronson Alcott, the father of Louisa May Alcott.
- I put you in bibliophile heaven by showing you The Sylvia Beach Hotel in Newport, Oregon, where every room is named after an author, and the Canterbury Booksellers Coffeehouse, bookstore, and B&B in Madison, Wisconsin.

I was astonished and delighted at what I learned. Our American literary heritage is rich and varied, and the number of literary sites in this country staggers the imagination. Another happy consequence of writing this book has been coming away incredibly encouraged by the enormous interest in literature in this country at a time when people keep proclaiming that reading is a thing of the past. I assure you it is not! In spite of the Internet, movies, and videos, people are reading more than ever before. When I was researching this book, I had the pleasure of watching long lines of teenagers waiting to purchase tickets for the Oregon Shakespeare Festival. At the Steinbeck Foundation in Salinas, California, I watched a movie about the author's life with a class of local fourth graders. Afterward, we discussed *The Red Pony,* the book they were reading in school.

I also loved the whimsical and quirky facts I uncovered in this project. Did you know, for instance, that the world's largest collection of Robert Browning's work is housed in Waco, Texas? Or that short story writer O. Henry's house is sitting smack dab inside the middle of a brewery in San Antonio? Or that the descendants of Papa's beloved six-toed cats are holding center stage and posing as Hemingway heroes at the Hemingway House in Key West, Florida?

Now, with all this elation goes some caveats. Let me, first of all, tell you how I chose the authors you will read about. It is a dubious honor to be an author in my book because the criterion is that they be dead. The reason for this is that I didn't want readers peering into Tony Hillerman's window or camping out in Anne Tyler's or William Styron's front yards. Writing is a private pursuit and should not be interrupted!

This book is subjective and has my favorite authors in it. You will note that Mark Twain appears seven times and Edgar Allan Poe shows up five times. I tried to put in as many women writers as I could find. I hope to introduce you to some authors you may not know and tell you new facts about those you do. I learned something new on every page and I want you to share my excitement.

Like all authors, I have been confined by words, time, and choices. This book could have gone on forever (sometimes it seemed as if it did), but deadlines are deadlines!

I tried to pick actual literary sites you could visit, so you could see the chair Emily Dickinson sat in, the room in which James Whitcomb Riley wrote *Little Orphan Annie,* and the town that inspired Sinclair Lewis to write *Main Street.* If I couldn't find a site, then I tried to find a related location that conveyed an incredible sense of place.

Finding B&Bs and deciding which to profile sometimes took the wisdom of Solomon. Excellent organizations, such as the Professional Association of Innkeepers International (PAII) and statewide bed and breakfast associations, were an enormous help. Whenever possible, I tried to use members of PAII and the statewide B&B associations because to be a member of these groups, the inn has to pass rigid inspections.

But sometimes geography is destiny. Places like New Orleans and Savannah have an embarrassment of riches, whereas a state like Alabama has surprisingly few. In Nebraska, you have to drive at least an hour after visiting Willa Cather's house in Red Cloud to The Kirschke House in Grand Island. In Waco, Texas, on the other hand, you can finish your last cup of coffee at the Judge Baylor House, then walk a mere two minutes to the Armstrong-Browning Museum.

Some of you may be surprised at how pricey particular inns have become; I have tried to include affordable ones whenever I could find them. I found many, but bed and breakfasts are often no longer the old Mom-and-Pop enterprises they used to be. Many can be quite sophisticated.

As much as I enjoyed researching this book, it was a monumental and sometimes daunting task. Literary sites usually stay put, but many of them go through massive renovations. Bed and breakfasts sometimes change owners at an alarming rate and have been known to go out of business. This is where you, the reader, come in. If in reading this book you find things that need updating, please notify me c/o Fulcrum Publishing, 350 Indiana Street, Suite 350, Golden, Colorado, 80401. I count on and appreciate your input. If you go to a place that delights you, let me know; on the other hand, if you find a spot, either a literary site or a B&B, that doesn't meet your expectations, let me know that too. But try to be kind, for, like Blanche Dubois, I depend on the kindness of strangers.

My main hope is that you will enjoy your visit to these literary sites and nearby bed and breakfasts. I want you to be as inspired as I was to read or reread the American classics with a new appreciation of how the authors' lives shaped their work. Remember, you are a crucial part of the literary process. After all, reading and learning about writers' lives is the ultimate interactive sport, for, as Ralph Waldo Emerson put it, "'Tis the good reader that makes the good book."

ALABAMA

The Oaks: Home of Booker T. Washington

1212 Old Montgomery Road
Tuskegee Institute, AL
36088-1914
(334) 727-3200

Who: Willie C. Madison, superintendent

When: 9:00 A.M.–5:00 P.M. every day except Christmas, Thanksgiving, and New Year's Day

How Much: Free; large groups should make reservations to tour the Oaks

Senior Citizen Discount: NA

Wheelchair Access: Yes

Directions: Contact the superintendent's office

What and Where: The Oaks, the Queen Anne–style Tuskegee home of Booker T. Washington, stands as a symbol of what this impressive man accomplished. Born a slave, Washington became one of the preeminent black leaders of his time. His great life work really began when, at age 25, he went to Tuskegee, Alabama, to create the Tuskegee Normal and Industrial Institute. When this visionary arrived in Tuskegee in 1881, the school was practically nonexistent—no funds, one dilapidated building, and no equipment. But the optimistic, practical, and energetic Washington didn't let these dismal prospects stand in his way. Rather, on rainy days when the roof leaked, the pragmatic Washington and his students used umbrellas in class to keep themselves dry. Under his tutelage, Tuskegee Normal and Industrial Institute grew to become a respected school of over 15,000 students, with a faculty of nearly 200, occupying 100 well-equipped buildings.

One of the more imposing buildings on campus is the Oaks, Washington's house, built, appropriately, of Institute bricks made by students and faculty. Here's what Washington said about his home: "The actual sight of a first class house that a Negro has built is ten times more potent than pages of discussion about a house that he ought to build, or perhaps could build."

Today the restored house is much the same as when the Washington family lived there. Visitors can see Booker T. Washington's certificate from Hampton Institute, along with a photo of the graduating class of 1875. Among his many awards are honorary degrees from Dartmouth and Harvard. There are photographs of two U.S. presidents and the king and queen of Denmark.

The home reflects the many interests of the Washington family. There is the piano that his daughter, Portia, an accomplished pianist, played for many dinner guests. Sons Booker Jr. and Ernest Davidson Washington enjoyed the stereopticon, dominoes, and table games, all of which are displayed in the parlor. In the den on the second floor are examples of functional furniture built by Institute students.

In his autobiography, *Up from Slavery,* Washington laments that he was able to spend only an average of six months out of each year in his beloved Tuskegee home. He relates what a special and refreshing time this was and how, after the evening meal, the family would often read or take turns telling stories and, "to me there is nothing on earth equal to that." He also unhappily admits that "the thing in my life which brings me the keenest regret is that my work keeps me for so much of the time away from my family, where of all places in the world, I delight to be."

When gravely ill in New York City, Washington insisted upon dying at the Oaks. He clung to life until he reached Tuskegee, and there, on November 14, 1915, he died. Three days later he was buried in the campus cemetery.

The Crenshaw Guest House B&B

371 North College Street
Auburn, AL 36830
(334) 821-1131

Bed and breakfasts are few and far between in the great state of Alabama, which makes us appreciate the Crenshaw Guest House all the more. One of its nice features is that the prices remain stable throughout the year, except during Auburn football weekends, which should come as no surprise. But as popular and colorful as Tiger weekends may be, there are other equally compelling reasons to visit this city. One of the main ones is the Booker T. Washington connection, which is important from literary, scientific, and cultural points of view.

The historic district is a beautiful setting for the inn, which is strategically located in the Old Main and Church Street area. The Wedgewood blue Victorian home is set among giant oak and pecan trees on a site once inhabited by Creek Indians. Built by Auburn University professor Bolling Hall Crenshaw, this graceful century-old structure features bay windows and delicate gingerbread trim. Rich architectural detail, tasteful period decor, and comfortable antiques (not an oxymoron) create a restful, pleasant atmosphere for guests.

Main-building bedrooms are on the first floor, each with a private bath and telephone. Referred to as the Bay, Oak, and Walnut Rooms, all three boast carved mantles and gleaming brass and porcelain and clearly establish a feeling of Old South hospitality. The carriage house, next to the garden, is a cozy recent addition. Here guest units, comfortable for as many as three people, are fitted with modern kitchenettes—perfect for visits of a longer term. All guests are provided with a complimentary breakfast basket and may help themselves to a variety of beverages and snacks around the clock.

Rates: $48–$75
Credit Cards Accepted: Visa, MC, AMEX
Number of Guest Rooms: 6
Number of Baths: 6
Wheelchair Access: No

Pets: No
Children: Yes
Smoking: No
Senior Citizen Discount: Yes
Directions: See brochure

ALASKA
and the Yukon

Jack London in the Klondike

The bold, strong tales of the struggle for survival in the Yukon and Alaska made Jack London's reputation; to this day, they still create most of our images of the colorful but brutal Alaska gold rush days of 1897–1898. In *Jack London: A Biography*, Richard O'Connor describes the author's first glimpse of Dawson: "As they swung around a final bend in the river, ... they came upon an unforgettable sight, Dawson, in the first flush of its boom. ... At the foot of the mountain was Dawson City, mostly a tent town spreading over the surrounding hills and swampy Flats. ... It took Jack only a few days to learn the depressing truth about a boom town; you had to be well-heeled to live in one."

The boomtown fascinated the young London with its spirited saloons and dance halls and the thousands of drifters, "shuffling aimlessly along, as directionless as himself."

London quickly realized that the real nuggets of gold were the true life stories of the old-timers and the hopeful newcomers who had come to the Klondike to win a treasure that would transform their lives. He traded in his pan of gold for a notebook and took notes about every impression, every sight and sound of this strange new world.

Jack London's Cabin

Dawson
(403) 993-6317

Who: The Klondike Visitor Association, (403) 933-5575, operates the museum and is open all year. You can also call the Yukon Visitor Centre at (403) 993-5566.

When: Open 10:00 A.M. to 6:00 P.M. from May 19 to September 21, but contact the Yukon Visitor Centre to confirm.

How Much: Free

Senior Citizen Discount: NA

Directions: Ask at the Yukon Visitor Centre at Front and King Streets.

What and Where: The history of the cabin is worthy of a Jack London short story. According to Ken Spotswood in *The History of Jack London's Cabin:*

> *The story of how the original cabin was discovered in the bush 120 kilometers from Dawson City—and how it was authenticated—is a masterful piece of detective work by Yukon author Dick North. ... The tale begins in September 1964, when North was visiting Rudy and Yvonne Burian at their homestead on the Stewart River. They were discussing London's story "To Build a Fire" in which a prospector froze to death on the*

left fork of Henderson Creek. The Burians maintained that London's story was based on a real life tragedy that had occurred on the Stewart River before London set foot in the Klondike in 1897. It was their opinion that London simply changed the location to an area that he was familiar with. When North quizzed them further, the couple said they had heard that London had, in fact lived and worked on the left fork. This first clue sent North to the mining recorder's office in Dawson where he scanned the record books. And there it was … London's claim read "Number 54 above discovery ascending the left fork of Henderson Creek."

Inspired by this discovery, North spent the next few years hunting for London's lost cabin. After much sleuthing, dog sledding in snow-blanketed wilderness, and frustrating wrong turns, North and his party found the cabin. There they found "a signature, written about five feet off the ground, on a log in the centre of the rear wall of the cabin which reads 'Jack London, miner author, Jan. 27, 1898.'"

Many visitors find that the most exciting part of their trip to the Jack London Cabin is meeting Dick North, who set up the museum and is currently the curator. North, who gives a daily interpretive talk about Jack London, set up a photo exhibit documenting London's arduous journey through the Klondike. The informative exhibit is located in the nearby museum.

Haeckel Hill Bed & Breakfast

1501 Birch Street
Whitehorse, Yukon, Canada Y1A 3XI
(403) 633-5625
(403) 633-5630 Fax
E-mail: bear@yknet.yk.ca
Website: http://www.yukonweb.wis.net/tourism/haeckel.htmld

Jack London is so identified with the Yukon Territory that you will feel his adventuresome spirit all around you. It was in the rugged Klondike that London found his "spiritual and writing home." As New Orleans inspired Tennessee Williams, the Klondike encouraged Jack London's muse.

In *Jack London: A Biography* by Richard O'Connor, it is reported that London said, "It was in the Klondike I found myself. There nobody talks. Everybody thinks. You get your true perspective. I got mine."

Although London, like the other explorers, had come in search of gold, the greatest gem he found in the Northwest Territory was wonderful material for his most famous books. One winter in the Yukon lasted him for years of writing. It provided him with the inspiration for *The Call of the Wild, White*

Fang, "To Build a Fire," and many other books and short stories.

A delightful and scenic spot to relive Jack London's adventures is the Haeckel Hill Bed & Breakfast. Innkeeper Leo Boon relates that Jack London came through Whitehorse and ran the White Horse Rapids on the Yukon Belle, the boat he and three companions built at Lindeman Lake. As in an excerpt from one of London's adventure stories, the men hurried over Lake LaBerge before the winter freeze.

At Haeckel Hill, you can hear the call of the wild and perhaps see the son of the wolf, but you can also enjoy clean, comfortable rooms with queen-size beds or nestle in a chair next to the sitting room fireplace. Begin your morning with a delicious breakfast while overlooking magnificent Mount McIntyre.

This is an outdoor person's paradise. Hike the trails that begin just out of the yard of the Haeckel Hill B&B. Enjoy a day hike that will give you a magnificent view of Whitehorse and Lake Laberge or stroll through the forest following the ski trails of Mount McIntyre. For a less strenuous activity, find a cozy spot on the sun deck or the garden patio and curl up with a copy of London's *Children of the Frost* or *Smoke Bellow* or just sit and enjoy the beauty of this hill, Thay Ta'w, whose name means eagles nest in Southern Tutchone.

Rates: $65–$95
Credit Cards Accepted: Visa, MC
Number of Guest Rooms: 4
Number of Baths: 4
Wheelchair Access: No

Pets: Yes
Children: Yes
Smoking: No
Senior Citizen Discount: No
Directions: See brochure

ARIZONA

---- ≡◊≡ ----

Tombstone National Historic Site

Tombstone Chamber of Commerce
104 South Fourth Street
P.O. Box 995
Tombstone, AZ 85638
(520) 457-9317
(520) 457-2458 Fax

Who: Barbara Johnson, director of the visitor center

When: Visitor center hours are 9:00 A.M.–4:00 P.M. Monday through Saturday, 9:00 A.M.–2:00 P.M. Sunday. Closed Thanksgiving and Christmas.

How Much: Admission charge for various sites

Senior Citizen Discount: No

Wheelchair Access: Limited

Directions: From I-10, take Exit 304 (Benson exit); drive south on Highway 80 for 23 miles to the town of Tombstone. Turn right onto South Fourth Street for one block. The visitor center is in the Old Bank Building at the intersection of Fourth and Allen.

What and Where: Tombstone, the city known as the "Town Too Tough to Die," is a genuine western town, the type of place where you expect the marshal (played by John Wayne) to come riding up in pursuit of a bunch of no-good varmints. Historically, the West's wildest mining town owes its beginning to Ed Schieffelin, who prospected the nearby hills in 1877. Friends warned him that all he would ever find would be his own tombstone. But instead of an Apache bullet he found silver—ledges of it. The town was originally dubbed Goose Flats, but the miners, with their tongues firmly planted in their cheeks, changed the name to Tombstone to commemorate the grim prophecy.

Tombstone quickly became the epitome of the lawless western town, the stuff that great cowboy songs and legends are made of. Tombstone was not an inappropriate name, for murders were part of everyday life, as were robberies, brothels, and saloons. Enter the most nefarious outlaws of the West, namely the Clanton gang. Shortly after, Wyatt Earp rode in, the original good guy in a white hat, and eventually Tombstone became the setting for the famous Earp-Clanton gunfight at the O.K. Corral.

What does any of this have to do with literature? In addition to the scores of movies made about the famous gunfight, romanticized versions of the town's history abound in print. Foremost is a nonfiction book by Walter Buns with the insidiously clever title, *Tombstone.* This is not to be confused with the novel *Tombstone* by Clarence Budington Kelland. Some of my other favorite titles are *I Married Wyatt Earp,* by

Glenn G. Boyer, *Doc Holliday*, by John Myers, *The Earp Brothers of Tombstone*, by Frank Waters, and *The Earps Talk*, by Alford E. Turner.

There is plenty of activity in today's Tombstone, much of it hokey, all of it fun if you are a western devotee. Many of the original buildings have been restored and the town itself is a Registered National Historic Landmark. You can visit the old Bird Cage Theatre at Sixth and Allen, which bills itself as "one of the West's most famous landmarks." This is the very spot where Wyatt Earp met his third wife, Sadie Marcus. The Tombstone Courthouse State Historical Monument and Museum (Toughnut and Third Streets) has exhibits about Wyatt Earp and other old-timers. The Tombstone Historama (Fourth and Fremont Streets) offers an electronic di-

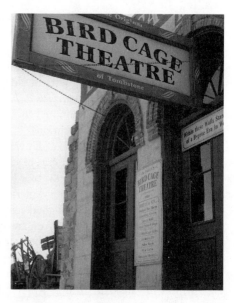

The Birdcage Theater in Tombstone, Arizona. Photo by David Donoho.

orama and film about Tombstone. The O.K. Corral (Allen at Fourth Street) features a restored stagecoach office where the big Earp-Clanton shoot-out took place.

There are amusing and unusual epitaphs at Boothill Graveyard (northwest of US 80) on the graves of some well-known outlaws. A few are fanciful, many are funny, and most are made up. Each month a major event is staged that depicts the western heritage from Wyatt Earp to Nellie Cashman (Angel of the Desert) to Vigilante Days; and every Sunday Old West shoot-outs are staged in the O.K. Corral on Allen Street.

Casa de San Pedro B&B

8933 South Yell Lane
Hereford, AZ 85615-9250
(520) 366-1300
(520) 366-0701 Fax
E-mail: 102157.1117@compuserve.com

The southeastern corner of Arizona is a magical place. First of all, the birding is magnificent, featuring a total of 335 species of birds, including the Green Kingfisher and Yellow-billed Cuckoo. Second, there is the majesty of the Chiricahua National Monument with its incredible rock formations and splendid solitude. Hiking there is almost a religious experience! Tombstone, as you have

read, is a rootin-tootin day of fun. So where to stay to enjoy all this diversity?

The Casa de San Pedro is in the perfect central location for all these activities, as well as Ramsey Canyon (for more birding) and Bisbee. The inn is such an attractive destination in its own right that you might just want to stay put. Casa de San Pedro is a Territorial-style inn that is built around a courtyard and fountain. It is beautifully decorated and furnished with hand-carved furniture from Mexico. Every effort has been made to capture the delightful atmosphere of the old inns of Spain and Mexico. Like guests in olden times, you will be treated as *invitados bein mirado* (highly regarded and honored guests) and lavished with personal attention.

Taking you from your work-a-day week and transporting you to another era are your congenial hosts, Chuck and Judy Wetzel. The Wetzels, escapees from corporate America, are delightful innkeepers with a good sense of humor. They will see to it that you are as enchanted with their inn and southeastern Arizona as they are.

There are ten courtyard guest rooms, each with a private bath. You can pretend

you are in your very own villa as you sit in a covered patio while enjoying the fountain and plants and watching the birds flitting about.

In the morning, the smell of fragrant teas and coffees will lure you to the dining room, where you will be served a full gourmet breakfast. Before or after your day's activities, you may want to hang out in the Great Room to plan your next hike or update your lifelist. On the other hand, you may just want to relax with a good book or marvel at the lovely purple mountains.

Anyone needing to pick up a gift should browse around the gift shop, stocked with nature-related items. Those who are on an extended trip will be pleased to know that laundry facilities are at their disposal. All in all, Casa de San Pedro is a delightful respite from twentieth-century life.

Rates: $95
Credit Cards Accepted: Visa, MC
Number of Guest Rooms: 10
Number of Baths: 10
Wheelchair Access: Yes

Pets: No
Children: Yes
Smoking: No
Senior Citizen Discount: No
Directions: See brochure

San Pedro B&B

3123 Thistle Road
P.O. Box 885
Sierra Vista, AZ 85636-0885
(520) 458-6412

Bob and Sue Walker are such congenial hosts at San Pedro B&B (not to be confused with Casa de San Pedro B&B) that you might have trouble breaking away to go visit Tombstone. At least that's the happy problem my husband, David, and I had on our recent visit here. Sitting around the beautiful pool on a lovely spring day while watching the large variety of backyard birds, it was difficult to consider doing anything more arduous than asking for another cup of coffee. Besides entertaining us with their nice sense of humor and informing us of the many activities in

the area, the Walkers fed us an enormous breakfast of cranberry juice, fruit, yogurt, an egg casserole with cheese sauce, biscuits and gravy and coffee cake. The meal was so gigantic, in fact, that we took the delicious coffee cake and fruit with us on our afternoon hike to the magnificent Chiricahua Mountains. Sue was raised in a family of twelve and told us she doesn't know how to cook for just two people!

The night before, David and I settled into the private, romantic *casita,* a spacious room with a private entrance, a private bath and shower, a microwave, a refrigerator, and a sitting area. The common room next to the casita includes a television, a pool table, and a small library. We were more interested in taking advantage of the relaxing hot tub and soaking under the magical Arizona starlight. The San Pedro B&B rooms are appointed with Southwestern furnishings and collectibles. One upstairs room in the main house offers a hall bath and an entrance onto the sun deck, where those famous Arizona sunsets can be viewed.

Don't just rush in and out of here, but plan to spend some time at this secluded two-story ranch house, which is located in a peaceful river valley within the San Pedro Riparian National Conservation Area. Its five-acre grounds, divided by the historic San Pedro River and surrounded by rolling hills and towering cottonwood trees, make it a perfect setting for bird-watching, hiking, or sightseeing. You can take in the unique ambience of the San Pedro Riparian National Conservation Area without leaving the B&B grounds. The riparian area is home to roughly half the number of known species in North America.

We whiled away a very pleasant hour or so on the Walkers' swing overlooking the San Pedro River. Besides visiting the historic and literary town of Tombstone, if you're a birder you could spend some time at the prime birding locations of Ramsey Canyon Preserve and Madera Canyon. Other activities include hiking the Coronado National Memorial, Chiricahua National Monument, or the Cochise Stronghold. Or you could explore the historic locations of Bisbee, Tombstone, and Fort Huachuca and the ghost towns of Gleeson, Charleston, and Pearce. Better yet, you could stay put and read some of the books you bought about Tombstone and the shoot-em-up days of the Old West.

Rates: $70–$80
Credit Cards Accepted: None
Number of Guest Rooms: 2
Number of Baths: 2
Wheelchair Access: No

Pets: No
Children: If older than 12
Smoking: No
Senior Citizen Discount: No
Directions: See brochure

Zane Grey Museum and Counseller Art

408 West Main Street, Suite 8
Payson, AZ 85541
(520) 474-6243

Who: Mel Counseller

When: 10:00 A.M.–4:00 P.M. Monday through Saturday, 11:00 A.M.–2:00 P.M. Sunday

How Much: Free, but donations gladly accepted

Senior Citizen Discount: NA

Wheelchair Access: Yes

Directions: From Highway 87 in Payson (Beeline Highway), turn west onto Main Street. The museum is on the right side of the street on the second floor of the Payson Visitors' Center.

What and Where: Skeptics who say that no one discusses or preserves the classics any more obviously do not know Mel and Beth Counseller. After the devastating Dude Fire of

1990 destroyed the Zane Grey Cabin, the Counsellers, former curators of the cabin, opened their own museum and dedicated it to "the preservation of Zane Grey lore."

As Beth Counsellor explained to me, "With or without a cabin the legacy continues. The essence and the impact of Zane Grey did not dissipate along with the ashes of his cabin. One has only to visit the locations of his Rim Country stories or of his cabin, or study the history of the area to see these things reflected with color and emotion in his novels. Grey was inspired by the environment he described in his eloquent nonfiction book *Tales of Lonely Trails,* which contains his Rim adventures of 1918 and 1919. In *Tales,* he lovingly refers to 'the heights and depths, its wild, lonely ruggedness, the color and beauty of Arizona land.'"

The Zane Grey Museum and Counseller Art is a combination of the life and writings of Zane Grey and the western art of Mel Counseller. The pervasive influence of Zane Grey on various aspects of Americana is well represented at the museum. Copies of each of his 84 books are available. The Counsellers have lovingly preserved mementos and photographs from the Zane Grey Cabin. Videos on the history of the cabin and Grey's colorful life are constantly running. In addition, visitors can see photographs depicting the life of Grey as a novelist and outdoorsman, as well as Grey letters, movie posters, and books.

The Counsellers, who are natural storytellers, will be delighted to share their knowledge and anecdotes of Zane Grey. If you want more information than a visit to the museum affords, the Counsellers also serve as guest speakers on cowboy art and conduct classes for Elderhostel, an adult education program. If you are a Western aficionado, save some time to look at Mel's art, which depicts cowboy scenes and western landscapes and wildlife. If you're just looking for local flavor, this is the place: Mel is considered one of Payson's most colorful personalities.

Kohl's Ranch Lodge

Highway 260
Payson, AZ 85541
(520) 478-4211

Too bad Zane Grey didn't have the pleasure of staying at Kohl's Ranch Lodge. He waxed rhapsodic enough about this gorgeous Tonto Rim area—no telling to what heights he may have been inspired had he come back from a long trail ride to the famous western hospitality of this fine hostelry. The Tonto Creek flows right past the inn and on its way through the largest ponderosa pine forest in the world. It's a toss-up as to who made who famous: the Mogollon Rim country, Zane Grey, or vice versa. Suffice it to say that, given the setting, it should come as no surprise that the atmosphere of Kohl's is casual and friendly. Guests enjoy swimming, fishing, and exploring forest trails on foot or horseback.

Nearby attractions are the Tonto Natural Bridge, the Tonto Fish Hatchery, and the Zane Grey Cabin site. Each season brings its own delights: summer contrasts of heat and shade; fall color with a snap to the air; winter, warming fireplaces and an occasional snow; and excellent spring fishing.

Main lodge rooms are contemporary western-style, many with fireplaces, and all are air-conditioned and with TV and telephones for those who (even if it's not their "druthers") must keep in touch with the outside world. Comfortable two-room cabins offering the same amenities are private getaways located directly next to the stream. The expansive lobby is a natural gathering place for visitors, and surely I need not specify the purpose of the Saloon and Dance Hall! The Roundup Room accommodates up to 50 people and is perfect for meetings or private parties. Another plus is the rustic Ranch House, with its own bar and small kitchen— just right for receptions and larger group activities. Of course, all this fresh air and natural beauty make anyone as aware of a growling stomach as of a well-turned bit of poetry or prose, so it is fitting that the Zane Grey Dining Room is one of the most popular areas within the confines of the lodge. This room's replica Old West hotel front is a great reminder of days gone by, and the stunning views outside the windows recall all there is to be enjoyed and savored today.

Rates: $75–$205
Credit Cards Accepted: Visa, MC, AMEX, Discover
Number of Guest Rooms: 46
Number of Baths: 46
Wheelchair Access: No

Pets: Inquire about Kohl's Kennels
Children: Yes
Smoking: Yes
Senior Citizen Discount: 20%
Directions: See brochure

Zane Grey in Sedona

Zane Grey spent the first part of his life obsessed with a desire to go West. When he finally accomplished this goal, he found his true spiritual home and spent the rest of his life writing about this fascinating region. The former dentist from New York City via Zanesville, Ohio, read and absorbed the history of the West. He then visited the area and assimilated its mystique. His writings allowed millions of readers to share his delight. One of the many western towns that he used as a setting for a novel was Sedona, Arizona, the magnificent red-rock country that has a unique sense of time and place. In the 1924 novel, *Call of the Canyon,* one of Zane Grey's characters says, "I never understood anything of the meaning of nature until I lived under these looming stone walls and whispering pines." The character is lovingly describing Oak Creek Canyon, which many chauvinistic Sedona residents think is far more spectacular than the Grand Canyon, 110 miles to the north. Oak Creek is known for its magnificently colored red, yellow, and white cliffs. The canyon is considered an oasis because of the cooling effects of the pine, cypress, juniper, cottonwood, and aspen trees. Along with the magnificent red-rock country to the south and the ghost town of Jerome nearby, Sedona truly evokes the world of Zane Grey.

Creekside Inn at Sedona

P.O. Box 2161
99 Copper Cliffs Drive
Sedona, AZ 86339
(520) 282-4992; (520) 282-0241; (800) 390-8621
(520) 282-0091 Fax

Now here's a memorable and comfortable experience. Creekside Inn at Sedona is snugly tucked on the very banks of beautiful Oak Creek, right in the heart of red-rock country. The mature sycamore trees of this area are renowned, and they line the creek and outline the flower-filled gardens of this pleasant, secluded place. All five guest rooms have

The Creekside Inn, Sedona, Arizona. Photo courtesy of the Creekside Inn.

a private bath, a patio, and contain an array of Victorian antiques that will warm a collector's heart. One of the three suites features a fireplace (not all guests come to Sedona in the summer), and the others overlook either the creek or the gardens. A deluxe breakfast is served, as are complimentary social-hour treats in the afternoon.

The living room is spacious and contains a book nook, and the wide veranda invites you to listen to the breeze and the gentle sounds of the running creek. For those of us with pent-up muscles that need relaxing (probably everyone in the reading audience), a rejuvenating Swedish massage is available from an on-call therapist. Strollers will love this location, which, though not exactly on the Gray Line route (but *is* on our Zane Grey adventure), is easy walking distance to some of the area's finest restaurants and shops.

Rates: $125–$275
Credit Cards Accepted: Visa, MC, AMEX
Number of Guest Rooms: 5
Number of Baths: 5
Wheelchair Access: Yes

Pets: No
Children: If older than 10
Smoking: No
Senior Citizen Discount: No
Directions: See brochure

The Lodge at Sedona

125 Kallof Place
Sedona, AZ 86336
(520) 204-1942; (800) 619-4467
(520) 204-2128 Fax

"Coffee Pot" is a double entendre for the people in Sedona. The high desert air makes one so appreciative of that first steaming hot brew early in the morning, to be sure. But it is the sight of the looming red sandstone formation known as Coffee Pot that provides a lifetime of inspiration. This landmark, visible from almost any point in the Sedona vicinity, is a highlight for guests approaching the Lodge at Sedona. One glimpse of this gorgeous two-and-a-half-acre setting lets the newcomer know that a treat is in store. The elegant yet rustic appointments in the native stone building include, among other things, a library and morning porch just perfect for that morning klatsch. The sumptuous breakfast that goes with the coffee

inspired one guest to write in the guest book, "The food was absolutely incredible, and we could hardly wait for breakfast each day." There are also afternoon appetizers to be enjoyed while gazing at the red rocks surrounding Sedona. Clearly, innkeepers Barb and Mark Dinunzio enjoy catering to their guests.

Thirteen guest rooms are beautifully decorated in themes that range from the Old West of the Lariat Room, with saloon doors and western memorabilia, to the Paisley Room, a name that speaks for itself, which includes a Jacuzzi, king-size bed, and a redwood deck set amid the pines. The natural beauty of Sedona has inspired artists and writers for over a century; now it is your turn to try to express the grandeur you feel—even if it is no more than a carefully worded post-card. A stay at the lodge will certainly be a good start. Don't discount that great cup of java and the fantastic view!

Rates: $120–$225
Credit Cards Accepted: Visa, MC, Discover
Number of Guest Rooms: 13
Number of Baths: 13
Wheelchair Access: One room

Pets: No
Children: By prior arrangement
Smoking: No
Senior Citizen Discount: No
Directions: See brochure

The Inn on Oak Creek

556 Highway 179
Sedona, AZ 86336
(520) 282-7896; (800) 499-7896
(520) 282-0696 Fax

When you enter The Inn on Oak Creek, you step into the setting of a Zane Grey novel. The "looming stone walls and whispering pines" from *Call of the Canyon* are right in your backyard. The new Inn on Oak Creek, once a well-known art gallery, takes full advantage of the natural splendor of its surroundings. Owners-innkeepers Pam Harrison and Rick Morris are justifiably proud of their achievement in creating such remarkable ambience within this special setting. Panels of glass provide open views of the rock escarpments and rushing waters of the creek. There's even a duck pond, for those of you who prefer nature in a more tranquil mode.

All eleven rooms have gas fireplaces, TVs with VCRs, phones, and private baths with whirlpool tubs and marble appointments. Most rooms have private decks with water views, and each room is individually decorated. What kinds of dreams might you have in the Trading Post Room, with its col-lection of Indian baskets, pots, and jewelry? Those lucky fishermen and women staying in The Angler's Retreat will enjoy rustic furniture and fly-fishing collectibles; they are encouraged to wet a line right off the private deck overlooking the creek.

After a hearty breakfast and just one final admiring view, guests choose among a variety of activities to fill the rest of the day in this unique area located between Sedona and Flagstaff. Just minutes away in the shops of Tlaquepaque are many of the Southwest's best art galleries. That photo opportunity you seek may occur on a hike, horseback ride, jeep tour, or in the gondola of a hot-air balloon. If you would prefer to spend the day relaxing, The Inn on Oak Creek has a private park on the creek that is tailor-made for guests like you. Complimentary refreshments and hors d'oeuvres will greet you upon your return. Zane Grey characters never had it so good!

Rates: $130–$205
Credit Cards Accepted: Visa, MC, AMEX, Discover
Number of Guest Rooms: 11
Number of Baths: 13
Wheelchair Access: Yes

Pets: No
Children: If older than 10
Smoking: No
Senior Citizen Discount: No
Directions: See brochure

The Grand Canyon

There are two beautifully written nonfiction books describing the exploration of the Grand Canyon. *The Exploration of the Colorado River of the West and Its Tributaries,* by John Wesley Powell, details the colorful adventurer's expedition through the Grand Canyon. This perilous scientific journey of 900 miles, which took ten months to complete, was filled with life-and-death adventures and was definitely not for the faint of heart:

We are three quarters of a mile in the depths of the earth, and the great river shrinks into insignificance, as it dashes its angry waves against the walls and cliffs, that rise to the world above; the waves are but puny ripples, and we but pigmies, running up and down the sands, or lost among the boulders.

In his spare but elegant book *Beyond the Hundredth Meridian,* Pulitzer Prize–winning author Wallace Stegner recounts the successes and frustrations of geologist John Wesley Powell. Here is a brief example of the hazardous journey:

In what they reported as exceedingly high water the boat party ran the Marble and Grand Canyons from Lee's Ferry to the mouth of Kanab Wash. By the time they arrived there on September 7, they were badly battered and pretty shaky. ... The water now was higher than it had been then; all the rapids, though they held fewer dangers from rocks, were of an unbelievable violence.

The Inn at 410 B&B

410 North Leroux Street
Flagstaff, AZ 86001
(520) 774-0088; (800) 774-2088
(520) 774-6354 Fax

My first contact with Sally and Howard Krueger, hosts at The Inn at 410, included an invitation to "unplug from the TV, phone, fax machine and the Internet." Now this may not appeal to everyone, but after a particularly frenetic week, it was just what I wanted. And this is the place to do it! Not only is this B&B an excellent example of casual country living, but the entire Flagstaff area is noted for wilderness beauty and Native American habitats dating back a thousand years, not to mention the unparalleled views of the Grand Canyon. *The Wall Street Journal* and *The New York Times* are relegated to a backseat position in no time flat. The open spaces of this part of America are indeed worthy of the song and story they have inspired: Wallace Stegner, Frank Waters, Zane Grey, Willa Cather, and John Wesley Powell are but a few of the writers who have attempted to put on paper the incomparable sense of place provided by this mountainous high-desert landscape. Distances become insignificant here; at a remove of 78 miles, The Inn at 410 is still one of the closest places to stay for a visit to Grand Canyon National Park.

The inn itself dates to 1894, although numerous additions and renovations have enabled it to keep pace with the times. It has been a private residence, a set of apartments, and a fraternity house in its previous incarnations; now it seems quite satisfied to accommodate guests in its four suites and five rooms. All have private baths, several have private entrances, fireplaces, and whirlpool tubs (all modern amenities need not be abandoned along with the fax machine!). A garden patio, gazebo, and sweeping front porch encourage home-baked cookie munching and pleasant conversation. The rooms themselves convey relaxation through their individual themes, which include Santa Fe, rustic cowboy, flowers (overlooking the patio garden, of course), Victorian teatime, arts and crafts, and vibrant country charm in shades of blue and bursts of yellow sunflowers.

The full-service breakfasts provide guests with the necessary fortification to face the great outdoors beyond the window pane. And come the end of the day, before opening that new book you just bought on Arizona, you may be in time for one of the readings held at the inn and sponsored by the Literacy

The Inn at 410 B&B, Flagstaff, Arizona. Photo courtesy of The Inn at 410 B&B.

Volunteers. One recent evening featured a program entitled "An Evening with Robert Burns" that included bagpipes and fiddles. Now what website can compete with that?!

Rates: $100–$155
Credit Cards Accepted: Visa, MC
Number of Guest Rooms: 9
Number of Baths: 9
Wheelchair Access: Yes

Pets: No
Children: Yes
Smoking: No
Senior Citizen Discount: No
Directions: See brochure

John Wesley Powell Memorial Museum and Visitor Information Center

6 North Powell Boulevard
Page, AZ 86040
(520) 645-9496
(520) 645-3412 Fax
E-mail: museum@page-lakepowell.com

Who: Julia P. Betz, executive director

When: Open 8:00 A.M.–6:00 P.M. Monday through Saturday and 10:00 A.M.–6:00 P.M. Sunday, April through October; 9:00 A.M.–5:00 P.M. Monday through Saturday, February 17 through March, and November through December 15; Closed from mid-December through mid-February

How Much: $1 per person for bus groups; free otherwise

Senior Citizen Discount: No

Wheelchair Access: Yes

Directions: The museum is located in the center of Page at the corner of Lake Powell

Boulevard. and North Navajo Drive (a Circle K and a Pizza Hut are directly across from it). For cars and normal-sized vehicles, park on the North Navajo side of the building. Large vehicles and those towing trailers or boats should park across the street behind the Pizza Hut.

What and Where: John Wesley Powell was the explorer who provided the first permanent record of discovery as a result of two hazardous trips down the Green and Colorado Rivers in 1869 and 1871.

The John Wesley Powell Museum, Page, Arizona. Photo courtesy of the John Wesley Powell Memorial Museum.

In *The Exploration of the Colorado River and Its Canyons,* Powell described how Glen Canyon came by its name: It was "… a curious ensemble of wonderful features—carved walls, royal arches, glens, alcove gulches, mounds and monuments. … We decide to call it Glen Canyon."

Glen Canyon vanished a quarter of a century ago when a hydroelectric dam was built on the Colorado River near Page, Arizona. The resulting man-made lake, known as Lake Powell, was named in tribute to the colorful one-armed Civil War veteran who led a survey party of nine on the first scientific expedition through the area.

The museum is funded by a nonprofit historical society started in 1969 by Page citizens to preserve and promote the story of Major Powell and the exploration of the Colorado River, the history of Page, and an appreciation for the Native American cultures of the area.

The museum has an extensive publication list, and if you want to know more about Powell, you might want to purchase *Into the Unknown: Major Powell's River Journey,* by Peter Anderson, *John Wesley Powell and the Great Surveys of the American West,* by Ann Gaines, *John Wesley Powell: The Story Behind the Scenery,* by Dan Murphy, or perhaps an audio- or videocassette such as *John Wesley Powell River Journals: The Grand Canyon of the Colorado* audiocassette or *New Beginnings: The Story of Page, Arizona.*

Visitors who purchase tickets from the museum for Lake Powell smooth-water float trips, scenic air flights, and jeep tours will be helping the museum. The various tour companies make a donation to the Powell Museum from each ticket sold. There is no extra charge to the visitor.

A Room with a View/A Bed and Breakfast Homestay

P.O. Box 2155
Page, AZ 86040
(520) 645-5763

When Ken and Marilee Earlywine named their bed and breakfast homestay, A Room with a View, they certainly were not exaggerating! Their newly constructed Southwest-style home has a spacious feeling accented by vaulted ceilings, skylights, and plenty of pristine windows to view the great sunrises, sunsets, and Vermillion Cliffs. Decks allow you to feel a part of that great outdoors that we so often read about but rarely get to experience. This home is located at the edge of town, near walking trails, with lake and canyon views that can best be described as "spectacular." It's easy to feel the adventurous spirit of John Wesley Powell in this natural setting.

Bats flit through the evening air, cottontails and jackrabbits abound, and early morning risers often catch glimpses of foraging owls and coyotes. The two guest bedrooms are named the Rose Room and the Southwest Room. Both contain sitting areas and have private baths. The Earlywines will share with you their thorough knowledge of the area and provide rib-sticking breakfasts that will carry you into whatever glorious experiences may lie ahead. Between the magnificent sunrise and marvellous sunset, something else wonderful is bound to happen.

A recent city ordinance requires guests to telephone the B&B upon their arrival in Page so that they can be escorted to the homestay by the owners. I don't know of any other community this side of Cameroons that has such an esoteric law. They will then be escorted to the homestay—by the owners, not the police!

Rates: $65–$79
Credit Cards Accepted: None
Number of Guest Rooms: 2
Number of Baths: 2
Wheelchair Access: No

Pets: No
Children: Yes
Smoking: No
Senior Citizen Discount: No
Directions: Page City ordinance requires guests to call ahead to be escorted to the homestay B&B.

CALIFORNIA

···· ☰✦☰ ····

Bret Harte in Arcata

Bret Harte was one of the few easterners who found himself in California by accident rather than by choice. When he arrived from New York in 1853 at the age of seventeen, it was to join his widowed mother and her new husband. Instead of participating in the gold-mining craze that afflicted so many of the local citizenry, he occupied himself with tutoring jobs and submitting maudlin poems to a weekly publication known as the *Golden Era*. Eventually he settled in the town of Union to be near his sister, Margaret. While there, he continued to support himself with various writing jobs, including a stint as assistant editor on the *Northern Californian*.

His genteel and aloof manner did little to endear him to the rough-and-tumble populace, which resented what it considered to be his superior ways. Things came to a head following the brutal February 1858 massacre of a band of coastal Indians by a vigilante group from nearby Eureka. Harte was so revolted by the savagery of this unwarranted attack that he wrote a scathing editorial denouncing it as butchery. This infuriated the paper's readers, many of whom considered his defense of the Indians something akin to treason. Understandably, Bret Harte's sojourn in Union came to an abrupt halt a few days later.

Today Union, since renamed Arcata, is a much more refined community. Arcata can boast that it is the home of Humboldt State University and currently is the only city in the country where the Green Party dominates the city council. The chamber of commerce provides maps if you feel like taking a self-guided tour of its historical spots. It is surprising that the one-time residence of F. B. Harte at 927 J Street still exists, but it is unfortunate that it is not open to the public.

Carter House Victorians

301 L Street
Eureka, CA 95501
(707) 444-8062; (800) 404-1390
(707) 444-8067 Fax

Mark Carter, the innkeeper at the elegant Carter House Victorians, is definitely in the right business. He loves keeping his Victorians in pristine shape and pampering his guests. Our lovely room was on the top floor of the hotel (there are two other Victorian B&Bs across the street). There was an inviting Jacuzzi in our room, which felt great on my aching back. The room was beautifully appointed, from the comfortable king-size bed to the VCR to the terrycloth bath robes in the attractive bath. The attention to detail here is perfect; nothing is overlooked. We found out later that visiting Hollywood royalty in the person of Morgan Freeman did indeed settle into this very room for the filming of the movie *Outbreak*.

Besides the good service, this is a wonderful location, situated in the heart of the redwood empire on the rugged Pacific

Northwest coast. Birders and nature lovers will enter an area of breathtaking, unspoiled natural beauty rich in rare flora and fauna.

The Carter House is located 300 miles north of San Francisco in a vast realm of primeval forest, home of the world's three tallest tree species. This pristine wilderness that calls to mind early California features secluded beaches, migrating gray whales, and stunning seascapes, not to mention the magnificent redwood forest. In addition, Humboldt County is home to the Arcata Marsh and Wildlife Sanctuary and the Humboldt Bay National Wildlife Refuge. Both these refuges and the many state and national parks within Humboldt County provide naturalists with myriad chances to immerse themselves in nature and to observe plant and animal life found only in this unique corner of the world.

The original Carter House, Eureka, California.

After roaming around Bret Harte territory in Arcata or roughing it in the wilderness, you can look forward to the gracious atmosphere of Carter House and a chance to recuperate. The Victorian mansion offers guests such amenities as in-room fireplaces, spa tubs, double-headed showers, minibars stocked with local specialty foods, televisions with VCRs, and CD players. Relax with fellow guests at the evening social hour while enjoying wine and appetizers, or take a tour of the organic gardens, where you can harvest produce for your dinner in Carter House's renowned restaurant before retiring with homebaked goodies.

Conscientious sight-seeing can work up quite an appetite. At the Carter House, food is abundant and delicious. Described by many food critics and satisfied guests as "offering the best breakfast in California," the Carter House dishes up an elegant spread of freshly squeezed orange juice followed by chunks of cantaloupe and honeydew in an orange-mint sauce, which consists of freshly diced mint leaves, Cointreau, and anise seed. Next is a hot pecan raisin bran muffin and a serving of eggs Benedict topped by hollandaise sauce that is pleasantly sharpened by the addition

of a bit of cayenne and black pepper. Be sure to leave room for the apple tart, an elegant creation of sautéed apples and almond filling encased in phyllo dough.

Next, of course, we all visited Arcata, one-time home of Bret Harte and full-time home to Humboldt College, whose library has an impressive collection of Bret Harte books. If these two activities don't interest you, you might consider a tour of the spectacular redwoods, kayaking, white-water rafting, tennis, or horseback riding. Vigorous exercise is strongly recommended for those wishing to indulge in an elegant dinner at the inn. As *Travel & Leisure* magazine puts it, "Some people come here just for the food."

I was in seventh heaven (I refrained from writing "hog heaven," you might note) at this culinary hot spot. It did, I am happy to report, live up to its reputation. We had two evenings of sterling food attended by Mark Carter, who knows his way around the table. On night one we started the meal off with baked cypress grove chèvre with nut crust, balsamic vinegar and roasted rosemary and squash cakes with creme fraiche; we moved on to a roasted pepper soup, followed by prawns sautéed in sesame, ginger, and soy and served with fresh vegetables and herbs. On night number two, we started with freshly caught Humboldt Bay oysters with asiago and fennel, moved on to a salad of freshly picked greens, and finished with a salmon steak barbecued in balsamic vinegar. Even though we were full, Mark talked us into sampling a dessert platter of strawberry shortcake, bread pudding, fruit cobbler, and three types of custard. Mark, who loves his home town of Eureka, wanted to show it to us. So we checked out some of the lively hotel bars. Then Mark showed us the rest of his properties. All the rooms are exquisite. I especially liked one of the lodgings that had an Art Deco flavor and reminded me of the setting for the PBS show about that great fictional detective, Hercule Poirot.

Rates: $95–$255
Credit Cards Accepted: Visa, MC, AMEX, Discover, Carte Blanche
Number of Guest Rooms: 19
Number of Baths: 19
Wheelchair Access: Yes

Pets: No
Children: Yes
Smoking: No
Senior Citizen Discount: No
Directions: See brochure

Angels Camp

Calaveras County Chamber of Commerce
(209) 736-4444; (800) 999-9039

Mark Twain's tall tale, "The Celebrated Jumping Frog of Calaveras County," put Angels Camp on the map. Everyone in town has a slightly different but equally colorful version about how Samuel Clemens came to write this yarn. How Clemens found his way to this tiny mining town is an interesting story in itself. It seems (or so the story goes) that the then-unknown author took a position on *The Californian,* Bret Harte's newspaper in San Francisco. Here he learned of the wealth of the Mother Lode, both in stories and in gold.

After a friend was charged with manslaughter, Clemens wrote a scathing article on the quality of police work in San Francisco. The struggling writer was advised to get out of town, and he fled for the Mother Lode in December 1864. It was a fortuitous move, for early in 1865, Mark Twain first heard the story of Jim Smiley's frog, which he transformed into his first widely popular work. The story appeared in the *New York Saturday Press* in November 1865 and was soon reprinted all over the United States and Europe. Twain achieved instant fame.

Angels Camp offers ample enjoyment for Mark Twain fans. The town is rightfully proud of its place in the author's heritage, and it shows. There are three sites you must see. First, head to the pretty Utica Park with its graceful trees and a statue of Mark Twain. This statue was donated to the town in 1954 by a film company making a movie on the life of Mark Twain that starred Frederick March.

Next, hop, skip, or jump down Highway 49 and head for the original site of Angels Camp, where Twain first heard the frog story. It's hard to miss, because there is a big bronze statue of Smiley's frog with a plaque that reads: Angels Camp, Home of the Jumping Frog, Romance, Gold and History. The locale of Mark Twain's famous story, *The Jumping Frog of Calaveras.* Frequented by Joaquin Murietta, Black Bart and other early day bandits.

The third stop is across the street at the original Angels Hotel. This is a California Registered Historical Landmark, with a marker that attests: Here Samuel Clemens first heard the yarn which was later to bring him fame as Mark Twain, author of *The Jumping Frog of Calaveras*.

Angels Camp is a fun town to poke around in, especially during the Jumping Frog Jubilee. Today it is a quiet mountain community, but you can easily imagine the liveliness of the saloons and the dance halls when gold fever possessed everyone in town. It was enjoyable to see the town decked out in its Calaveras splendor, and every storefront was painted with a picture either of a frog or Mark Twain. The hillside perspective gives a wonderful view of the town and its century-old buildings.

Twain devotees will also want to head for the town of Murphys. There in the hallway of the Murphys Hotel are photographs of Mark Twain; the ballroom is filled with still more pictures of the humorist. Twain's signature appears on the register at the front desk (along with that of Horatio Alger). My favorite piece of memorabilia, though, was a framed soliloquy where Twain discusses "being good" and decides to let "good enough" alone.

Jumping Frog Jubilee

P.O. Box 489
Angels Camp, CA 95222
(209) 736-2561

Who: Diane Bauman

When: The event starts at 11:00 A.M. on the Thursday before the third weekend in May and continues from 9:00 A.M.–11:00 P.M. on Friday, Saturday, and Sunday.

How Much: $7, $8, and $9 on Thursday, Friday, and Saturday/Sunday, respectively, for adults. Juniors 6 to 12 years old are $2 less.

Senior Citizen Discount: Free

Wheelchair Access: Yes

Directions: Call for directions

Frog jumping at Angels Camp, Calaveras County, California. Photo courtesy of Finley Holiday Films.

What and Where: A few miles from Angels Camp is "Frogtown," where the jumping contest is held. Entrants for the famous frog jump arrive from all over the world, including frog participants from Mexico, Canada, China, Britain, South Africa, and Germany. Bring your own frog or rent one at the fair. The top fifty frogs in the qualifying trials advance to the Grand Finals in the International Frog Jump for a chance at the winning title.

This colorful contest was started in May 1928 when the Angels Boosters Club developed and organized a big celebration on Angels Camp's Main Street, based on Mark Twain's story of the jumping frog of Calaveras County. An estimated 15,000 frog fans and 20 frogs turned out for the festivities. The winning frog, Pride of San Joaquin, jumped a convincing 3 feet 9 inches.

The current world-record frog jump was set in May 1986 by Rosie the Ribiter, who jumped an impressive 21 feet 5 $^3/_4$ inches, beating the previous world record by 4 $^1/_2$ inches.

Tips on Catching and Jumping a Frog
The Calaveras County Jumping Frog Jubilee judges offer the following advice for would-be frog jockeys: "When you're on the stage preparing for the jump, have a container of warm water available. Dip the frog in the water immediately before it jumps for the judges. Once your frog is placed on the starting pad he may not be touched, although you may jump up and down, shout, blow on him or do anything else to get him to jump. Almost as amusing as the unpredictable frogs are the wild antics of the jockeys as they urge their croakers on to victory with kicks, stomps, and yells."

Mark Twain Cabin—Jackass Hill
Tuolumne County Museum

P.O. Box 299
Sonora, CA 95370
(209) 532-1317

Who: Front desk

When: 10:00 A.M.–4:00 P.M. Sunday through Friday, 10:00 A.M.–3:30 P.M. Saturday

How Much: Donations welcome

Senior Citizen Discount: NA

Wheelchair Access: Yes

Directions: Call for directions

What and Where: Located on Highway 49 between Sonora and Angels Camp is the cabin on Jackass Hill where Mark Twain lived with his friends Jim Gillis and Dick Stoker. The hill was named "Jackass" in the late 1840s because of the large numbers of donkeys teamsters parked on the hill on their supply trips to the Mother Lode mining camps. In *Roughing It*, Twain describes his cabin: "We lived in a small cabin on a verdant hillside, and there were not five other cabins in view over the wide expanse of hill and forest."

The Wedgewood Inn

11941 Narcissus Road
Jackson, CA 95642
(209) 296-4300; (800) WEDGEWD [933-4393]
E-mail: wedgewd@depot.net

If you've been meaning to take time out to smell the roses, The Wedgewood Inn is the ideal place to start. The lovely English country gardens contain 100 rose bushes, so you'll have plenty of time to contemplate. If you are not of a meditative nature and want to do more than smell the roses (like perhaps grow them at your own house), all the rose bushes are labeled, and you can take notes.

I for one was delighted to nestle inside the bell-roofed gazebo, sip some lemonade, and read a murder mystery. The five-acre retreat filled with oaks and pines made a much-needed respite from "civilization and its discontents."

If you find that even reading is too much of an effort in this tranquil setting, there are four Pawley Island double hammocks with your name on them. Here you can nap to your heart's content or listen to the lilting fountains or to the thirty different varieties of birds. On the other hand, if the setting puts you in mind of an English novel and you feel the urge for a spot of croquet or horseshoes, you've come to the right place.

The Wedgewood Inn reflects the personalities of its innkeepers, Jeannine and Vic Beltz. Jeannine, who is most gracious and hospitable, tells me over tea in her living room that "I have always had a hospitality lifestyle. Between being a full-time mother of three, children's coordinator of a Bible study fellowship, and the wife of an IBM executive, I have always loved to entertain guests and to cook. Running a B&B just seems an extension of my existing lifestyle."

As for Vic, a former electronic engineer at IBM in San Jose, he keeps the guests amused with his dry sense of humor and runs the place as efficiently (but not as dryly) as, well, an IBM plant. He also is the gardener, the expert on gold prospecting, and the proud owner and displayer of "Henry," the resident Model T Ford.

Jeannine used two themes while decorating the inn: spinning wheels and wedding dresses. There are family members' wedding dresses in many of the guest rooms and spinning wheels throughout the inn. The furnishings of The Wedgewood have been collected over a period of 37 years; many are gifts from Vic's parents, who themselves have been collectors for 60 years.

My favorite items in the inn were the dolls, all in excellent condition, and all cuddled by a Beltz somewhere along the line. Our room, the Victorian Rose, features lace curtains, family heirlooms, a bay window overlooking the rose garden, and the most comfortable mattress I have ever slept on. The truffle fairy thoughtfully left chocolates on our pillow every night.

The formal breakfast on fine bone china begins with a prayer by Vic. The morning we were leaving he included a request for safe travel. Then, like a fantasy of all dessert-loving people, we were actually served the last course first. You know the expression "Life is short. Eat dessert first." Well, the Beltzes don't just talk about it. The baked pear with raspberry sorbet began our morning repast and was followed by a cranberry frappé, a delicious quichelike dish called O'Brien's sausage bake, a tomato topped with zucchini and pine nuts, and currant oatmeal scones with Texas peach Amaretto honey butter.

You won't go hungry in the afternoon after you have explored Angels Camp and the rest of the gold country. We shared baked garlic and brie, gourmet fruit and nut nibbles, and The Wedgewood's signature drink, Crantea, cranberry juice and tea.

The Beltzes always give their guests a going-away present when they leave. We got a pretty red silk rose. As we were leaving, I heard one of the guests say to some newcomers checking in, "They really pamper you here." It's true; they really do.

Rates: $90–$155
Credit Cards Accepted: Visa, MC, AMEX, Discover
Number of Guest Rooms: 6
Number of Baths: 6
Wheelchair Access: No

Pets: No
Children: No
Smoking: No
Senior Citizen Discount: No
Directions: See brochure

Dunbar House, 1880

271 Jones Street
P.O. Box 1375
Murphys, CA 95247
(209) 728-2897; (800) 692-6006
(209) 728-1451 Fax

The beauty of this area of the country is characterized by its magnificent forests and tree-laden hillsides. The Costas have acknowledged this by naming the rooms of Dunbar House, 1880 after the most regal of the stately monarchs. The Cedar Suite was once the original owner's sewing room and adjoining sun porch, a tranquil setting that extends into the inn's garden area. Sequoia, the former library, remains elegant, and as in all the rooms, showcases a wonderful wood-burning stove. Upstairs is the Ponderosa, originally the master bedroom, with a grand view of the town and of the garden below. Sugar Pine Suite was once the bedrooms of all five Dunbar sons, who somehow left their joyous boyhood energy in the very woodwork of the place. Willis Dunbar, patriarch of the family, was a local businessman and ran a large ranch nearby while also serving in the state assembly. Sitting on his front porch, you fully expect to see a horse and buggy pull up to the gate. Today this is still quite possible, for the town of Murphys has its own equestrian taxi service.

Rates: $115–$155
Credit Cards Accepted: Visa, MC, AMEX
Number of Guest Rooms: 4
Number of Baths: 4
Wheelchair Access: No

Pets: No
Children: If older than 10
Smoking: No
Senior Citizen Discount: No
Directions: See brochure

The Sharpsteen Museum

1311 Washington Street
Calistoga, CA 94515
(707) 942-5911; (707) 942-6960

Who: Marlys Gilmore

When: 10:00 A.M.–4:00 P.M. daily during daylight saving time, 12:00–4:00 P.M. daily during standard time. Closed Thanksgiving and Christmas.

How Much: Free

Senior Citizen Discount: NA

Wheelchair Access: Yes

Directions: Highway 29 north from Napa about 22 miles

What and Where: The Sharpsteen Museum is a delightful small museum that dramatically transports you back to the early days of Calistoga and the Napa Valley. The elegant 1860s hot springs resort of publisher, soldier-of-fortune, and pioneer Sam Brannan comes to life in extraordinary scale-model dioramas, the focal point of the museum.

This 32-foot-long display depicts life in the opulent resort that gave Calistoga, "the Saratoga of the Pacific," its name.

The museum is the brainchild of Ben Sharpsteen, an Academy Award–winning animator, producer, and director for Walt Disney Studios, who retired to the Napa Valley after an illustrious career working on such beloved Disney projects as *Fantasia, Cinderella, Alice in Wonderland, Pinocchio,* and *Dumbo.*

There is much to see in this charming little museum, but for our purposes you might want to concentrate on the Robert Louis Stevenson exhibit and bronze sculpture, recreating his stay in Calistoga. It was while he and his new bride, Fanny, were living on the slopes of Mount St. Helena that Stevenson wrote *The Silverado Squatters.*

Robert Louis Stevenson State Park

Silverado District
Department of Parks and Recreation
20 East Spain Street
Sonoma, CA 95476
(707) 938-1519; (707) 938-1406

Who: Visitors' center

When: Every day, all year

How Much: $2 for adults

Senior Citizen Discount: No

Wheelchair Access: No

Directions: See below

What and Where: North of Calistoga, up an incredibly winding hill, lies the beautiful Robert Louis Stevenson State Park. The road, State Highway 29, leading to the park is scenic, but be warned that it is a "Dramamine Express."

David and I took the lovely (but steep) hike on a lush, tree-lined trail. At the trailhead is a plaque that points out that RLS, intrigued by Napa wine makers, stage drivers, and hunters created lively characters still enjoyed today.

Having just read *Treasure Island* for the third time, we were intrigued to learn that Mount St. Helena, where we were hiking, was Stevenson's model for *Treasure Island*'s Spyglass Hill.

Farther up the hill was another plaque that read: After months of roughing it, RLS left notebooks overflowing with description of local scenes and people which enriched not only *The Silverado Squatters,* but his later writing as well.

Foothill House

3037 Foothill Boulevard
Calistoga, CA 94515
(707) 942-6933; (800) 942-6933
(707) 942-5692 Fax

Let's start with the late afternoon and wine appreciation hour at Foothill House. After all, this *is* the famed Napa Valley, and Doris and Gus Beckert know how to put first things first. Their wine and cheese is served in the sunroom and comes with a spate of oenophile information from these friendly, knowledgeable innkeepers, including fascinating references to the entire wine-making process and its various stages. The setting, too, calls for a series of toasts to stately redwoods, a rock garden, and waterfall that play out against the background view of beautiful Mount St. Helena. Redwood prevails here, most accommodations include private decks and patio funiture, and all rooms have private entrances as well as private baths. The descriptive names of the rooms derive from the dominant color in the handmade quilt covering each of the queen-size four-poster beds: Lupine Suite (blues and greens), Redwood Room (rusts with gold and green accents), and Evergreen Suite (teal with a touch of persimmon). Quails's Roost, the elegant and fully equipped separate cottage, is all warm gray, cream, and raspberry. Laura Ashley fabrics are visible throughout, as are Jacuzzi tubs, ceiling fans, and wood-burning fireplaces.

And that second "B" in B&B is not given short shrift here, either! Doris, a graduate of San Francisco's Culinary Institute, serves gourmet breakfasts with a flair that includes her trademark garnishes of edible flowers. Everything about this remodeled farmhouse, its setting, and its hosts will prompt yet another toast at the end of a satisfying day: *Salud,* and perhaps even an impulsive "Kiss the cook!"

Rates: $135–$250
Credit Cards Accepted: Visa, MC, AMEX, Discover
Number of Guest Rooms: 4
Number of Baths: 4
Wheelchair Access: No

Pets: No
Children: Yes
Smoking: No
Senior Citizen Discount: No
Directions: See brochure

The Silverado Museum

1490 Library Lane
P.O. Box 409
St. Helena, CA 94574
(707) 963-3757
(707) 963-0917 Fax

Who: Edmond Reynolds, Director

When: 12:00–4:00 P.M. Tuesday through Sunday

How Much: Free

Senior Citizen Discount: NA

Wheelchair Access: Yes

Directions: To reach the Silverado Museum from either the north or the south, take Highway 29 (which becomes Main Street in St. Helena) to Adams Street. Turn east and proceed to Library Lane. Take a left to the museum, which is the large white building on the right.

What and Where: The Silverado Museum is devoted to the life and work of Robert Louis Stevenson and houses one of the world's most distinguished collections of Stevensoniana. It is within a few miles of the abandoned bunkhouse at the old Silverado Mine, where RLS spent his honeymoon in 1880. *The Silverado Squatters* is his account of those days.

The museum was the realization of the dream of one of America's foremost bibliophiles, Norman Strouse. As a young man, Strouse read *The Silverado Squatters* and became a great Stevenson aficionado and collector. After retiring as chairman of the board of the J. Walter Thompson Advertising Company, he moved to St. Helena, where he established the museum. Strouse's extraordinary personal collection of Stevensoniana became the nucleus of an ever-growing collection.

Country Garden Inn

1815 Silverado Trail
Napa, CA 94558
(707) 255-1197
Website: http://www.napavalley.com/countrygarden

There are books everywhere you look at the very English Country Garden Inn. Lisa Villiers Smith, the innkeeper of the Country Garden, is rather like a delightful literary character herself. With her dry British wit and propensity for spoiling her guests, she could have stepped from the pages of Oscar Wilde or Noel Coward. Interestingly enough, Lisa told me that her family does indeed have Old World literary connections. It seems her parents were the proprietors of a hotel in Somerset, England, where Coleridge first read his poem, *The Rime of the Ancient Mariner.*

I strongly urge you to go on a long fast before checking in, because the supply of food never ends. The morning begins with an English breakfast of delicious fresh fruit (raspberries, kiwi, strawberries), scones with homemade jams, and coffee cake, followed by scrambled eggs, "bangers," tomatoes, English muffins, eggs Benedict or a fluffy omelette filled with peppers, mushrooms, cheese, and tomatoes. Wash the whole feast down with a flute of complimentary champagne.

After your visit to the Silverado Museum, pop back to the inn for a spot of afternoon tea. The tea service will put you in mind of a scene from P. G. Wodehouse; you almost expect Jeeves to be doing the serving as Bertie Wooster fumbles in the background, making some nonsensical remark. You will feel you have been transported across the pond to Brown's Hotel as you sip your tea and enjoy the shortbread, gingersnaps, chocolate chip cookies, and chocolate cake.

Pretend you're in a Jane Austen novel and take a turn around the enchanting rose garden or amble along the river. Have a look at the large aviary containing more than thirty exotic bird species from all over the world. Stroll back for happy hour, hosted on the backyard patio. Help yourself to some sherry or wine and choose from a variety of cheeses, homemade chutney, olives, spicy green beans, and sun-dried tomato spread. Like most B&Bs, the Country Garden Inn does not offer dinner, which may be a blessing, because a groaning board of sweetmeats—fudge, truffles, mints, macaroons, fruit, and amaretto cake with dessert wines—is provided in the evenings. Top off the epicurean day with a nightcap of wine and spicy deviled almonds roasted with cayenne pepper.

On our last visit to our favorite storybook inn, my husband and I stayed in the large, luxurious two-story Riverbank

Cottage. We watched the sun set from our own private relaxing Jacuzzi. After a delicious dinner at the Napa Valley Grille, we returned and cozied up to the fireplace. I got lost in the pages of *Treasure Island*, while David was held captive by *Kidnapped.*

Rates: $125–$210
Credit Cards Accepted: Visa, MC, AMEX
Number of Guest Rooms: 10
Number of Baths: 10
Wheelchair Access: Yes

Pets: No
Children: No
Smoking: No
Senior Citizen Discount: No
Directions: See brochure

Jack London State Historic Park

2400 London Ranch Road
Glen Ellen, CA 95442
(707) 983-5216

Who: Park staff

When: The park is open 10:00 A.M.–5:00 P.M. during standard time, 10:00 A.M.– 7:00 P.M. during daylight saving time. The Museum is open 10:00 A.M.–5:00 P.M. daily except for Thanksgiving, Christmas, and New Year's Day.

How Much: $5 per vehicle

Senior Citizen Discount: $1 off for those older than 62

Wheelchair Access: Yes

Directions: See brochure

What and Where: Begin your Jack London sojourn with a visit to the House of Happy Walls, which was built by Jack's widow, Charmian London, in 1919–1922. This small and formal home, with its Spanish-style roof and walls of fieldstone, is where Charmian lived whenever she was not traveling abroad or staying with relatives. As she stated in her will, this dwelling was to be used as a museum housing the collection of London photographs and exhibits. Happy Walls also serves as the park visitor center, as well as a gift shop that sells many of the prolific author's best-known works.

Give yourself at least an hour and a half for the dramatic one-mile trip to the intriguing Wolf House. The stroll leads you through a lovely mixed forest of Douglas fir, California buckeye, redwoods, buttercups, poppies, and myriad birds and wildlife.

When I came upon the remains of Wolf House, I was shocked by how much of it remained and how magnificent the house might have been. This ill-fated dream house of Charmian and Jack London was designed by Albert Farr, the renowned San Francisco architect, and was to have been a showcase that would remain standing for a thousand years. The successful author had spent about $80,000 when, on August 22, 1913, his dreams and his newly constructed house went up in smoke. A dismissed ranch hand, London's brother-in-law, and former admirers who were angered by London's renunciation of socialism were suspected of arson, though the cause of the fire remains a matter of speculation. We can only speculate about what the house might have looked like had it been completed. Stone walls complete with window openings, fireplaces, and other details appear little changed by the passage of time. With a little help from the park's brochure and some imagination, I could picture the long outdoor pool that was to have been stocked with mountain bass. It was not difficult to visualize the large library, London's large workroom, and the fireproof vault in the basement that was designed to house his collection of manuscripts and other valuables. The outline of the two-story living room with its alcove for Charmian's grand piano can be discerned, along with the dining room designed to seat as many as 50 people.

Other interesting sites at the park include London's grave and the half-mile-long trail that circles the center of the 1,400 acres of land that London called his "Beauty Ranch." Many of the buildings were designed and built by London himself as part of his determination to develop and demonstrate new agricultural techniques that could be shared with farmers everywhere. I particularly liked the Cottage, London's study, in which he wrote many of his later novels and stories. The glassed porch to the right of the front door is where Jack London died on November 22, 1916.

Campbell Ranch Inn

1475 Canyon Road
Geyersville, CA 95441
(707) 857-3476; (800) 959-3878
(707) 857-3239 Fax
Website: http://www.campbellranchinn.com

If your special criteria for a perfect B&B includes a room with a view, the Campbell Ranch Inn fits that request completely. Along with the spectacular 35-acre sweep of Sonoma County wine country comes a 20-by-40-foot swimming pool, a hot tub, and a regulation-size tennis court. All sorts of recreation is available nearby, including Lake Sonoma, redwood parks, the Russian River, and the Mendocino coast. The ways to exercise or exhaust yourself (depending on your frame of mind) are many, but the thought of a masseuse available in your own bedroom when you return to the inn is quite comforting, to say the least.

A full breakfast is served from a menu perhaps already preserved in Mary Jane Campbell's own *Campbell Ranch Inn Cookbook*. I highly recommend the egg puffs with green chile or the ham and pineapple–stuffed French toast. Each evening, a homemade pie or cake is served to guests as well. The inn has four spacious rooms in the main house plus a separate cottage. All beds are king-size, and all rooms have private baths. Host Jerry Campbell offers an added treat for those guests interested in model trains—and I am finding that their number is legion! An HO-gauge buff, Jerry does not need much encouragement to show his train room in full operation. Then there's the greenhouse, and the show pigeons, and more. Do yourself a favor, and find out why I revise my original statement from a "room with a view" to "a ranch you *must* view."

Rates: $100–$225
Credit Cards Accepted: Visa, MC, AMEX
Number of Guest Rooms: 4 guest rooms and 1 cottage
Number of Baths: 5
Wheelchair Access: No

Pets: No
Children: Yes, though young children are discouraged due to the inn's peaceful atmosphere.
Smoking: No
Senior Citizen Discount: No
Directions: See brochure

Gaige House Inn

13540 Arnold Drive
Glen Ellen, CA 95442
(707) 935-0237; (800) 935-0237
(707) 935-6411 FAX

Jack London's Valley of the Moon is just an hour away from San Francisco. Known to us as Sonoma Valley, it is the perfect backdrop for readers with a penchant for history, a weakness for London's literary lure of adventure, and an oenophile's keen fondness for good wines! Complete the perfect vacation package by combining all the above with a trip to Glen Ellen and a stay at the Gaige House Inn. Innkeeper Ken Burnet will see to your needs with great efficiency and good humor and will be quick to inform you that each of his nine guest rooms contains several volumes of Jack London's works. Don't expect rugged adventurism in your bedroom decor, however. All accommodations are elegantly appointed, with a focus on Ralph Lauren linens and eclectic artwork collected on the owner's various global treks. Of special note is the Gaige Suite, with sunny windows on three walls, a wraparound deck overlooking the lush garden and full-sized swimming pool, and a blue-tiled bath that is easily the size of entire hotel rooms! The

The Gaige House, Glen Ellen, California. Photo courtesy of the Gaige House Inn.

three Garden Rooms also open onto a deck and are only steps away from the same perfectly manicured lawn and 40-foot pool. All guests enjoy a special luxury—the comfort of hand-ironed bed linens—an amenity I thought had gone the way of other niceties from an earlier century. The morning coffee is Peet's, the orange juice fresh-squeezed, and the bountiful breakfast served at private tables or on the glorious sun-filled terrace.

Rates: $125–$245
Credit Cards Accepted: Visa, MC, AMEX, Discover
Number of Guest Rooms: 9
Number of Baths: 9
Wheelchair Access: No

Pets: No
Children: No
Smoking: No
Senior Citizen Discount: No
Directions: See brochure

John Steinbeck Library

305 Lincoln Avenue
Salinas, CA 93901
(408) 758-7311

Who: Mary Jean S. Gamble, archivist

When: 10:00 A.M.–9:00 P.M. Monday through Wednesday, 10:00 A.M.–6:00 P.M. Thursday through Saturday. Closed on Sunday. Call ahead for a tour of the archives.

How Much: Free

Senior Citizen Discount: NA

Wheelchair Access: To the Steinbeck Room

Directions: Heading south to Salinas on US 101, take the Main Street exit to downtown. The library is one block south of the Monterey County Courthouse.

Heading north on US 101, take the Main Street exit and make a U-turn at the first light so that you'll be heading downtown. The library is one block south of the courthouse.

What and Where: The Steinbeck Collection, started in 1960, now consists of over 30,000 items, including John Steinbeck's original letters, photographs, first editions, numerous newspaper and magazine articles, and assorted memorabilia. Staff members are available to assist visitors and researchers during regular business hours. A tour can be arranged for school groups and other organizations by making advance reservations. A guide to the library's John Steinbeck Collection was published in 1979. Copies of the guide may be purchased at the library.

Jack Patton, former editor of the *Salinas Californian,* presented a gift of Steinbeck first editions and a voluminous file of Steinbeck-related newspaper clippings to the library in 1964. This launched the extensive John Steinbeck Archives, which is well used by the northern California community, as well as by a large number of researchers, students, and devotees of Steinbeck throughout the world.

The highlight of the archives is the original holographic manuscript of *The Pearl,* written in pencil and ink on 67 folio leaves. Composed in January and February 1945 with the working title *The Pearl of La Paz,* this last substantial privately owned Steinbeck manuscript is still in fine condition. We can see how the original and published versions differ. Steinbeck obviously realized change was in order, for at the head of the first leaf he wrote, "Trial sheet:—to be thrown away." Everything from numerous word changes to the general arrangement of the chapters and paragraphs are on display. There are also many passages and sentences in the manuscript that were completely altered or dropped from the published version. The manuscript ends differently than the published version. Juana and Kino rest with their child on a cliff as their pursuers approach them. Kino raises his hand to touch his wife and child, and suddenly there is a flash of rifle fire. Steinbeck added the closing passage that describes Juana and Kino returning to La Paz after the murder of their child, Coyotito, with Kino tossing the pearl back into the ocean.

Other interesting items in the collection include a recording of Steinbeck reading from his works, over 200 photographs of the author from infancy, a fifth-grade reader signed and dated by Steinbeck, the author's letters and postcards, the unrevised proof of *East of Eden,* the galley proof and typescript of *Steinbeck: A Life in Letters,* and over 150 hours of taped interviews with people who knew Steinbeck, as well as interviews with people who are familiar with the Salinas Valley and Monterey area settings used by Steinbeck in his work.

Some of the many limited or rare editions one might see are Steinbeck's acceptance speech for the Nobel Prize in Literature; a copy of *Cannery Row* inscribed by the author; *Tortilla Flat,* one of 500 advance copies; *The Red Pony,* three of 699 numbered copies signed by the author; chapter 34 from *East of Eden;* and a copy of *The Sea of Cortez,* inscribed and signed by authors Ed Ricketts and John Steinbeck.

National Steinbeck Center

371 Main Street
Salinas, CA 93901
(408) 753-6411
(408) 753-0574 Fax

Who: Patricia Leach, executive director

When: 10:00 A.M.–4:00 P.M. Monday through Friday, 10:00 A.M.–2:00 P.M. on Saturday. Closed on holidays unless prior arrangements are made.

How Much: Free for individuals, $2 per person for tour groups of 10 people or more.

Senior Citizen Discount: NA

Wheelchair Access: Yes

Directions: From US 101 (heading either north or south) exit west on John Street, which leads to south Main. Take south Main north to Old Town Salinas. The center is on the corner of San Luis and Main Streets.

What and Where: The John Steinbeck Center Foundation was founded in 1983 by a group of Salinas residents who wanted to share the author's life with his huge circle of admirers. It has grown to the point where it now offers an impressive array of events and activities based on John Steinbeck's writing, his life, and his times. The foundation also offers Steinbeck Country tours of Monterey and Salinas, literary performances and programs, a February 27 Steinbeck birthday party, and a museum featuring displays of the author's many works and his colorful life. A special project, Steinbeck in the Schools, provides movies, visual aids, speakers, and tours of Steinbeck Country to help students learn about the author's works.

The staff at the foundation is extremely enthusiastic about plans for the new $8.5 million Steinbeck Center Museum. As Sue Almond, the office administrator, explained to me: "The new Steinbeck Center is being built in tribute to a belief John Steinbeck shared with his native city … the belief that the arts should be enriching to the community and relevant to everyday life. … This will be literature and culture come alive."

When the new center opens in 1998, I will be particularly excited about making the acquaintance of Rocinante, the truck Steinbeck drove across the United States in 1960 in *Travels with Charley*. In this best-seller, Steinbeck explained that Rocinante was not mean or ugly-natured like some cars he'd owned. Because of her purring motor and perfect performance, he treated her like the honest bookkeeper, the faithful wife, and except, for meticulous routine maintenance, he ignored her.

The center also contains a display of posters featuring films made from Steinbeck novels. James Dean starred in *East of Eden*, Dorothy Lamour starred in *A Medal for Benny*, and Jayne Mansfield headed up the cast of *The Wayward Bus*. Much to my surprise, Steinbeck also wrote the screenplay for *Viva Zapata;* in the movie, Marlon Brando was cast in the role of the Mexican hero.

There is a compact bookstore featuring many of the author's works as well as fun souvenirs such as Steinbeck tee shirts, magnets, coloring books—all profits go to a good cause, the new Steinbeck Center Foundation.

Steinbeck Festival

371 Main Street
Salinas, CA 93901
(408) 753-6411
(408) 753-0574 Fax

Who: Patricia Leach, executive director

When: 10:00 A.M.–4:00 P.M. Monday through Friday, 10:00 A.M.–2:00 P.M. on Saturday. Closed on holidays unless prior arrangements are made.

How Much: Free for individuals, $2 per person for tour groups of 10 people or more.

Senior Citizen Discount: NA

Wheelchair Access: Yes

Directions: From US 101 (heading either north or south) exit west on John Street to south Main. Take south Main north to Old Town Salinas. The Steinbeck Center is on the corner of San Luis and Main Streets.

What and Where: Steinbeck aficionados from around the globe flock to Salinas on the first Thursday in August for a marathon weekend of tours, films, panel discussions, and special events. A festival dinner held on the future site of the National Steinbeck Center provides the perfect backdrop for people of many nations and diverse cultures to fulfill one of Steinbeck's dreams and join in a common passion.

The 1996 Steinbeck Festival XVII, titled Celebrating Steinbeck's Salinas Valley, paid homage to the author's *The Valley of the World*. To quote Steinbeck: "I think I would like to write the story of this whole valley, of all the little towns and all the farms and ranches in the wilder hills. I can see how I would like to do it so that it would be The Valley of The World."

Highlights of the 1996 gala included the Doc Ricketts's lab tour, the Red Pony bus tour, an Ag tour that focused on the history of the area's $2 billion agricultural industry (many leaders said proudly, "We were the Grapes of Wrath"), and a keynote presentation on John Steinbeck by Sam and Timothy Bottoms, the stars of the TV miniseries *East of Eden*. Some of the many presentations: The Fall of Patriarchy in The Winter of Our Discontent: Steinbeck's Men; A Beer Milkshake, the Human Incongruities in Steinbeck's Valley of the World; and The History of Salinas Valley. Among the activities, which stretched over four full days, were showings of Steinbeck plays, movies, and an opportunity to view Rocinante of *Travels with Charley* fame.

The Steinbeck House

132 Central Avenue
Salinas, CA 93901
(408) 424-2735

Who: Front desk

When: 10:00 A.M.–2:30 P.M. Monday through Friday, 11:00 A.M.–2:30 P.M. on Saturday. Closed Sunday. Closed for major holidays, including the Wednesday through Sunday around Thanksgiving, and from December 21 through January 13.

Lunch Information: Luncheon is served at 11:45 A.M. and again at 1:15 P.M. Monday through Friday by reservation: (408) 424-2735. Reservations are held for 14 minutes. Lunch costs $7.50; dessert $3.00; coffee, tea, milk $1.00; wine and beer available.

How Much: Admission is free

Senior Citizen Discount: NA

Wheelchair Access: No

Directions: Call for directions

The Steinbeck House, Salinas, California. Photo by David van Hulsteyn.

What and Where: The Steinbeck House, boyhood home of John Steinbeck, bills itself as the "home of the boy down the street, who, with some kind of extra magic gained immortality for himself and the valley of green gold." The literature about the home of the Pulitzer and Nobel Prize–winner tells visitors that the author was raised in a house filled with lively discussion and good books.

Steinbeck immortalized this home in his semiautobiographical novel *East of Eden:* "On an impulse he turned off Main Street and walked up Central Avenue to number 130. ... it was an immaculate and friendly house, grand enough but not pretentious, and it sat inside its white fence surrounded by its clipped lawn and roses and cotoneasters lapped against its walls."

John Steinbeck, the third of four children, was born on February 27, 1902, to John Ernst and Olive Hamilton Steinbeck, in the room immediately to the left as you enter the home's front door. Here's how the author describes this room in *East of Eden:* "The pleasant little bedroom was crowded with photographs, bottles of toilet water, lace pin cushions, brushes and combs and the china and silver bureau-knacks of many birthdays and Christmases."

Today the house is a charming restaurant that features fresh produce from the fields of the famous Salinas Valley. Since 1971 the restaurant has been run by a group of what one volunteer described as "civic-minded, enthusiastic women who share a common interest in gourmet cooking." All profits go toward the maintenance of the Steinbeck House and to Salinas Valley charities. Expect a pleasant meal in an attractive environment, but do not assume that the servers and other members of the Valley Guild will be concerned with John Steinbeck lore. The literature you are given at the house has information about what you are to see. Read, don't ask.

After lunch, browse around the Best Cellar, the basement shop featuring books (including many Steinbeck first editions) and gift items. Here you can also see the bed that belonged to John's parents. Throughout the house there are pictures of John and his siblings, as well as his baby cup and signet ring.

If you don't want to leave town without seeing every Steinbeck landmark, then don't miss the Steinbeck gravesite at 768 Abbott Street. The author's ashes are buried under the leaning oak in the Hamilton family plot in the Garden of Memories.

Old Monterey Inn

500 Martin Street
Monterey, CA 93940
(408) 375-8284; (800) 350-2344
(408) 375-6730 Fax

If God is in the details, you'll be in heaven at the Old Monterey Inn. The innkeepers, Gene and Ann Swett, are perfectionists, and it shows.

The elegant 1929 Tudor-style manor house is beautifully appointed, and your every need is anticipated. Ann's mother was an interior designer and obviously passed her skills on to her daughter. The inn always has a feeling of fresh touches and up-to-the-minute decor because the Swetts redecorate every three years.

Longtime Monterey residents, the Swetts are very involved in preserving the beauty and history of their historic community, and as Ann told me over tea in their formal living room, "The thrust of doing the inn is to preserve the building. People just don't build houses like this anymore." There is also a sentimental attachment to the house because the Swetts raised their six children here.

Allow time in your literary peregrinations to enjoy the gardens at the Old Monterey Inn. My husband pronounced the gardens "exquisite." The focal point of the garden is the magnificent gnarled 400-year-old live oak. The acre of English garden is ablaze with pink oleander, wisteria, and a field of impatiens. Keeping our literary journey in mind, I could picture Miss Marple and her chums having a spot of tea in this lush yard, so reminiscent of St. Mary Mead. As I sipped my iced tea in this lovely secret garden, I thought the sign on the lawn, One is nearer God's heart in a garden than any-where else on earth, could have been written with this B&B in mind.

Our room, the floral-enhanced Ashford Suite, was made for romance, with its king-size bed, bay windows overlooking the blooming wisteria, and inviting fireplace. The next morning we enjoyed our breakfast in bed of delicious no-fat French toast, fruit, juice, and coffee. It was a sybarite's heaven.

You can't go wrong in any of the ten elegant guest rooms. The Garden Cottage is the perfect place for a secluded honeymoon with its cozy fireplace, canopied king-size bed, and splendid garden vistas. To keep in the spirit of this book, try the library, with its large stone fireplace, perfect reading nook, and book-lined walls. Capture the experience of a turn-of-the-century safari or pretend you're Ernest Hemingway in the Serengeti Room, with its antique travel mementos, relaxing whirlpool bath, and warming fireplace.

The Swetts host a wine and hors d'oeuvres hour every afternoon, when you can discuss, among other things, where you will have dinner that evening. My husband and I did just that and had a delicious meal at Roy's Restaurant at the Inn at Spanish Bay. While enjoying the evening sunset over the water, we happily ate our fresh fish served with a Euro-Asian flair. Before dinner we worked up an appetite by driving the beautiful 17-Mile Drive, stopping along the way for strolls at Bird Rock, Seal Rock, and the Lone Cypress, one of California's most familiar landmarks.

Rates: $190–$270
Credit Cards Accepted: Visa, MC
Number of Guest Rooms: 10
Number of Baths: 10
Wheelchair Access: No

Pets: No
Children: No
Smoking: No
Senior Citizen Discount: NA
Directions: See brochure

Seven Gables Inn

555 Ocean View Boulevard
Pacific Grove, CA 93950
(408) 372-4341

Robert Louis Stevenson called the Pacific Grove–Monterey area "the greatest meeting of land and water in the world." A charming place from which to enjoy this magical meeting is the Seven Gables Inn. Its spectacular rocky-point setting offers dramatic views of the ocean and coastal mountains from every room.

The inn has many literary connections. It was built by people from Salem, Massachusetts, to resemble Hawthorne's famous House of Seven Gables. To pay homage to this author, there is naturally a Hawthorne Room.

Next door to the Seven Gables is the Grandview Inn with its Robert Louis Stevenson and John Steinbeck Rooms. These two authors never lived in the house, but the rooms were named to reflect the rich literary history of the area. Ask your helpful innkeepers, the Flatleys, to point you in the direction of Monterey's RLS House, on 530 Houston Street, where you can learn about his stay here in 1879. As on his other California trips, Stevenson was cooling his heels, waiting for his beloved, Fanny Osbourne, to get her divorce so he could marry her.

Even though this inn is very elegant, it is very relaxing. Every afternoon at 4:00 P.M. an English high tea is served on the sunporch or outdoors on the patio. You might read a little Steinbeck or Stevenson as you sip your tea and eat the delicious homemade treats and imported cakes. An inn specialty is the generous sit-down breakfast served with classic elegance in the grand dining room. Silver platters of fresh fruit, yogurt, and a variety of homemade breads, cakes, or apple cobbler are served along with fine teas and coffees.

If you are an antique aficionado, you will appreciate the Flatley family's collection of fine European antiques. All the guest bedrooms are bright and sunny, and each has its own private bath. The beds are first-rate, the reading lights are excellent, and the rooms are beautifully appointed. All have attractive sitting areas and ocean views.

If you have time to spare after visiting Steinbeck country, enjoy the scenic wonderland that surrounds you. There is Carmel-by-the-Sea, Big Sur, Point Lobos, and the spectacular migration of the gray whales (October through March). A special treat is the year-round presence of frolicking sea otters. You absolutely must save half a day for the spectacular new Monterey Bay Aquarium: It is truly awe-inspiring. Remember you are directly across from Steinbeck's Cannery Row.

A quick caveat: This inn is rated four stars in the *Mobil Travel Guide* and is on an American Express TV commercial, so make your reservations early.

Rates: $125–$225
Credit Cards Accepted: Visa, MC
Number of Guest Rooms: 24
Number of Baths: 24
Wheelchair Access: Yes

Pets: No
Children: If older than 12
Smoking: No
Senior Citizen Discount: No
Directions: See brochure

The Huntington Library, Art Collections, and Botanical Gardens

1151 Oxford Road
San Marino, CA 91108
(818) 405-2141; (818) 405-2274 for directions

Who: Call info line

When: Summer hours, 10:30 A.M.–4:30 P.M. daily except Monday; rest of the year, 12:00 noon–4:30 P.M. Tuesday through Friday and 10:30 A.M.–4:30 P.M. on weekends. Closed Mondays and holidays.

How Much: $7.50 per adult; $4.00 per student; free for children under 12. On the first Thursday of each month admission is free for everyone.

Senior Citizen Discount: $6 for seniors

Wheelchair Access: Yes

Directions: From Los Angeles take I-110 (which becomes Arroyo Seco in Pasadena), turn right (east) on California Boulevard, and drive several blocks to Allen Avenue. Turn right (south) on Allen to the museum entrance.

Refreshments: The restaurant is open Tuesday–Friday 12:00 to 4:00 P.M., Saturday and Sunday 11:30 A.M. to 4:00 P.M. Light meals, pastries, drinks, and sandwiches are available. Tea is served in the Rose Garden Room Tuesday–Friday from 12:00 to 4:00 P.M., Saturday and Sunday from 10:45 A.M. to 4:00 P.M. For reservations call (818) 683-8131.

Bookstore: Located in the entrance pavilion, the store carries a variety of books, art, botanical prints, notecards, and gift items related to the Huntington collections. Open Tuesday–Friday, from 12:00 noon to 5:00 P.M., weekends from 10:30 A.M. to 5:00 P.M.

What and Where: Few places in the world offer the combination of treasures for both visitors and scholars that the Huntington does. The 130-acre botanical gardens feature specialized areas for roses, palms, camellias, and herbs, as well as Japanese, subtropical, desert, and jungle plants. The art collections are distinguished by one of the most important collections in the United States of British art of the late eighteenth and early nineteenth centuries, and by a small but fine collection of American paintings and decorative art. The library has a rich collection of rare books, manuscripts, and photographs that spans ten centuries of history and literature in Britain and America.

The nearly 2,000 scholars (called "readers") who use the library's research materials each year are attracted by what one scholar has called "perhaps the most wonderful research environment in the world."

The library has records unequaled in the United States for the study of medieval England. The collection contains several thousand English medieval documents of great historical, literary, and religious interest. For me, the literary landmark is the Ellesmere manuscript of Geoffrey Chaucer's *Canterbury Tales*. Handwritten on vellum, the manuscript is elaborately decorated with portraits of the twenty-three pilgrims, and one is thought to be a likeness of Chaucer himself. Its fame rests not only on its handsome presentation—it is one of the best-preserved English literary manuscripts in existence—

but also on the importance of its text. The Ellesmere manuscript is the earliest complete copy of Chaucer's original text, made within a decade or so of the poet's death.

Perhaps the most important medieval document in the library's collection is a very early copy of the Magna Carta, the first guarantee of rights and liberties in England. The Huntington's collection of more than 54,000 incunabula is the second largest in the United States, after the Library of Congress. The earliest book in the collection is a Gutenberg Bible, the first important book printed using movable type. The Huntington's Gutenberg is one of twelve surviving copies printed on vellum and one of three vellum copies in America.

The Huntington also holds and often displays fifteenth-century editions of Aristotle, Pliny, Euclid, and Dante, important for their influence on the course of intellectual history in the Renaissance and exquisite in their craftsmanship.

The library's collection of early Shakespeare editions remains unsurpassed by any other library in the world. The "First Folio," entitled *Mr. William Shakespeare's Comedies, Histories, and Tragedies,* contains 36 plays, 20 of them printed for the first time. This is unquestionably the most important resource relating to the Bard's texts.

The Huntington also holds other masterpieces produced during the Elizabethan period, including rare early copies of Spenser's *The Faerie Queene,* Milton's *Paradise Lost,* and John Bunyan's *Pilgrim's Progress,* for two centuries the most popular book in the English language.

The library's manuscripts and first editions of English literature from the eighteenth to twentieth centuries include works by some of Britain's most celebrated poets and novelists: Alexander Pope, Jonathan Swift, Robert Burns, Henry Fielding, William Blake, Lord Byron, Charles Dickens, William Makepeace Thackeray, and Anthony Trollope. There is a large collection of letters and writings by well-known English literary figures. Dickens is represented by nearly 1,000 letters; Percy Bysshe Shelley by notebooks with characteristic sketches, experimental rhymes, and bits of verse later incorporated into his poems; Robert Louis Stevenson by the journals of his voyages to the South Seas and California; and Alfred Lord Tennyson by many poems, including part of *In Memoriam.*

The Huntington has the largest collection of letters, documents, and papers of the Founding Fathers located outside the great East Coast repositories. One of the most notable of these is the manuscript of Benjamin Franklin's autobiography. George Washington's genealogy is written in the first president's own handwriting (1792).

Thomas Jefferson's letters and printed works detail his activities as a political philosopher and social scientist, as a statesman who brought about the Louisiana Purchase, as a patron of education and a scientist, as a Virginia plantation owner gloomy about troubles over slavery, and as the inventor of a copying machine (a reduced-scale replica is frequently on display).

Henry Edwards Huntington had a deep interest in Robert E. Lee and a deeper interest in Abraham Lincoln. He acquired a fine set of early letters Lee wrote to his wife, Molly, and a later series written to his favorite cousin, Martha Williams. The Lincoln collection includes more than 200 letters and manuscripts by the 16th president. Associated with the Lincoln collection are the letters, books, and documents of Civil War nurse Clara Barton and of Civil War soldiers and their families.

Another treasure in the library is John James Audubon's famous *Birds of America.* For its commanding size, vividness of depiction, and scientific accuracy, it is an unparalled publication. Audubon's original goal was to draw every American bird from nature in its actual size. Audubon published the work himself, issuing engravings to subscribers in sets of five.

The Huntington Library and Botanical Gardens, San Marino, California. Photo by Bob Schlosser.

There is a remarkable collection of California literature at the Huntington, featuring the writings and correspondence of Ambrose Bierce, Bret Harte, John Muir, Joaquin Miller, and Mary Austin. In addition, the library possesses Jack London's manuscripts, correspondence, scrapbooks, photographs, and first editions, as well as his personal library. Numbering some 30,000 items, the London collection contains the manuscripts of almost all of his works—even the charred pages of the manuscript of *The Sea Wolf,* which burned in the fire that followed the 1906 San Francisco earthquake.

The library holds most of the early editions of the works of American writers of consequence before 1900, and it also has important holdings of the works of major twentieth-century American authors such as Conrad Aiken and Wallace Stevens.

The collection of 45,000 manuscripts and many rare printed books includes the manuscript and proof sheets of Henry David Thoreau's *Walden;* Edgar Allan Poe's first book of poems, composed when he was 14 (now the rarest of his works); poems by Walt Whitman; the manuscript of Mark Twain's *The Prince and the Pauper;* and first editions of many classics of American literature, such as Herman Melville's *Moby-Dick* and Mark Twain's *The Adventures of Huckleberry Finn.*

The founder of the library, Henry Edwards Huntington, was a man who always loved books and art and who "wanted to give something to the public before he died." He created a trust in 1919 that became the Huntington Library, Art Collections, and Botanical Gardens. He gave to this trust all his books, manuscripts, and art objects, the library building, his residence, and gardens, and ultimately $10 million in endowment funds.

AUTHOR'S NOTE: A special treat is having tea in the Rose Garden Tea Room. The setting does justice to any that Oscar Wilde or Agatha Christie could conjure up: We sat overlooking stately trees and a multitude of roses, drank delicious tea, and enjoyed a marvelous selection of tea sandwiches, scones, and desserts. Call (818) 683-8131 for more information.

Will Rogers State Historic Park

1501 Will Rogers State Park Road
Pacific Palisades, CA 90272
(310) 454-8212

Who: Michael Allan

When: 8:00 A.M. to sunset every day except Thanksgiving, Christmas, and New Year's Day

How Much: $5 per car

Senior Citizen Discount: $4

Wheelchair Access: No

Directions: Call for directions

What and Where: Will Rogers's ranch became a state park in 1944, following the death of his wife, Betty. After touring Rogers's home, spend some time on the grounds. There is an audio tour of the park with which you can learn about the blacksmith shop, the roping area, the polo cage, and the stable. For walkers, the two-mile loop trail to Inspiration Point is particularly popular; there are also a nature trail and longer hikes. The more sedentary might prefer to enjoy the small picnic area and nature center.

I encourage readers to watch the charming movie about Will Rogers's life at the visitor's center. The film includes some great footage of the Ziegfeld Follies with Rogers performing his amazing rope tricks. As a movie star, his silent films were only moderately successful. He decided that he could do better on his own, so he started his own company to produce *The Ropin' Fool*. This movie "broke him," and he had to return to the Follies. He then added lectures, radio shows, and writing to his repertoire. Always an enthusiast for a new medium, he became a big advocate of "talking pictures" and, as it turns out, became one of the leading box office attractions of his day.

Will Rogers's house reflects his personality. Who else would have a mounted, roped calf in his living room? It seems that he had the disconcerting habit of practicing his roping on people and furniture. One of his exasperated friends retaliated by sending him a roped cow. Another friend sent him a cigar-store Indian because he felt Rogers "needed another Indian to talk to." Both of these gifts are prominently displayed in the living room.

On the mantle, over the beautiful stone fireplace in the living room, is the head of a Texas longhorn steer, the breed Will Rogers's rancher father raised in Oklahoma. The steer was a gift from Amon Carter. The living room is filled with Charles Russell bronzes and Native American rugs. Our guide told us that there are 18 different tribes represented in the living room.

I particularly enjoyed seeing his study with his 1926 Remington typewriter. We learned that Rogers had a typewriter on his desk and another one in his car. Above his writing desk are maps where he charted his extensive trips. Other not-to-be-missed items are the walls of photographs featuring W. C. Fields; Douglas Fairbanks; Will Rogers, Jr., doing pony tricks; portraits of Betty and their three children, Will Jr., Mary, and Jim. The most chilling picture is one of Will and Wiley Post standing by a plane in Fairbanks, Alaska, two hours before the crash that killed them both.

The house was left with the family's items intact to reflect the daily life of Will and Betty—so much so that I expected members of the Rogers family to pop in and ask us to stay for dinner. The dining room table remains permanently set on the off-chance that such friends as Walt Disney or Spencer Tracy might drop by to partake of one of the Rogers's legendary barbecues. Sheet music belonging to Betty, once a piano teacher, remains on her piano.

Will Rogers was an enthusiastic horseman. Polo was frequently played at his ranch. This tradition continues today, and visitors may occasionally see teams in competition. Betty's will specified that the polo grounds were to remain open to the public.

Literary Los Angeles

Los Angeles evokes such a sense of place that I must briefly mention some authors who used it as a wonderfully effective backdrop for their fiction. Can you imagine Raymond Chandler placing his hard-boiled mysteries in any other setting? His detective, Philip Marlowe, investigated the underbelly of L.A. in his classic crime novels *The Big Sleep; Farewell, My Lovely;* and *The Long Goodbye.* These would have been very different books if they had been set in Des Moines, Iowa.

The definitive Hollywood novel is Nathanael West's *The Day of the Locust,* chronicling the death of the American dream seen through the eyes of movieland losers. F. Scott Fitzgerald's unfinished final novel, *The Last Tycoon,* depicts the life of a wealthy young Hollywood producer. Hooray for Hollywood!

Inn at Playa del Rey

435 Culver Boulevard
Playa del Rey, CA 90293
(310) 574-1920
(310) 574-9920 Fax

When I called my Los Angeles friend, David Beckett, and told him my husband and I were at a serene inn overlooking birding wetlands and boats, he informed me in no uncertain terms that there were no such places in L.A. and that I had finally landed where he knew I would end up all along, in the home for the bewildered.

But this time my opera singer–actor friend was wrong. There is such a place in L.A., and its name is the Inn at Playa del Rey. At night we opened the door to our balcony to let the gentle sea breezes cool us, and in the morning we awoke to lilting birdsong.

The Inn at Playa del Rey is that all-too-rare phenomenon—a sanctuary in the middle of a sprawling city. As Susan Zolla, the amusing and charming innkeeper, told me over a delicious breakfast, "As you can see, great egrets come close enough to the breakfast room each morning that we have begun calling them our 'regulars.' The blue herons stand off in the distance in a sentrylike perch as though guarding the back entrance to the wetlands."

After we had explored the wonderful Will Rogers State Historic Park, we came back to this retreat and joined other guests

One of the rooms at the Inn at Playa del Rey.
Photo courtesy of the Inn at Playa del Rey.

for wine, fruit, and cheese at the hors d'oeuvres hour. The light and airy contemporary inn lends itself to civilized conversation and relaxation. This is no accident, for the architect, drawing on memories of favorite Cape Cod retreats, created a human sanctuary, bringing the beauty of the natural surroundings inside the inn. Nowhere is this more evident than in the guest rooms. As I was luxuriating in the Jacuzzi, I could see colorful sailboats through the open window.

The staff is first-rate. We dragged in after driving almost 500 miles from Napa and were in a severe state of car lag. The cheerful attendant at the front desk showed us to our room and then returned five minutes later with some freshly baked chocolate chip cookies for us. Equally important, the staff gave us great directions to both the Will Rogers Historical State Park and the Huntington Library.

Now you may ask, Is the Inn at Playa del Rey close enough to our literary sites? The answer is, Yes, as close as anything in L.A. is to anything else. You can avoid the freeway to the Will Rogers State Historic Park. The Huntington Library is about 25 minutes away on the freeway. My feeling is that in southern California driving long distances is part of the job description. Therefore, travelers should stay in the most tranquil, comfortable surroundings possible. Trust me, this is the place.

Rates: $95–$225
Credit Cards Accepted: Visa, MC, AMEX, Discover
Number of Guest Rooms: 22
Number of Baths: 22
Wheelchair Access: Yes

Pets: No
Children: Yes
Smoking: No
Senior Citizen Discount: No
Directions: See brochure

Channel Road Inn

219 West Channel Road
Santa Monica, CA 90402
(310) 459-1920
(310) 454-9920 Fax
E-mail: channelinn@aol.com

The history of this house is as volatile and unique as the beaches and mountains that surround it. Designed by architect Frank Kegley in 1910, today it remains a rare West Coast example of shingle-clad Colonial Revival and is listed in many architectural books as such. Originally located on Second Street, the home was built by Scottish entrepreneur Thomas McCall, who amassed a fortune in Texas oil and cattle and moved to California with his wife, Helen, and six daughters. His many civic interests keep his name alive in the community today. After the death of his daughter, Mary, 11, in 1962 the house was sold, moved from Second Street to its present location, and acquired a third story. It was never completed, however, and for 12 years, ravaged

by weather and vagrants, it stood abandoned. Its renovation and current good health seem appropriate to the original McCall spirit.

The spirit of the time, too, is evident in the Channel Road Inn interior. Evocative of the elegant lifestyle of the 1930s, the expansive rooms are filled with photos of the McCall family and memorabilia of that time. All 14 guest rooms have different furniture styles and decor, from wicker to four-posters and quilts. The coffee is fresh and strong, the muffins and breads are homemade, the service is decidedly special, and each guest is catered to with care and attention. The rejuvenating force that gave this handsome building a second chance can certainly be felt. Let's hope it will rejuvenate you too!

Rates: $95–$225
Credit Cards Accepted: Visa, MC, AMEX
Number of Guest Rooms: 14
Number of Baths: 14
Wheelchair Access: Yes

Pets: No
Children: Yes
Smoking: No
Senior Citizen Discount: No
Directions: See brochure

Literary San Francisco

Sir Arthur Conan Doyle

Everyone loves San Francisco, and Sir Arthur Conan Doyle was no exception. After visiting America's favorite city, he exclaimed: "San Francisco has always been one of my dream cities, for it has the glamour of literature, without which matter is a dead thing."

In 1923, the renowned creator of Sherlock Holmes was in town to deliver several lectures on psychic research and spiritualism, subjects he embraced late in life, after the death of his son in World War I. In his informative book *The Literary World of San Francisco and Its Environs* (no self-respecting San Francisco bibliophile should be without this guidebook), author Don Herron tells us that on his speaking tour, Doyle and his family stayed a week at The Clift Hotel. Though clearly not a B&B, The Clift Hotel, 495 Geary Street, (415) 775-4700, is an elegant hotel where you should take afternoon tea or have a martini in the beautiful cocktail lounge. Or maybe both.

If you are a genuine Sir Arthur Conan Doyle fan, you will want to go to Pacific Heights, 2151 Sacramento Street, where a plaque on the house reads, This house, built in 1881, was once occupied by Sir Arthur Conan Doyle.

In true innovative San Francisco style, this statement is just a bit of an exaggeration, because Conan Doyle actually spent only two hours here visiting a Dr. Abrams before heading off for Muir Woods. But like so much in the city by the bay, it's good local color.

If you are a Sherlock Holmes buff (and who isn't?), you can't possibly leave town without a visit to the Sherlock Holmes Public House and Drinking Salon at the Holiday Inn at Union Square, at the corner of Sutter and Powell. It's definitive San Francisco—a good learning experience and a room with a view. Before or after browsing around 221B Baker Street, spend some time gazing at the bay from the wonderful rooftop looking west to the Pacific. After touring this extremely hilly city, you deserve to stop for a drink and some complimentary hors d'oeuvres. But first stroll around the rather extensive display put up by the San Francisco branch of the International Baker Street Irregulars. Some of the highlights include a replica of the living room of 221B at five o'clock on a foggy evening in 1897, Holmes's famous violin, his purple dressing gown, Dr. Watson's desk, Holmes's huge pipe collection, and, fittingly, a portrait of his creator, Sir Arthur Conan Doyle.

Mark Twain

Prior to his arrival in San Francisco, Mark Twain had gained a degree of acclaim in Nevada for his anecdotal writings. Unfortunately, the *Enterprise* and the *Golden Era* didn't pay well enough to support him, let alone cover the losses he had accumulated as a mining speculator. In order to level his financial playing field, he hired on with a city newspaper known as the *Morning Call,* where he was required to do those things a reporter was normally expected to do: cover court cases, chase after volunteer firefighters, examine police records. One of the more sensational stories he wrote during his brief tenure on the *Call* had to do with the murder of a Private Kennedy in the Fort Mason barracks (now a youth hostel). For the most part, however, he found this line of work to be, as he describes it, "fearful drudgery, soulless drudgery … ." So it was that after a mere four months he returned to the *Golden Era* and, later, began writing for the *Californian* and the *Chronicle,* all of which gave his creative style freer rein. During this time he also developed a friendship with Bret Harte, a writer whose style and wit were more finely honed; the association was an essential stage in Twain's evolution into the author nonpareil he became.

For a number of reasons, very little remains of the buildings that were present during Mark Twain's three-year stint in San Francisco. First, as he noted in his later years in Hartford, the 1906 earthquake and fire finally repaid the *Call* for the drudgery it had imposed upon him by gutting its office building; unfortunately, Providence got a little carried away and leveled almost the entire city. What little remained of Twain's haunts after this devastation gave way to "progress" in 1959 when entrepreneurs decided that the Transamerica Building would be a better use of the space formerly occupied by the *Golden Era* offices. Thus it was that the "Monkey Block," which had served as a focus for Twain and Harte, along with Robert Louis Stevenson, Jack London, and Ambrose Bierce disappeared, leaving only a vague reminder of its literary opulence.

City Lights Bookstore
261 Columbus Avenue
San Francisco, CA 94133
(415) 362-8193

I have to confess that as a girl growing up in superstraight Indiana, I was fascinated by beatniks (and in fact wanted to be one). I wished to forgo my prim and proper basic black dress, white gloves, and string of pearls and hit the nearest coffeehouse and listen to Beat poetry.

With this in mind, on my first trip to San Francisco I headed straight to City Lights Bookstore. Now, many years later, whenever I am in San Francisco I still like to hang out at City Lights. This is time travel at its very best—enter the door and it's the sixties again.

Lawrence Ferlinghetti opened City Lights Bookstore in 1953 in North Beach, the first all-paperback bookstore in the United States. It has always been the home of Beat writers, political activists, and poetry. Ferlinghetti, who is best known for his poem *The Coney Island of the Mind,* named his bookstore for the classic Charlie Chaplin movie. As I was strolling around the large shop, I thought, Where else could you find an entire section of Beat literature, or an equally large one of Surrealism? It's much more than a bookstore. It calls itself a "Literary Meetingplace," and it also serves as a publishing house, specializing in poetry and the republication of forgotten or out-of-print classics.

Then there's the publishing history that put this beatnik bookstore on the literary map. According to Don Herron in *The Literary World of San Francisco and Its Environs,* "After Ginsberg's Six Gallery reading of 'Howl' in October 1955, Ferlinghetti sent him a note, repeating Emerson's message to Whitman upon reading *Leaves of Grass*: 'I greet you at the beginning of a great career.' But Ferlinghetti added a line: 'When do I get the manuscript'?"

Ginsberg gave Ferlinghetti his manuscript, but before it made its way to the shelves of City Lights it was seized by U.S. Customs in England in 1957, and when it finally came to San Francisco, local police arrested Ferlinghetti. After a long controversial trial that summer, a judge ruled that *Howl* was not obscene. City Lights was known from that day forward as the bastion of artistic freedom in San Francisco, maybe the country.

The other writer intimately associated with City Lights is Jack Kerouac, who was the ringleader of the Beat Generation. Kerouac's autobiographical novel, *On the Road,* is about his spiritual quest while on a cross-country tour of America. This book, which wannabe Beats loved and their parents abhored, was a chronicle of excesses of alcohol, drugs, and sex. Although City Lights and the city of San Francisco honored Kerouac by naming a street after him (formerly Adler Alley), the author ended his life as a very conservative and bitter alcoholic. He denounced his friends Ginsberg and his traveling buddy Neal Cassady (immortalized as Dean Moriarty on *On the Road)* for protesting the Vietnam War and experimenting with LSD.

Before you leave this neighborhood, you must hang out for a while at Vesuvio Cafe at 225 Columbus, next door to City Lights. Known as "a gathering place of the people of North Beach since the days of 1949," the place is a living scrapbook of literary happenings. Picture if you will Dylan Thomas drinking a few pints before going on his lecture tour, or the wild and crazy Kerouac, who got so drunk one night that instead of meeting fellow writer Henry Miller in Big Sur, he spent the night at Vesuvio's.

At the Vesuvio Cafe, San Francisco's beloved columnist, the late Herb Caen, often liked to hang out with the Beats of North Beach. After *On the Road* was a huge commercial success, Caen wrote in his column that both Sputnik and the Beats were "far out," and as he linked the two together, he coined the term "beatnik."

Dashiell Hammett Tour
P.O. Box 8755
Emoryville, CA 94662
(510) 287-9540

If you're a *Maltese Falcon* fan, you absolutely cannot leave San Francisco without seeing the very spot where Sam Spade's partner, Miles Archer, was shot with a .38 by the seductive but deadly Brigid O'Shaughnessy. Only in San Francisco would this fictitious act be commemorated by a brass plaque.

The tour is four hours of good fun and entertainment. You sense the flavor of the trek when you show up in front of the old main library and meet leader-writer Don Herron, who is appropriately clad in a snap-brim hat and trench coat. The games begin as Herron leads you over the fog-shrouded hills stalked by Sam Spade, the Continental Op, and other legendary characters created by San Francisco's most famous mystery writer. When you finish this tour, there is nothing you will not know about Hammett's days in the city by the bay. During the three-mile walk you'll visit every haunt where Hammett is known to have lived in the city and the majority of locales from *The Maltese Falcon.*

This is your chance to play detective as you shadow Sam Spade in his quest for the fabulous figurine of a mysterious black bird. Prowl the back alleys where the Continental Op, Hammett's longest-running detective, met the opposition over the barrel of his blazing .38.

Author and historian Herron is a lively guide, and along the way, he recites excerpts from Hammett's novels to give the tour some added zip. He also tells you stories about the author's work as a Pinkerton detective on the lurid Fatty Arbuckle rape-murder case; about his five-month prison term, a result of his refusal to testify in 1951 before the House Committee on Un-American Activities; his tempestuous relationship with Lillian Hellman; and his enervating attacks of tuberculosis.

If you're more of a do-it-yourselfer or an armchair detective or traveler, pick up a copy of *The Dashiell Hammett Tour* by Don Herron. You can order a copy of this book from City Lights Bookstore.

John's Grill
63 Ellis Street (between Stockton and Powell)
San Francisco, CA 94103
(415) 986-3274

You may have noted a certain culinary theme to this book; the author finds it necessary to take refreshment after exploring literary sites. So it is always a pleasure when I can report to you on an eating establishment that combines literature *and* food and drink. John's

Grill is such a place, and it is shrine for *Maltese Falcon* fans. As a matter of fact, John's Grill was a setting in Hammett's famous novel.

Where else could you find the Bloody Brigid, a special drink that arrives in a souvenir glass complete with a falcon emblazoned on it? Or how can you leave town without sampling Sam Spade's Chops, which includes rack of lamb, baked potato, and sliced tomatoes? In case you're wondering what the connection is, surely you remember that Spade pops into John's Grill right before going on the crazy car chase down to 26 Ancho in Burlingame. He phones the car company, asking for a car with a driver who'll keep his mouth shut and, "Have him pick me up at John's, Ellis Street, as soon as he can make it." And are the lamp chops authentic? You bet your black bird they are. Hammett reports, "He went to John's Grill, asked the waiter to hurry his order of chops, baked potato, and sliced tomatoes, ate hurriedly, and was smoking a cigarette with his coffee" when the driver pulled up. If Sam Spade research makes you think of drinking rather than eating, Dashiel Hammett's favorite drink was supposedly a double vodka martini with a twist.

Here's a little history about John's Grill, supplied, of course, by our leading Hammett expert, Don Herron. John's, which opened in 1908, is the only surviving restaurant mentioned in *The Maltese Falcon*. To live up to its literary obligation, on January 16, 1976, John's transformed the second floor into the Maltese Falcon Dining Room. It's great fun; you almost feel as if you are stepping into the frames of the movie *The Maltese Falcon*, starring Humphrey Bogart. There are wonderful still pictures of Bogie gracing the walls and a glass case containing books by and about Hammett, and, naturally, a facsimile of the legendary black bird.

Bret Harte

There is so much literary history in San Francisco that it would take an entire book to do it justice. As a matter of fact, there are several out there. I have already mentioned Don Herron's book; another you must have in hand as you tromp up and down the hills of this historic city is *Literary Hills of San Francisco*, by Luree Miller. It's a marvelous guide and is filled with biographies that will thrill bibliophiles. For instance, using Miller's guide, I went straight to Post Street to the Bohemian Club's building, where I saw the large bas-relief depicting the lively pioneer characters created by Bret Harte. After Harte fled Arcata (see page 18), he started his journalistic life again as a typesetter on the *Golden Era* in San Francisco. Then, in 1868, he became the founding editor of the *Overland Monthly*, a literary journal that became popular with East Coast readers. After Harte published his stories "The Luck of Roaring Camp," "The Outcasts of Poker Flat," and "Tennessee's Partner," he became an overnight literary hit. He left San Francisco for the East and then moved on to Europe. Most critics feel Harte did his best work in California.

Robert Louis Stevenson

Robert Louis Stevenson, too, has a monument in San Francisco, located on Washington Street at Portsmouth Square. Inscribed with an excerpt from his *Christmas Sermon*, it is decorated with *Treasure Island*'s galleon, the *Hispaniola* in full sail. There is something rather touching about this memorial to Stevenson because it was erected by his friends. This is a lively place to visit because it's smack dab in the middle of Chinatown and the people-watching is a major attraction.

Portsmouth Square is an appropriate spot for a Stevenson monument because it was here in 1879 that the sickly, impoverished author would sit on a bench writing his novels.

He would also think about his paramour, the controversial Fanny Osbourne, a California native he met in France. It was his pursuit of the married Osbourne that brought the lovesick Stevenson to California in the first place.

There is another plaque at 608 Bush Street, where Stevenson lived while waiting for the love of his life to get her divorce in Oakland. It was here that he wrote *From Jest to Earnest*, essays about Benjamin Franklin. In spite of a kindly landlady, Mary Carson, he became quite ill here. Certainly his poverty, coupled with his anxiety about his beloved Fanny, made his tuberculosis worse. When he started hemorrhaging, Fanny moved him from this address to a hotel near her home in Oakland. In 1880 Fanny's divorce became final and the couple was finally able to get married and move to Stevenson's homeland, Scotland. Nine years later the author returned to the United States as a celebrity—his adventure books had brought him fame and fortune. He and Fanny sailed from the Golden Gate to Samoa, where he died at the young age of forty-four.

San Francisco's Literary Hotels

Once in a while you're entitled to stay in a hotel, especially in San Francisco, where there are a multitude of literary hotels. Again from Don Herron's informative book, I learned about the following hotels, where you might see the ghosts of the great writers who once visited:

The Palace Hotel (2 Montgomery Street) played host in 1882 to the 27-year-old Oscar Wilde, who, decked out in his silk "dandy" clothes, signed in as "O. Wilde and servant." He may have dressed like a fop, but at a dinner at the Bohemian Club he apparently drank the members under the table. Rudyard Kipling checked into the Palace in the late 1880s and called the hotel "a seven-storied warren of humanity." He probably didn't have such kind words about Ambrose Bierce, then of the *San Francisco Illustrated Wasp*, who rejected Kipling's short stories.

The Clift Hotel (495 Geary Street), where Sir Arthur Conan Doyle stayed (see page 43), is also known as one of the many possible haunts of Casper Gutman, of *Maltese Falcon* fame. However, there are many other candidates for this post. The staff of the St. Francis swears Gutman (whom they seem to regard as a real person) was one of their guests. Other Hammett aficionados insist that the Sir Francis Drake was the model for Gutman's hotel. For you literary trivia fans, in the book the hotel is named the Alexandria.

The St. Francis's (335 Powell Street) guest registry lists the names of Edna St. Vincent Millay, Tennessee Williams, Damon Runyon, Ring Lardner, and H. L. Menken. In his book, Don Herron reports that in this very hotel, "over lunch in the Mural Room in 1943 Ernest Hemingway persuaded Ingrid Bergman to star in the film of his novel *For Whom the Bell Tolls.* ..." The St. Francis even rates a passage in Sinclair Lewis's classic *Babbitt,* where three traveling salesmen declare that it is "a swell place, absolutely A-1."

At the Fairmont Hotel (California and Mason Streets), Dashiell Hammett decided to see how the other half lives and borrowed money to live there extravagantly. Trying to impress and entertain his friends, he rented a suite, but by the end of the week had blown so much money that he had to borrow cash to pay for his trip back to the Big Apple. In 1936, right after he won the Nobel Prize, Eugene O'Neill checked into the Fairmont.

The Mark Hopkins (1 Nob Hill) also has a rich literary history. The colorful Gertrude Stein and her companion Alice B. Toklas stayed here as part of their United States tour in 1935.

But writers always have an opinion on everything and are not reluctant to speak or write their minds. Raymond Chandler was not so enamored of San Francisco hostelries, and in 1948 he declared, "San Francisco I liked, but its hotels stink."

San Francisco's Literary Streets

Where else but San Francisco would you find streets named after authors? I think it's a wonderful tradition that more cities should emulate. Here are some of the writers you can expect to meet on a street sign:

Jack London Street (formerly Center Street)
Jack Kerouac Street (formerly Adler Alley)
Mark Twain Plaza (formerly western end of Merchant Street)
Frank Norris Street (formerly eastern half of Austin Street)
Dashiell Hammett Street (formerly Monroe Street)
Ambrose Bierce Street (formerly Aldrich Street)
William Saroyan Place (formerly Adler Alley, east of Columbus)
Kenneth Rexroth Place (formerly Tracy Place)

The Archbishop's Mansion

1000 Fulton Street
San Francisco, CA 94117
(415) 563-7872; (800) 543-5820

One of the rooms at The Archbishop's Mansion, San Francisco, California. Photo courtesy of The Archbishop's Mansion.

For years I was never certain what people meant when they spoke of "the sophisticated elegance and privacy of a small European hotel." It took the Archbishop's Mansion to show me what that phrase is really describing. Here, truly, is a blend of modern efficiency and Old World charm. Built in 1904 for the archbishop of San Francisco himself, it is today one of the grandest of the city's Historic Landmark homes. The vivid mixture of distinctive styles might in a less-expansive setting prove overwhelming, but here the flow of second French empire, belle epoque, Victorian, and Louis XIV all seems quite appropriate. The lavish splendor of the original three-story open staircase, complete with carved mahogany columns, seems only fitting when we see it terminate in a 16-foot dome of stained glass. Eighteen fireplaces do not seem ostentatious after one has become accustomed to the delicate design of the Aubusson carpet—the detail of which is repeated in the glorious plaster ceiling above. There are no shoddy behind-the-scenes sculleries here. Nothing is frayed or worn. The integrity of the restoration is complete, from chandeliers to tester beds to claw-foot bathtubs. It is a lesson in luxury and in personal comfort.

All 15 rooms have private baths; some include fireplaces; some are suites. As a reminder that the city's renowned opera house is close by, all rooms are named for famous romantic operas: La Bohème is appropriately cozy and French; the Don Giovanni suite includes a grand parlor and overlooks the manicured lawn of Alamo Square. Continental breakfasts are brought to guests' rooms. Some of the public areas in the hotel are designated "common" rooms, but the description seems inadequate in a building of such splendor. For me, the experience of staying at the Archbishop's Mansion and having a chance to see the Bechstein player piano once owned by Noel Coward is grand in every sense of the word.

Rates: $129–$385
Credit Cards Accepted: Visa, MC, AMEX, Discover, Diners Club
Number of Guest Rooms: 15
Number of Baths: 15
Wheelchair Access: No

Pets: No
Children: Yes
Smoking: No
Senior Citizen Discount: 10% for AARP members
Directions: See brochure

Spencer House

1080 Haight Street
San Francisco, CA 94117
(415) 626-9205
(415) 626-9230 FAX

Never underestimate the power of a woman (write that down, it has a ring to it!) or a good word-of-mouth advertising campaign. If you've got it, you don't need to flaunt it: People will just know a good thing when they hear about it. This certainly explains the success of Spencer House, a B&B that began without a sign or brochures, and with an unlisted telephone number. Located in the Haight, a major intersection of the 1960s hippie counterculture, this reserved, gray Queen Anne mansion has a timeless air about it that may have kept it from total disintegration more than once in earlier days. When current owners Barbara and Jack Chambers decided to spend two years of their life on the home's restoration, they also made the major decision to do things just right. Haunting the waysides and side streets all over England and France, they found wonderful antiques, fabrics, and silver. These items were chosen with such care that they appear to have always been in place, just so, at Spencer House.

The six bedrooms and baths are furnished with fine attention to detail, from the feather ticking to the vaseline glass–globe light fixtures. The scent of morning coffee leads guests to the kitchen, filled with burnished copper and instantly memorable. A formal breakfast includes three to four courses set off by candles, crisp linens, and silver pieces, some of which one must guess over to figure out the original use and purpose. But as for the inn itself: sterling! No two ways about it!

Rates: $105–$175
Credit Cards Accepted: Visa, MC, AMEX
Number of Guest Rooms: 6
Number of Baths: 6
Wheelchair Access: No

Pets: No
Children: Yes
Smoking: No
Senior Citizen Discount: No
Directions: See brochure

COLORADO

Helen Hunt Jackson:
Colorado Springs Pioneers Museum

215 South Tejon Street
Colorado Springs, CO 80903
(719) 578-6650
(719) 578-6718 Fax

Who: Matt Mayberry, public programs coordinator

When: 10:00 A.M.–5:00 P.M. Tuesday through Saturday, 1:00–5:00 P.M. on Sunday, May through October

How Much: Free

Senior Citizen Discount: NA

Wheelchair Access: Yes

Directions: The museum is located south of downtown Colorado Springs in the historic El Paso County Courthouse. From I-25, take the Bijou Street exit east to Tejon Street; take Tejon south five blocks to the museum.

What and Where: Author Helen Hunt Jackson is one of Colorado Springs's most beloved and well-known literary figures. As progressive in her thinking as today's feminists, Jackson was a woman well ahead of her time. Respected as an astute businesswoman, she commanded a salary equal to her male peers. She was versatile and wrote travelogues, children's stories, historical accounts, and poetry, as well as one novel.

A childhood filled with tragedy turned Jackson to a literary career. Born in Amherst, Massachusetts, in 1830, the author's young life was filled with death and sadness. Her mother died of tuberculosis when Helen was 13. Her father died three years later. In 1852 Helen married Edward Hunt, an up-and-coming scientist and naval officer and had two children. But unhappiness struck again with the death of her infant son, Murray. Then Captain Hunt was killed in an accident while testing an underwater apparatus. Before she could recover from these heartaches, Rennie, her nine-year-old son, died. Helen turned to writing as a means of dealing with her sorrow.

Like so many others of her time, Helen was persuaded by her doctor to move to the West "to recover her health." She stayed briefly in Denver, then moved permanently to Colorado Springs. She initially found the "rough community" rather dismal but eventually discovered herself in the thick of the intellectual and social center of what was then called the West's "Little London" society. Besides creativity and intellectual stimulation, Helen found love in Colorado Springs. In 1875, at the age of 45, she married William Sharpless Jackson, an officer of the Denver and Rio Grande Railway

Company and founder of the El Paso County Bank.

The newlyweds established a residence in Jackson's recently constructed home at 228 East Kiowa Street. Mr. Jackson wanted his sophisticated bride to be comfortable, so he extensively remodeled his home to accommodate her tastes and to provide a spectacular view of Cheyenne Mountain.

Three rooms of this house have been preserved and are on display at the Colorado Springs Pioneers Museum, along with numerous furnishings and memorabilia from Helen Hunt Jackson's life. Her study, the living room, and dining room are preserved as Helen knew them.

The visitor can learn how Helen became impassioned with improving the life of the Native American. Her fervent support of Native Americans resulted in the writing of *Ramona,* her only novel, in 1884, the story of a lovely young woman of mixed Scottish and Indian ancestry and her Native American lover. The story was a huge success but unfortunately did little to improve the lot of American Indians.

Holden House 1902 B&B Inn

1102 West Pikes Peak Avenue
Colorado Springs, CO 80904
(719) 471-3980
(719) 471-4740 Fax
E-mail: holdenhous@aol.com

Resident owner-innkeepers Sallie and Welling Clark have lovingly restored this once-neglected 1902 Colonial Revival Victorian home and carriage house. The extensive 1986 renovation included a new foundation, plumbing, heating, wiring, and landscaping. Guests can appreciate the project by thumbing through the Holden House before-and-after photo album. Many of the inn's furnishings belonged to Sallie's grandmother, family treasures that include a parlor stove, silver tea service, and a 200-year-old Gaudy Welsh tea set. There is an eclectic collection of Victorian and traditional furnishings throughout the inn.

The Holden House, Colorado Springs, Colorado. Photo courtesy of the Holden House.

The original owner of the home, Isabel Holden, and her husband, Daniel, owned considerable mining interests in the Colorado boomtowns of Aspen, Cripple Creek, Leadville, Silverton, Goldfield, and Independence. The six guest rooms therefore take their names from these holdings. If you've read Frank Waters, you no doubt have a good idea of what life was like in "The Springs" and in the mountains for poor workaday miners and the strike-it-rich entrepreneur alike. Helen Hunt Jackson's husband, too, made his mark in the Rockies, leading the expeditions that surveyed the fourteeners, as detailed in Wallace Stegner's *Angle of Repose.*

Sallie is known for her creative breakfasts with delectable names, such as eggs fiesta, German puff pancakes, and ruffled crepes Isabel (ruffled? yes!). Daily maid service, guest telephones, freshly baked cookies, and turn-down service are just a few of the Holden House special touches. Resident cats Mingtoy and Muffin are the real owners of the inn and are such characters that you may consider them featured entertainment.

One last note of interest: The Holden House living room contains an authentic Van Briggle tile fireplace. The Van Briggle pottery factory, located on what is now the nearby campus of Colorado College, was especially famous for its Art Deco artistry, still admired by collectors the world over.

Rates: $105–$115
Credit Cards Accepted: Visa, MC, AMEX, Discover, Diners Club, Carte Blanche
Number of Guest Rooms: 5
Number of Baths: 5

Wheelchair Access: Yes
Pets: No
Children: No
Smoking: No
Senior Citizen Discount: No
Directions: See brochure

Two Sisters Inn—A B&B

Ten Otoe Place
Manitou Springs, CO 80829
(719) 685-9684; (800) 2SIS-INN

Two Sisters Inn, Manitou Springs, Colorado. Photo courtesy of Two Sisters Inn.

Manitou Springs marks the ascent to Pikes Peak and, like its Indian name, reflects both a respect for and a joy in natural wonders. Writers of geography, history, and fiction have used it as a setting. It's the kind of place Hollywood would invent if it weren't here already. And right at the beginning of the pleasant town's self-guided walking tour is the Two Sisters Inn—how convenient! The relaxed, refreshing mood is set by innkeepers Wendy Goldstein and Sharon Smith, who work in tandem so well that many guests

consider them to be the sisters in the inn's name. However, the original "two sisters" were the siblings who, in 1919, established the Sunburst boardinghouse that is now transformed into a rose-colored Victorian bungalow suitable for weary travelers and energetic area visitors alike.

The five-bedroom B&B has both private and shared baths and includes a honeymoon cottage filled with white wicker and sunshine. In the main house an attractive stained-glass front door opens into a living room featuring a native greenstone fireplace. From here one steps into the old-fashioned parlor with fainting couch (red velvet, of course) and an 1896 piano. The library attracted my attention—it contains an entire wall of cookbooks. Compliments on their breakfasts and evening treats should inspire them to write one of their own. Manitou Springs is also famous for its sparkling mineral waters. Too bad our excellent hostesses can't bottle the bubbly atmosphere they've created at the Two Sisters. What a winner that would be!

Rates: $63–$100
Credit Cards Accepted: Visa, MC,
   Discover
Number of Guest Rooms: 5
Number of Baths: 4
Wheelchair Access: No

Pets: No
Children: If older than 10
Smoking: No
Senior Citizen Discount: No
Directions: See brochure

The Hearthstone Inn

506 North Cascade Avenue
Colorado Springs, CO 80903
(719) 473-4413; (800) 521-1885
(719) 473-1322 Fax

My literary consultant, Ruth Holmes, had a real treat when she went to research the Hearthstone Inn for me. Here is her report on her stay:

"Welcome back" was the first thing I saw on The Hearthstone Inn's brochure, but little did they realize that I took this as a very personal invitation, because I actually lived in one of these two glorious "Victorian ladies" that together constitute this prime B&B. As is the story with most imposing homes of the period, the Hearthstone houses have undergone many transitions. My family lived in a ground floor apartment (now part of the Fireside Room) in the 1950s—that's when the Air Force Academy was nothing more than a sign on the windswept prairie: Future Home of. Returning all these years later, I was delighted with the variety of pastel colors used on the ouside of the inn and almost teary to see the same fireplace, the same oval stained-glass window, the same latticed entryway to what I had once called home.

Now, as then, spacious Cascade Avenue remains a noteworthy address, connecting the century-old prosperous downtown area with the beauty of Colorado College and the homes of those prospectors who made it good in the Pikes Peak gold and silver rushes. The mountain itself looms grandly behind the Hearthstone (did you know it was the inspiration for "America the Beautiful," which was written here in Colorado Springs and is note-worthy because it is so much easier to sing than our national anthem?) and many of the inn's windows have a perfect view of the "purple mountains' majesty." Also of note is the home of author Helen Hunt Jackson, but to find it you must enter the Pioneer Museum, located in the stately brick Old Courthouse downtown. The Jackson house is a proud acquisition and was moved almost in toto—books, china, mantel, doorjambs, and all.

Guests at the Hearthstone have 25 rooms from which to choose. Each, of course, is totally different from its neighbor, and the names reflect a theme: Conservatory, Hideaway, Solarium, Coachman's Retreat. Most accommodations have private baths, some even private porches—which makes for a leisurely breakfast in the summer—and others have wood-burning fireplaces—great for creating atmosphere in the winter. All rooms are furnished with antiques of walnut, oak, and cherry. A most satisfying breakfast is included in the price of each room. A sample menu might include eggs Florentine with fresh melon wedges and spicy apple cake, or a sausage and potato pie, hot pumpkin fritters, and seasonal berries. Lunches are also served, and conferences and special events are a regular part of the staff's special training and expertise. Puzzles, games, a piano, and ever-renewed fresh coffee encourage guests to congregate; however, when you prefer, in these lovely connected ladies there is always a quiet place, too. Thomas Wolfe wrote, "you can't go home again," but my return visit to the house at 506 North Cascade was an exception to that rule.

Rates: $85–$155
Credit Cards Accepted: Visa, MC, AMEX
Number of Guest Rooms: 25
Number of Baths: 23 private, 2 shared
Wheelchair Access: Yes

Pets: No
Children: Yes
Smoking: No
Senior Citizen Discount: No
Directions: See brochure

Willa Cather: Mesa Verde National Park

P.O. Box 8
Mesa Verde, CO 81330
(970) 529-4461

Who: Superintendent, Mesa Verde National Park

When: Mesa Verde National Park is open all year, but on a limited basis in winter. Weather permitting, interpretive services are offered throughout the year. The Dwelling Museum is open from 8:00 A.M.–5:00 P.M. every day from March through November. Guided tours are from 9:00 A.M.–5:00 P.M. at half-hour intervals.

How Much: Admission to the park is $5 per private vehicle or $2 per person.

Senior Citizen Discount: One-time charge of $10 for those older than 62

Wheelchair Access: Yes

Directions: See brochure

What and Where: Mesa Verde, Spanish for "green table," is so called because of its comparatively level top, heavily forested with piñon and juniper trees. Located in southwestern Colorado, the site is considered one of the nation's major archaeological preserves. Trips to the archaeological sites are conducted daily. Under the guidance of ranger-interpreters, visitors are allowed to enter some of the outstanding ruins.

Although Mesa Verde is a fascinating place in its own right, for our literary purposes, it is the site known as Cliff City in Willa Cather's novel, *The Professor's House.* Here's how Tom Outland, one of the protagonists, describes his beloved sacred land and the people who lived there:

> But the really splendid thing about our city, the thing that made it delightful to work there, and must have made it delightful to live there, was the setting. The town hung like a bird's nest in the cliff, looking off into the box canyon below, and beyond into the wide valley we called Cow Canyon, facing an ocean of clear air. ... Once again I had that glorious feeling that I've never had anywhere else, the feeling of being on the mesa, in a world above the world.

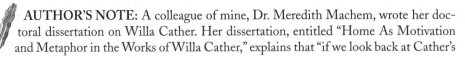 **AUTHOR'S NOTE:** A colleague of mine, Dr. Meredith Machem, wrote her doctoral dissertation on Willa Cather. Her dissertation, entitled "Home As Motivation and Metaphor in the Works of Willa Cather," explains that "if we look back at Cather's

biography, we can see that Blue Mesa in *The Professor's House* is Mesa Verde and nothing else. Cather had spent a rhapsodic time at Cliff Canyon in Mesa Verde." According to Dr. Machem,

The cliff dwellings were quite symbolic to Cather because she felt that the time she lived in was "out of joint." As many critics have noted, one of her major themes is materialism versus idealism, the commercial valueless present versus the cultured meaningful past. Her intellectual homelessness in the twentieth century caused her to search further and further into the past for a civilization that embodied traditions and customs of merit. In The Professor's House, *such a place was the culture of the cliff-dwellers.*

Machem points out that "in *The Professor's House,* the ideal civilization is dead and gone and there is no prospect of deterring the ravages of the modern world." Machem shows how the professor idealizes the Blue Mesa:

The professor's ramshackle house is exactly the opposite of those houses on Blue Mesa, the Cliff Dweller Village which Tom Outland, his student, found in a canyon. ... Everything about the Cliff City bespeaks beauty, harmony, symmetry, proportion, and design. There is no clutter, no useless ornamentation, no contradiction in the ancient village.

    The differences in setting between the professor's and Tom's sanctuaries point up the difference between the modern civilization and the ancient. The professor's house is "almost as ugly as it is possible for a house to be; square, three stories in height, painted the color of ashes"; the cliff dwellings, in contrast, are beautiful brightly colored buildings which are orderly and comfortable. Almost everything in professor St. Peters' old house is in disrepair or inconvenient in some other way; on the mesa everything is in order and intact.

Machem discusses how *The Professor's House* is an autobiographical work:

Cather went through a crisis similar to the professor's when she found that her life's work was over and done. For the most part, she had told the stories of the heroic people whom she knew, of those who had brought traditions, values, and specific treasures with them from the old world to the new and who had thus humanized their places. With the passing of the generation of settlers and the mechanization of modern society, houses no longer reflected the identities of their owners. The new materialism homogenized all people and made their lives mediocre and meaningless. To restore meaning, one had to look to other civilizations and other times. Cather juxtaposed present and past, the wasteland and the ideal society in The Professor's House, *her most interesting and experimental novel.*

Kelly Place

14663 Road G
Cortez, CO 81321
(970) 564-3125; (800) 745-4885

Where to begin when describing Kelly Place? The temptation is to start with its archaeological significance in the big picture of this special part of the world known as the Four Corners. After all, this is the setting of Willa Cather's *The Professor's House*. Ancient ruins

Artist's rendition of Kelly Place. Artwork courtesy of Kelly Place.

abound; there are over 25 documented Anasazi sites on this 100 acres of famous McElmo Canyon. A full-time archaeologist teaches classes here, overseeing the excavation and restoration. The bordering "landlord" is the Bureau of Land Management, with 6,000 acres of pristine not-for-sale real estate. From 14,000-foot mountains to cliff dwellings, river rafting to covered wagon trips—Kelly Place can accommodate almost any wish list for the western traveler.

But there's more! Established by botanist George Kelly, who designed the Denver Botanic Gardens, and beautifully maintained for the last 15 years by owners Rodney and Krisie Carriker, this property is also a unique oasis in the high desert. Apricot and apple orchards, vineyards and flowering gardens—horticultural delights to please all the senses abound.

The lodge itself is an adobe-style building with courtyards. The eight bedrooms all have private baths and queen-size beds. As you would expect, the atmosphere is relaxed, the food is hearty, and at night you can reach up and almost touch the stars.

Rates: $69–$99
Credit Cards Accepted: Visa, MC, Discover
Number of Guest Rooms: 10
Number of Baths: 10
Wheelchair Access: No

Pets: No
Children: Yes
Smoking: No
Senior Citizen Discount: No
Directions: See brochure

Silver River Adobe Inn

P.O. Box 3411
3151 West Main
Farmington, NM 87499
(505) 325-8219; (800) 382-9251

Only 20 miles from the Colorado border, Farmington is an entrance to that magical Four Corners area, unique on the map (four states adjoin here at right angles), homeland of the ancient Anasazi, territory rife with legend and natural settings of unbelievable space and grandeur. Pick a direction, any direction, and you're adventure bound! Choosing the Silver River Adobe Inn as your point of reference is a good move, because it is situated directly on the San Juan River, route of myth and transportation for centuries. The inn is perched, quite literally, on a sandstone cliff some 30 feet above the water, and a new guest addition has a sitting area right there over the water! Built in traditional northern New Mexico style, the building maintains that charm that resides innately, it seems, in architecture of this kind: rough adobe bricks, Mexican tile countertops, small paned windows, and plenty of handcrafted pine woodwork. The stories from this area will energize you—works by Frank Waters, Willa Cather, Tony Hillerman—yet the simple adobe, piñon-scented fireplaces, and the whispering river will impart a tranquillity found nowhere else.

Rates: $65–$125
Credit Cards Accepted: Visa, MC, AMEX
Number of Guest Rooms: 3
Number of Baths: 3
Wheelchair Access: Yes

Pets: No
Children: If older than 12
Smoking: No
Senior Citizen Discount: No
Directions: See brochure

Blue Lake Ranch

16919 State Highway 140
Hesperus, CO 81326
(970) 385-4537
(970) 385-4088 Fax

Literary muses abound at the Blue Lake Ranch. Arriving in this magical world, a bed and breakfast inn some 20 miles west of Durango, Colorado, is like stepping into a novel by Colette. There are rooms crowded with colorful flowers, a kitchen table set with the seasonal delights the ranch has produced. Everywhere are the reassuring odors of good food cooking. And, as Colette would have wanted, the windows of the garden room are filled with pots of herbs, lemon and lime trees, and sweet geraniums. These simple pleasures gave Colette a sense of peacefulness. Half a century later, they do the same for me.

Because of the splendid gardens here, English authors spring to mind, perhaps Beatrix Potter or Wordsworth. Since there are grazing herds of sheep, I thought of the tales of the kindly Yorkshire veterinarian James Herriot in *All Creatures Great and Small.* Supply your favorite author, bring her book, and laze away the day in this peaceful, secluded spot. Because the literary site in this area is Mesa Verde, which inspired Willa Cather's *The Professor's House,* that book would be perfect mood reading.

At the ranch there are gardens everywhere and seemingly hundreds of varieties of flowers, and the eponymous blue lake around which peacocks strut their stuff.

The rooms echo this peaceful garden scenery, especially our favorite, the spacious Garden Room. This huge suite, glowing in its yellow and pink decor, is luxurious, with a pink-and-white chaise lounge and loveseat, antique writing desk, huge wooden armoires, and old family pictures. From every room there are unparalleled views of the beautiful La Plata Mountains, which form a backdrop to the lake.

We awoke in the morning to the lilting sounds of classical music and the sight of birds flitting about the lush gardens. Breakfast was in a tropical greenhouse overlooking another of the gardens. The convivial atmosphere was conducive to civilized conversations with strangers who quickly became friends.

Summer breakfasts feature a traditional European buffet of muesli, three big wheels of cheese, two kinds of meat, yogurt, two types of homemade bread with homemade jam, fresh fruits, coffee, tea, and juice.

Winter breakfasts are hardier, perhaps omelettes with cheese and pesto sauce with piñon nuts and homemade sausage, or French toast with huge boysenberries.

On our several visits, we were served these delicious repasts by innkeepers Shirley and David Alford. Shirley, an M.D. and native of Durango, uses her exceptional organizational skills to keep this gem of an inn running. David is the gardener and cook, as well as a full-time dad to their daughter and son. At first glance, David's 6-foot 4-inch frame wouldn't seem to indicate a man who loves to garden, putter around in the kitchen, and, most of all, make his guests feel welcome.

The country gentleman's lifestyle is a natural evolution for this former social worker, who spent every childhood summer on his grandparents' farm on Lake Erie. "We had a wonderful garden. I have this image of my grandmother with armloads of peonies and irises," Alford said one morning while refilling our coffee cups. "Of course, as a child, I didn't realize how much work a garden was. My grandmother had gardeners—men to dig, she called them—and all she did was pick the flowers. Now that I have my own ranch, I realize that I am the man to dig."

Alford's stunning gardens are not just for looks. Blue Lake is a working ranch. After Alford has finished whipping up breakfast, he turns his attention to one of his other enterprises: preserving and selling heirloom seeds—varieties that would become extinct if someone didn't keep them growing. The Flanders poppies, one type of seed Alford sells, cover an entire hillside on the ranch with intense red and black hues. The seeds came from neighbors—three elderly sisters whose grandmother originally brought the seeds from France.

Alford also breeds lambs and markets a wide array of edibles, such as vanilla bean honey; lavender jelly; peach and raspberry jam; sage, dill, and garlic vinegar; and edible flower garnish. If, as Shakespeare says, "There's rosemary, that's for remembrance," who could ever forget Blue Lake Ranch?

Rates: $60–$245
Credit Cards Accepted: None
Number of Guest Rooms: 12
Number of Baths: 12
Wheelchair Access: No

Pets: No
Children: Yes
Smoking: No
Senior Citizen Discount: No
Directions: See brochure

Oscar Wilde in Leadville

Leadville seems an odd place for the literati to gather, but gather they did in this mining town at 10,188 feet. Even by Colorado Rocky Mountain standards, Leadville is considered to have a rigorous, some would say inhospitable, climate. It is hard to imagine Oscar Wilde in this Wild West setting, but according to *The Colorado Book*, by Eleanor M. Gehres, Sandra Dallas, Maxine Benson, and Stanley Cuba, Wilde was on a lecture tour through the United States in 1882, and the only things he liked in this country were Walt Whitman and the Rocky Mountains. Here's what Oscar Wilde, one of the world's great wits, had to say about Leadville in his essay, "Impressions of America,"

> *From Salt Lake City one travels over the great plains of Colorado and up the Rocky Mountains, on the top of which is Leadville, the richest city in the world. It has also got the reputation of being the roughest, and every man carries a revolver. I was told that if I went there they would be sure to shoot me or my travelling manager. I wrote and told them that nothing that they could do to my travelling manager would intimidate me. They are miners—men working in metals, so I lectured to them on the Ethics of Art. I read them passages from the autobiography of Benvenuto Cellini and they seemed much delighted. I was reproved by my hearers for not having brought him with me. I explained that he had been dead for some little time which elicited the enquiry, "Who shot him?" They afterwards took me to a dancing saloon where I saw the only rational method of art criticism I have ever come across. Over the piano was printed a notice: PLEASE DO NOT SHOOT THE PIANIST. HE IS DOING HIS BEST.*
>
> *The mortality among pianists in that place is marvelous. Then they asked me to supper, and having accepted, I had to descend a mine in a rickety bucket in which it was impossible to be graceful. Having got into the heart of the mountain I had supper,*

the first course being whisky, the second whisky and the third whisky. … So infinitesimal did I find the knowledge of Art, west of the Rocky Mountains, that an art patron—one who had in his day had been a miner—actually sued the railroad company for damages because the plaster cast of Venus of Milo, which he had imported from Paris, had been delivered minus the arms. And, what is more surprising still, he gained his case and the damages.

Wallace Stegner in Leadville

In *Angle of Repose*, his lyrical, beautifully written novel based on the lives of his grandparents, author Wallace Stegner shows the reader the impact Leadville had on his characters, Oliver Ward, a mining engineer, and Susan Ward, a writer-illustrator. They first see Leadville from their seat on a narrow-gauge train.

Susan says, "The train's so little, after the Santa Fe. If I should draw us now, I'd take a position away behind and above, and show us as a teeny little toy disappearing into these enormous mountains."

"Hang around a while," Oliver said. "When we get to Slack's and pick up the team we'll be an even teenier speck disappearing into even bigger mountains."

"Deeper and deeper into the West. They call Leadville the Cloud City, don't they?"

Later, when the couple is settled in their log cabin, Susan thinks about her new mountain home:

The thin air smelled of stone and snow, the sun came through it and lay warm on her hands and face without warming the air itself. Up, up, up. There was no top to this pass. Oliver said it crested at more than thirteen thousand feet. They were long past all trees, even runted ones.

Later in the Leadville chapter, Stegner introduces the beloved Colorado author Helen Hunt Jackson:

One morning a knock came on the door, and Susan opened it to see a stout, bright-eyed, self-assured little lady standing there: Helen Hunt Jackson, sent to her like a valentine by their mutual friend Augusta. As a literary lady married to a mining engineer, and resident in the West, Mrs. Jackson could hardly have been more reassuring to Grandmother.

The Leadville Country Inn

127 East Eighth Street
P. O. Box 1989
Leadville, CO 80461
(719) 486-2354; (800) 748-2354

Picket fence, clapboard and shingle siding, and cozy front porch all lend a first impression of hospitality and warmth that is not contradicted. Upon entering the Leadville Country Inn, an additional sensory impression probably will be the heavenly aromas wafting from the kitchen, because almost all guests comment on the wonderful food provided in the "breakfast" half of "B&B." Skeptics, of course, may say that anything tastes good at an altitude of over 10,000 feet, but don't believe them. I am enough of a cook to realize the difficulty of high-altitude baking and therefore am even more impressed by the fare provided at the Leadville Country Inn. The town itself is noted for its mining history and in recent years has become a year-round destination for outdoor enthusiasts, history buffs, and antiquers. The inn provides amenities appreciated by all of these guests and has a long list of quotable recommendations to prove it.

Rates: $47–$149
Credit Cards Accepted: Visa, MC, AMEX, Discover, Diners Club
Number of Guest Rooms: 9
Number of Baths: 9
Wheelchair Access: No
Pets: No
Children: If older than 10
Smoking: No
Senior Citizen Discount: No
Directions: US Highway 24 becomes Harrison Avenue in Leadville; turn east on Eighth Street.

The Apple Blossom Inn

120 West 4th Street
Leadville, CO 80461
(719) 486-2141; (800) 982-9279

The five Senn sisters must have made a joyful noise when they were growing up. They've all gone off to their own endeavors now, but innkeeper Maggie Senn, one of the sisters, has recalled fond memories by naming half the guest accommodations in the Apple Blossom after her four sisters: Elizabeth, Kate, Amy, and Julia Rooms. A nice touch, don't you think? Since all beds are made up with four pillows, I also imagine the great pillow fights that may be commemorated.

The library is yet another guest room, once the office of the original owner, banker A. V. Hunter. Five stained glass windows and a parquet floor make this special, much as Estelle's room is memorable for its Victorian fireplace, sitting area, and private bath. The Rose and Spring Rooms share a bath but keep their own individual appeal. The inn retains much of its 1879 ambience, due mainly to the handsome original appointments: crystal and brass light fixtures, Florentine tile fireplace surrounding beveled mirrors, intricately carved woodwork, and brilliantly colored stained-glass windows. The inn, in fact, is named for the eye-catching window design of eleven apple blossoms with garnet centers.

Full breakfasts are served—always a welcome notation—and packed lunches are available for on-the-go guests. The old-fashioned cookie jar, refilled daily, must also be a reminder of those days when five small hands dove into it upon returning home from school.

Maggie runs a "green inn," with recycling and conservation programs in place, and a portion of each room rental is donated to such nonprofits as the National Trust for Historic Preservation, Public Broadcasting Service, World Hunger Relief, Amnesty International, and the Wilderness Society. Our conscientious hostess sets a good example; we can learn the finer lessons of conservation and familial affection from her at the Apple Blossom Inn.

Rates: $59–$128
Credit Cards Accepted: Visa, MC, AMEX, Discover, Diners Club
Number of Guest Rooms: 7
Number of Baths: 5
Wheelchair Access: No
Pets: No
Children: Yes
Smoking: No
Senior Citizen Discount: Yes
Directions: See brochure

CONNECTICUT

* ─ ◊ ─ *

The Harriet Beecher Stowe Center

73 Forest Street
Hartford, CT 06105
(860) 525-9317; (860) 522-9258
(860) 522-9259 Fax

Who: Visitor center

When: Memorial Day through Columbus Day, 9:30 A.M.–4:00 P.M. Monday through Saturday and 12:00 noon–4:00 P.M. Sunday. Closed on Monday the rest of the year.

How Much: $6.50 for adults; $2.75 for children ages 6 through 16

Senior Citizen Discount: Yes

Wheelchair Access: Yes

Directions: Call for directions

What and Where: The last residence of Harriet Beecher Stowe, whose *Uncle Tom's Cabin, The American Woman's Home,* and other writings made her one of the most successful authors of nineteenth-century America, was one of the first Victorian house restorations in the country. Guided tours provide an intimate glimpse into the life of the Stowe family, including some of Mrs. Stowe's paintings, her writing table, family and professional memorabilia, period furnishings, and historical gardens. Seasonal displays showcase holiday settings and household events.

The Stowe House and neighboring Mark Twain House are reminders of an era when this part of Hartford—called Nook Farm—was home to many national figures in the arts and social reform. These include Isabella Beecher Hooker, suffragist and women's rights leader; John Hooker, lawyer and abolitionist; William Gillette, playwright and actor, famous for his portrayal of Sherlock Holmes.

Built in 1871, the Stowe House is a fine example of the then-popular "cottage" style, exemplifying a comfortable, rather than ostentatious, style of living. The kitchen, patterned after a model advocated by Mrs. Stowe and her sister, Catherine Beecher, in their book *The American Woman's Home,* boasts all the modern conveniences of the period. Mrs. Stowe lived here from 1873 until her death in 1896.

Also on the property is the home of Katharine S. Day, grandniece of Harriet Beecher Stowe and benefactor of the Stowe-Day Foundation, who purchased this building in 1939 as part of her effort to preserve elements of the Nook Farm area. Today the 1884 Day House, with its handsome period interior, provides changing gallery space for the holdings of the Stowe Center and the Stowe-Day Library, a major research collection focusing on cultural and family history, social reform, women's studies, and decorative arts. Researchers are welcome by appointment. Public forums, live performances, and reading/discussion groups are all part of the educational facility commitment of the Stowe Center.

Mark Twain's House

351 Farming Avenue
Hartford, CT 06105
(860) 493-6411

Who: Visitor center

When: From Memorial Day through Columbus Day, 9:30 A.M.–5:00 P.M. Monday through Saturday, 11:00 A.M.–5:00 P.M. Sunday; during the rest of the year closed on Tuesday, open from 12:00 noon–4:00 P.M. on Sunday. Closed on major holidays.

How Much: $7.50 for adults; $3.50 for children ages 6 to 12

Senior Citizen Discount: $7

Wheelchair Access: Yes

Directions: Map on brochure

What and Where: What will you find at Mark Twain's Hartford, Connecticut, home? Perhaps it was best described by a tour guide who deftly noted, "It's one-third river boat, one-third cathedral and one-third cuckoo clock." And an elaborate river boat–cathedral–cuckoo clock it is.

When Samuel Clemens moved to Hartford with his new bride, he hired architect Edward Tuckerman Potter and interior designer Louis Tiffany to create a house in which he would be comfortable. "Avoid plain walls at all costs," he cautioned his builders. Potter and Tiffany's finished product was an intricate blend of American, Oriental, Turkish, and Indian style, with Twain's exuberance flooding every room and passageway. It cost $100,000 (in 1876) to build, and almost that much to maintain every year.

This was the only home Twain stayed in for any length of time. The author was a restless soul who lived in every part of the United States and traveled the globe several times over. But for 17 years—the 17 years that he was surrounded by his three daughters, Susy, Clara, and Jean—he stayed put in this one house and here wrote his greatest works.

The library is one of the main rooms of the house. A huge carved wooden mantle surrounds its fireplace. The Clemenses had the mantle brought from Scotland, where it was salvaged from an ancient castle. Across it, Twain had carved a quote from Emerson: "The ornament of a house is the friends that frequent it."

And friends the Clemenses did have. On many an evening a whole host of Twain's literary friends attended dinner parties in the large, elaborate dining room, then retired to the library, where Twain's three daughters acted out scenes of their father's work. Their stage was the rounded solarium that adjoined the library.

Twain could have used the library to write in, or he could have used the cozy second-story room that had been designed to be his study, but where he ended up, where he produced the manuscripts of his greatest works, was the third-story billiard room with his desk shoved up against a plain wall (one of the few plain walls in the whole house). From midmorning until dinner time Twain sat, writing page after page, as he completed one manuscript after another: *Roughing It, The Gilded Age, The Adventures of Tom Sawyer, A Tramp Abroad, The Prince and the Pauper, Life on the Mississippi,*

The Adventures of Huckleberry Finn, A Connecticut Yankee in King Arthur's Court.

Fortunately or unfortunately, writing was not Twain's only interest. He had a curiosity about gadgets. (Twain was one of the first writers to use a typewriter.) And the gadget that interested him most was the Paige typesetting machine. This machine, Twain was sure, would revolutionize the printing industry and make him a wealthy man. In reality, what it made him was bankrupt, for he lost over $300,000 in a venture to promote its use in publishing.

In 1891 Twain closed up his house and moved his family to Europe, where they could live more cheaply. Then, for two years he went on lecture tours around the world, charming audiences in Europe, India, South Africa, and Australia. In the end he returned to the United States an international hero.

But Twain's popularity and financial comeback were eclipsed by a personal tragedy. While he and the rest of his family were visiting England, his daughter Susy, then 26 years old, contracted spinal meningitis at home and died in Connecticut before her parents were able to see her again. After that, the house in Hartford contained too many memories. Twain closed it and put it up for sale. After several years on the market it sold, finally, for a mere $28,000. From then on it switched hands several times, being a private home, a boys' school, a storage warehouse, an apartment house, and a branch of the Hartford Library. In 1955, however, the Mark Twain Memorial Foundation began restoration work, bringing the mansion back to the splendor of the days of Mark Twain.

Butternut Farm

1654 Main Street
Glastonbury, CT 06033
(860) 633-7197
(860) 659-1758 Fax

If you want the experience of staying in a house that is older than the United States of America, you might consider Butternut Farm. Through careful renovation, innkeeper Don Reid has rediscovered the original wide brick fireplaces, the broad floorboards, and the paneling on many of the walls of this 1720 house. Even the hinges have been hammered by hand. To complement the architecture, Mr. Reid has furnished his bed and breakfast with eighteenth-century Connecticut antiques and landscaped the grounds with flower and herb gardens.

There's no hyperbole in the name. Butternut Farm is a farm with prize dairy goats, pot-bellied pigs, a llama, and Mr. Reid's flocks of chickens, doves, ducks, and geese. A full breakfast, including eggs (fresh from the henhouse), milk, cheese, and homemade jams, is served in the original kitchen or in a cozy breakfast room.

The overnight accommodations include two rooms with private baths, plus a suite and an apartment, each with a private bath.

Butternut Farm is a ten-minute drive from Mark Twain's Hartford home.

Rates: $70–$90
Credit Cards Accepted: AMEX
Number of Guest Rooms: 5
Number of Baths: 5
Wheelchair Access: No
Pets: No
Children: Yes
Smoking: No
Senior Citizen Discount: No
Directions: See brochure

Simsbury 1820 House

731 Hopmeadow Street
Simsbury, CT 06070
(203) 658-7658; (800) TRY-1820

It is always the best season of the year at the Simsbury 1820 House! For instance, the Fourth of July means an ice cream social on the great lawn, with music and festivities continuing a turn-of-the-century tradition. Decorations and amenities change with the season, but the attention to detail of host Wayne Bussey and his knowledgeable staff remains constant. The graciously restored country manor overlooks the center of this historic town and was once home to Gifford Pinchot, father of the American conservation movement.

Listed on the National Register of Historic Places, the inn retains the integrity of its original design yet offers modern accommodations for its guests. The 34 bedrooms are decorated in reproduction fabric and furniture of the eighteenth and nineteenth centuries. Overstuffed chairs and four-poster beds bespeak comforts of a bygone era, and private baths, phones, televisions, and air conditioning provide the luxuries of our current age. Simsbury 1820 House features a restaurant that has received national acclaim, assuring you a menu of outstanding variety.

Rates: $110–$150
Credit Cards Accepted: Visa, MC, AMEX, Discover
Number of Guest Rooms: 32
Number of Baths: 32
Wheelchair Access: Yes

Pets: Yes
Children: Yes
Smoking: Yes
Senior Citizen Discount: 10% for AARP members
Directions: Brochure contains map

Manor House

P.O. Box 447
Maple Avenue
Norfolk, CT 06058
(860) 542-5690

"There's so much to see and do in this area," say Manor House innkeepers Diane and Hank Tremblay, but frankly, this large turn-of-the-century home and its garden are so beautiful it would seem enough just to sit quietly and admire the view. This Victorian English Cottage–style mansion was built for the leisure class of an earlier era—that Gilded Age Mark Twain described so succinctly. And there is actually a Twain connection here, for he often summered in Norfolk. That home, alas, burned to the ground a decade ago, but still standing and directly across from

Manor House is the handsome Episcopal Church of the Transfiguration, which Twain attended when he was in town. In fact, one of his daughters gave a concert to raise money for the irreplaceable Louis Comfort Tiffany stained glass windows in the church.

Tiffany windows also grace Manor House, and along with the antiques, fireplaces, and a grand piano, lend the charm of a bygone era to this very special place. Ainsworth Rand Spofford built this home in 1898. He was Abraham Lincoln's librarian of Congress, charged with collecting and collating two copies of every book printed in the United States.

Manor House menus change daily and include such hearty fare as orange waffles, French toast with raspberries, and poached eggs with lemon butter and chive sauce. The accompanying honey is harvested from hives in the splendid perennial garden. All guest rooms have private baths; additional amenities include balconies, fireplaces, and a Jacuzzi. Located only a short drive from Edith Wharton, Herman Melville, and yet more Mark Twain territory, I still say that Manor House itself will be difficult to leave or to match.

Rates: $85–$190
Credit Cards Accepted: Visa, MC, AMEX, Discover
Number of Guest Rooms: 8
Number of Baths: 8
Wheelchair Access: No

Pets: No
Children: If older than 12
Smoking: No
Senior Citizen Discount: Yes
Directions: See brochure

Eugene O'Neill: The Monte Cristo Cottage

325 Pequot Avenue
New London, CT 06320
(860) 443-0051
(860) 443-5378 Fax

Who: Lois McDonald, assistant curator

When: Memorial Day through October 10:00 A.M.–5:00 P.M. Tuesday through Saturday, 1:00–5:00 P.M. Sunday; guided tours are available at 10:00 A.M., 12 noon, 2:00 P.M., and 4:00 P.M.

How Much: $4 for adults and students

Senior Citizen Discount: No

Wheelchair Access: No

Directions: Call for directions

What and Where: One of America's greatest playwrights, Eugene O'Neill, was born in a New York hotel, but the place he called home was the Monte Cristo Cottage in New London, Connecticut. O'Neill worked as a reporter for the local paper until he was hospitalized with tuberculosis. Recovering, he decided to become a playwright instead of the poet he had planned to be. Leaving a trail of broken hearts behind him, the handsome young man left New London to study drama at Harvard. O'Neill went on to win four Pulitzer Prizes and the Nobel Prize for literature.

But it was the playwright's father, the actor James O'Neill, who created Monte Cristo Cottage. The well-known matinee idol named the cottage after his most popular role, the swashbuckler Edmond Dantè's in *The Count of Monte Cristo*. The product of a wretched Irish childhood, the elder O'Neill was a penny-pincher who expected to end up in the poorhouse. In 1884 he purchased this property, an 1840 farmhouse and a one-room school, remodeling the farmhouse into a Victorian stick-style house with a porch, a front staircase, and a tower with a "witch's hat" roof. Curator Sally Pavetti describes the cottage as a modest house, resembling the Cabot family home in Eugene O'Neill's *Desire Under the Elms*.

The elegant windows in the front parlor provide a glimpse into the writer's imagination. O'Neill's masterpiece, *Long Day's Journey into Night*, and his only comedy, *Ah, Wilderness!* are set in this very room, which is called "the sitting room" in his plays. It has been meticulously restored according to his stage directions. Nothing is in the parlor that is not specified in the scripts. It is interesting to note that O'Neill said that *Ah, Wilderness!* was a nostalgic dream of what he wished his adolescence might have been.

Eugene O'Neill felt great affection for the Monte Cristo Cottage because it was the only permanent home he ever knew. The O'Neill family were theater gypsies and tagged along with James, staying in second-rate, dingy hotels. As a matter of fact, it was in the hotel of his birth, the Barrett House in New York, on Broadway and 43rd Street, that one of the defining moments of Eugene's life took place. The hotel doctor prescribed morphine for his mother Ella's postnatal pain, and she never failed to remind her son that her lifelong addiction was because of his birth.

Permanent displays feature not only the playwright and the New London connection, but also his father (James O'Neill's stage sword is on display); his daughter, Oona, who became the fourth and last wife of Charlie Chaplin; and the playwright's tempestuous third wife, Carlotta Monterey O'Neill. Louis Schaeffer, O'Neill's biographer, called their marriage a "Strindbergian nightmare."

Eugene O'Neill died in a Boston hotel in 1953. His last words were, "Born in a goddam hotel room and dying in a hotel room."

Eugene O'Neill Theater Center

305 Great Neck Road
Waterford, CT 06385
(860) 443-5378
(860) 443-9653 Fax

Who: Box office, (860) 443-1238

When: Summer only; there are matinee and evening performances.

How Much: $8 to $12

Senior Citizen Discount: No

Wheelchair Access: Yes

Directions: Call box office

What and Where: The Eugene O'Neill Theater Center is a thespian's dream come true. The center's many and varied offerings include the National Playwrights' Conference, the National Music Theater Conference, the Cabaret Symposium—which is targeted at cabaret performers—and the National Puppetry Conference, which is highly recommended by Pinocchio, Punch and Judy, and friends.

Twice a year the center hosts the National Theater Institute. Students receive college credits in theater while living on site for 13 weeks. As the Bard of Avon reminds us, "The play's the thing!"

Lighthouse Inn

6 Guthrie Place
New London, CT 06320-4206
(860) 443-8411; (800) 678-8946
(860) 437-7027 Fax

A view of the lighthouse, to paraphrase Virginia Woolf, lends a necessary perspective to anyone's life. Here's an opportunity to test this statement and have a glorious good time doing it. The Lighthouse Inn is one of those timeless beachfront mansions of another era that has retained its beauty and dignity with a usefulness that assures its future as well. Listed by the National Trust for Preservation as one of the Historic Hotels of America, this 1902 Mediterranean-style country house was built by steel magnate Charles S. Guthrie. It overlooks Long Island Sound and still retains its private beach. Originally named Meadow Court because of the surrounding fields and wildflowers, the formal grounds and gardens were designed by noted landscape architect Frederick Law Olmsted, who also designed New York's Central Park.

The mansion itself forms a half circle that allows every room a view (are we back to Ms. Woolf again?) of either the gardens or the sound. Meadow Court in its heyday was a focal point for society functions as well as a retreat for film stars such as Bette Davis and Joan Crawford. The inn has been in operation since 1927, and the 27 mansion rooms and 24 carriage-house rooms are finely appointed with antiques, fireplaces, and private baths. For 70 years, the experienced staff has hosted events, from festive weddings to professional business conferences. The Mansion Restaurant is known throughout the state and boasts a Sunday brunch to rival anything in Connecticut. Enjoy the views, the beach, the food, the gardens, and be aware that the stately white lighthouse is presiding over and subtly influencing it all.

Rates: $75–$255
Credit Cards Accepted: Visa, MC, AMEX
Number of Guest Rooms: 50
Number of Baths: 50
Wheelchair Access: No

Pets: No
Children: Yes
Smoking: Yes
Senior Citizen Discount: No
Directions: See brochure

DISTRICT OF COLUMBIA

Literary Washington, D.C.

Since its founding in 1800, the nation's capital has attracted writers the way Paris has always drawn lovers. Granted, many of them didn't stay long, but the authors who came to visit or work in Washington make up an impressive who's who of America's greatest writers.

Some traveled through briefly, chronicling their experiences during times of war and peace; others came to work as bureaucrats for the government or simply to tour the city and its monuments. A few drank their way through the Foggy Bottom, giving the city's nickname a whole new meaning.

Whatever their purpose in sojourning here, literary lions such as Edgar Allan Poe, Walt Whitman, Mark Twain, Willa Cather, Louisa May Alcott, Zora Neale Hurston, Langston Hughes, and a card catalogue of others left their influences on a city known more for its love of politics than of prose.

Perhaps William Faulkner's description of his 1954 visit to Rockville, Maryland, for his daughter's engagement aptly explains why so many creative souls came—and quickly left—the capital: "It was the damnedest collection of prosperous concerned stuff-shirt Republican senators and military brass hats and their be-upholstered and be-coiffed beldames as you ever saw," he wrote. "Fortunately, hardly any of them ever heard of me, so I was let alone."

In 1842, Edgar Allan Poe arrived on a publicity tour in order to collect subscriptions for a proposed literary magazine as well as to secure a job in a federal customs house. His backers arranged a lecture and a visit with President John Tyler, touting Poe as one of the most "powerful, chaste and erudite" authors of his time. But after downing too much port his first night in town, followed by a mint-julep spree with Civil War photographer Mathew Brady, Poe missed both appointments. He left after five days, jobless and without a single subscription, branded unreliable by the magazine's backers.

Mint juleps were all the rage that year. Charles Dickens also came to Washington in 1842 on a tour of the States, which he described in his *American Notes*. He dined at the home of author and orator Daniel Webster, feasting on opossum served Virginia style—stuffed with chestnuts—and mint juleps. He stayed up late toasting one of Webster's guests—New York writer Washington Irving, who was preparing to travel to Spain on a diplomatic assignment.

Emily Dickinson's 1855 visit with her father, a Massachusetts congressman, was much more sedate. (Yes, she did occasionally leave Amherst.) She stayed at the Willard Hotel and visited George Washington's grave at Mount Vernon, which stirred her poetic soul: "One soft spring day we glided down the Potomac in a painted boat, and jumped upon the shore ... hand in hand we stole along up a tangled pathway 'til we reached the tomb," she wrote.

The outbreak of the Civil War in 1861 brought a number of writers who helped tend wounded Union troops lying in army encampments and in the hospital wards that filled the city. Louisa May Alcott arrived from Boston to serve in the nurses' corps, but after six weeks she contracted typhoid fever and returned home with her health permanently damaged by the mercury compound prescribed as a cure. Alcott's *Hospital Sketches* contains the letters she wrote from Washington describing the horrors of war.

When Walt Whitman went down to Washington in 1862 from New York, *Leaves of Grass* was already in its third edition. His brother George had been seriously wounded during the first battle of Fredericksburg, and Whitman hurried to his side on the battlefield, where he encountered the unbelievable suffering he later described in *Specimen Days and Collect*. While his brother recovered, Whitman settled in Washington, secured a part-time job as an army paymaster, and wrote occasional articles about the war for *The New York Times* in order to earn a meager salary. But most of his energy went to comforting wounded soldiers in makeshift hospitals throughout the city, delivering food, newspapers, and books, reading them Bible passages, and writing their letters home.

Whitman's presence became familiar to the soldiers, but the long, exhausting hours and his inadequate income contributed to a physical breakdown in 1864. Doctors sent him home to Brooklyn to recuperate for six months. He returned the following year and spent seven years working and writing in Washington, producing *Drum-Taps*, a volume of poems containing the revered odes to Lincoln, "When Lilacs Last in the Dooryard Bloom'd" and "O Captain! My Captain!" and a number of other works. He also continued adding constant revisions to his opus, *Leaves of Grass*. In 1873, while living in a tiny attic room across the street from the Treasury Department, he suffered a severe stroke and left Washington for his brother's house in Camden, New Jersey, where he continued working until his death in 1892.

Mark Twain paid a brief visit to postwar Washington in 1867 at the invitation of Senator William Stewart of Nevada, whom he had met during his days in the mining camps out West. He was supposed to serve as secretary and speechwriter for Stewart but after a few weeks was fired because he spent more time enjoying the senator's cigars and whiskey and finishing *The Innocents Abroad*. He left in 1868, thoroughly disgusted with politicians: "It could probably be shown by facts and figures that there is no distinctly American criminal class except for Congress," he said.

Twain may have despised the demeanor of Washington's politicos, but he must have been impressed by their fashion because he allegedly started wearing his trademark white suits during his stay here. The house he occupied sat at F and 14th Streets, NW, but was torn down to make way for Garfinckel's, a popular department store that went out of business in 1990.

In 1877 Bret Harte was invited to Washington to edit a new magazine called *The Capital*. The 1870 publication of his collection of short stories, *The Luck of Roaring Camp and Other Sketches*, had launched him so quickly into fame that he quit his teaching job in California, traveled east, and started writing fiction for *The Atlantic Monthly*. But financial backing for *The Capital* never materialized, and after several months living in a hotel, Harte was appointed U.S. consul in Germany, then Scotland. He spent the rest of his life in London.

Frances Hodgson Burnett, who was born in England and raised in Tennessee, held court as a legendary hostess in Washington during the late 1800s. Her residence at 1219 I Street NW (where she wrote *Little Lord Fauntleroy*) became a spectacular salon visited by Oscar Wilde during his American lecture tour of 1882. (Wilde's outrageous attire consisted of a black-silk claw hammer coat, a flowered waistcoat, knee breeches, silk stockings, and broad-buckled patent leather pumps, which allegedly shocked the staid Washingtonians.) Today a parking lot occupies the site of Burnett's former home.

From 1886 to 1890 Burnett lived at 1730 K Street NW, where she continued to host her famous salons until she and her husband, optometrist Dr. Swann Burnett, built a grand residence at 1770 Massachusetts Avenue NW, where she wrote more than 50 books before her death in 1924.

Ambrose Bierce brought his dark humor to the capital in 1899 and stayed ten years as a feature writer for newspapers owned by William Randolph Hearst. "Bitter Bierce" may have found inspiration here for some of the entries in his *Devil's Dictionary*, including *capital*, "the seat of misgovernment," and *diplomacy*, "the patriotic act of lying for one's country." He liked to hobnob at the bar of the old Army-Navy Club with his Baltimore friend, H. L. Mencken, and hosted Sunday brunches at his home in the Olympia Apartments (at 16th and Euclid Streets NW). But in 1910 he left Washington and vanished in Mexico during the revolution, becoming a legend as the Old Gringo. "Good-bye—if you hear of my being stood up against a Mexican stone wall and shot to rags please know that I think that a pretty good way to depart this life," he wrote to his sister. "It beats old age, disease or falling down the cellar stairs. To be a Gringo in Mexico—Oh, that is euthanasia."

Novelist Willa Cather, who lived a much happier life than Bierce, also worked as a journalist during the several months in 1900 she lived in Washington. She came to translate French materials for a cousin who taught at what became George Washington University and to compose columns for newspapers in Pittsburgh and Nebraska.

Marjorie Kinnan Rawlings, Pulitzer Prize–winning author of *The Yearling*, grew up in Washington at the house that still stands at 1221 Newton Street NE. (It is closed to the public.) The farm her father owned near Rock Creek in Maryland undoubtedly shaped her strong connection to nature. The daughter of a U.S. Patent Office examiner, she won a two-dollar prize in 1907 at age 11 for a story submitted to the *Washington Post*'s children pages, to which she frequently contributed.

Humorist James Thurber spent some of his early years in the area when his father brought the family from Ohio in 1901 so that he could work as secretary to an Ohio congressman. The Thurbers spent two winters living at 2031 I Street NW, one block away from the house of young Stephen Vincent Benét, a celebrated Washington poet whose *John Brown's Body* won the Pulitzer Prize in poetry in 1929. The two summers his family spent in a cottage in Falls Church, Virginia, forever changed Thurber's life. "It was there that, one Sunday, I was struck by an arrow fired by my older brother," Thurber wrote to a friend. "He was seven, and I was six and Robert was four, and I'm sure we all threw up together."

The arrow struck Thurber's left eye, destroying his sight in that eye. Frances Burnett's husband, Dr. Swann Burnett, eventually removed the eye. But this experience did not destroy Thurber's happy recollection of his Washington days. "I always think fondly of Washington and Fall's Church and have enough memories of both places, most of them fond, to fill a book," Thurber wrote.

Thurber returned to Washington during World War I to work as a code clerk at the State Department. One of his colleagues was Benét, who often lunched with Thornton Wilder when the playwright worked for the War Industries Board.

Washington played an influential role in the Harlem Renaissance movement of the 1920s, and Howard University attracted both Zora Neale Hurston and Langston Hughes. Hurston arrived from Florida as a Howard freshman in 1919. She spent two years working on the college literary magazine and published her first short story before moving on to New York City's Barnard College. She also worked as a manicurist at a barbershop at 14th and G Streets, where businessmen and politicians made up her regular clientele. "I learned things from holding the hands of men like that," Hurston wrote in her autobiography, *Dust Tracks on a Road*. "I heard many things from the White House and the Senate before they appeared in print. They probably were bursting to talk to somebody, and I was safe."

Poet Hughes had just finished sojourning in Mexico, Africa, and Europe when he came to Washington in 1924, hoping for a scholarship to Howard. The university never gave him one. But he stayed for 14 months, writing and publishing poems while working in a Laundromat, an oyster house, and busing tables at the Wardman Park Hotel, where he met poet Vachel Lindsay when Lindsay gave a reading at the hotel. Hughes put three of his own poems on Lindsay's table in the dining room, and Lindsay read them to his audience, promptly pronouncing Hughes to be a genius. Many of Hughes's poems reflect rhythms of the life on Seventh Street, Washington's black neighborhood, where the sermons of storefront preachers mingled with the strains of blues and jazz.

World War II brought another wave of writers, including Pulitzer Prize–winning playwright Robert Sherwood, who served as a speechwriter for Franklin Roosevelt, and John Steinbeck, who often visited the White House.

Pulitzer Prize–winning poet Archibald MacLeish served as a cultural advisor to Roosevelt and as Librarian of Congress from 1939 to 1944. MacLeish introduced a program inviting annual poetry consultants to the Library of Congress that continues today. Southern authors Allen Tate and Robert Penn Warren served as the first two consultants. MacLeish also joined poet Robert Frost in securing the 1958 release of poet Ezra Pound from Washington's St. Elizabeth's Hospital for the Insane. Pound had been hospitalized in 1946, deemed mentally unfit to stand trial for treason after he was accused of delivering anti-Semitic broadcasts for the Fascists in Italy during the war.

One of America's much-loved short story writers, Katherine Anne Porter, visited Allen Tate while he served as the Library of Congress's poetry consultant from 1943 to 1944. In 1960, after the publication of her only novel, *Ship of Fools*, Porter moved permanently to Washington, residing at 3601 49th Street NW until 1975. She died in 1980 in a nursing home in Silver Spring, Maryland.

Environmentalist Rachel Carson, whose publication of *Silent Spring* in 1962 alerted the world to the dangers of insecticides, also was drawn to Silver Spring, where she lived from 1946 until her death in 1964. After the war she wrote radio scripts about sea creatures for the Federal Bureau of Fisheries.

Washington continues to attract literary lions from around the world, who come to teach, write, and visit a city of monumental inspiration. Most likely, they all make at least one mandatory visit to two of the world's greatest libraries, the Folger Shakespeare Library and the Library of Congress. Before leaving, you should peruse the shelves here, too—or at least a portion of them. You'll find more books here than just about anywhere else in the world.

The Folger Shakespeare Library

201 East Capital Street SE
Washington, D.C. 20003
(202) 544-7077; (202) 544-4600

Who: Registration desk

When: The Exhibition Hall and Elizabethan Theater are open from 10:00 A.M. to 4:00 P.M. Monday through Saturday. The library is not open to the public; researchers must call to register: (202) 675-0306.

How Much: Free, but contributions are appreciated

Senior Citizen Discount: NA

Wheelchair Access: Yes

Directions: Call for brochure

What and Where: Located one block from the U.S. Capitol, The Folger Shakespeare Library houses the planet's largest collection of Shakespeare's printed works. As if that's not enough, the library contains rare Renaissance manuscripts on everything from law to theology to the arts; 50,000 paintings, drawings, engravings, and prints; and musical instruments, costumes, films, and an Elizabethan theater (where the Shakespeare Theater performs). The Elizabethan garden is filled with the scent and colors of herbs and flowers grown during Shakespeare's time.

Philanthropist and oil tycoon Henry Folger amassed the library's impressive collections, starting with $1.25 down payment on a $107.50 set of Shakespeare's works he made as a student at Amherst College after attending a lecture. The lecturer was Ralph Waldo Emerson, and his eloquent admiration for the Bard profoundly changed Folger's life. For more than 40 years Folger and his wife scoured the world for artifacts of the Elizabethan era and treasures connected to William Shakespeare.

The Folger's collections receive constant attention from scholars and educators and are shared with the public through displays and interpretative programs. Annual exhibits, medieval and Renaissance music concerts by the Folger Consort, and readings by contemporary writers from around the world draw 200,000 visitors each year.

You can tour the collections and archives Monday through Saturday at 11:00 A.M. and the garden every Saturday from April through October at 10:00 A.M. and 11:00 A.M.

The Library of Congress

101 Independence Avenue SE
Washington, D.C. 20540
(202) 707-5000

Who: Librarian (202) 707-5205; public affairs office (202) 707-2905

When: 8:30 A.M.–9:00 P.M. Monday, Wednesday, and Thursday; 8:30 A.M.–5:00 P.M. Tuesday, Friday, and Saturday

How Much: Free

Senior Citizen Discount: NA

Wheelchair Access: Yes

Directions: See brochure

What and Where: The Library of Congress, the national library of the United States, houses more than 500 miles of books in three buildings—truly a bibliophile's dream. With more than 16 million books and 100 million newspapers, maps, and other items published in more than 400 languages, this repository is the world's largest library.

Founded in 1800, the library contains treasures such as a Gutenberg Bible and the Giant Bible of Mainz, as well as many historic documents, such as the manuscript collections of the country's first 23 presidents and other prominent Americans.

You can see maps and atlases that explorers and navigators used to chart the world and outer space, as well as the latest developments in software and databases. You can also look up your family history in the local history and genealogy section and locate just about any book ever written by your favorite author.

The Library of Congress is open daily except Christmas and New Year's Day and schedules monthly exhibits, poetry readings, concerts, and daily tours. For information, write or call.

Kalorama Guest House at Kalorama Park

1854 Mintwood Place NW
Washington, D.C. 20009
(202) 667-6369
(202) 319-1262 Fax

Kalorama Guest House at Woodley Park

2700 Cathedral Avenue NW
Washington, D.C. 20008
(202) 328-0860
(202) 328-8703 Fax

As a former resident of Washington, I know one of the secret delights of this town is its beautiful tree-lined neighborhoods. Staying at either location of the Kalorama Guest House lets you experience the pleasure of charming neighborhoods in this very pretty city, which one of my acquaintances described as looking like a giant park.

Each of the guest houses is located in a quiet residential area close to downtown Washington. Both locations are close to our literary sites (the Folger and the Library of Congress), not to mention the White House, the Capitol Building, and the wonderful museums of the Smithsonian.

If you like embassy-hopping, you are a quick walk down Kalorama Road to the French embassy, the Chinese embassy, and the stately Massachusetts Avenue diplomatic residences. You can walk to the Woodley Park Zoo (home of the world's cutest panda bears). At Woodley Park you can ride the beautiful and efficient underground Metro and connect to National Airport, Union Station, and the Smithsonian museums. When I was showing a friend of mine from New York City around, he thought the Metro was a wonderful destination in its own right.

Both of the Kalorama Guest Houses have a European touch that will provide you a home away from home at a surprisingly

One of the rooms at the Kalorama Guest House, Washington, D.C. Photo courtesy of the Kalorama Guest House.

moderate rate. Because the hosts of both places are year-round residents, they will have lots of insider tips to make your stay more enjoyable.

Hostess Tami Wood has made these charming Victorian townhouses comfortable with brass beds with plush comforters, warm Oriental carpets, plants, and turn-of-the-century artwork. The parlor is the place to enjoy your continental breakfast each morning and your sherry sip in front of a crackling fire every afternoon. For dinner, you are minutes away from some of Washington's best ethnic restaurants.

Kalorama Guest House at Kalorama Park

Rates: $50–$120
Credit Cards Accepted: Visa, MC, AMEX
Number of Guest Rooms: 31
Number of Baths: 19
Wheelchair Access: No

Pets: No
Children: Yes
Smoking: No
Senior Citizen Discount: 10%
Directions: Brochure contains map

Kalorama Guest House at Woodley Park

Rates: $50–$120
Credit Cards Accepted: MC, AMEX, Discover
Number of Guest Rooms: 19
Number of Baths: 14
Wheelchair Access: No

Pets: No
Children: Yes
Smoking: No
Senior Citizen Discount: 10%
Directions: Brochure contains map

FLORIDA

Marjorie Kinnan Rawlings and Dudley Farm State Historic Sites

South County Road 325 in Cross Creek
Route 3, Box 92
Hawthorne, FL 32640
(904) 466-3672; (904) 466-9273
(904) 466-4743 Fax

Who: Valerie Rivers, park manager

When: The park is open from 9:00 A.M. to 5:00 P.M. Tours of the home are hourly on the hour (except for noon) from 10:00 A.M. to 4:00 P.M. Tours are not offered in August, September, or on Thanksgiving, Christmas, and New Year's Day.

How Much: $2 per adult, $1 for children ages 6 to 12; free for children under 6.

Senior Citizen Discount: No

Wheelchair Access: Yes, upon request

Directions: See map in brochure

What and Where: The Marjorie Kinnan Rawlings State Historic Site has been listed on the National Register of Historic Sites since 1970. It is a microcosm of Florida farmland and marshland that represents a history, culture, and architecture from a rural Florida that has all but vanished.

Marjorie Kinnan Rawlings in her garden, Hawthorne, Florida. Photo courtesy of Marjorie Kinnan Rawlings and Dudley Farm.

Each tour is limited to ten people. A waiting time is not unusual, and afternoon tours are often filled. The yard, grove, and nature trails remain open throughout the year. School groups and those interested in arranging a workshop or seminar should call or write for information.

AUTHOR'S NOTE: I felt a sense of kinship when I read in one of Rawlings's letters, "I was doomed to write." A most inspiring experience was to sit in her old barn and read her scrapbooks.

My favorite item was an article describing how Rawlings met Ernest Hemingway. At a restaurant, she sent a note to his table, "If you are Ernest Hemingway, will you come over and have a drink with us?" To which Hemingway replied, "If you are Marjorie Rawlings, I would be happy to."

The Herlong Mansion

402 Northeast Cholokka Boulevard
P.O. Box 667
Micanopy, FL 32667
(352) 466-3322

The town of Micanopy (pronounced mick-án-opee), Florida, and the Herlong Mansion immediately put one in a literary frame of mind. After visiting the Marjorie Rawlings home, I hunkered down on the front porch of the Herlong Mansion, sipped some mint ice tea, munched some chocolate chip cookies, gazed at the lush cypress trees in the front yard, and read Rawlings's autobiography, *Cross Creek*. Rocking on the inviting front porch of the mansion and feeling the lovely spirit of Marjorie Rawlings all around, I felt the shades of several other southern characters.

I pictured Atticus Finch, taking time off from his legal duties in *To Kill a Mockingbird* so he could pull up a chair to set a spell. Later, while strolling around the lovely small town of Micanopy, my mind flipped through the pages of Truman Capote's *A Christmas Memory*. In several of the old historic homes I could picture the young Truman with his cousin, Miss Sook Faulk, baking their holiday fruitcakes. I could almost smell the fragrance of the spices and feel the warmth of the kitchen. Micanopy is the kind of a town that transports you to an earlier time, another era. For years, visiting Florida, I wondered whatever became of the Old South. The best of it is in Micanopy and the Herlong House.

My husband and I enjoyed our southern respite in a cozy cottage (separate from the main house) featuring a beautiful antique wood headboard, wood shutters, and an old wooden chest. The next morning we were treated to a delicious breakfast of fresh fruit, bran muffins, sausage, and Herlong Decadent Bread, which the personable innkeeper, Sonny Howard, describes as a combination of French toast and bread pudding. Take time to linger in the dining room to admire the glass collection, the beautiful chandeliers, and the fresh flowers. Have another cup of coffee while Sonny entertains you with his after-breakfast talks about the Herlong ghost or the Underground Railroad at the Herlong. If there is a receptive audience, you will probably hear about the secret room that may have been a hiding place for a band of Seminole Indians, a retarded member of the Herlong family, or a stash of moonshine. Sonny is a raconteur, so don't be in too big a hurry to hit the road or you'll miss a delightful part of the breakfast show. He admits that all his tales are speculative, but he doesn't want to know the truth lest it ruin his stories!

This sleepy southern town is home to two excellent restaurants, Wild Flowers Cafe and The Cottage Cafe. At Wild Flowers, we feasted on a Caesar salad (profiled in *Gourmet* magazine) followed by chicken marsala as the main course. As one who no longer eats veal, I appreciated the fact that Wild Flowers offers chicken as a substitute meat in all its veal dishes. If this gourmet restaurant that eschews fried food was a surprise in rural Florida, imagine my amazement when I tried The Cottage Cafe, with its Brazilian fare. The Churrasco (sirloin steak grilled with spices) or the black beans and rice are comparable to anything I've found in big cities.

Save some time to stroll around Micanopy and browse through the 17 antique shops. Don't be surprised if you feel the ghost of Marjorie Rawlings all around because the film *Cross Creek* was made on these very streets.

Rates: $50–$160
Credit Cards Accepted: Visa, MC, AMEX
Number of Guest Rooms: 12
Number of Baths: 12
Wheelchair Access: Yes

Pets: No
Children: Yes
Smoking: No
Senior Citizen Discount: 10% for AARP members on weekdays
Directions: Brochure contains map

Thurston House

851 Lake Avenue
Maitland, FL 32751
(407) 539-1911
(800) 843-2721

Thurston and Hurston can easily be confused, especially when both are associated with the same small town of Maitland, Florida. Zora Neale Hurston grew up in Eatonville, the first incorporated African American township in the United States, just next door to the not much larger city of Maitland. Her colorful folktales and reminiscences reflect the tenor of her life there.

Thurston House has an entirely different background but is definitely a perfect place to stay if you are visiting the Hurston National Museum of Fine Art or the annual (January and February) Zora Neale Hurston Festival of the Arts and Humanities in Eatonville. The Winter Park area of Florida was extremely popular a hundred years ago with wealthy families whose fortunes were made in the North and who sought a second home in a sunnier clime. In 1885, Minneapolis businessman Mr. Thurston built a winter "cottage," now operating as a guest house. Four bedrooms, each with private bath, overlook a wonderful property, which includes its own private lake and landscaping dotted with exotic shrubs and other flora, including orange, tangerine, and camphor trees. Here is a special setting that allows its guests to "imagine" themselves into another time, another era. How grand to leave reality behind even for just this brief, shining moment!

Rates: $100–$110
Credit Cards Accepted: Visa, MC, AMEX
Number of Guest Rooms: 4
Number of Baths: 4
Wheelchair Access: No

Pets: No
Children: If older than 12
Smoking: In designated areas
Senior Citizen Discount: 10%
Directions: See brochure

Ernest Hemingway Home and Museum

907 Whitehead Street
Key West, FL 33040
(305) 294-1575, bookstore
(305) 294-1136, office

Who: Linda Larson, curator

When: 9:00 A.M.–5:00 P.M. every day

How Much: $6.50 for adults, $4 for children ages 6 to 12

Senior Citizen Discount: No

Wheelchair Access: First floor only

Directions: From Florida mainland, US 1 becomes Roosevelt, which becomes Truman. Follow Truman until you come to Whitehead Street, turn right, and stop at 907 Whitehead.

What and Where: Key West is filled with literary ghosts, none more spirited than Ernest Hemingway and Tennessee Williams. As local writer David Kaufelt, who escorted us on a splendid literary tour of the island, put it, "Tennesee Williams is the secret bougainvillea in the island while Hemingway is the marlin swimming around the island."

How did Hemingway, Key West's most famous literary lion, come to live in this sleepy but captivating island paradise? His friend John Dos Passos told him that Key West was the Garden of Eden. After a six-year stint in Europe, where he wrote *The Sun Also Rises,* Hemingway was ready to return to the States. A run of bad luck made the young author anxious to head for sunny climes. After accidentally pulling a skylight on his head, losing a suitcase filled with manuscripts, and suffering from an anthrax infection, he was ready for a change of scenery. When his editor, Maxwell Perkins, suggested that Hemingway and his second wife, Pauline, return to America the long way, by ship, Hemingway took his advice. He agreed with Perkins that a "slow, recuperative trip via Cuba" was what the doctor ordered.

Hemingway was scheduled to pick up a new yellow Ford runabout, a present from Gus Pfeiffer, Pauline's uncle, the richest man in Piggot, Arkansas. The car was supposed to be waiting for the young couple when they docked, and they were to drive to Piggot. However, because of a mix-up with the ferries that were delivering the car, the Ford was held up in Miami. Trevor and Morris Ford, the Key West dealership, tried to make amends for the inconvenience by arranging for the successful author and his wife to stay at the company apartment until his car arrived. Hemingway was not pleased but was so exhausted from the trip that he reluctantly accepted the offer. He and Pauline moved into 314 Simonton, a small apartment overlooking the azure waters of the Gulf of Mexico. By the time the car arrived at the end of the week the Hemingways had decided to stay put: They were hooked on Key West.

The easygoing village was exactly the type of place Hemingway was looking for, an inspirational paradise in which to finish writing his second novel, *A Farewell to Arms.* He quickly got hooked on deep-sea fishing and despite Prohibition, found he could carouse and drink the evenings away at Sloppy Joe's Bar. Hemingway was delighted with his Key West existence and even set one of his novels, *To Have and Have Not,* here, but Pauline did not share his enthusiasm. She was tired of apartment living, and after the birth of their two sons, Patrick and Gregory, with a collection of servants, the family simply needed more room. After the successful publication in 1929 of *A Farewell to Arms,* the couple decided to make Key West their permanent home. When Pauline admired the European architecture of a fixer-upper at 907 Whitehead Street, her generous and wealthy Uncle Gus bought the house as a present for the princely sum of $8,000.

The house needed major renovation and the first priority was Hemingway's study. He was attracted to the house because it had a second building behind the main house that was the ideal spot for a writer's study. He turned it into the perfect male—some would say macho—writer's retreat. There are the obligatory hunting trophies mounted on the walls. The floor is imported brown, white, and gold Cuban tile. Hemingway carefully lined the walls with shelves, filling them with his favorite books, and in the middle of the room he placed a plain round table. Even though many Hemingway scholars say he preferred to write in longhand, his Royal typewriter, sitting on the table, looks as if it has performed mighty service.

On a leather-covered stick chair purchased from a cigar factory, the very disciplined author would follow a strict regimen each and every day. Around 6:00 A.M. every morning he would settle down to work in his study. "When I'm working on a book or a novel, I write every morning as early as possible." He wrote until he reached a point "where I still had some juice left and know what will happen next," and then he stopped and tried to survive until tomorrow. "I'm happy only when I write," Hemingway allegedly told a *New York Times* reporter. The author was obviously very happy in his new digs, because it was here that he wrote *Death in the Afternoon, Green Hills of Africa, To Have and Have Not,* and the first pages of *For Whom the Bell Tolls.*

After a six-pencil morning, he fixed himself some lunch and then joined the "mob" at Sloppy Joe's for some carousing or fishing. In 1931 he helped turn himself into a major celebrity by building a wall around his house to make him seem more intriguing. This ploy worked, and *Life* magazine thereafter covered every step he made.

Key West Literary Seminar Writers' Walk

Don't miss this excellent Writers' Walk; it was the highlight of my trip to Key West. Novelist David A. Kaufelt, author of the *The Fat Boy Murders* series and many other novels, is a knowledgeable and very amusing tour guide. He made this eccentric, lively, literate city come to life, and his witty repartee, filled with anecdotes, was great fun. He takes you on a one-hour guided walk straight into the heart of the writer's Key West. He shows you Tennessee Williams's first residence on the island, Robert Frost's cottage, and other places of literary interest. He weaves into the one-mile, one-hour walk a fascinating literary history of the island, onetime home to poets Wallace Stevens and Elizabeth Bishop and playwrights Tennessee Williams and James Kirkwood. Kaufelt pointed out that the idiosyncratic architecture of Key West seems to have nurtured the talents of more writers per capita than any other city in the country. Seven Pulitzer Prizes have been presented to the island's writers, and currently over 100 published writers reside, full- or part-time, in Key West.

When I asked if today's writers had critique or support groups, Kaufelt answered with a sly grin, "In Key West, writers meet only at parties!"

A wonderful addition to your Key West tour is the book *Key West Writers and Their Houses: The Influence of Key West and Its Architecture on 20th-Century Poets and Writers from Ernest Hemingway to Thomas McGuane,* by Lynn Misuko Kaufelt. This beautiful book by David Kaufelt's wife is great to read while you're in Key West or in your favorite armchair back home. It was full of good information about Key West writers as well as excellent photographs of their houses.

Tours are given on Saturday and Sunday, December through May, and cost $10, tax not included. You may purchase tickets from Key West Island Books, which is located at 513 Fleming Street. For the Saturday tour, meet at Heritage House, 410 Caroline Street, at 10:30 A.M. For the Sunday tour, meet at Hemingway House, 907 Whitehead, at 10:30 A.M. For more information, contact Jeanette Manning, Miles Frieden, or Sue Marshall at 419 Petronia Street, Key West, FL 33040; (305) 293-9291.

Blue Parrot Inn

916 Elizabeth Street
Key West, FL 33040
(305) 296-0033; (800) 231-BIRD
(305) 296-5697 Fax

When I saw the (800) 231-BIRD number given for the Blue Parrot Inn, of course I was hooked. Those of you familiar with my book *The Birder's Guide to B&Bs* recognize my penchant for all things beaked and feathered. "We're in the middle of Old Town, just two blocks from Duval Street, where everything happens," says affable innkeeper Frank Yaccino.

The Inn has ten guest rooms, each with a private bath. The house itself is a wonderful example of Bahamian style, with a two-story wraparound porch, all gingerbread and painted railings. Built in 1884, it was the home of one of those infamous wrecker captains who made fortunes on their daring and initiative in salvaging shipwrecks from the often wrathful seas. The heated pool is literally steps away from the residence—a great place to work on a tan or to find a shady palm frond to shade you and your current best book. Breakfast is an extended continental buffet style, as laid-back and satisfying as everything else in balmy Key West. Homemade muffins are a regular treat, with quiche running second, according to a guest poll. It's of course a movable feast and may be enjoyed poolside, roomside, or porchside. By the way, there *is* a resident parrot named Rhapsody, as well as Cleo, the inn cat. But don't worry about fights and raucous squalling; Cleo is terribly well-mannered, and the parrot is not real!

The Florida Keys are the only car-accessible islands of the Caribbean, and the three-and-a-half-hour drive from Miami is a world-class tour in itself: The Gulf of Mexico is on one side of the turnpike, the mighty Atlantic on the other. Getting there is definitely part of the fun!

Rates: $70–$160
Credit Cards Accepted: Visa, MC, AMEX, Diners
Number of Guest Rooms: 10
Number of Baths: 10
Wheelchair Access: Yes

Pets: No
Children: If older than 16
Smoking: Yes
Senior Citizen Discount: 10%
Directions: See brochure

Papa's Hideaway

309 Louisa Street
Key West, FL 33040
(305) 294-7709; (800) 714-7709
(305) 294-1034 Fax

You must admire a town that celebrates sunset every day of the year. It's a festive tradition bound to adjust your aura and put some perspective on your karma. What could be more appropriate, especially when the view is from the southernmost tip of land in all the United States and the sun melts down the sky and into the endless expanse of ocean with a warm orange flush and a strange green flash. The unusual penchants and talents of the locals are obvious everywhere—everything seems to fit in while nevertheless remaining decidedly different. The architecture, for instance, is a crazy blend of Victorian gingerbread, Bahamian, Spanish, New England, and southern plantation. But it works. Walking or cycling the tight plant-lined streets is delightful, and although a visitor is never quite sure where he is, it is impossible to stay lost. All paths lead to beach, harbor, or ocean, and even Papa's Hideaway can be readily found.

Rooms are decorated in themes from the Pulitzer Prize– and Nobel Prize–winner's novels, and there is a choice of spacious studio apartments in the Guesthouse or two-bedroom units in the Cottage. All have fully equipped kitchens and room for extra guests. Hammocks and chaise lounges are de rigueur, and the effort of choosing among Jacuzzi, lap, or standard pool options may keep you prone. To revive, there's always the complimentary morning pastry served with an espresso or cappuccino. That should keep you wired until it's again time for that special sunset celebration.

Rates: $79–$195
Credit Cards Accepted: Visa, MC, Discover
Number of Guest Rooms: 5
Number of Baths: 5
Wheelchair Access: No

Pets: No
Children: Yes
Smoking: No
Senior Citizen Discount: No
Directions: On confirmation sheet

Authors of Key West Guest House

725 White and Petronia
Key West, FL 33040
(305) 294-7381; (800) 898-6909

Does visiting a place designated as Mile Marker 0 make you feel you've come to the very end of the world? It should, because the road to Key West ends near a spit of land at the edge of the Atlantic Ocean. People who live on the Keys commute over the ocean, driving to the Florida mainland on the world's longest causeway. They refer to their homes and destinations by mile marker numbers, a most reasonable system in a geography composed more of water than of land. Perhaps that Mile Marker 0 sign is a lure for people who like to live on the edge, both literally and literarily, because many of our favorite authors came, saw, and were conquered by the ineffable charm of Key West.

Authors of Key West Guest House is a guest house made up of nine rooms and cottages, each dedicated to a specific literary figure who at some time lived in the Keys. Each accommodation contains works and memorabilia of its namesake. Two cottages, designed in the local Bahamian conch style, were originally living quarters to cigar makers, once a part of a thriving local business in the early part of the century. One of these conch cottages does homage to playwright and Pulitzer Prize–winner Tennessee Williams, the other to Papa Hemingway, winner of both the Pulitzer and the Nobel Prizes in literature.

Four deluxe rooms span the upper level of the main house, all of which have private baths and Bahama fans and open onto a sundeck. Thornton Wilder is represented here (although Key West is not exactly a mirror image of *Our Town*). *A Chorus Line*'s Jimmy Kirkwood is next. President Harry ("The buck stops here") Truman loved the Keys, so different from the hectic pace of

Washington, D.C., or the Heartland stability of Independence, Missouri. A photographic collage depicting the era of our 33rd president has been put together with care. To round out this diverse group is John James Audubon, author of *Audubon Florida* as well as the incomparable *Birds of North America*, and arguably the most renowned and respected resident of the Keys. Framed reproductions of his bird sketches lend a unique touch to this room. Three poolside rooms evoke the figures of Carson McCullers, James Leo Herlihy, and Lillian Hellman, all of whom used the Deep South as inspiration.

A simple yet satisfying continental breakfast is provided, but the real treat is a visual one as you stroll the wooden walkways that lead to a red brick patio and adjacent pool. Surrounded by palm trees, hibiscus bushes, and brilliant red bougainvillea vines, a visitor gains insight into what it is that brought so many who have come before him home—home to Key West.

Rates: $79–$165
Credit Cards Accepted: Visa, MC, AMEX, Discover
Number of Guest Rooms: 15
Number of Baths: 15
Wheelchair Access: Yes

Pets: No
Children: No
Smoking: No
Senior Citizen Discount: No
Directions: See brochure

GEORGIA

Sidney Lanier Cottage

935 High Street
P.O. Box 13358
Macon, GA 31208-3358

Who: Katherine C. Oliver

When: 9:00 A.M.–1:00 P.M. and 2:00 P.M.–
4:00 P.M. Monday through Friday, 9:30
A.M.–12:30 P.M. on Saturday

How Much: $3 adults, $1 students over 12,
$.50 children ages 6 to 12

Senior Citizen Discount: $2.50

Wheelchair Access: Yes

The Sidney Lanier Cottage, Macon, Georgia.
Photo courtesy of the Sidney Lanier Cottage.

Directions: From I-75, take Exit 52. Turn
left onto Forsyth Street (one way) and
go straight through three traffic lights.
At the third light, turn left onto Orange Street. Soon you will see an old brick church
at the corner of Orange and High Streets. Turn right onto High Street and drive until
you reach 935.

What and Where: Sidney Clopton Lanier was born February 3, 1842, in this gabled,
whiteframe Victorian cottage. Although most of us know Lanier as a poet, at the cottage, I learned that he was recognized as a linguist, mathematician, lawyer, soldier,
teacher, and musician. He spent the later years of his short life in Baltimore playing
first flute in the Peabody Symphony Orchestra. His poetry reflects his devotion to
music, and in a manual, *The Science of English Verse* (1880) he discusses his theory of the
relationship between music and poetry.

Among Lanier's best-known poems are "The Marshes of Glynn," "The Crystal,"
"Trees, and the Master," "Corn," "The Symphony," "Sunrise," and "Song of the
Chattahoochee." Many of these verses dealt with social issues of the day such as the
growing commercialism of post–Civil War America and the plight of the impoverished
farmer. A complete collection of his poems, edited by his wife, has been republished in
easily readable type by the Middle Georgia Historical Society and is available at the
Lanier Cottage.

The cottage is filled with Sidney Lanier memorabilia, including his silver flute, his
wife's wedding dress, and many portraits. The decor of the cottage is typical of the early
nineteenth century.

In front of the cottage is a large live oak tree planted in 1932 by the Vineville Garden Club and dedicated to the poet, who died in 1881 of tuberculosis at the age of 39.

If the cottage whets your appetite for Sidney Lanier and you'd like to commune with his ghost, you might consider going on "Sidney's Old South Historic Tours." The tour brochure suggests that you will "take a tour with the spirit of Sidney Lanier." Many southern stories and surprises are promised, along with a tour of Macon's famous historic district. There are tours daily every day but Sunday at 10 A.M. and 2 P.M., starting from the terminal station. Call (912) 743-3401.

1842 Inn

353 College Street
Macon, GA 31201
(912) 741-1842; (800) 336-1842

In the morning the 1842 Inn delivers a continental breakfast to your room, complete with flowers and a paper. In the evening, the inn, the recipient of a four-diamond lodging award, offers complimentary appetizers. There is also a turn-down service with imported chocolate mints placed on your pillow and shoe shines while you slumber.

This Greek Revival antebellum house will give you the illusion of having been transported to a plantation, but twentieth-century creature comforts will bring you back to reality. There are insulated walls that provide absolute privacy. Blackout linings in the draperies are appreciated by late sleepers. Some rooms even have a second television to view while you relax in a whirlpool bath.

All 21 rooms offer an eclectic blend of Oriental rugs, fine antiques, and deluxe linens and towels. It is a winning combination. The beds are all king- or queen-size period reproductions with custom mattresses.

Judge John J. Gresham, cotton merchant and founder of the Bibb Manufacturing Company, built this charming house in 1842. The house has been beautifully restored and features elaborate mantels, crystal chandeliers, graceful columns, and oak parquet floors inlaid with mahogany. The place is elegantly run, thanks to the owner, Aileen Hatcher.

The Sidney Lanier Cottage is only a short walk away. Afterward, you could stroll over to Macon's historic district, take a walking tour, attend the Cherry Blossom Festival in March, or just sip a mint julep in the Taft State Room at your elegant inn. The message is, "Enjoy."

Rates: $95–$155
Credit Cards Accepted: Visa, MC, AMEX
Number of Guest Rooms: 21
Number of Baths: 21
Wheelchair Access: Yes

Pets: No
Children: If older than 12
Smoking: Yes
Senior Citizen Discount: 10% for AARP members
Directions: See brochure

Ina Dillard Russell Library:
Flannery O'Connor Collection

Georgia College and State University
Campus Box 43
Milledgeville, GA 31061
(912) 453-4047
(912) 453-6847 Fax

Who: Nancy Davis Bray

When: Fall and spring hours: 7:30 A.M.–10:00 P.M. on Monday through Thursday, 7:30 A.M.–5:00 P.M. on Friday, 12:00 noon–5:00 P.M. on Saturday, 1:00 P.M.–10:00 P.M. on Sunday. Summer hours: 7:30 A.M.–8:00 P.M. on Monday through Thursday, 7:30 A.M.–12:00 noon on Friday, 1:00–5:00 P.M. on Saturday; 2:00–8:00 P.M. on Sunday. Call ahead to see the O'Connor collection.

How Much: Free

Senior Citizen Discount: NA

Wheelchair Access: First floor only

Directions: From the north, take 441 south. At Milledgeville, do not take the bypass but head into town. Continue across the railroad tracks to Montgomery and turn left at Clark Street, where the library is located. From the south, head into town on 22, which will turn into Montgomery. After a short distance in town, 22 will veer off but stay on Montgomery until you reach the Clark Street intersection and the library.

What and Where: "The writer operates at a peculiar crossroads where time and place and eternity somehow meet. His problem is to find that location" (Flannery O'Connor, "The Regional Writer").

It is worth it to visit the Flannery O'Connor Collection just to take in her wonderful quotes and witty anecdotes. One of my favorites is how the suffer-no-fools author answered one of her critical readers. It seems that the author's first fan letter "was from an old lady who wrote, 'I do not like your book. It has left a bad taste in my mouth.' I wrote her back and said, 'You were not supposed to eat it.'"

Hailed as one of Milledgeville's most accomplished native daughters, O'Connor was actually born in Savannah. Milledgeville, however, became her primary residence for the majority of her creative life. Graduated from Georgia State College for Women (now Georgia College) with a B.A. in 1945 and from the Writers Workshop at the University of Iowa with an M.F.A. in 1947, O'Connor lived on the East Coast for a number of years. When she contracted lupus in 1951, she returned to Milledgeville, where she and her mother, Regina Cline O'Connor, settled at Andalusia, the family farm north of town. Here she wrote many of her stories, published in such magazines as *The Kenyon Review, Harper's*, and *The Sewanee Review.*

Initially stymied by her fiction, critics now seem to understand the profoundly Christian vision that underlies her work. Shortly after the publication of *The Violent Bear It Away*, O'Connor wrote, "I can wait fifty years, a hundred years for it to be understood."

The Flannery O'Connor Collection was established shortly after the first publication of O'Connor's short story "The Geranium" in 1946. At that time the collection consisted of early items from O'Connor's student days at Peabody High School and Georgia State College for Women. Although she is remembered primarily for her fiction, O'Connor was also an accomplished cartoonist; her cartoons from the college newspaper, literary magazine, and yearbook are on display.

In addition to over 6,000 pages of manuscripts, O'Connor's personal collection of over 700 books and journals is housed in the library.

In 1971 the Flannery O'Connor Memorial Room was started by friends and alumni to honor this distinguished graduate of Georgia College. It is furnished in the Victorian style of the 1870s. Much of the furniture was a gift of Regina O'Connor and was brought to the room from Andalusia, the farm where O'Connor wrote most of her fiction.

Hinson House

200 North Columbia Street
Milledgeville, GA 31061
(912) 453-3993

There is something magical about the South. Everyone is a storyteller and there is such a rich history that there are many stories to tell. When you stay at the Hinson House (circa 1890), you will discover the grace and elegance that was the Old South. You will be within close proximity to the Flannery O'Connor Collection, not to mention to historic architecture and lovely gardens. You'll want to visit Memory Hill Cemetery, where Flannery O'Connor and many of the other illustrious men and women who shaped the region are buried.

The spacious guest rooms at the Hinson House feature private baths, TVs, and telephones. There are several rooms set aside just for reading (Flannery O'Connor, no doubt) or relaxing. Then there's the wonderful porch complete with rockers on which to laze away a summer day. If you are in a more ambitious mood, ask innkeeper Karen Rowell-Hinson to tell you about illustrated walking tours, narrated trolley rides, tours of the governor's mansion, or information on antiques, golf, or tennis.

Rates: $75
Credit Cards Accepted: Visa, MC
Number of Guest Rooms: 3
Number of Baths: 3
Wheelchair Access: No

Pets: No
Children: No
Smoking: No
Senior Citizen Discount: No
Directions: See brochure

Flannery O'Connor Childhood Home

207 East Charlton Street on Lafayette Square
Savannah, GA 31401
(912) 238-9796

Who: Robert Jones

When: 1:00–4:00 P.M. Saturday, 1:00–5:00 P.M. Sunday

How Much: $2 donation

Senior Citizen Discount: No

Wheelchair Access: No

Directions: Call for directions

What and Where: There is much about Savannah to admire and enjoy. Any city whose convention and visitors bureau's phone number is (800) 444-CHARM is my kind of town. This historic city is a walker's paradise and *Le Monde* just voted it "The Most Beautiful City in North America." The 21 original public squares laid out more than 250 years ago by Savannah founder James Oglethorpe are magnificent. Low-country food is legendary and history abounds. You must visit the Juliette Gordon Low Girl Scout Center, the birthplace and girlhood home of the founder of the Girl Scouts of America.

But let's turn our literary attention to the birthplace of Flannery O'Connor. Thrice the winner of the O. Henry Award and also a posthumous winner of the National Book Award, in 1972, O'Connor was born in Savannah on March 25, 1925. The O'Connor house dates from 1855, when it was constructed as one of a pair of row houses, each only 20 feet wide. The O'Connor family occupied the three top floors. The O'Connor home was purchased in 1989 for the specific purpose of maintaining it as a memorial to Flannery O'Connor and as a literary center for Savannah. Hugh Brown, of the Armstrong State College English department, believes that although O'Connor's literary career began after she left Savannah, the home and neighborhood she grew up in had a formative influence on her.

Literary programs are held throughout the year, except in summer (the house is not air-conditioned). There are public readings of O'Connor's works, as well as readings and lectures about other southern authors.

Take some time to stroll around the neighborhood that shaped Flannery O'Connor's childhood. Step across the square to the Cathedral of St. John the Baptist, where she was baptized, made her first communion, and was confirmed. East of the square, on the site of the present-day Cathedral School, was Saint Vincent's Grammar School, which she attended from grades one through five.

Since Savannah is such a quirky, whimsical, and fun city, I would be remiss if I didn't end this discussion with some local literary trivia. If you like a good literary ghost along with a delicious meal, don't leave town without eating at The Pirate's House, located in a 1734 building. Local legend has it that the building is haunted by Captain Flint, after whom Long John Silver, in Robert Louis Stevenson's *Treasure Island,* named his parrot. If you listen very carefully, you can hear Captain Flint calling for his rum and denouncing the rogues who robbed him of his treasure. If all this pirate lore increases your appetite, you can return for more ghost sightings and elegant gourmet fare at 45 South, another restaurant in the same haunted building.

No trip to Savannah would be complete without a visit to the Bonaventure Cemetery. Many locals say, with a twinkle in their eyes, that Savannah has more interesting dead people than live ones. Here in the dense oak forest complete with romantic Spanish moss are the graves of native sons Johnny Mercer, the Tin Pan Alley songwriter, and the poet Conrad Aiken. Of course, any devotee of the recent best-selling book by John Berendt, *Midnight in the Garden of Good and Evil,* knows that the cemetery is an integral part of the steamy, well-written story that has put Savannah, for better or worse, on the map. If you want to take a look at the cemetery through the eyes of *The Garden of Good and Evil* as well as catch a glimpse of the shrimp boats featured in the movie *Forrest Gump*, contact Tapestry Tours at (800) 794-7770.

Ballastone Inn and Townhouse

14 East Oglethorpe Avenue
Savannah, GA 31401
(912) 236-1484; (800) 822-4553

There is something about Savannah that exudes charm, hospitality, and those things that represent the best of the Old South. The Ballastone Inn typifies the best of Savannah. The minute you walk in the door, you will be handed a glass of sherry. Shoes left outside your door will be polished overnight, and you will find a cozy terrycloth robe in the bathroom. Every night chocolates and cordials magically appear at your bedside. The well-trained staff will serve your breakfast at whatever time you choose in your room, in the double parlor, or in the courtyard. They will arrange everything from restaurant reservations and theater tickets to sight-seeing tours and airline flights. With this type of service, you may never want to go home.

Bride and *Glamour* magazines voted the Ballastone one of the most romantic bed and breakfasts in the nation. When Paul Newman stayed here, he wrote in the guest book, "A delightful slice of the old South. A gentle reminder that all does not necessarily go well with the Yankees."

The ceiling fans, four-poster and canopy beds, marble-topped tables and dressers, cheval mirrors, and comfortable loveseats are elegant reminders of the genteel past. Modern conveniences such as air-conditioned rooms, 24-hour concierge service, and an elevator have not been overlooked. As the Ballastone brochure promises, if you stay here, you will "return to the romance of the Old South."

Rates: $100–$215
Credit Cards Accepted: Visa, MC, AMEX
Number of Guest Rooms: 18
Number of Baths: 18
Wheelchair Access: No
Pets: Yes
Children: If older than 12

Smoking: Yes
Senior Citizen Discount: Check regarding conditions
Directions: From I-95, take I-16 east. The second red light is Oglethorpe Avenue. Turn right on Oglethorpe; the inn is five blocks ahead on the left.

The Eliza Thompson House

5 West Jones Street
Savannah, GA 31401
(912) 236-3620; (800) 348-9378

There are two things I love about visiting the South: One is the sense of history and the other is the graciousness. The Eliza Thompson House in Savannah scores on both counts.

According to Civil War lore, the beautiful red-haired Eliza was one of Savannah's most highly regarded hostesses. Her reputation apparently caught the attention of General William Tecumseh Sherman. Legend has it that Eliza was one of the reasons Sherman spared Savannah on his infamous March to the Sea. Another is that Sherman dealt leniently with Savannah in order to offer it to President Lincoln as a Christmas present. Whatever the reason, you will be glad that this lovely house in this gem of a city was saved.

The graciousness of the Eliza Thompson House is certainly intact. You can imagine yourself in a bygone era sitting in the beautifully landscaped courtyard next to a flowing fountain while taking afternoon tea. You can enjoy civilized conversation with fellow guests during the wine and cheese reception from 5:00 to 7:00 P.M.

The inn is a warm melding of the traditions and charms of the last century with the comforts of today. The blend of old and new is evident in the rich elegance of gleaming pine floors and period furnishings combined with the comforts of direct dial phones, color television, and a private bath. This is the best of both worlds.

The main house has 12 guest rooms; Miss Eliza's Carriage House contains 11 more rooms. You will be sure to dine in style. Every morning a complimentary newspaper is provided with the deluxe continental breakfast. Save room for lunch, because one of Savannah's star restaurants, Mrs. Wilkes, serves a southern lunch fit for the likes of Rhett Butler.

Rates: $89–$179
Credit Cards Accepted: Visa, MC, AMEX
Number of Guest Rooms: 23
Number of Baths: 23
Wheelchair Access: Yes

Pets: No
Children: Yes
Smoking: No
Senior Citizen Discount: 10% for AARP members
Directions: Brochure contains map

Forsyth Park Inn

102 West Hall Street
Savannah, GA 31401
(912) 233-6800

You can probably find fancier inns in Savannah but none is more cheerful and friendly. Owners Virginia and Hal Sullivan are the epitome of gracious southern hospitality. Every evening they will invite you to join them on the patio or in the parlor for a visit and offer you wine chilled in an elegant silver bucket.

The Forsyth is located in Forsyth Park, Savannah's largest and most opulent park, filled with moss-laden oaks, blooming azaleas, scented magnolias, lighted monuments, and a sparkling fountain.

The inn is a hop, skip, and a jump from the historic riverfront and its antique shops, museum homes, and many good restaurants. Two of my favorite restaurants are the elegant 45 South, with its continental flair, and the Pirate's House, with its typical Savannah dishes.

The rooms at the inn take you back to the pampered lifestyle of the landed gentry of the nineteenth century. All nine rooms feature period furnishings with four-poster king- and queen-size beds, unique fireplaces, antique marble baths or whirlpool tubs, and carefully preserved architectural details. Lovebirds may prefer the private carriage cottage nestled in the courtyard.

Save some time to stroll around Savannah. As one of our tour guides put it, "Savannah is like a beautiful baby—Everyone loves her."

Rates: $115–$185
Credit Cards Accepted: Visa, MC, AMEX, Discover
Number of Guest Rooms: 10
Number of Baths: 10
Wheelchair Access: No

Pets: No
Children: Yes
Smoking: Yes
Senior Citizen Discount: Yes
Directions: See brochure

Atlanta-Fulton Library: Margaret Mitchell Display Collection

One Margaret Mitchell Square
Atlanta, GA 30303
(404) 730-1700; (404) 730-4636

Who: Front desk

When: 10:00 A.M.–5:00 P.M. Monday, 10:00 A.M.–8:00 P.M. Tuesday through Thursday, 10:00 A.M.–5:00 P.M. on Friday and Saturday, 2:00–6:00 P.M. on Sunday

How Much: There is a charge for nonresidents to check out books.

Senior Citizen Discount: NA

Wheelchair Access: Yes

Directions: From I-85, take Exit 96 (International Boulevard) and stay in the left-hand lane. At the Spring Street exit, you will be on the backside of P Street Plaza. The library is in the next block at the corner of Carnesie Way and Forsyth Street.

What and Where: Atlanta is proud of its native daughter Margaret (Peggy) Mitchell Marsh and has an interesting artifact collection honoring her memory. Her novel *Gone with the Wind* was widely translated and you can see foreign editions in many languages, including Latvian, Arabic, and Slovakian. There are portraits of the author from childhood through adulthood, and photographs, tickets, and guest cards from the lavish opening celebration of the movie *Gone with the Wind*. You can see the typewriter Mitchell used to write her epic novel and a facsimile of an original typewritten page, as well as her entire personal library.

Atlanta Historical Society Library and Archives

130 West Paces Ferry Road
Atlanta, GA 30305
(404) 814-4040; (404) 814-4000

Who: Front desk

When: 10:00 A.M.–5:30 P.M. Monday through Saturday, 12:00 noon–5:30 P.M. on Sunday

How Much: $7 for adults, $5 for students older than 17; $4 for juniors ages 6 to 17

Senior Citizen Discount: $5

Wheelchair Access: Museum only

Directions: See brochure

What and Where: This library and archives is located in McElreath Hall and includes much to interest fans of Margaret Mitchell and *Gone with the Wind.* You can see the typing table and clipboard the author used while writing her enormously popular book. There are photographs of Mitchell as well as publicity shots of Clark Gable, Vivien Leigh, Olivia de Havilland, and Hattie McDaniel taken during the filming of the movie. The collection includes the personal correspondence of Margaret Mitchell, articles she wrote as a reporter for the *Atlanta Journal,* and many more mementos.

Emory University:
Robert W. Woodruff Library

Special Collections
(404) 329-6887

If you can't get enough *Gone with the Wind* memorabilia or are a serious researcher, check out the library at beautiful Emory University, where you can look at items concerning the production of the legendary movie.

The Margaret Mitchell House

999 Peachtree Street, N.E. Suite 1940
Atlanta, GA 30309-3964
(404) 249-7012
(404) 249-9388 Fax

Who: Nancy Tao

When: Public tours from 9:00 A.M. to 4:00 P.M. Saturday and Sunday only; call for expanded hours in fall 1997. Museum shop open daily, from 9:00 A.M. to 5:00 A.M.

How Much: $6 for adults, $5 for students with valid ID, $4 for children ages 7 to 12, and free for children 6 and under

Senior Citizen Discount: $5

Wheelchair Access: NA

Directions: The Margaret Mitchell House is conveniently located at the corner of 10th and Peachtree Streets in the heart of Midtown Atlanta. To purchase tickets, enter through the visitor's center located at the corner of Peachtree and Peachtree Place. The house is adjacent to the Midtown MARTA Station and is accessible from I-75/85 off Exit 10.

What and Where: Listed on the National Register of Historic Places, the Margaret Mitchell House, birthplace of *Gone with the Wind*, is a turn-of-the-century, three-story Tudor Revival mansion where Margaret Mitchell lived and wrote her Pulitzer Prize–winning book. Margaret (known as Peggy) Mitchell lived in the house between 1925 and 1932 following its conversion to a 10-unit apartment building. She and her husband, John Marsh, lived in apartment #1.

When the Margaret Mitchell House opened on May 16, 1997, keynote speaker Tom Wolfe, author of *The Right Stuff* and *Bonfire of the Vanities*, described the universal appeal of Mitchell's work by proclaiming *Gone with the Wind* one of the greatest literary works of all time.

The docent-led tour of the house is a one-hour experience featuring archival exhibits and exclusive photographs that tell the story of Margaret Mitchell beyond her famous novel. The tour begins in the visitor's center with "It May Not Be Tara," a locally produced movie about her life. Highlights of the house include the Front Room where Peggy's typewriter and desk were located and where she wrote the majority of her book. Here you will be informed that she and John loved to entertain and frequently had their friends over for parties. She would toss a towel over her typewriter before guests arrived to ensure privacy about her writing. Another interesting anecdote the docents will tell you is that in 1926 John, tired of always lugging books home for his wife to read, brought her a second-hand portable Remington typewriter. As he presented his gift to her, John said, "Madam, I greet you on the beginning of a great new career." His idea was that because Peggy had basically read every book in the public library she would need to write one of her own!

And what a career it was! Describing *Gone with the Wind*, Margaret Mitchell explained, "If the novel has a theme it is that of survival. ... What qualities are in those who fight their way through triumphantly that are lacking in those who go under ... ? I only know that the survivors used to call that quality 'gumption.' So I wrote about the people who had gumption and the people who didn't." Margaret Mitchell might have been describing herself because as you will discover after touring her home, this lively, outspoken writer certainly had gumption!

Oakwood House Bed and Breakfast Inn

951 Edgewood Avenue Northeast
Atlanta, GA 30307
(404) 521-9320
(404) 688-6034 Fax
E-mail: oakwoodbnb@aol.com

"History has never stood still here," say Judy and Robert Hotchkiss, hosts, owners, and next-door neighbors of Oakwood House. Built in 1911 and named in our own day for the giant oak tree presiding regally over the backyard, this building has had a colorful and somewhat checkered history. At various times it has housed a boardinghouse, been used for storage, cut up into apartments, transformed into offices for an international charter company, and housed interesting characters such as marriage counselors and film and video makers. The current owners have lived next door since 1978, and Judy maintains a writing office in the inn. Homey touches are welcomed by travelers, such as the washer and dryer and off-street parking—remember, we're talking Big City here. Four private guest rooms and a ground-level suite are available. Each room has a private modern bath and telephone. The house is reminiscent of *Our Town* and contains the pleasant and requisite wall-size bookcases and warm brick hearths. Lace curtains and shutters go with the territory, and help maintain that special down-home aura that we are all so glad to recognize at the end of a long day's journey. The continental breakfast features healthy baked goods and fresh fruits. And even in winter, the backyard oak is wonderful.

A table setting at the Oakwood House. Photo courtesy of Oakwood House Bed and Breakfast.

Rates: $70–$150
Credit Cards Accepted: Visa, MC, AMEX, Discover
Number of Guest Rooms: 6
Number of Baths: 6
Wheelchair access: Yes

Pets: No
Children: Yes
Smoking: No
Senior Citizen Discount: No
Directions: See brochure

The Whitlock Inn

57 Whitlock Avenue
Marietta, GA 30064
(770) 428-1495
(770) 919-9620 Fax

The Whitlock Inn's hostess, Alexis Edwards, says it best: "Here in historic Marietta we hold onto anything that's old: our houses, our furniture, our recipes and our accents. It's this holding on to the best of the past that makes this area in and around the square one of the most beautiful cities in the state." Couple this description with one look at the gorgeous inn itself, and you'll be hooked. Built as a private residence in 1900, this stately two-story white clapboard structure is a standout, particularly notable for its columned and banistered porches and the four tall brick chimneys that seem to stand guard as sentinels keeping time at bay. A large ballroom, two dining rooms, and two parlors attest to a different lifestyle but fit perfectly with the objectives of its current incarnation, which are to provide the finest services for guests, whether it be for an evening of pleasurable relaxation, a business function, or a memorable wedding. The gardens, too, are for the use and enjoyment of guests and include access to a beautiful and somewhat secluded roof garden. Five bedrooms with private baths and unique decors are available, and I'm happy to say that each contains that old-fashioned staple, a ceiling fan.

Rates: $75–$125
Credit Cards Accepted: Visa, MC, AMEX, Discover
Number of Guest Rooms: 5
Number of Baths: 5
Wheelchair Access: No

Pets: No
Children: If older than 12
Smoking: No
Senior Citizen Discount: No
Directions: See brochure

Inn Scarlett's Footsteps

40 Old Flat Shoals Road
Route 18, Pike County
Concord, GA 30206
(770) 884-9012
Website: http://www.gwtw.com

"I'll think about it tomorrow" might be the second-best-known line in Margaret Mitchell's *Gone with the Wind* (we all recognize Rhett's "Frankly, Scarlett ..." as numero uno), but it may not be the right reaction to the latest *Gone with the Wind* craze. It may make you too late to reserve a room, or to reserve a collectable portion of the Hollywood facade used in the 1939 movie that has never lost its appeal. Innkeeper K. C. Bassham purchased the MGM Tara facade when she was contemplating the opening of a B&B. Inn Scarlett's Footsteps is the result, and it, too, is proving to be a blockbuster. Unrestorable pieces of the set will be cut into small strips and encased in lucite with a color picture of the plantation home of practically everybody's favorite true-grit heroine. A certificate of authenticity will be included, and a percentage of the money received will be donated to the Clayton County Historical Society and the Margaret Mitchell House. The inn itself provides guided tours by costumed Southern belles, Civil War—excuse me, The Recent Unpleasantness Between the States—reenactments, a museum, carriage rides, a carriage house gift shop, *and* a place to spend the night! Upon reading K. C.'s literature, I vividly recalled a scene that impressed me when I first saw this film classic (is there anyone who has seen it only once?). The brochure reads: Dream of an eighteen-inch waist as you glide down the grand staircase. I think that image alone is worth the trip, don't you?

Rates: $65–$99
Credit Cards Accepted: Visa, MC, AMEX
Number of Guest Rooms: 5
Number of Baths: 5
Wheelchair Access: No

Pets: No
Children: If older than 10
Smoking: No
Senior Citizen Discount: No
Directions: See brochure

HAWAII

—+·—≡◆≡—·+—

Jack London's Island of Hawaii

After the roaring success of *Martin Eden, Call of the Wild,* and *White Fang,* Jack and Charmian London sailed their sailboat *Snark* to Hawaii. They visited Hilo on the big island in 1911 and were overwhelmed by island hospitality. They were wined, dined, and entertained every night and invited to a reception given by Queen Liliuokalani. London recorded these adventures in his book *The Cruise of the* Snark, and Charmian wrote her own book, *Our Hawaii,* a volume of memories, after her husband's death.

Shipman House B&B

131 Ka'iulani Street
Hilo, HI 96720
(808) 934-8002; (800) MAP-THIS; (800) 627-8447

Don't worry about the plane fare—once you've seen and heard the charms of the Shipman House Bed & Breakfast you'll decide that it's not just bird-watchers who need a checklist of unforgettable sightings. Known by local children as The Castle, and thereby assured of historical record for generations to come, this frame Victorian mansion is one of the last of its kind in the state of Hawaii. It is listed on both the National and State Registers of Historic Places, and judging by the number of people who approach it with camera at the ready, it is probably Hilo's most photographed residence. Owned by the Shipman family since 1901, it has been restored to its original elegance by a Shipman great-granddaughter and her husband, Barbara-Ann and Gary Andersen. Only a family member could recreate the experience of life with the Shipmans, a gracious, unpretentious hospitality that seems harder and harder to find today.

The house itself, located on the five and a half acres of what is known as Reed's Island, boasts the requisite double parlor, library, conservatory, billiard room, and second-story ballroom. The exterior is breathtaking, with a round three-story tower, wraparound veranda, and four curved bay windows. The porte cochere's high step accommodated turn-of-the-century horse-and-buggy arrivals. In the 1930s the Shipmans installed what may have been Hilo's first elevator, still in use today. Other buildings in the complex include a two-room guest cottage, servants' quarters, and a garage. The B&B guestrooms are those traditionally used by visitors and include the guest cottage and a first-floor room in the main house furnished with antique koa twin beds, mosquito netting, a ceiling fan and a private bath. Barbara-Ann is quite emphatic when she says, "I do not believe in skimpy breakfasts," thus endearing herself forever to most inveterate travelers. An expanded continental buffet is served on the lanai and is sure to offer assorted local fruits (twenty varieties of fruit tree are grown on the premises), coffee (Kona, of course), homemade breads, muffins, popovers, coffee cake, pancakes, and more.

The Shipman family has a fascinating history that is too long to relate here, but it is their connection with Jack London that first attracted my attention. The literary adventurer and his equally adventurous wife were month-long guests of the Shipmans while their sailboat *Snark* was under repair in Hilo Bay. A copy of London's letter of introduction is in the house library, and he has been quoted as saying, "To me, Mother Shipman is the first lady of Hawaii." After her husband's death, Charmian returned again and again, and considered this her island home. The Shipmans are mentioned in her books.

Rates: $130
Credit Cards Accepted: Visa, MC, AMEX
Number of Guest Rooms: 3
Number of Baths: 3
Wheelchair Access: No

Pets: No
Children: No
Smoking: No
Senior Citizen Discount: No
Directions: See brochure

Mark Twain at Hawaii: Volcanoes National Park

Mark Twain visited the famous volcano, now Hawaii Volcanoes National Park, in 1866. He seemed to think he was going to the ends of the earth—which, come to think of it, he was—and seemed more surprised to find a comfortable shelter that he described as "a neat little cottage with four bedrooms, a large parlor, and dining room" than at the spectacular sight of the volcano itself. He must have been somewhat impressed by the incredible Hawaiian volcano, because he wrote that Vesuvius was as a soup kettle compared to Kilauea. You can read more about Twain's island adventures in *Roughing It* or in a book published by the Hawaii Natural History Association, P.O. Box 464, Makawao, HI 96768, entitled *Mark Twain's Letters from Hawaii*.

Chalet Kilauea–The Inn at Volcano

998 Wright Road
Volcano Village, HI 96785
(808) 967-7786; (800) 937-7786
E-mail: bchawaii@aol.com

Any place that offers a Tree House Suite, a twenty-four-hour-a-day Jacuzzi, and a private chef is my kind of place. No wonder Jack London and Mark Twain liked this island so much!

If you like to get away from it all, Chalet Kilauea, The Inn at Volcano, a unique and beautiful bed and breakfast inn 1.5 miles from the entrance to Hawaii Volcanoes National Park, is your kind of place. You can rent one of the six luxurious vacation homes and find your own island paradise. You have full use of the inn plus an intimate home with your own private phone and TV with VCR. In the Hoku Mana House you have both an ocean view and a mountain view. From this contemporary home with modern Polynesian furnishings you have a spectacular view of Mauna Loa and Mauna Kea, the island's two 14,000-foot peaks. There are two bedrooms, each with a queen bed and private bath. If you feel like whipping up your own Hawaiian luau, a full kitchen awaits your creative culinary talent.

Hosts Lisha and Brian Crawford believe in service and it shows, from the attention to detail (monogrammed bathrobes, flowers in every room, and welcome chocolates) to the variety of environments from which guests can choose for their stay. When you want to step into someone else's life for a change, try one of their exotic theme rooms. The Continental Lace Suite is for the hopeless romantic. Lace curtains, French oil paintings, and a canopy bed make this the ideal room for a honeymoon couple. It also features a double Jacuzzi tub. There is also the Out of Africa Room, filled with baskets, masks, and other African pieces collected during the Crawfords' travels. You could choose the Oriental Jade Room, a delightful space where gold and jade make up the color scheme and antique Chinese screens enhance the atmosphere. Then there is my favorite,

the Tree House Suite, which includes a two-story unit with a king-size bed and color cable television; you look over hundreds of trees from the upstairs window. An adult tree house is every grown-up kid's fantasy!

Attention to detail shows in the candlelight two-course full gourmet breakfasts served at the Chalet as well. The first course includes juices and fruits of the season, and a second course might be smoked salmon and bagels, Indian curry with grilled tomato, or Hawaiian sweet bread French toast. Top this off with Kona coffee and a selection of international teas, and you will be ready for a day at the volcanoes. If you return to the inn between 4:00 and 5:00 P.M., afternoon tea awaits you, and you can top that off with a dip in the Jacuzzi on the premises. This is the Big Island at its best!

Rates: $125–$395
Credit Cards Accepted: Visa, MC, AMEX, Discover, Diners Club, Carte Blanch, JCB
Number of Guest Rooms: 12
Number of Baths: 12

Wheelchair Access: No
Pets: No
Children: Yes
Smoking: No
Senior Citizen Discount: Yes
Directions: See brochure

My Island Bed and Breakfast

P.O. Box 100
Volcano, HI 96785
(808) 967-7216
(808) 967-7719 Fax

My curiosity was piqued when I realized that the candles, kerosene lamps, and flashlights at My Island were not just decorations. As host Gordon Morse succinctly puts it, "Electrical service in Volcano is not guaranteed." He also suggests that guests not get excited over a slight earthquake now and then. "We live atop a rock 'n roll volcano, and this house has stood up to it all for over 100 years. Some eruptions have actually been seen (and heard!) from our bedroom windows." Umbrellas by the front door are also necessities, because an annual rainfall of 150 inches can

mean nine inches in 12 hours. A roof catchment system prevails in Volcano, for there is no commercial water system. Rainwater is stored in redwood tanks and pumped back into the house. The water is the softest in the world, so your shampoo will go a long, long way.

Does all of this sound rather daunting? I certainly hope not, because My Island is worth the adventure and the trip. Set amid a five-acre estate lush with trees and flowers beyond description (in this limited space) is a three-story house, the oldest in the Volcano community. *Haleohu* ("house in the mist") earns its name when trade-wind clouds settle on 4,000-foot Kilauea, one of the most active volcanoes on Earth. Built around 1886 by the Lyman family, early missionaries, this sturdy house is replete with pleasantries and oddities, such as the hand-poured windowpanes with wonderfully distorted glass. There are no clothes closets, for early settlers hung their few belongings on pegs, much as was done in Colonial America.

Breakfast is served family-style and is an all-you-can-eat delight. Six bedrooms, three in the main house (including an attic dormitory), a three-bedroom garden unit, and a separate three-bedroom vacation home are available. Your hosts, Gordon and Joann Morse, and My Island's manager, their daughter, Kii, are 30-year residents who delight in sharing their knowledge of island life with guests. I can't help but add that there are no screens on the windows at My Island, because this spectacular area has no mosquitoes, termites, or other creepy-crawly critters. That certainly wins points in my book!

Rates: $40–$100
Credit Cards Accepted: None
Number of Guest Rooms: 5
Number of Baths: 5
Wheelchair Access: Yes

Pets: No
Children: Yes
Smoking: No
Senior Citizen Discount: No
Directions: See brochure

Rosy's Rest

76-1012 Mamalahoa Highway
Holualoa, HI 96725
(808) 322-REST

The Kona Coast is justifiably noted for its ocean views and broad expanses of rich farmland. Macadamia nut farms flourish here, and Kona is to coffee what Kleenex is to tissues. And for those who seek the charm of old Hawaii—well, here we are. Rosy's Rest takes advantage of all this natural beauty and provides a panoramic view of miles of fabulous shoreline. A country cottage look prevails, inspired by the Ohia "twig" beds. All rooms have private baths. An added delight is that this B&B is within walking distance of the quaint village of Holualoa, home to many artists and brimming with pleasant galleries and shops.

Rates: $75–$85
Credit Cards Accepted: None
Number of Guest Rooms: 2
Number of Baths: 2
Wheelchair Access: No

Pets: No
Children: Extra charge
Smoking: No
Senior Citizen Discount: No
Directions: See brochure

IDAHO

—•— ≍◆≍ —•—

Ernest Hemingway's Sun Valley

Hemingway had a long-standing love affair with the state of Idaho. It had everything he was looking for—good hunting, beautiful scenery, congenial companions, and a clean, well-lighted place to work. Parts of the state reminded him of the Spain of his youth.

Hemingway initially traveled to Sun Valley in September 1939 as the guest of Union Pacific Railroad chairman Averell Harriman. The celebrity author had been informally invited to the Sun Valley Lodge to help promote the new ski resort. Although Hemingway sometimes claimed to shun publicity, my guide in Key West, Florida, claimed "Papa" was a promotion hound. In Idaho, the public Hemingway seemed to shine, and he was in a promotional film entitled *Sun Valley and the Hunter*. The movie, on videotape, can be seen at the Ketchum Community Library.

Hemingway and his paramour, Martha Gellhorn, the glamorous blonde journalist he'd met at Sloppy Joe's Bar in Key West, stayed in Suite 206 at the Lodge. It was in this room with its spectacular view of the mountains that Hemingway worked on *For Whom the Bell Tolls*. Today the hallways of the Lodge are filled with historic photos, several of which show Hemingway at his portable typewriter on the balcony.

In the fall of 1940 Idaho once again became Hemingway's escape hatch. Known as a congenial host and a man who liked to party, the author was sometimes too popular for his own good. After hosting a steady stream of company, which included the Gary Coopers and Dorothy Parker, Hemingway headed for Idaho. This time he and Martha went on a week's pack trip into the wild Middle Fork region of the Salmon River. The couple had such a good trip that they decided to tie the knot in Cheyenne, Wyoming.

In 1941 the entire Hemingway clan (complete with Ernest's three sons) descended on Sun Valley. In the fall, Martha, the boys, a few locals, and Ernest went on a rare hunt for antelope in eastern Idaho's Pahsimeroi Valley. This incident was later turned into the Hemingway short story "The Shot." Soon after, Ernest and Martha were divorced.

After the end of World War II in 1946, Hemingway returned to Sun Valley with his new wife, Mary. The couple were the guests of honor at a special showing of the movie version of Hemingway's short story "The Killers." The movie, starring Burt Lancaster, was one of the few adaptations of his works that Hemingway liked. The premiere was held at the Sun Valley Opera House. A respite in Cuba kept the Hemingways from Sun Valley until the fall of 1947.

Whenever the author was in town, the press was never far behind. Lillian Ross, a writer for *The New Yorker*, came to town to interview Ernest, who was working on *The Garden of Eden*.

It was 1958 before Ernest and Mary returned to Sun Valley. In between bird hunting and fishing he worked on *A Moveable Feast*. He played out the last chapter of his life in Sun Valley and committed suicide in 1961. Hemingway is buried in the Ketchum cemetery. His presence is still felt in the valley he loved so much, and he continues to be a living legend in Idaho and throughout the world.

The Hemingway House

What and Where: The house in which Hemingway died is closed to the public, but it can be seen from the west side of Highway 75, 0.75 mile north of Ketchum. At the Saddle Road Extension, exit. The house, with distinctive green trim and a green balcony, is uphill on your left.

The Hemingways settled into the Topping house in the fall of 1959, after fleeing from the tumultuous political situation in Cuba. Mary and Ernest were attracted by the spectacular views, the blond woodwork throughout, and an oversized modern kitchen and large stone fireplace. The author followed his morning writing routine, this time using a special stand-up desk in his room where he worked overlooking Adam's Gulch, Ketchum, and the majestic mountains.

After Ernest's suicide, his widow, Mary, maintained the family home until the mid-1980s. Because she and her husband were both nature lovers, she willed the property to The Nature Conservancy, and after her death in 1986 it became the organization's state headquarters. The next year The Nature Conservancy established the 14-acre Hemingway Preserve on the property that protects a mile of the Wood River.

Hemingway's Grave at the Ketchum Cemetery

What and Where: You can also visit "Papa's" grave in the Ketchum Cemetery, north on Highway 75 between Knob Hill Park and the Bigwood Golf Course. The larger-than-life author's grave is marked by a large but simple marker flanked by two evergreen trees. His fourth wife, Mary, is buried by his side.

The Hemingway Memorial

What and Where: A lovely memorial featuring a bronze bust of Ernest Hemingway, mounted on a stone pedestal, stands simply and elegantly in a grove of aspens and willows overlooking Trail Creek.

Hemingway's biographer, A. E. Hotchner, suggested building this tribute to his friend. The monument was dedicated in a festive manner, very much in keeping with the author's style. The gala event took place on July 21, 1966, the 67th anniversary of Hemingway's birth. An orchestra played Mozart, Idaho's governor was in attendance, *Atlantic Monthly* editor Robert Manning addressed the crowd, and when the ceremony was over everyone went to the Trail Creek Cabin for a party hosted by Mary Hemingway.

Inscribed on a plaque on the pedestal is the now-famous epitaph Hemingway wrote in memory of a friend. Read it and you'll find yourself thinking of the author himself:

... and above the hills
the high blue windless sky
Now he will be a part of them forever.

Povey Pensione

128 West Bullion
Box 1134
Hailey, ID 83333
(208) 788-4682; (800) 370-4682

Some people think that bed and breakfasts have turned into ultrachic and pricey hotels, and many people think Ketchum is on its way to becoming another Aspen or Vail. Not to worry. If you still like your B&Bs to be inexpensive, homey, and charming, you'll want to try the Povey Pensione. As owner Terrie Davis explained, "We wanted to keep our pensione simple and friendly. Our inn fits in perfectly with Hailey, which is the cutest little walking town."

The rates at Povey Pensione are quite reasonable, but there is no skimping on service or first-class food. Breakfasts of French toast or German puff pancakes filled with fruit are presented in such a picture-perfect fashion that guests often take snapshots of the breakfast table. Terrie always uses colorful fresh flowers and lots of fruit. Who can blame shutterbugs for wanting to capture this winning still life? The breakfast time slot is leisurely and for your convenience. You can choose any time between 8:00 and 10:00 A.M. to break your fast.

Everything at Povey Pensione is done with the guest in mind. The four spacious bedrooms, each furnished with period antiques, are private, well-insulated rooms. "We tried to provide quiet rooms that have a place for our guests to sit and relax," explained Terrie Davis. "When my husband and I bought the 1890 John Povey home, we completely rebuilt it to keep the historical features but to make it comfortable."

The location could not be better—only 13 miles south of Sun Valley. In addition to world-class skiing, the area offers boating and fishing, hiking, mountain biking, and golfing. To view the Wood River Valley in blissful tranquility, ski or bike the trail to Ketchum, visiting the Hemingway Memorial along the way. You'll understand why "Papa" Hemingway returned to Idaho again and again.

Rates: $60
Credit Cards Accepted: Visa, MC
Number of Guest Rooms: 4
Number of Baths: 2
Wheelchair Access: No

Pets: No
Children: If older than 12
Smoking: No
Senior Citizen Discount: No
Directions: See brochure

River Street Inn

100 Rivers Street West
Sun Valley, ID 83353
(206) 726-3611; (800) 954-8585 Ext. 1020
(208) 726-2439 Fax
E-mail: riverst@sprynet.com

I'm a real sucker for breakfast in bed. A tempting tray of pastries and a delicious morning entree brought bedside is just one of the many ways guests are pampered at the River Street Inn. A leisurely afternoon tea and relaxing Japanese soaking tubs are two more ways Sun Valley's first B&B lives up to its reputation as a luxurious home away from home. Add spacious parlor suites with queen-size beds, walk-in showers, cable television, in-room phones, and small refrigerators and you have the setting for a romantic, sybaritic weekend.

Nature is never far away, for the French doors open onto a deck nestled among aspens and cottonwoods. The deck offers an ideal spot for early-morning bird-watching or late-night stargazing. Many of the guest rooms overlook Trail Creek, and others have clear, magnificent views of Bald Mountain.

Innkeeper Amy Smith explained the appeal of her country inn, which has been in business for 11 years. "It's a very comfortable place that is not overly done. We have a great location and guests can walk to any-place in Ketchum."

"One of our main attractions," Smith adds, "is the weather. They call this place Sun Valley for a reason."

There is plenty to keep you busy in Sun Valley. In the winter, try the world-famous downhill and cross-country skiing. In the summer and fall, play golf or indulge in white-water rafting, fly fishing, mountain biking, canoeing, horseback riding, or hiking in the lovely Sawtooth National Recreation Area. Bob and Janet Ford, peripatetic friends of mine, just returned from a trip to the Sun Valley area, and they said the biking and hiking are first-class here. Good cooks who also know their way around restaurants, the Fords reported that "the Ketchum Grill was a favorite of ours. It had a nice porch to sit on and watch the town. We thought it offered great food for a reasonable price, including several game dishes."

Rates: $130–$185
Credit Cards Accepted: Visa, MC, Discover, AMEX
Number of Guest Rooms: 8
Number of Baths: 8
Wheelchair Access: No

Pets: Yes, with a $10 pet charge per room
Children: Yes
Smoking: No
Senior Citizen Discount: Yes
Directions: See brochure

Ketchum Korral Motor Lodge

310 South Main Street
Box 2241
Ketchum, ID 83340
(208) 726-3510
(800) 657-2657

"A foolish consistency is the hobgoblin of little minds," wrote Ralph Waldo Emerson. Although this book hopes to offer readers information about the best B&Bs, exceptions must be made. Ketchum Korral Motor Lodge is such an exception.

Hemingway himself stayed at the Ketchum Korral (then the MacDonald Cabins) in 1946 and 1948. The Hemingway Cabin (or the Large Cabin), where the author stayed, is graced with framed letters

Hemingway wrote to his family about the cabins. One of them tells how he found some wonderful cabins that he felt would be cozy and comfortable. The Ketchum Korral served as a base camp for the author's fishing and hunting trips. The very congenial owner, Norma Schneider, is delighted to talk about the valley and its most famous resident.

"We get a lot of people who come here to see where Hemingway stayed," Schneider told me.

Even if you're not a Hemingway fan, there is plenty to keep you occupied in Ketchum. As Schneider, a California transplant, explains, "Everything I love is here. There are one hundred miles of paved hike and bike trails. In the summer you can take wonderful float trips. In the fall there is a gorgeous Indian summer. The mountains here remind me of the mountains in Switzerland."

"We appeal to people who want to get away from it all," Schneider tells me. " Our cabins are more down-home. We don't offer as much frou-frou stuff as the fancier places, just magnificent scenery and friendly service."

Rates: $50–$125
Credit Cards Accepted: Visa, MC, AMEX, Discover
Number of Guest Rooms: 17
Number of Baths: 17
Wheelchair Access: Yes

Pets: With deposit
Children: Yes
Smoking: Yes
Senior Citizen Discount: No
Directions: See brochure

ILLINOIS

＋◆ ≡◆≡ ◆＋

Carl Sandburg State Historic Site

331 East Third Street
Galesburg, IL 61401
(309) 342-2361

Who: Carol Nelson

When: 9:00 A.M.–5:00 P.M. every day except for Christmas, New Year's Day, and Thanksgiving

How Much: Suggested donations of $2 for people over 18, $1 for those 18 and younger

Senior Citizen Discount: No

Wheelchair Access: Yes

Directions: In Galesburg, follow the brown directional signs

What and Where: When Carl Sandburg, the world-renowned poet and biographer and recipient of two Pulitzer Prizes, died at the age of 89, his ashes were sent, as he had requested, to be buried in the backyard of the simple workingman's cottage in which he was born. At 331 East Third Street in Galesburg stands the three-room house that Sandburg's father, a Swedish immigrant who worked on the Chicago, Burlington and Quincy Railroad, bought for his family in 1873. It's a modest house, typical of a railroad laborer's home. Inside, the parlor, the kitchen, and the bedroom contain simple furniture and many personal belongings of the Sandburg family. Behind the house is a small wooded park. Underneath Remembrance Rock, at the center of the site, lie the ashes of the poet who gave America back to herself.

Sandburg knew Galesburg as only a boy in the late 1800s could know it. He carried newspapers, delivered milk, harvested ice, laid bricks, and shined shoes in Galesburg's Union Hotel. He and his group of friends, the "Dirty Dozen," palled around together, occasionally getting themselves into trouble. Once Sandburg and his friend French Juneau heard that William Jennings Bryan was going to be speaking in Monmouth, Illinois, only 16 miles away, so the two of them rode the cowcatcher of the train going to Monmouth and back.

When Sandburg became 17, he grew restless. "I hated my home town and yet I loved it. And I hated and loved myself about the same as I did the town and the people. I came to see that my trouble was inside myself more than it was in the town and the people … I decided in June of 1897 to head West … I would become a hobo."

It wasn't until many months later that he returned to "the only house in the United States where I could open a door without knocking, and walk in for a kiss from the woman of the house."

Soon after that, he volunteered to serve in the Spanish American War. When he returned home to Galesburg he attended Lombard College and became a member of the college's Poor Writers' Club. His professor, Phillip Green Wright, believed in Sandburg's writing ability to the extent that he printed his student's first book of poems, *In Reckless Ecstasy*, on a simple press he had in his basement.

When Sandburg finally left Galesburg for good, he moved to Wisconsin, where he wrote and distributed political pamphlets in sympathy with the plight of the American worker. After marrying Lillian Steichen, he moved to Chicago, where he worked as a journalist covering labor issues. It wasn't until he was 38 that his creative writing finally began to pay off. At that point, he found himself on the brink of what would be a career as one of America's most loved poets, storytellers, and historians.

When you visit Galesburg, you might want to see other remnants of Sandburg's boyhood. His second home is at 641 East South Street. His third home is at 806-810 East Berrien, where he slept with his brother in the long attic room.

Old Seventh Ward School (Now Douglas School), at 435 East Third Street, was where Sandburg attended elementary school. "As a child, I attended school here, and was in Miss Margaret Mullen's room. There I learned about numbers and how they could slip and slide away from you."

Brook Street Fire Station, at 550 East Brooks Street, is where Sandburg served as a fireman to help support himself during his college years.

The CB&Q Tracks and Shop area now has a Railroad Museum, at the corner of Seminary and Mulberry, which is open noon to 5:00 P.M. Memorial Day through Labor Day. (One of Sandburg's milk-route customers was Frank Bullard, the engineer who, during Sandburg's boyhood, set the world's record for train speed.)

The front of Knox College is Old Main, where Abraham Lincoln and Stephen Douglas gave the fifth of their famous debates. Sandburg wasn't alive during Lincoln's lifetime but as a boy had a thirst for knowledge about the great statesman and would ask questions about Lincoln of the older people about town who had actually known him. Near the end of his life Sandburg wrote a six-volume account of Abraham Lincoln's life, a work for which he received the Pulitzer Prize in history.

Seacord House

624 North Cherry Street
Galesburg, IL 61401
(309) 342-4107

While railroad workmen lived in humble cottages near the rail yards, the more affluent members of Galesburg lived in the elegant section of town known as Society Hill. Among them was Wilken Seacord, the superintendent of the railroad and a prominent citizen, who built a beautiful three-story Eastlake Queen Anne home on Cherry Street. While Mr. Seacord lived there, a young Swedish American boy, Charlie

Line drawing of the Seacord House by Annette Lindeman.

Sandburg, delivered his newspapers to his porch.

The Seacord House is now a bed and breakfast that has retained the elegance and style of the late 1890s. The walls have wallpaper in keeping with the period; the windows are draped with lace curtains. The large high-ceilinged rooms are furnished with the family antiques of Gwen and Lyle Johnson, Seacord House's owners. There is a wraparound front porch where you can relax in the porch swing. In the backyard is a patio where you can sit and listen to the birds.

Each of the three guest rooms is furnished with a waterbed for your sleeping comfort and cooled with ceiling fans. Two guest rooms have private sinks.

Breakfast is served each morning at the round oak table in the dining room or, weather permitting, on the brick patio in the backyard. If you're in luck, you'll hit a day when Lyle Johnson serves up his famous special-recipe waffles. Otherwise, you'll have to settle for some delicious stuffed French toast, or some of Gwen's orange-pecan or cheese and bacon muffins, along with fresh fruit, fruit juice, and your fill of coffee.

"It's a slow pace of life in Galesburg," notes Gwen Johnson. "The people are friendly and the whole culture is personalized." Take time to stroll the neighborhood around Seacord House, where fine Victorian homes line the brick streets. Let yourself slow down and take in the town of Carl Sandburg.

Rates: $35–$40
Credit Cards Accepted: Visa, MC, Discover
Number of Guest Rooms: 3
Number of Baths: 1
Wheelchair Access: No

Pets: No
Children: Yes
Smoking: No
Senior Citizen Discount: No
Directions: Call for directions

Edgar Lee Masters: Oak Hill Cemetery

1000 Main Street
Lewistown, Illinois 61542
(309) 547-3006 Ext. 12

Who: Information (309) 547-4300

When: Call to obtain tour times

How Much: Free

Senior Citizen Discount: NA

Wheelchair Access: No

Directions: Call for directions; brochures available at city hall

What and Where:

Where are Elmer, Herman, Bert, Tom and Charley,
The weak of will, the strong of arm, the clown, the boozer,
*   the fighter?*
All, all are sleeping on the hill.
One passed in a fever,

One was burned in a mine,
One was killed in a brawl,
One died in a jail,
One fell from a bridge toiling for children and wife—
All, all are sleeping, sleeping on the hill.

So wrote Edgar Lee Masters in the opening of his famed *Spoon River Anthology*. Spoon River was based on a real town, Lewistown, Illinois, where Masters spent his adolescence, and the people in his story are based on the real people who lived and died in Lewistown and the surrounding area. Although the book was published in 1915, it was forbidden in Lewistown until 1972. That was when the last of the characters' immediate descendants passed on.

"We always have to explain to tourists," noted David Boyd, Lewistown's tourism chairman, "that Edgar Lee took a great deal of poetic liberties with the characters in the Anthology. That, fortunately or unfortunately, the good characters come from Petersburg and the bad characters come from Lewistown." (Petersburg, a town 35 miles to the south of Lewistown, was where Masters lived during his early childhood.) Mr. Boyd has reason to comment. Two *Spoon River* characters, Granville Calhoun and Hamilton Green, were based on his great-grandfather. And the other characters? It would be a good idea to get hold of a copy of John Hallwas's *Annotated Spoon River Anthology* (which can be found at Copperfield's Bookstore in Macomb, Illinois). Hallwas identifies nearly all the characters from the *Anthology* and gives their burial location.

"All, all are sleeping, sleeping on the hill." Oak Hill Cemetery is over 150 years old now. It's a real place where the citizens of Lewistown are buried, among them the townspeople from whom Masters developed his characters. Twice a year, locals, dressed in period clothes, assemble at the cemetery to read epitaphs from the *Spoon River Anthology:* on Edgar Lee Masters' Day, during the first weekend in June, and during the Spoon River Fall Festival, during the first two weekends in October.

The places where Masters gathered his stories still exist. Rasmussen Blacksmith Shop, just a couple of blocks from his boyhood home, was where old and young alike gathered on cold winter days to warm themselves by Mr. Rasmussen's potbellied stove. Plenty of gossip and many stories were passed from person to person as they huddled there warming themselves, and young Edgar Lee was listening. (The Rasmussen Blacksmith Shop is now open free to the public from 10:00 A.M. to 5:00 P.M. April through October. For other months, arrangements can be made through Lewistown's Historical Society at 309-547-2081.)

Masters's father was a lawyer in town. His law office still stands (although it is now occupied). Edgar Lee did some office work for his father as a boy and apprenticed under him as a young adult. Without question, he collected some of his stories from his father's confidential files.

Then there's the Lewistown Courthouse, a building from which Abraham Lincoln delivered his Return to the Fountain speech in 1858, and to which one of Masters's characters, Silas Dement, set fire in 1894. (Two columns from the burned courthouse were re-erected in the Oak Hill Cemetery. The present courthouse was built in 1897 on the grounds of the previous one.)

There are other streets and buildings which Masters's characters passed by during the span of their lives in "Spoon River": the old hotel, the Presbyterian church, Peavine Railway Depot, the *Fulton Democrat*. All are nestled close together in the old part of

Lewistown. It's an easy walk, during which you can imagine Spoon River's citizens, who walked here a hundred years before.

Masters left Lewistown and eventually moved to Chicago, where he became a member of the law firm of Clarence Darrow, the eloquent criminal defense lawyer who defended John Scopes in the "Monkey Trial" of 1925. Later, Masters moved on to New York.

He died in 1950 and was buried on another hill, Oakland Cemetery, just outside of Petersburg, the town where he spent his earliest years. Edgar Lee Masters's childhood home in Petersburg can be visited daily. It is located on the corner of Eighth and Jackson Streets and is open every day between 1:00 P.M. and 5:00 P.M., except Mondays.

The Oaks

510 West Sheridan
Petersburg, Illinois 62675
(217) 632-5444

On a bluff overlooking Edgar Lee Masters's village of Petersburg stands a nineteeth-century Victorian mansion surrounded by five and a half acres of wooded lawn. It was built by Senator Edward Laning, a well-known lawyer of the town. Years later his grandson would become good friends with Edgar Lee Masters, and the mansion, named The Oaks, would have a place in one of Masters's books, *The Sangamon.*

Senator Laning hired John Carver, a locally famous builder, to build this Italianate Victorian, which includes a three-story walnut staircase, unique plasterwork ceilings, original interior shutters, and no less than seven fireplaces.

The Oaks, now a bed and breakfast, can be an elegant addition to your tour of Spoon River country. Its owners, Susan and Ken Rodgers, invite you to stay in one of five individually furnished rooms. The Edward Laning Suite includes two spacious rooms with a magnificent view of Petersburg. An eclectic mixture of antiques and Italian furniture adorn the rooms, along with private fireplace and bath.

Miss Martha's Bedchamber, named after Senator Laning's daughter, features wicker furniture, a fireplace with a carved wooden mantel, original shutters, and a queen-size bed.

Master John's Quarters, named after Laning's son, contains a walnut Eastlake double bed, matching marble-topped dresser, the original marble sink, and a fireplace.

Olivia's Guest Room is a suite located on the third floor. In it you will find two double beds and graceful period furniture. It has its own bath and a private sitting room, including TV and VCR.

The Maid's Quarters, which is secreted away above the kitchen, is furnished with oak antiques and rose-and-ivory wallpaper. If you stay in the Maid's Quarters, you can sit and enjoy the evening in your private screened-in porch or relax in the whirlpool of your private bath.

The downstairs of the mansion includes a library, a parlor, and two dining rooms, all trimmed in walnut with intricate plasterwork and moldings and with three beautiful marble fireplaces.

In the afternoon you are welcomed with a repast of tea and cookies or wine and cheese. In the morning the Rodgerses serve a full gourmet breakfast in one of their elegant dining rooms. If you like, you may also partake of a seven-course dinner served by candlelight. (The cost of dinner ranges from $15 to $25, depending on which entree you prefer. Dinner is available to The Oaks guests any night of the week. It is available to the public, by reservation, on Friday and Saturday evenings only.)

Rates: $70–$115
Credit Cards Accepted: Visa, MC, Discover
Number of Guest Rooms: 5
Number of Baths: 4
Wheelchair Access: No

Pets: No
Children: Yes
Smoking: No
Senior Citizen Discount: Yes
Directions: See brochure

The Ernest Hemingway Foundation

339 North Oak Park Avenue
Oak Park, IL 60303
(708) 848-2222

Who: Jennifer Whealer, executive director

When: 1:00–5:00 P.M. Wednesday, Friday, and Sunday; 10:00 A.M.–5:00 P.M. on Saturday

How Much: $4 for adults, $3 for youths

Senior Citizen Discount: $3

Wheelchair Access: No

Directions: Take I-290 to Harlem Avenue exit; take Harlem Avenue north to Chicago Avenue. Go east on Chicago Avenue to Oak Park Avenue, then south on Oak Park Avenue for approximately one block to 339 Oak Park.

What and Where: Ernest Hemingway was my favorite author when I was a journalism major in college, so I was interested in visiting the Hemingway Foundation to see if I could learn how he developed his spare, realistic literary style. I certainly was able to witness the evolution of his writing style from his first published work at age 12 in 1911 to excerpts from his Nobel Prize acceptance speech in 1954. There is an interesting six-minute video of Papa's high school years as well as a literary wall featuring first-edition book jackets.

There is much to learn here about the complex life of Hemingway. His childhood diary is on display, as is a letter from nurse Agnes von Kurowsky terminating their engagement. Anyone who has read any of Hemingway's work knows the influence of nature on his writing. According to a display at the foundation, his father, an avid sportsman, passed on a love of the natural world to Ernest.

Don't miss the week-long Hemingway birthday celebration held around July 21, Papa's birthday. This festive week includes writers' workshops, lectures, and other activities. For more information, call (708) 848-2222.

There must be something in the water in this literate midwestern town, because many well-known authors were born here. Edgar Rice Burroughs, considered Oak Park's "second most famous author," lived in the village from 1911 to 1919 at 821 Scoville, 414 Augusta (where he wrote 11 novels), 700 North Linden, and 325 North Oak Park Avenue. In 1912, Burroughs published *Tarzan*, which not only was a best-seller but has been equally popularized by a series of movies. In an ironic statement, Burroughs told an interviewer in 1929, "I know nothing about the technique of story writing, and now after 18 years of writing, I still know nothing about technique—I was writing because I had a wife and two babies, a combination that does not work well without money."

Other Oak Park authors include Charles MacArthur, coauthor of the classic *The Front Page*, and Dorothy Thompson (Mrs. Sinclair Lewis) whom Lewis called "the best newspaperman in the country."

Finally, spend at least an extra day, maybe two, to enjoy the magnificent genius of architect Frank Lloyd Wright. You can tour his home and studio and view the exteriors of 13 buildings designed by Wright , including famous examples of the "Prairie House." To get an in-depth picture of this fascinating man and his work, I recommend taking the audio tour. Save some time for the Ginkgo Tree Bookshop at the Wright Home; I guarantee you can buy something wonderful for everyone on your Christmas list.

The Write Inn

211 North Oak Park Avenue
Oak Park, IL 60302
(708) 383-4800

Jazz, bathtub gin, and the Charleston. Not to mention Art Deco, Frank Lloyd Wright, Hemingway and Fitzgerald. If you're "hung up," as they say, on the twenties, this is the place for you. The Write Inn opened in 1926 as the Oak Park Manor. This architectural gem of the famed Frank Lloyd Wright Historic District was home to many literary figures, who, like Vincent Starrett, found the character of the hotel an excellent creative atmosphere for writing. Starrett's talents and titles were many: poet, reporter, founding member of the Baker Street Irregulars, chief editor of the *Chicago Daily News*—he was also popular as the resident bookman of The Write Inn.

Today he would have no trouble recognizing the rooms filled with period furniture and accessories and restored mosaic and marble floors in the public area, and he'd probably applaud the modern conveniences, which include fax machines, meeting rooms, and coffee service—all important for a writer's well-being. The room selection is large, with parlor rooms, period suite, standard and family rooms, and even an entire wing on the top floor that can accommodate 14 guests. Although there is also a new and spacious elevator, I have the feeling Starrett (and perhaps you as well) would prefer the smaller period model that is still working after all these years.

Rates: $55–$155
Credit Cards Accepted: Visa, MC, AMEX, Discover, Diners Club
Number of Guest Rooms: 65
Number of Baths: 65
Wheelchair Access: Yes

Pets: Yes
Children: Yes
Smoking: Yes
Senior Citizen Discount: 10% for AARP members Sunday through Thursday
Directions: Brochure contains map

Literary Chicago

Chicago is known for great jazz, innovative architecture, Lake Michigan, the Art Institute, and American literature. Because you are only about 20 minutes away from the Windy City when you are in Oak Park, you might want to think about some of Chicago's literary giants. Unfortunately, you will need to use your imagination because there are no sites to visit. Recently, while driving into Chicago, I listened to a Carl Sandburg audiotape featuring his *Chicago Poems,* and the city came alive from his perspective. He is the ultimate chronicler of the Chicago scene, and I recommend reading or listening to his poem "Chicago" as you gaze at the skyline:

> *Hog Butcher for the World,*
> *Tool Maker, Stacker of Wheat,*
> *Player with Railroads and the Nation's Freight Handler;*
> *Stormy, husky, brawling.*
> *City of the Big Shoulders:*

Many Chicago writers, including Sandburg, cut their teeth as newspaper reporters. Ben Hecht and Charles MacArthur wrote the definitive newspaper play, *The Front Page,* depicting the madcap, exciting life of a big-city reporter. Theodore Dreiser was a newspaperman, and *Dawn,* his autobiographical novel, describes this life. Others member of the Fourth Estate are the *Chicago Tribune's* popular columnist Ring Lardner and the *Chicago Daily News* columnist Eugene Field.

The other great Chicago tradition is muckraking. In *The Jungle,* a book guaranteed to make you never want to eat a hot dog or hamburger again, Upton Sinclair took on the brutal horrors of the Chicago stockyards.

INDIANA

—◦— ≡◆≡ —◦—

James Whitcomb Riley Museum Home

528 Lockerbie Street
Indianapolis, IN 46202
(317) 631-5885

Who: Sandra Crain

When: 10:00 A.M.–3:30 P.M. Tuesday through Saturday, 12:00 noon–3:30 P.M. on Sunday. Closed during major holidays and during the first two weeks of January.

How Much: $2 for adults, $.50 for children ages 7 through 17, free for children under 6

Senior Citizen Discount: $1.50 for seniors 65 and older

Wheelchair Access: First floor only

Directions: Call for directions

What and Where:

> *Such a dear little street*
> *It is nestled away*
> *From the noise of the city*
> *And heat of the day.*

This is how James Whitcomb Riley described his Victorian house, the place the poet spent the last 23 years of his life. Riley, a lifelong bachelor, was a paying guest of his longtime friends, Major and Mrs. Charles L. Holstein.

The house is considered one of the finest historic preservations in the United States. It gives the visitor a glimpse of the life of urban, upscale Victorians in the shadow of downtown Indianapolis. Due to the foresight of a group of Riley's friends, including Booth Tarkington, the house was purchased from the estate of Mrs. Charles L. Holstein soon after her death on October 18, 1916.

Italianate in style, the elegant home is in pristine condition and features wall-to-wall carpeting, hand-carved solid woodwork, and faux marble fireplaces.

The house is extremely Victorian (translation: stiff) but has some fascinating period pieces. Don't miss the petticoat mirror, a device essential to the proper Victorian lady, who always had to consult a glass to make certain no petticoats and no ankles showed. Also of the era is the fainting couch in one of the bedrooms. I discovered why fainting couches were all the vogue in Victorian times: Many women wore punishing corsettes pulled as snug as possible and consequently, fainting was common! Our tour guide pointed out that in proper Victorian homes the kitchen doors were always closed, because Victorian women simply did not go into the kitchen!

The ladies did venture forth into the dining room, and the Lockerbie Street dining room features one of the best sideboards of the era. In this formal dining room it took three servants to get the food to the table, which was beautifully set with fine china and Reed and Barton silver. At each place setting was an orange cup, which our guide informed us was to be used only when company called, because oranges were considered delicacies.

The library, Riley's favorite room, contains his books, as well as a portrait of his friend Joel Chandler Harris of Uncle Remus fame.

Riley's bedroom seems to be ready for his return. There are cookies and tea waiting for him, and his famous top hat is on the bed. His desk and favorite pen are awaiting inspiration. Hanging above the fireplace is one of Riley's favorite items: a Wayman Adams painting of his beloved poodle, Lockerbie.

The James Whitcomb Riley Museum Home. Photo by Bass Photo Co., Inc.

A special treat is to visit the Riley House during the month of December, when the entire house is beautifully decorated in the Victorian manner. It is so well done and "Victorianally correct" that even Queen Victoria would be amused.

The Nuthatch B&B

7161 Edgewater Place
Indianapolis, IN 46240
(317) 257-2660
(317) 257-2677 Fax
E-mail: nuthatch@netride.com

After Joan Hamilton's divorce, her Canadian Methodist minister father gave her some advice that has been the cornerstone of her life. "You need to read. It will save your life."

Joan has been reading or working with books ever since. She went to Louisiana State University and earned a master's degree in library science, then went to Tulane University and worked in the university's rare-book room. She was one of only two women to receive a Lilly Fellowship in rare books at The Lilly Library at Indiana University. After she married Bernie Morris, a college professor, she went into the bookstore business.

When Bernie retired from the Department of Psychology at Purdue University, Joan decided she wanted to be home with him. Voilà, the bed and breakfast was born!

Bernie and Joan are a dynamic duo, Bernie with his New York wit and storytelling ability and Joan with her amazing finesse in the kitchen. She grows all her own herbs, and her breakfasts are something to write home about. We started with fresh plums topped with a delicious orange sauce. Then we feasted on an egg and potato frittata covered with fresh herbs picked from Joan's herb garden. The potatoes were grown by a friend of Joan's and were "dug up last week." There were two varieties of organic tomatoes. As a Hoosier myself, I am a sucker for homemade jams and jellies. Joan offered two varieties, both wonderful. To top the homemade toast, we had our choice of lemon verbena jelly made from herbs from the garden right outside the kitchen, or raspberry-blueberry jelly. For the sake of good reporting, I chose both. Just when I thought I could not eat another bite, Joan brought out a coffee cake. I rose to the occasion and made room.

Even though there are books everywhere at the Nuthatch, as well as pictures of illuminated manuscripts, after eating Joan's breakfast I headed for her huge cookbook collection. The shelves held such tempting titles as *The Hoosier Cookbook, The Kansas Cookbook, The Los Angeles Cookbook, The Gardener's Cookbook,* and a large section of cookbooks devoted to Thai, Chinese, Vietnamese, and Southeast Asian cuisine.

As Joan and I sat on the back porch overlooking her lovely view of the White River, she explained how she got hooked on cooking. "It all started with herbs. When I first moved to Indianapolis, there was no place to get fresh herbs." So she did what any self-respecting culinary artist would—she grew her own.

"I started with basil and moved on to growing my own Thai herbs, keffir lime, Thai ginger plant, and three kinds of Thai basil.

If I couldn't eat it, I wouldn't grow it," explained my genial hostess as we sipped Italian cream sodas and watched the nuthatches, the inn's namesakes, flit around the porch. "I loved stuff that smelled good."

After her first trip to Hong Kong, Joan was an instant convert to Oriental food. This affinity for spicy Asian food has sent her halfway around the world to learn ancient methods of preparation. After three trips to Thailand and Indonesia, she was ready to share this fiery, exotic fare with Indianapolis. Now, through seminars, TV cooking shows, and classes at the library, she teaches the meat-and-potatoes crowd how to fix a Thai dinner party menu featuring fiery beef salad, chicken with Thai basil, and delicious black sticky rice pudding. For B&B gourmets, if four of you book the entire Nuthatch (there are only two rooms), you'll win a free cooking class. Bon appetit!

Sometimes I think many B&Bs are almost too elegant these days; therefore, I liked the casual, somewhat rustic feel of the Nuthatch. With the lovely river setting I felt as if I were in a resort, not a city. My husband felt as if he were back in his boyhood home in upstate New York as we settled into the appropriately named Adirondack Suite. A circular staircase led to our suite, a comfortable room with fireplace, old wicker furniture, Indian rugs, and the double pleasure of an attached greenhouse and a private terrace.

Rates: $80–$95
Credit Cards Accepted: Visa, MC, AMEX, Discover, Diners Club
Number of Guest Rooms: 2
Number of Baths: 2
Wheelchair Access: No

Pets: Yes
Children: If older than 12
Smoking: No
Senior Citizen Discount: Yes
Directions: See brochure

Old Northside B&B

1340 North Alabama Street
Indianapolis, IN 46202
(317) 635-9123; (800) 635-9127

The Old Northside of Indianapolis is a historic neighborhood where citizens of wealth and prominence built mansions a century ago. It therefore seems most fitting that our handsome inn takes its name accordingly. Snug in the middle of this area of handsome homes and prestigious addresses is the Romanesque Revival brick house built in 1885 by Herman C. DeWenter. DeWenter was a German immigrant who became a prominent Indiana industrialist. The original wood floors and handcarved cherry woodwork attest to his attention to detail, and the present owners contracted skilled European craftsmen to paint new murals on the ceilings and walls. Unique theme rooms have been carefully designed and include the Theatre Room, decorated with old playbills, posters, and vintage traveling luggage, and a Jacuzzi tub of which even Sarah Bernhardt would have been envious.

Naturally we stayed in the Literary Room, which contains memorabilia from the golden era of Hoosier literature, highlighting authors read the world over, including Booth Tarkington, Lew Wallace, and James Whitcomb Riley. Guests can curl up with a book in front of the working fireplace or carefully thumb through pages while relaxing in the large Jacuzzi tub. I leafed through Tarkington's *Claire Ambler*, Riley's *Rhymes of Childhood*, and Wallace's *Ben-Hur*. The book theme predominates in this room, with its book-emblazoned bedspread, throw rug, and draperies.

No one needs a hint as to how the Bridal Room is designed, and racing fans need no clues about the Indy Room's memorabilia and the sport that put Indiana on the map. An old brick wall of the building has even been left exposed, just to add to the nostalgia accumulated here. A common area for guests that is particularly popular is the music room, with its baby grand piano, antique organ, and collection of somewhat unusual stringed instruments.

And as for breakfasts, be prepared for a treat, but don't bring your book or newspaper to the breakfast table. Innkeeper Susan M. Berry has some ground rules, and as she mischievously whisked the morning paper from one of her guests' hands, she asked him, "Didn't your mother tell you it is not polite to read at the table?"

Susan's full breakfasts please both the palate and the eye. She asks that you not spoil it by asking about calories! Seated on a pleasant outside porch on white wicker furniture, we were served banana-nut muffins, an artistically presented fruit plate, and banana crepes with flowers and herbs.

While enjoying coffee with Susan in this attractive urban setting, I discovered that she had been a concert pianist. "I got burned out, but I still love music. That's why I created the music room."

The music room reflects Susan's Ukrainian background, and in her determined manner she imported Ukrainian artists to create Old-World elegance. With its Russian balalaika, Ukrainian bondura, and Ukrainian Easter eggs and icons, the music room is beautiful and makes a nice change from the usual Victoriana at most B&Bs. A large portrait of Susan is the centerpiece of the room.

"I'm a Stress-A personality and am multitalented," Susan told me as she poured me another cup of java. "I work twenty-two hours a day, seven days a week. My goal is to create the most luxurious hotel in town."

Rates: $75–$165
Credit Cards Accepted: Visa, MC, AMEX, Discover
Number of Guest Rooms: 5
Number of Baths: 5
Wheelchair Access: No

Pets: No
Children: If older than 10
Smoking: No
Senior Citizen Discount: Yes
Directions: See brochure

The Lilly Library

7th Street, south of the Showalter Fountain
Indiana University
Bloomington, IN 47405
(812) 855-2452
(812) 855-3143 Fax

Who: Any librarian

When: 9:00 A.M. to 6:00 P.M. Monday through Friday and 9:00 A.M. to 1:00 P.M. on Sunday, except for major holidays

How Much: Photo identification necessary, no charge

Senior Citizen Discount: NA

Wheelchair Access: Yes

Directions: Call for directions

What and Where: The Lilly Library at Indiana University has one of the finest collections of rare books in the United States. The New Testament of a Gutenberg Bible and Audubon's *Birds of America* are on permanent display in the Main Gallery. One page of the *Birds of America* is turned each week. The library is named to honor the family of Eli Lilly, who started the pioneer Indiana pharmaceutical company. The roots of this extensive collection of modern literary manuscripts go back to the gift of J. K. Lilly Jr.'s library to the university in 1956. Lilly had a small number of choice items, including Barrie's *Peter Pan*, Edgar Lee Masters's *Spoon River Anthology*, Archibald MacLeish's *J. B.*, and one notable collection—a large group of manuscripts of Hoosier poet James Whitcomb Riley.

    Among the many extraordinary original manuscripts are *The Adventure of the Red Circle*, autographed by author Sir Arthur Conan Doyle; the Introduction to *The Cry for Justice* by Jack London; Edith Wharton's *The Age of Innocence* with corrections in the author's own hand; F. Scott Fitzgerald's *The Vegetable: A Comedy;* Ernest Hemingway's "Homage to Ezra"; D. H. Lawrence's "Accumulated Mail"; the page proofs for the English edition of Virginia Woolf's *Mrs. Dalloway* with the changes made by the author for the American edition; Theodore Dreiser's *Dawn;* Ian Fleming's *Casino Royale;* Jack Kerouac's *Scripture of the Golden Eternity;* T. S. Eliot's "Ezra Pound"; Ted Hughes's *The Hawk in the Rain;* Allen Ginsberg's "Gods dance on their own bodies"; Sylvia Plath's "Night Walk"; and Booth Tarkington's *Bimbo the Pirate*. Also included are Sylvia Plath's suprisingly cheerful childhood letters.

    Naturally, rare manuscripts such as these call for special ground rules. Materials may be used by anyone who presents current picture identification and completes a registration card. All personal property that is nonessential to your research must be stored in lockers. Only pencils may be used in the Reading Room, and, obviously, all materials must be handled with care.

Scholars Inn Bed and Breakfast

801 North College Avenue
Bloomington, IN 47404
(800) 765-3466

What could be better after doing some research at the Lilly Library than staying at the appropriately named Scholars Inn? Located just five blocks from the downtown area and close to all university activities, the Scholars Inn is an elegant restored brick mansion blending the past with the present in a friendly, comfortable atmosphere.

The 100-year-old mansion features Oriental rugs, antique furnishings, and a European breakfast served every morning in the elegant Gathering Room. The five bedrooms have original hardwood floors, pillow-top mattresses, cable TV with HBO, and phones. Of course, for literary purposes as well as comfort, you'll want to try the Gene Stratton Porter Room, with its king-size bed, antique wardrobe, and Jacuzzi. If you are a basketball fan (and you have to be in Indiana, known for "Hoosier Hysteria"), you'll want to stay in the Charles Austin Beard Room, which contains the schoolmaster's wardrobe from the movie *Hoosier*. This room also features a spacious master bedroom with a king-size bed and a striking marble bathroom.

If you are staying here for scholarly or business purposes, you can take advantage of the fax machine, private phone, and corporate rates. If your schedule permits, visit Brown County State Park in Nashville, Indiana, for some great scenery and antique and gift shopping.

Rates: $69–$135
Credit Cards Accepted: Visa, MC, AMEX
Number of Guest Rooms: 5
Number of Baths: 5
Wheelchair Access: No

Pets: No
Children: If older than 12
Smoking: No
Senior Citizen Discount: No
Directions: See brochure

Limberlost North:
Gene Stratton Porter State Historic Site

1205 Pleasant Point, Box 639
Rome City, IN 46784
(219) 854-3790

Who: Front desk

When: Open from the third week in March to December 15 from 9:00 A.M. to 4:30 P.M. Tuesday through Saturday, 1:00 to 4:30 P.M. on Sunday. Closed Monday.

How Much: $2 suggested donation

Senior Citizen Discount: No

Wheelchair Access: Call ahead

Directions: Call for brochure

What and Where: Wildflower Woods, now known as the Gene Stratton Porter State Historic Site, reflects the unique personality of its owner. When the Limberlost Swamp near her Geneva home was drained for farmland, destroying Porter's area for nature study, she decided to move her workshop permanently to the place in northern Indiana where she had vacationed as a teenager. She and her husband purchased 150 acres along the shores of Sylvan Lake and called their property Limberlost North—Wildflower Woods. The vast virgin forest, as well as Porter's personal gardens, provided a rich source of material for her nature studies, photography, and writing.

You get a good sense of place when you enter through the lovely formal gardens designed by Porter and hear the inviting bird sounds echoing throughout. You almost expect "the Bird Woman" (the author's sobriquet) to magically appear. If she did make a surprise visit, she would be pleased to note that her gardens are maintained following her original map and plant listings. The flowers that Gene and her pharmacist husband, Charles, planted are still flourishing. The trees she wrote about so lovingly in many of her books are still standing stately and tall.

The Cabin in Wildflower Woods, designed by Gene Stratton Porter, is a two-story cabin with exterior walls of Wisconsin cedar logs. As you enter, note the hallway paneled in wild cherry that grew on the property. Among the many interesting features of the home is a living-room fireplace that contains a number of miniature carved stone Aztec heads collected in Mexico by Charles Porter. The Friendship Fireplace in the living room is designed of Indian artifacts and stones from a variety of states. Above the fireplace are photos of Gene Stratton Porter, her daughter, Jeannette Porter Meehan, and the author's husband, Charles Dorwin Porter. On the mantel are pictures of her parents, Mark and Mary Stratton.

The house has 14 rooms: six rooms and a photographic darkroom on the first floor and seven bedrooms on the second. The dining room is particularly attractive, with its cherry paneling, corner fireplace, and Gene's nature photographs. The author's study features her personal library, copies of her work, many family photographs, and an interesting fireplace made from native puddin' stone. Take some time to browse in the gift shop with its well-stocked collection of the author's books.

AUTHOR'S NOTE: Gene Stratton Porter, like Elnora, the heroine of *A Girl of the Limberlost,* was brave, resourceful, and resilient. Porter's attire must have caused quite a stir in conservative, proper Indiana. She went to her nature studies dressed in a knee-length khaki skirt, high leather hiking boots, and a blouse and hat of neutral colors to blend into the landscape. Packing a revolver for protection against massasauga rattlers, she was often seen lugging a camera and tripod into the woods.

The Olde McCray Mansion Inn

703 E. Mitchell Street
Kendallville, IN 46755
(219) 347-3647

Just seven miles away from the historic Gene Stratton Porter State Historic Site is the town of Kendallville, a friendly Hoosier community of about 7,500. Here you will find yourself in Indiana's lake district, an area that contains 100 beautiful lakes. A short stroll from the McCray Mansion brings you to Bixler Lake Park, where you have your choice of two beaches, picnic areas, playgrounds, ball fields, and 100 acres of open park land. If you are an old-car enthusiast, you might want to visit the Auburn-Cord-Dusenburg Museum, 15 miles down the road.

Or you might just want to relax with a Gene Stratton Porter book at the beautiful and gracious Colonial McCray Mansion.

Rates: $52–$57
Credit Cards Accepted: Visa, MC, AMEX, Discover
Number of Guest Rooms: 5
Number of Baths: 4
Wheelchair Access: No

The early-1900s home is situated on a shady tree-lined street and has three full floors plus a basement game room. A favorite feature is the spectacular stairway of walnut and oak, which winds its way from the game room to the second floor. There is a formal living room, a stately walnut library, a formal dining room and a cheery breakfast room where guests are served a continental breakfast. The second floor offers a choice of five large and comfortable bedrooms and four baths.

Pets: No
Children: Occasionally
Smoking: No
Senior Citizen Discount: No
Directions: Brochure contains map

The Book Inn B&B

508 West Washington
South Bend, IN 46601
(219) 288-1990
Website: http://members.aol.com./bookinn/

I like a place where books dominate, so I was obviously in bibliophile heaven at The Book Inn, a B&B and bookstore.

The inn is an elegant destination in its own right. It is one of the earliest residences in South Bend's historic district and is listed as an outstanding example of Second Empire architecture by the Indiana Historic Site Preservation committee. If you are a French Victorian buff, you will find something to delight your eye everywhere you look—irreplaceable hand-hewn butternut woodwork, 12-foot ceilings, and entry doors with double leaf wood and applied decoration.

But as a bookaholic I gravitated toward the volumes that are everywhere. The living room is a treasure trove for book hounds like me. There were old rare tomes on the fireplace mantel and intriguing titles such as *The Smithsonian Book on Books* and *The Library*, a children's book, within easy reach on a sprawling coffee table.

Line drawing of The Book Inn B&B by Mary Louise Moscan.

Every nook and cranny held a book display, and for those of us who need a twelve-step program for our reading addiction, there were racks of magazines, desks with book designs on them, wall hangings of books, and quotes about books. I wanted to stay a week!

David and I stayed in the Louisa May Alcott Room, a sunny, cheery corner room with a king-size bed, decorated in soft greens and plenty of chintz. After a delicious dinner at the Morris Inn on the Notre Dame campus, I snuggled in for my annual reading of *Little Women*, thoughtfully provided by the innkeepers, as were the other Alcott books. A nice touch in the room were the pictures of Louisa May. Other literary bedrooms include the Jane Austen, also with a king-size bed, rose-colored wallpaper, and a grand view of the grounds of Tippecanoe Place next door, a restaurant and former home of auto industry mogul Clement Studebaker. Of course, there is a Charlotte Brontë Room with a queen-size bed and cozy sofa nook (that rhymes with book, which I'm certain is no coincidence).

Then, for the ultimate booklovers treat, I walked downstairs after my continental breakfast to browse through the quality used bookstore, a wonderfully eclectic collection of mostly nonfiction books with a good selection of mystery fiction, children's books, classics, and cookbooks.

Inns reflect the personalities of the innkeepers, and so it should come as no surprise that Peggy and John Livingston are as delightful as the wonderful combination of vocations they have concocted. Peggy, a lively, friendly former third-grade teacher, decided to open a bookstore after the youngest of her four children went off to college. "When I was trying to think what to do next, I decided that I was happiest at a bookstore or a library."

After attending a seminar in San Francisco entitled How to Open a Used Bookstore, Peggy opened the Book Bungalow in Terre Haute, Indiana, and got hooked on the used bookstore business. When John, an attorney, relocated the family to South Bend, Peggy decided to try a bookstore and B&B.

"I like the guests I get," Peggy told me as we sipped tea in the formal dining room. "I always learn so much about the world of books from my guests. With each guest, I talk about a different author. It's particularly interesting when the Charlotte Brontë Society stays with me. John and I have lived all over the country and we love to travel. The beauty of running a B&B is that it's like traveling without having to pack."

The beauty of staying at The Book Inn should be obvious by now. Adding another B to B&B is a novel idea that really works.

Rates: $80–$150
Credit Cards Accepted: Visa, MC, AMEX
Number of Guest Rooms: 5
Number of Baths: 5
Wheelchair Access: No

Pets: No
Children: Yes
Smoking: No
Senior Citizen Discount: No
Directions: See brochure

IOWA

⊷ ⊱❖⊰ ⊶

Mark Twain: Keokuk Public Library

210 North 5th Street
Keokuk, IA 52632
(319) 524-1483

Who: Shirley Dick

When: 9:30 A.M.–9:00 P.M. Monday through Thursday, 9:30 A.M.–6:00 P.M. Friday and Saturday

How Much: Free

Senior Citizen Discount: NA

Wheelchair Access: Yes

Directions: Contact the library

What and Where: Even though there is not a great deal to see in Keokuk, you can feel the wit and charm of Mark Twain all around you. In many ways, this is where the young Sam Clemens got his start. According to an excellent brochure provided by the Keokuk Public Library: "In 1855 Samuel Clemens came up river to pay a visit to his older brother, Orion Clemens, who operated the Ben Franklin Book and Job Printing Office, located at 52 Main (later 202 Main). Orion had recently married Mollie Stotts, a Keokuk girl."

Orion talked Sam into staying in Keokuk, offering room, board, and five dollars a week as incentive. During his two years in Iowa, Sam began his illustrious career as an after-dinner speaker. At a printer's banquet held in celebration of the birthdate of Benjamin Franklin, the humorist wowed his first crowd. The *Keokuk Post* reports that Clemens's maiden speech at the Ivins House on January 17, 1856, was by all accounts hilarious. "Sam Clemens was loudly and repeatedly called for, and responded in a speech replete with wit and humor, being interrupted by long and continued bursts of applause."

Clemens received his first paycheck for his writing in Keokuk, always a red-letter day for any writer. He received five dollars (which was considered good payment at that time) from the *Keokuk Post* for three farcical travel letters, presumably written by Thomas Jefferson Snodgrass. The first letter, dated October 18, 1856, was a satiric account of Snodgrass's trip downriver to St. Louis.

In late 1856 the peripatetic Clemens took his leave of Keokuk. But he returned as a guest lecturer for the Library Association meeting held at the Chatam Square Church. On April 8, 1867, he delivered his new but already famous Sandwich Islands lecture and was paid the large sum of $35.00.

The world-renowned writer, now known as Mark Twain, paid three more visits to Keokuk in the 1880s, once on a lecture tour, once doing research for his book *Life on the Mississippi,* and once to buy a house for his mother, Jane Clemens. This house, located at 626 High Street, can be viewed from the street, but it is now a private residence.

Keokuk River Museum

P.O. Box 400
Keokuk, IA 52632
(319) 524-4765; (319) 524-6491

Who: Robert L. Miller

When: 9:00 A.M.–5:00 P.M. (last tickets sold at 4:30) every day from April 1 through October 31

How Much: $1.50 for adults 14 and older, $.75 for children ages 6 through 13, and free for children under 6

Senior Citizen Discount: No

Wheelchair Access: No

Directions: South Second Street to Johnson Street; take Johnson Street to the riverfront. Boat is plainly visible at Victory Park.

What and Where: If you want to discover the charm of Mark Twain's Mississippi, visit the Keokuk River Museum, which immediately transports you to the era of river steamboats. As a matter of fact, the museum is located on the *George M. Verity,* a real sternwheel steam towboat that operated from 1927 through April 1960 on the Mississippi River system. The *Verity* was the first of four steamboats built for the revival of river transportation and was the first to move barges from St. Louis north to St. Paul.

The Grand Anne

816 Grand Avenue
Keokuk, IA 52632
(319) 524-4310; (800) 524-6310

The Grand Anne is aptly named; not only does it refer to the Grand Avenue location, but it is also a magnificent example of Queen Anne style, favored by so many renowned architects at the turn of the century. Mention of its two-acre grounds and 22 rooms does not begin to describe it, but those of you who know the period and design will nod appreciatively at double parlors, pocket doors, conservatory, coffered ceiling, reception hall, and grand staircase. The library contains a special collection and display of the golden days of aviation. Guests are encouraged to browse here, and to enjoy the entire house, including the enticing porches, formal garden, and croquet lawn.

Four second-floor rooms are reserved for visitors. Judge Huiskamp's Chambers is a tower suite with sitting room offering spectacular views of the rolling Mississippi just across the street. An eclectic array of furniture includes a queen-size bed and sofa bed, as well as a private bath. Carol's Lookout is country French, with a queen-size antique bed with matching vanity, wicker table and chairs, and the original marble-top sink in the bath. An eight-foot Eastlake headboard attracts attention in Clyde's Retreat, which also has a bath. The western decor Cowboy Room offers a full-size futon and cowboy kitsch design; it is only available in conjunction with Clyde's Retreat, with which it shares a bath.

The Grand Anne Inn. Photo courtesy of The Grand Anne.

Hostess Dana McCready maintains a high level of comfort for her guests, and satisfying breakfasts, designer robes and towels, fresh flowers, and down comforters add to your enjoyment. You are in the heartland of the nation, and both Keokuk and the Grand Anne intend to give you a warm welcome.

Rates: $65–$90
Credit Cards Accepted: Visa, MC, AMEX
Number of Guest Rooms: 4
Number of Baths: 4
Wheelchair Access: No

Pets: No
Children: If older than 12
Smoking: No
Senior Citizen Discount: No
Directions: See brochure

LOUISIANA

＋・━◆≡・＋

Kate Chopin's Cloutierville

Kate Chopin was way ahead of her time. The 1899 publication of *The Awakening,* her novel about a woman's sexuality and desire for self-fulfillment, was rejected by Victorian America—banned in her hometown St. Louis as well as other cities.

Chopin received harsh criticism from readers who accused her of being as immoral as the novel's protagonist, Edna Pontellier, who leaves her husband to set up a painting studio and have a brief affair. The outcry against the book seems absurd today, but the reaction shook her deeply and kept her relatively isolated, by choice, from the literary world.

A visit to Chopin's former home in Cloutierville, Louisiana, reveals much about this strong-willed, fiercely independent author, who was born in 1851 in St. Louis and raised by three generations of widows. At 19 she married Oscar Chopin, a Creole from Louisiana, and settled for ten years in New Orleans. The couple had six children. When Oscar's business failed in 1879, the Chopins moved to his family's plantation in Cloutierville, where he ran the plantation and general store.

Tucked away in Natchitoches Parish (pronounced Nak'-uh-tush for those unfamiliar with Creole), at the southern tip of the Cane River Lake, the tiny village of Cloutierville is surrounded by antebellum homes, bayous, and lakes. Chopin described the area as "a little French village … simply two long rows of very old frame houses facing each other across a dusty roadway."

The Chopins' home, built by slaves between 1806 and 1813 for Alexis Cloutier, today houses the Bayou Folk Museum, established in 1965 to honor the bayou folk who lived here during the 1800s and the author who immortalized them in her writing. Surrounded by graceful magnolias and a wrought-iron and brick fence, the Chopins' two-story home originally was built with handmade brick, heart cypress and heart pine, square wooden pegs, and *bousillage,* a mixture of mud and Spanish moss. The ground floor, with its dirt floors, originally served as a storage area. The family lived on the second floor, which remains accessible from a side stairway to the upper balcony. They occupied a large living room, where Chopin wrote her stories surrounded by friends and family, as well as a master bedroom and three small bedrooms.

Some of the original features remain, including the double French doors opening onto the front balcony, glass panes, and upstairs wainscoting. The restored furnishings were found in the Cane River area.

The Chopin plantation general store once stood to the north of the house. After Oscar died suddenly of swamp fever in 1882, Kate briefly took over operation of the plantation and the store, then disposed of the property in order to return to St. Louis with her children to take care of her widowed mother.

In 1890 she published her first novel, *At Fault,* which foreshadowed the themes of independence and will she developed further in *The Awakening.* In 1894 she published a compilation of short stories entitled *Bayou Folk,* which celebrated the Creole traditions and superstitions of the longtime inhabitants of the Cane River country.

After the disappointing reception to *The Awakening*, Kate did not stop writing completely. She published several short stories before her death in 1904, from a brain hemorrhage that struck her after visiting the St. Louis World's Fair.

Today her reputation as a masterful writer has been restored, and the story of Edna Pontellier continues to inspire women struggling to balance careers, children, and marriage with their own desires and needs. "I would give up the unessential; I would give my money, I would give my life for my children, but I wouldn't give myself," Edna says in *The Awakening*.

Kate never abandoned herself. Standing in Cloutierville, it's easy to conjure up an image of this formidable woman on horseback in her favorite attire, a blue riding habit with a train fastened up at the side, as she explored the swamps and canebrakes around Cloutierville or danced to music in her living room, full of a passion for life.

Kate Chopin Home and Bayou Folk Museum

243 Highway 495
Cloutierville, Louisiana 71416
(318) 379-2233

Who: Amanda Chenault

When: 10:00 A.M.–5:00 P.M. Monday through Saturday, 1:00–5:00 p.m. on Sunday, year-round except for major holidays

How Much: $5 for adults, $3 for students ages 13–18, $2 for children ages 6–12

Senior Citizen Discount: $4

Wheelchair Access: No

Directions: Call for directions

What and Where: The Association for the Preservation of Historic Natchitoches, P.O. Box 2248, Natchitoches, LA 71457. For tour information, call Saidee Newell at (318) 352-0447 or Maxine Southerland at (318) 352-8604.

    The Association for the Preservation of Historic Natchitoches offers annual tours of historic homes and plantations during the second weekend in October. For $12, you can take the Cane River Country Tour and visit the Kate Chopin Home and Bayou Folk Museum, as well as the St. Augustine Church, the Melrose Plantation, which dates back to 1796, and the Cherokee Plantation, built before 1839. Or visit some of the oldest homes in Natchitoches on The Town Tour, which also costs $12.

Breazeale House Bed and Breakfast

926 Washington Street
Natchitoches, LA 71457
(318) 352-5630; (800) 352-5631

With visits to several hundred B&Bs behind me, I have wondered why there haven't been any ghosts behind the wainscoting. Finally, here is a hint of one. Innkeepers Willa and

Jack Freeman attest to guests experiencing some inexplicable activities, which seem to focus on "unknown occupants." This bucolic Southern setting seems just the place for a ghost to haunt—I wouldn't mind coming back here myself!

Then, too, the Breazeale House has a connection with writer Kate Chopin, and her stories float eerily through my memory, evoking long-gone images from Louisiana's past. Chopin was the sister-in-law of Congress-man Phanor Breazeale, for whom the house was built. She spent some time here, and I'm sure was always a welcome guest. President William Howard Taft was also an overnight guest of the congressman. The beautiful three-story house was built in the late 1800s and features eight bedrooms, nine stained glass windowpanes, 11 fireplaces, and no partridge in a pear tree but two staircases and several other architectural attractions. It is also recognizable to many as the house used in the film version of *Steel Magnolias*.

Rates: $55–$75
Credit Cards Accepted: Visa, MC, AMEX
Number of Guest Rooms: 4
Number of Baths: 4
Wheelchair Access: No

Pets: No
Children: Yes
Smoking: No
Senior Citizen Discount: No
Directions: Brochure contains map

William Faulkner's New Orleans

William Faulkner opens his novel *Absalom, Absalom!* with the lines, "They went to New Orleans," and indeed Faulkner himself enjoyed a rich New Orleans history. The steamy, romantic city, "the city that care forgot," had a major influence on this great southern writer's work. As a matter of fact, many Faulkner scholars feel that New Orleans was a pivotal point in the author's career. He arrived as a fired postal worker and overly romantic poet and left a published novelist. By the time he moved to Oxford, Mississippi, he had already started mapping out the landscape for his famed Yoknapatawpha County.

Besides placing *Absalom, Absalom!* in New Orleans, Faulkner also wrote *Mosquitoes*, a satire of his adopted city. He seemed to thrive on the atmosphere of this sensuous town; today you can retrace some of his steps by hanging out at a few of his favorite haunts that are still very much alive. He drank coffee at the Cafe du Monde on Decatur Street and dined at the then-cheap Galatoire's and Arnaud's. Of course, you can't leave New Orleans without a visit to Faulkner's House at 624 Pirate's Alley, the well-stocked, wonderful bookstore with a large section, appropriately enough, devoted to Faulkner. This narrow three-story building with its plant-filled wrought-iron alcoves is where the author wrote *Soldier's Pay*, his first novel.

There is a controversy about what type of person Faulkner was during his sojourn in New Orleans. According to the interesting book *Literary New Orleans*, edited by Richard S. Kennedy, it depended "on which 'famous Creole' one believes, that he was either a delightful and trustworthy friend and companion or a vain arrogant man who forgot his old friends when he became famous."

Tennessee Williams's New Orleans

Tennessee Williams put New Orleans on the literary map, and for 45 years the author and his beloved adopted city enjoyed a productive, symbiotic relationship.

When he first arrived, he described himself as a migrating bird going to a more congenial climate. Tom Williams moved to New Orleans in December 1938 for a number of reasons. First of all, he was anxious to escape St. Louis and the unhappy family life he wrote about in his thinly veiled autobiographical play, *The Glass Menagerie*. Second, he had been told that the WPA Writers Project was looking for workers, but when he arrived he found that there were no jobs.

But he immediately fell in love with this seductive city and declared New Orleans his "spiritual home." He knew he had to stay on, so he took a job waiting tables in the French Quarter. He recognized that New Orleans would feed his creativity and later said, "I found the kind of freedom I had always needed and the shock of it, against the Puritanism of my nature, has given me a theme, which I have never ceased exploiting."

He loved the Bohemian atmosphere of his new home, but in spite of the constant stimulation he wrote faithfully every day. It was in New Orleans that Tom Williams died and Tennessee Williams, the brilliant playwright, heavy drinker, and infamous homosexual emerged.

Like George Washington, Williams is said to have slept in many places (in the Big Easy). Some say his first apartment was a cell-like roach-infested garret at 431 Royal Street that cost three dollars a week. Others claim his first New Orleans residence was at 722 Toulouse Street. Still others swear that the Pulitzer Prize–winning playwright first lived on Bourbon Street.

Tennessee Williams was peripatetic; between writing projects, he loved to travel. He kept New Orleans as his spiritual home but maintained a residence in Key West. After an extensive trip to Europe, he returned to New Orleans in 1951. Accompanied by his 94-year-old grandfather, the Reverend Walter Dakin, the two gentlemen stayed at the Monteleone Hotel. Williams apparently liked staying at this hotel (the birthplace of Truman Capote) because from the back rooms he had a view of the Mississippi and, as all writers know, one needs something to stare at when the words don' t flow (and the river does). His grandfather was a congenial companion who wasn't the least bit judgmental. He thoroughly enjoyed the colorful lifestyle of the "city that care forgot" and didn't seem to disapprove in the least of his grandson's unconventional lifestyle. Williams seem to gain solace from the reverend's spiritual presence and sometime just sat by his side to get inspiration. The playwright would work for four or five hours on *Camino Real,* the drama of the moment, and then he and his grandfather would have a leisurely lunch at Antoine's, Galatoire's, or Arnaud's before spending the rest of the afternoon strolling around the French Quarter.

He must have enjoyed sauntering around the city in which he set *A Streetcar Named Desire, Suddenly Last Summer,* and *Vieux Carre.* The two-time Pulitzer Prize–winner remarked that more than half his best work had been written in New Orleans. Williams put his unique stamp on this town, and everywhere you look you see the ghosts of Blanche DuBois, Stella, and Stanley, and even a streetcar named Desire.

Literary New Orleans

As I was walking around the Big Easy smelling the smells, listening to the sounds, enjoying the sights, I thought to myself, How could writers not like New Orleans? It is writer's heaven. It's steamy, sexy, romantic, with good music, great food, fabulous bars. I have always lamented not being a southerner because southerners are born storytellers.

When I was chatting with the delightful Rosemary James, the co-owner (along with James de Salvo) of the Faulkner Bookstore, she explained why southerners were put on this earth to write. The South, she told me, was settled by the Irish, the Welsh, the Scots, and the Huguenots, all of them great drinkers. The Irish in particular are natural raconteurs, and the more they imbibed, the greater their stories became.

Save some time for some heavy browsing and spending at the wonderful Faulkner House Bookstore at 624 Pirate's Alley; if you are a bibliophile, you will love this place. Don't leave without purchasing *New Orleans Stories, Great Writers on the City,* and *Literary New Orleans,* edited by Richard S. Kennedy. Of course, you may want to embellish your Faulkner and Williams collection as well as pick up tomes by Truman Capote, Zora Neale Hurston, and Kate Chopin. Faulkner House has the definitive collection of out-of-print books by southern writers.

Finally, take time to visit the Frances Parkinson Keyes House and Garden at 1113 Charters. Keyes, who wrote historical romances based on fact, is best known for her New Orleans novel *Dinner at Antoine's.* The million copies it sold helped her pay for the restoration of her beautiful home. The house is worth a visit, even though Keyes's fame did not outlive her. Besides admiring her doll collection and enjoying the beautiful patio, I was interested to learn that Keyes was awarded the French Legion of Honor for writing, and as assistant editor of *Good Housekeeping* she interviewed Mussolini, Lon Chaney, and Mary Pickford. In her role as hostess she gave a cocktail party for the Duke and Duchess of Windsor.

I could not leave this literary city without mentioning the following:

- Truman Streckfus Persons was born in New Orleans at the Monteleone Hotel. Later, and better known as the colorful Truman Capote, the author came back to his birthplace and wrote the acidic *Music for Chameleons.*
- Sherwood Anderson lived at 715 Governor Nicholls, and it was here that he wrote "Many Marriages." Anderson was the literary social director of his adopted city, and at his home at one time or another gathered William Faulkner, Lillian Hellman, John Dos Passos, and F. Scott Fitzgerald. There was, in true New Orleans tradition, lots of drinking and swapping stories at the Anderson household. If only walls could talk, we would proably have several juicy novels from these soirees.
- Lillian Hellman was a hometown girl, and her best known work, *The Children's Hour,* was written while she was living at 1718 Prytania Avenue. This drama about the devastating effects of a child's charge of lesbianism against two of her teachers was the crowning jewel in Hellman's literary career.
- 2900 Prytania is where F. Scott Fitzgerald rented an aparment while revising the galleys of his first novel, *This Side of Paradise.* The pristine, tiny white house overlooks an old cemetery, which fascinated the young Fitzgerald. The cemetery is built in keeping with the Louisiana custom, with the crypts and graves built above the ground. There is a practical reason for this, of course, other than to intrigue young novelists. In Louisiana the water table is just beneath the ground surface.
- John Dos Passos, whose short story "Funiculi Funicula" is set in New Orleans, lived at 510 Esplanade Avenue, at the northeast end of the French Quarter.

Dauphine Orleans Hotel

415 Dauphine Street
New Orleans, LA 70112
(504) 586-1800; (800) 521-7111
(504) 586-1409 Fax

The historic Dauphine Orleans Hotel was in existence in 1814 when the drums of General Jackson's army, bound for the Battle of New Orleans, echoed from the walls of the French Quarter. A few short years later, John James Audubon painted many of the plates in his *Birds of America* here, in the heart of the French Quarter. As a matter of fact, the Audubon Room, now the hotel's main meeting room, is the very cottage where the famous naturalist painted.

The recently renovated Dauphine Orleans Hotel is spacious and luxurious. The evening hospitality begins with cocktails and appetizers in the Bagnio Lounge, the spot where May Bailey and her ladies of the evening once plied their thriving trade. A red lantern in the doorway and the original license issued to the bordello are prominent mementos of the building's colorful past.

The staff and owners of the Dauphine Orleans are proud of the many amenities they offer. Each beautifully appointed room includes a well-stocked minibar, hair dryer, and cable television. A favorite feature is the guest library. The hotel encourages guests to keep unfinished library books with their best wishes. At dinnertime, while you are are out feasting at one of New Orleans splendid restaurants or are enjoying a Sazerac, the Dauphine Orleans Hotel staff will be turning down your bed and leaving a treat on your pillow.

Next morning, you can laze over your ample continental breakfast while you read your complimentary paper. Later, after a day of sightseeing in the Big Easy, a dip in the outdoor swimming pool is a great way to relax.

There are many activities in New Orleans in addition to the literary sites. Absorb the jazz scene on Bourbon Street or enjoy a beignet while you stroll along the levees of the mighty Mississippi. Take in the spectacular new Aquarium of the Americas or visit Musee Conti, the fabled wax museum. Of course, sampling as many restaurants as possible is always my number-one priority!

Rates: $79.95–$389.00
Credit Cards Accepted: Visa, MC, AMEX, Discover, Diners Club
Number of Guest Rooms: 111
Number of Baths: 111
Wheelchair Access: Yes

Pets: No
Children: Yes
Smoking: Yes
Senior Citizen Discount: Yes
Directions: See brochure

Lafitte Guest House

1003 Bourbon Street
New Orleans, LA 70116
(504) 581-2678; (800) 331-7971

This city is all about atmosphere and hospitality. You won't be disappointed in this inn, because the Lafitte Guest House is as much New Orleans as Blanche DuBois, beignets,

One of the rooms at the Lafitte Guest House.
Photo courtesy of the Lafitte Guest House.

and voodoo queens. You will get the New Orleans feeling of graciousness when you are served afternoon wine and cheese in the parlor. Your continental breakfast can be served in your room, on the balcony, in the parlor, or in the courtyard. Food, drink, and charm is why this city is so popular.

The four-story French manor house, built in 1849, is on the National Register of Historic Places and is filled with fine antiques and paintings collected from around the world. A step into the spacious entrance parlor is a step back in time, or perhaps into your own fantasy. New Orleans, with its carnival atmosphere, is truly a city of make-believe.

No guest at Lafitte Guest House will have to worry about being comfortable. All 14 rooms are carpeted and have either queen- or king-size beds. They are decorated in period furnishings, many with the original black marble mantels over the fireplace and crystal chandeliers. The most popular rooms seem to be the ones with the four-poster beds with full or half-testers.

The staff is informal but efficient. A book of menus is available to help you pick the perfect restaurants, whether you want morning coffee and beignets, red beans and rice, or étouffée. We were steered to lunch at Mr. B's Bistro, where I had the world's messiest (but best) barbecued shrimp, and dinner at the award-winning Bayona's, where I had sautéed salmon with choucroute and gewürztraminer sauce and orange-scented crepes. Yum!

Rates: $59–$165
Credit Cards Accepted: Visa, MC, AMEX, Discover
Number of Guest Rooms: 14
Number of Baths: 14
Wheelchair Access: No

Pets: No
Children: Yes
Smoking: No
Senior Citizen Discount: Yes
Directions: See brochure

Terrell House

1441 Magazine Street
New Orleans, LA 70130
(504) 524-9859

New Orleans is so rich in atmosphere that it is the perfect spot for writers. Or, in our case, visitors who want to learn about famous authors. The Terrell House is a good place to begin your literary journey.

The Terrell House gets you in the proper southern mood because it is a renovated mansion. Built by Richard Terrell, a New Orleans cotton merchant, the Terrell House is today an inn with antebellum grace. You will enjoy the marble fireplaces, gaslight fixtures, Oriental carpets, antique chandeliers, and a fabulous courtyard. This is the real New Orleans, from the exquisite furniture to the site on Magazine Street, where locals shop and eat. The furniture in two rooms are pieces from the studio of Prudent Mallard, the French-trained craftsman whose workshops on Royal Street were patronized by the city's elite in the 1840s and 1850s.

The Terrell House looks loved and cared for because it is. The owners, past and present, scout all over the globe for antiques that will shine in this showplace. The pièce de résistance is a delightful collection of children's bedroom furniture, which looks perfect in its new home in the parlor.

The original carriage house has been converted into four guest rooms, each furnished with period antiques. All open onto or overlook the courtyard. The servants' quarters, located over the kitchen, is the most unusual room and features brick walls, hardwood floors, Oriental carpets, and an ornate period bed.

Southern hospitality abounds in this gracious mansion. A continental breakfast is served in the dining room, and in the evening you are invited to a hospitality hour in the parlor or the courtyard.

Its location is an appealing feature of the Terrell House. Originally known as Faubourg Ste. Marie, the Lower Garden District is the oldest purely residential neighborhood outside the French Quarter. Many of the homes here were built during the height of the Greek Revival craze of the 1820s to 1850s. Magazine Street, also called the Street of Dreams, is the real New Orleans. You will enjoy strolling and visiting in the antique shops, art galleries, jazz clubs, and restaurants. I discovered that we were dangerously close to one of my favorite New Orleans restaurants, Commander's Palace. David and I had a superb dinner here highlighted by great food and excellent service. I had the Commander's Creole Favorite with turtle soup au sherry, the chef's special salad, Lyonnaise gulf fish, and a fabulous bread pudding soufflé. Whoever wrote "You don't know what it means to miss New Orleans" must have had this dessert in mind!

Rates: $85–$200
Credit Cards Accepted: Visa, MC, AMEX
Number of Guest Rooms: 10
Number of Baths: 10
Wheelchair Access: Yes

Pets: No
Children: Yes
Smoking: No
Senior Citizen Discount: No
Directions: See brochure

The McKendrick-Breaux House

1474 Magazine Street
New Orleans, LA 70130
(504) 586-1700; (888) 570-1700

Talk about a phoenix rising from the ashes! When Lisa and Eddie Breaux first began the renovation of this Magazine Street property, part of the building didn't even have floors. There had been so many remodelings that they were uncertain of the original house plan and literally tore the place down in small segments in order to reconstruct the building according to the first owner's plans. Then there was that unsightly bar next door, which, with great imagination, became a courtyard. The whole story would resemble Cinderella's

if there wasn't such an incredible amount of work involved.

Once upon a time in 1865 there was a wealthy Scottish immigrant by the name of Daniel McKendrick who built a three-story masonry home in Greek Revival style in what was then part of the Sapry Plantation, now known as the Lower Garden District. Today the property consists of the main house, a courtyard, and a second building. Five spacious bedrooms, each with private bath, attest to the life of ease and elegance enjoyed

A room at the McKendrick-Breaux House. Photo courtesy of the McKendrick-Breaux House.

by a chosen few in earlier times. A pleasant continental breakfast is served in the antique-filled double parlor, and the plant-filled patio is inviting for sipping coffee or trying on glass slippers. The Breauxes assure their guests that this is their home as well as an inn; therefore, the key words are comfort (for their guests) and accessibility (to local amenities). Despite the grueling labor and anxious moments spent during the renovation, Lisa and Eddie do seem to be living happily ever after.

Rates: $70–$130

Credit Cards Accepted: Visa, MC, AMEX

Number of Guest Rooms: 5

Number of Baths: 5

Wheelchair Access: No

Pets: No

Children: Yes

Smoking: No

Senior Citizen Discount: Yes

Directions: See brochure

Longfellow Evangeline State Park

1200 North Main Street, Highway 31
St. Martinsville, LA 70582
(318) 394-3754

Who: Information center

When: 8:30 A.M.–5:00 P.M. every day except major holidays, tours on the hour

How Much: $2.50 for adults (ages 13 and older)

Senior Citizen Discount: Free for those over 61

Wheelchair Access: In visitor's center

Directions: Call for directions

What and Where: You've certainly read Longfellow's famous love poem *Evangeline,* but did you know that this mighty epic was based on a true story? The character Evangeline was in reality Emmeline Labiche and Gabriel was Louis Arceneaux, who made their separate ways to St. Martinville after being expelled from the well-known "forest primeval."

Longfellow first heard this tale from a Salem minister, the Reverend Horace Conolly, during a dinner party at which Nathaniel Hawthorne was also a guest. As a matter of fact, Conolly hoped that Hawthorne would tell the story of the lovers. When Hawthorne declined, the author suggested that Conolly approach Longfellow. The poet liked the subject matter and in 1847 published the poignant *Evangeline: A Tale of Acadie.* The poem is a history lesson as well, for it tells the story of the 1775 expulsion by the British of the French inhabitants of Acadia, now Nova Scotia, and their migration to Louisiana. "Cajuns" is a corruption of "Acadian."

When you're visiting the 157-acre park on the banks of Bayou Teche, you'll want to stop by the Acadian House Museum, which features a one-room cabin with displays showing the lifestyle of the Acadians who settled this area. Historical features include the authentic hand-pegged Acadian weaving loom and the interpretive displays of the culture and plantation life of Acadians and Creoles. For those with a more romantic bent, the cabin is allegedly the home of Evangeline's Gabriel (Louis Arceneaux). If you have time, visit the Olivier Plantation, the nineteenth-century home of a wealthy French Creole family.

Save some time to stroll around the town of St. Martinsville where, among other sights, you should see the statue of Evangeline in the churchyard of St. Martin of Tours Catholic Church. The statue was modeled on the actress Dolores del Rio, who played the lead in the 1929 movie *Evangeline*, filmed at nearby Catahoula Lake.

The Old Castillo Hotel

220 Evangeline Bouldevard
P.O. Box 172
St. Martinsville, LA 70582
(318) 394-4010; (800) 621-3017
(318) 394-7983 Fax

Like the waters of the historic Bayou Teche that glide nearby, time seems to pass more slowly in St. Martinsville. Here stands the legendary Evangeline Oak, a living tribute to one of America's most famous stories of love won and lost.

Close by this reminder of fidelity and faith is another historic site, the warm red-brick Greek Revival Old Castillo Hotel. Three stories of elegance, balconies, and shutters adorn the almost unchanged facade of the hotel constructed in the 1830s for M. Pierre Vasseur. A local advertisement announced the opening of the Union Ballroom, which offered a "room for ladies," for gumbo,

and a "room for men," designated for games and liquors.

Some time later, management was transferred to Madame Edmond Castillo, widow of a well-known steamboat captain, under whose guidance the hotel became noted for hospitality and gala balls. The building was later purchased by the Sisters of Mercy, who, for almost a century, operated a school for girls here.

In 1987 the Holinses bought and renovated the property, which, since 1979, has been listed on the National Register of Historic Buildings. Today The Old Castillo Hotel and its inclusive La Place D'Evangeline Restaurant are again landmarks of hospitality.

Rates: $50–$80
Credit Cards Accepted: Visa, MC, AMEX
Number of Guest Rooms: 5
Number of Baths: 5
Wheelchair Access: Yes

Pets: No
Children: Yes
Smoking: Limited
Senior Citizen Discount: No
Directions: Brochure contains map

Maine

Edna St. Vincent Millay's Whitehall Inn

52 High Street, Box 558
Camden, ME 04843
(207) 236-3391; (800) 789-6565

When Edna St. Vincent Millay graduated from high school, her future seemed uncertain at best. She wanted to make a career of music or poetry, but the prospects for an untutored girl at that time weren't very bright. College was out of the questions for financial reasons: Millay's mother, who was a poet and musician, valued culture above all else, but on her salary as a practical nurse it was all she could do to make ends meet. Fortunately for us, she did manage to instill in her three daughters a love for books, music and the theater. We could best describe Mrs. Millay by paraphrasing Erasmus: When she had a little money, she bought books; if she had some more, she bought food and clothing.

As luck would have it, a kind fate helped to define Edna's career. It seems that her sister, Norma, who worked during the summer at Whitehall Inn, convinced Edna to come to a party at the resort to celebrate the end of the season. As part of the program, Edna reluctantly agreed to read *Renascence,* a poem she had written in high school. The opening lines describe the rugged coastline that she loved so much. A vacationing professor from Cincinnati, struck by Edna's passion and sensitivity, told a wealthy friend about her who in turn offered to pay Edna St. Vincent Millay's tuition to Vassar University.

At Vassar, Edna was a bit of a misfit. When she was a child, her mother was sometimes gone from the house for days on end as a home nurse. The girls, then, got the run of the house, coming and going as they pleased. For supper they could fix a pan of fudge, if that's what they wanted. But at Vassar there were rules. And rules, according to young Miss Millay, were for ignoring if they didn't make any sense. She was perpetually on the brink of being expelled because of her nonconformity. It was only through the intercession of the college president that she managed to complete the four-year program.

After graduation she moved to New York City, where she supported herself by writing short stories under the name of Nancy Boyd and performing as an actress and playwright with the Provincetown Players. When Greenwich Village became too upscale, she moved to Paris to associate with other expatriates like Hemingway, Fitzgerald, Stein, Pound, and Masters.

But, growing homesick, she returned to America. Here she fell in love with Eugen Boissevain, a widower whose first wife had been a well-known champion of women's rights. The relationship gave the author the time and serenity she needed to write. It is perhaps no coincidence that within four months after her marriage she published *The Harp Weaver and Other Poems,* for which she was awarded the Pulitzer Prize. The book was dedicated to her mother, the free-spirited single parent who first gave Edna poetry and music.

Edna and Eugen spent the next 23 years together on their farm in New York. The marriage lasted until 1949, and they died within 14 months of each other.

The hills near Whitehall Inn in Camden, Maine, will give you a sense of the rugged land which nurtured this romantic poet. They help you live the experience that Edna St. Vincent Millay called *Renascence*.

Whitehall Inn

52 High Street, Box 558
Camden, ME 04843
(207) 236-3391; (800) 789-6565

Whitehall Inn was originally built in 1834 by a sea captain. When the captain died, his widow supported herself by taking in houseguests. In the years that have followed, the inn has grown into a charming resort of 50 rooms.

It is easy to see why the Whitehall Inn is so appealing to the thousands of guests who visit every year. Here in the village where the mountains meet the sea, the inn provides a quiet, magical place from which you can experience the craggy Maine coast. Just sitting on a rocking chair on the veranda, you can feel the fresh ocean breezes come in from Penobscot Bay.

Inside the inn one summer evening many years ago, Edna St. Vincent Millay nervously recited her poem *Renascence*. Today in one of the parlors, which is dedicated to this Maine poet, you'll find many of her books, along with an unpublished manuscript and a reproduction of the first draft of *Renascence*.

The Whitehall Inn. Photo courtesy of the Whitehall Inn.

"We are part of a community that is steeped in culture, the sea and the belief that we should work hard and respect one another," is the philosophy of the innkeepers, the Dewings. In this tradition, the Dewing family of Whitehall Inn and their staff do their best to ensure you will have a memorable stay.

Rates: $70–$145
Credit Cards Accepted: Visa, MC
Number of Guest Rooms: 50
Number of Baths: 48
Wheelchair Access: Yes

Pets: No
Children: Yes
Smoking: No
Senior Citizen Discount: No
Directions: Brochure contains map

Blue Harbor House, A Village Inn

67 Elm Street
Camden, ME 04343
(207) 236-3196; (800) 248-3196
(207) 236-6523 Fax
E-mail: balidog@midcoast.com

The Blue Harbor House. Photo by Tom Bagley.

I just love it when a B&B advertises "bicyles available." Even if what I want to do is shop or sit in a rocker on the front porch, I find that bicycle-oriented innkeepers have a great sense of humor and are really connected with the wishes of their guests. All this is certainly true of Dennis Hayden and Jody Schmoll, innkeepers at Blue Harbor House. Camden can best be viewed and appreciated from a variety of perspectives (not the least of which is from a bike), including the sea.

The harbor is "snug"; the town is "quaint." Ordinarily I would hesitate to use these hackneyed terms, but not with

Camden. Many of us know it as the setting for the film version of Rodgers and Hammerstein's *Carousel*—no sound stage could match the authentic clapboard houses, the river that rushes through the center of town and down to the sea. A stay at Blue Harbor House allows you to greet the morning on the sun porch, where the windows frame Mount Battie, spectacular in any season and considered the inspirational setting for Edna St. Vincent Millay's poem *Renascence*.

All Blue Harbor House guestrooms have private baths, with beds of all sizes, some with canopies. The carriage house suites offer private entrances and sitting rooms. Breakfasts at the inn are just what one would expect in Maine: lobster quiche and blueberry pancakes, for starters. For dinner, by reservation only, guests may choose a candlelight feast or a traditional Maine lobster feed with corn on the cob and all the trimmings. Either choice will leave you singing, "It was a real nice clambake" and wishing you could stay just a few days longer in this picture-postcard village by the sea.

Rates: $85–$135
Credit Cards Accepted: Visa, MC, AMEX, Discover, Diners Club
Number of Guest Rooms: 10
Number of Baths: 10
Wheelchair Access: No

Pets: Yes
Children: Yes
Smoking: No
Senior Citizen Discount: No
Directions: See brochure

MARYLAND

⊷ ⊷ ⊱⊰ ⊶ ⊶

Westminster Hall and Burying Ground:
The Edgar Allan Poe Monument and Grave

519 West Fayette Street
Baltimore, MD 21201
(410) 706-2072
(410) 706-0696 Fax

Who: M. J. Rodney

When: The cemetery is open daily during daylight hours. Reservations are required for tours of the catacombs and cemetery; these are given on the first and third Friday and Saturday of each month from April through November.

How Much: $4 per adult and $2 per child under age 12

Senior Citizen Discount: $2

Wheelchair Access: Yes

Directions: From the south, take I-95 north to I-395 (Russell Street). At Fayette Street turn west and drive for one block to the corner of Greene and Fayette. Westminster Hall is on the left side of the street. From the north, take I-95 south to Exit 53, which is Russell Street. Follow directions as before.

What and Where: Can you think of a spookier way to spend Halloween than touring Edgar Allan Poe's final resting place? As a matter of fact, a trip through the Baltimore catacombs is a journey through one of Poe's horror stories. The faint of heart better spend the evening at Camden Yards watching the Orioles rather than tiptoeing through the tomb of the creator of "The Raven." Some scholars feel that a particular enormous tomb at Westminster is the one Poe described in "The Premature Burial." It is thought that the author of the macabre might have wandered through these catacombs, in his time an open graveyard, at night and conjured up his terrifying tales. Perhaps he was inspired by grotesque tales that the homeless of his day used the tombs as sleeping quarters. Legend has it that many of these impoverished souls were accidentally trapped inside the tombs and suffocated to death. It is indeed a Poe-like scenario.

Poe's own death was as mysterious as many of his stories, and his final days remain shrouded in mystery. Returning alone to Baltimore from a trip from Richmond to New York, he was found in a semiconscious condition in a doorway on Lombard Street. The cause of his death is unknown, but it's thought he was suffering from pneumonia in addition to a precarious mental and physical condition. He died at the age of 40 on October 7, 1849, and was buried beside his beloved wife, Virginia, and Maria Poe Clemm, his aunt.

If you're more of an architecture buff than a horror fan, you might enjoy the extraordinary construction of the church on arches above the tombs, creating the amazing catacombs below the building.

Betsy's B&B

1428 Park Avenue
Baltimore, MD 21217
(410) 383-1274
(410) 728-8957 Fax

What do F. Scott Fitzgerald, Gertude Stein, and Edith Hamilton all have in common? Why, residences in Baltimore's Bolton Hill, of course. This community had its beginning as Mt. Royal, Bolton, and Rose Hill, the estates of three prominent Baltimore families. Following the Civil War, housing development in the area boomed with the introduction of sewers and horse-drawn cars. By the twentieth century Bolton Hill was an example of style and elegance. Many other patrons of the arts lived here but as was a common story, the Depression changed life on these graceful tree-lined streets. Urban blight eventually was conquered by "rehabbers," who rekindled the old neighborhood spirit and succeeded in having the area designated a historic district.

And the perfect place to absorb and appreciate this heady brew of history and literary heritage is right there, waiting for you. Betsy's B&B is a four-story "petite estate" set proudly among other red-brick row houses adorned with the white marble "stoops" (entrance steps) that are a trademark of this city. Six carved marble mantels will attract your admiration, as will the detailed ceiling medallions and an entry hall floor of alternating strips of light oak and lustrous dark walnut. Satisfying breakfasts are held in the dining room of the fine old house. All rooms have private baths, and French doors open onto a private garden and deck, where guests are welcome to stroll or relax in the tree-shaded hot tub. Indeed, this is a house—and a neighborhood to awaken anybody's muse.

Rates: $65–$85
Credit Cards Accepted: Visa, MC, AMEX, Discover
Number of Guest Rooms: 3
Number of Baths: 3
Wheelchair Access: No

Pets: No
Children: Yes
Smoking: No
Senior Citizen Discount: No
Directions: See brochure

Twin Gates B&B Inn

308 Morris Avenue
Lutherville, MD 21093
(410) 252-3131

They are stone, by the way, the twin gates that give this well-designed and immaculately restored early Victorian residence its

name. Just minutes from Baltimore's many attractions or the tranquility of places like the Ladew Topiary Gardens in Hartford

County, Maryland, this 1857 clapboard beauty contains six guest rooms that look out over porches and garden, offering balconies and snug window seats. Each room is decorated in a unique style, from the California Suite and the Pride of Baltimore Room to the Cape May and the Maryland Hunt. The wide front porch of Twin Gates, the attractive garden gazebo, and the third-floor library bring forth all of one's latent powers of relaxation. (Some of us have almost forgotten that gazebo means "gaze," and "relax" should mean much the same thing!) In the elegant dining room Gwen serves her famous heart-healthy breakfasts, a feat that has put her on the national speakers' circuit. Hard to believe, but those egg soufflés and peach crepes with raspberry sauce are actually good for you! All in all, departing through those handsome stone gates will leave you with a sense of satisfaction that should balance the feeling of anticipation you had upon arriving. It's just that kind of a place.

Rates: $95–$155
Credit Cards Accepted: Visa, MC, AMEX
Number of Guest Rooms: 6
Number of Baths: 6
Wheelchair Access: No

Pets: No
Children: Ages 12 and over
Smoking: No
Senior Citizen Discount: No
Directions: See brochure

Celie's Waterfront B&B

1714 Thames Street
Baltimore, MD 21231
(410) 522-2323; (800) 432-0184
(410) 522-2324 Fax

Innkeeper Celie Ives has eight quick reasons why her B&B is an excellent place to stay, but, really, once the bustling waterfront neighborhood has pulled you in, especially if you have viewed it from the fourth-story roof deck, she might as well just move on and tell you what's good for breakfast. Then there's Celie's great-great-grandmother to recommend the place. True, it is only her portrait over the fireplace, but she has quite a way about her and seems to set the tone for what goes on here. Located in the heart of the Fell's Point harbor community, this beautiful three-story inn has been designed and built with your comfort in mind. Each of the seven rooms has a private bath and offers a choice of bed sizes. Skylights, fireplaces, whirlpool tubs, private balconies, and harbor views are additional features. Breakfast can be served on the roof deck, in your room, on your balcony, in the courtyard, in the gar-

A table setting at Celie's Waterfront B&B. Photo by Curtis Martin.

den, or by a crackling fire in the dining room.

Celie herself is a compelling reason to stay at this lovely B&B. When my husband

and I first met her, she was sporting an Oriole's baseball cap, so it was love at first sight. My husband, who was born in Baltimore, ventures back yearly to see the Orioles play, so when he read Celie's brochure, "Cal (Ripkin) and Celie's both broke records this year! You've read about his success. Now read all about ours," David, a dyed-in-the-wool Ripkin fan, was hooked. Because our stay in town always includes a trip to the old ball game, we were pleased that the Water Taxi and Harbor Shuttle provide a unique means of getting to Oriole Park at the elegant new Camden Yards during the season.

Baltimore has been an exciting, livable city for several centuries. The historic Fell's Point harborside village dates to 1730, the site of a colonial shipyard that produced the grand seafaring clipper ships. The frigate *Constitution*, the oldest U.S. Navy ship still afloat, is berthed at nearby Harborplace. A short walk down cobblestoned streets will present a view of many original old houses built in Federal, Greek Revival, and early Victorian styles. Specialty shops and "chop" and coffeehouses abound. In such an atmosphere, with such pleasurable accommodations as are provided at Celie's, your main decision will certainly be how to juggle your time so as to stay just a bit longer. Great-great-grandmother would approve.

Rates: $94.50–$175.00
Credit Cards Accepted: Visa, MC, AMEX, Discover
Number of Guest Rooms: 7
Number of Baths: 7
Wheelchair Access: Yes

Pets: No
Children: If older than 10
Smoking: No
Senior Citizen Discount: No
Directions: See brochure

MASSACHUSETTS

———— ※◆※ ————

Emerson House

Cambridge Turnpike at Lexington Road
Concord, MA 01742
(508) 369-2236

Who: Barbara Mongan

When: From mid-April through October, 10:00 A.M.–4:30 P.M. Tuesday through Saturday, 2:00–4:00 P.M. on Sunday

How Much: $4.50 for adults, $3 for children ages 6 to 17

Senior Citizen Discount: $3

Wheelchair Access: No

Directions: Call for directions

What and Where: In the very town from which the first shots of the Revolution were heard, there lived some of America's greatest writers: Henry David Thoreau, Nathaniel Hawthorne, Bronson Alcott, Louisa May Alcott, and their mentor, the Sage of Concord, Ralph Waldo Emerson. It would not be unusual to find them all in Emerson's study, volleying ideas back and forth. Other writers, John Greenleaf Whittier, Henry Wadsworth Longfellow, Henry James, Bret Harte, Charles Sumner, and Walt Whitman, traveled to Concord to talk with Emerson in his home. Who was this man who attracted and inspired so many of the great literary minds of his day?

Before Emerson came to Concord he was a Unitarian minister in Boston, as his father had been. But after a year and a half in the pulpit, Emerson left the ministry forever in search of some understanding of what a human being truly needs in order to thrive.

In his early life Emerson had known a fair amount of loss. His father had died when Emerson was a boy. Two of his four brothers suffered from mental illness. Another died of tuberculosis. He himself suffered from lung disease and temporary blindness. His young first wife, Ellen, died just seventeen months after their marriage, as did his first son, Waldo, to whom he dedicated his poem "Threnody."

When Emerson moved to Concord in 1835 he brought with him his second wife, Lydia Jackson, as well as the seminal ideas of what was to be his great contribution to American Transcendentalism.

Visiting Ralph Waldo Emerson's home, you will find it essentially as it was when he died in 1882. In the front parlor, the Transcendental Club met and developed and published *The Dial*, an influential literary magazine of its day.

In the book-lined study Emerson passed endless hours shaping his thoughts by sharing them with other writers and philosophers. Emerson fiercely believed that the only way to understand the past was to read the writers that have gone before. His bookshelves are actually trays with handles on them. He couldn't stand the thought of losing his collection of books should the house catch fire, so he put them on trays, making them easy to move in a hurry. The house did catch fire, in 1872, and the books were spared. "When I open a good book," Emerson once noted, "say, one which opens a literary question, I wish that life was 3,000 years long."

Emerson wrote in a rocking chair by the window of his study. He set a large atlas across the arms of the chair and used it as a writing surface as he rocked gently back and forth, putting thought to paper. From time to time he'd look up and gaze outside the window as travelers passed by, going to and from Concord on the Cambridge Turnpike. "I am not solitary whilst I write," he once commented, "though nobody is with me."

Bronson Alcott, a friend and fellow philosopher, was the founder of a Utopian commune called Fruitlands. When the commune failed about a year after its inception, Emerson persuaded the Alcott family to come to Concord to live. He even offered his home to the family until its fortunes were restored, but Mrs. Alcott declined this particular offer. The family acquired a house of its own but always felt welcome at Emerson's home. Louisa May, one of the daughters, was constantly borrowing books from Mr. Emerson's library. Years later, when she wrote *Little Women*, she used Emerson's persona for the character of Mr. Lawrence, the old gentleman who lived next door and always looked after the family.

At one time Henry David Thoreau was the Emerson family's handyman. He chopped their wood and did the gardening. The land on which Thoreau built his cabin on Walden Pond actually belonged to Emerson. The latter would often visit, then go by himself to a rocky ledge in a wooded spot, where he played his flute and wrote in his journal.

Alcott and Thoreau once had the idea of surprising Emerson with a close-to-nature summerhouse. Instead of using logs, they built it from rustic branches hung with moss. The project was to illustrate the nature of curves, but the structure was too damp ever to be used.

Sleepy Hollow, northeast of town, was once a field where Emerson, Hawthorn, Alcott, and Thoreau would sometimes meet by chance while taking their separate strolls among the wildflowers. Now Sleepy Hollow is a cemetery where these friends have come together again, this time to rest on Author's Ridge.

Across the street from Emerson's house is the Concord Antiquarian Museum. The Emerson family gave the land for the museum with the understanding that a fireproof room would be built to house the contents of Emerson's study. Also in the museum are the contents of Thoreau's Walden Pond cabin. The museum is open mid-March to October from 10 A.M. to 4:30 P.M. on Monday through Saturday and 2:00 P.M. to 4:30 P.M. Sunday; the rest of the year, it is open from 10:00 A.M. to 4:30 P.M. on Saturday and 2:00 P.M. to 4:30 P.M. on Sunday.

Orchard House: Home of the Alcotts

399 Lexington Road
Concord, MA 01742
(508) 369-4118
(508) 369-1376 Fax

Who: Stephanie Upton, director

When: 10:00 A.M.–4:30 P.M. Monday through Saturday from April through October; 11:00 A.M.–3:00 P.M. Monday through Friday, 10:00 A.M.–4:30 P.M. on Saturday, 1:00–4:30

P.M. on Sunday from November through March. Closed January 1–15 and on Easter, Thanksgiving, and Christmas.

How Much: $5.50 for adults, $4.50 for students, $3.50 for children ages 6 to 17

Senior Citizen Discount: $4.50 for seniors age 62 and older

Wheelchair Access: First floor only

Directions: From I-95 take exit 30B (Route 2A West). Follow 2A West to where it forks, and bear right onto Lexington Road. Orchard House is on the right approximately one mile from the center of Concord.

What and Where: By the time the Alcott family moved to Concord, they had lived in 22 places in 21 years. Bronson Alcott, Louisa May's father, was a man of great philosophical vision whose plans never quite worked out the way he hoped. In Boston he established a school based on child-centered education. "Look to the child to see what is to be done, rather than to his book or system." Perhaps it was an idea before its time, because the school closed within five years of its inception. Then he spearheaded Fruitlands, a utopian commune near Harvard, Massachusetts, where philosophers and writers tried to elevate their understanding of life through simple honest farm work. As it turned out, many writers and philosophers don't know a hawk from a handsaw, and Fruitlands folded.

Ralph Waldo Emerson, who had publicly supported Bronson Alcott's endeavors, invited the family to move to Concord, even offering to put them up in his own home. The Alcotts came but were able to gather together the 1,000 dollars that bought them their own piece of land, 12 acres on which stood two dilapidated houses. Bronson joined the houses and renovated them into a home that would serve the Alcotts for the next 20 years.

Louisa May had three sisters who are easily identifiable as the March sisters in her book *Little Women*. Anna, the oldest, was Meg in the book; Louisa May was Jo; Abigail May was Amy; and Beth, who died at age 22, remained Beth.

When you walk into Orchard House, scenes from *Little Women* seem to appear everywhere. The wedding of Meg and John Brook took place in the parlor (as did the real wedding of Anna and John Pratt). Louisa May's "mood pillow" still sits on the parlor settee. The girl had a volatile temperament and used the pillow to give her family fair warning of how to deal with her on any given day. If it was pointed up, she was in a good frame of mind. If it was pointed down, it was best to avoid her.

The dining room often served as a stage where the Alcott girls put on plays, ranging from original melodramas to the works of Shakespeare and Dickens.

The cluttered study, with stacks of books and busts of Socrates and Plato, belonged to Mr. Alcott. On the round table in the corner sits one of his projects, a reader for the blind. (He and a friend were in the process of copying *Little Women* for the blind just before his death.)

The kitchen was Mrs. Alcott's domain. As Louisa once wrote, "All the philosophy in our house is not in the study, a good deal is in the kitchen where one fine old lady thinks high thoughts and does good deeds while she cooks and scrubs." Louisa bought the soapstone sink for her mother with the first royalties of *Little Women*.

Upstairs are the bedrooms. May, the artist of the family, covered the walls of her room with pencil and ink drawings. (She later moved to Europe, married a Swiss businessman-musician, and settled in Paris, where she became a noted copyist.)

Louisa and Anna shared a room until Anna got married. Thereafter, it was Louisa May's haven: a quiet, private place where this romantic, emotional young woman could sit and write. There is a semicircular desk between the two windows where Louisa wrote for up to 14 hours a day. She taught herself to write with both hands so that when one hand became tired, the other could take over. Always foremost in her mind were her family's financial problems and how she could help through her writing. The first book she published was a children's storybook that she dedicated to her little friend, Ellen Emerson, daughter of the great philosopher. Next she wrote *Hospital Sketches*, a description of her experience as a nurse during the Civil War. The autobiographical novel *Work* told of a young single woman, Christie, and her daring attempt to live independently during the 1800s. When Louisa turned 30, under the pen name of A. M. Barnard she began writing gothic thrillers.

Finally her publisher, Thomas Niles, suggested that she write a book for girls. A book for girls? Her reaction was rather negative. "Never liked girls or knew many except for my sisters but our queer plays and experiences may prove interesting, though I doubt it."

Mr. Niles must have said something to convince her to give it a try. So during the summer of 1868, Louisa May Alcott sat at the desk in her bedroom and, in the span of three months, wrote *Little Women*.

Louisa never married. "I'd rather be a free spinster and paddle my own canoe," she wrote. In addition to writing seven other novels (*Little Men, An Old Fashioned Girl, Eight Cousins, Rose in Bloom, Under the Lilacs, Jack and Jill,* and *Jo's Boys*), she took an active interest in women's rights and female suffrage, and she became the guardian of her sister May's baby, Lulu, when May died weeks after giving birth.

Today Orchard House still sits as it did over 150 years ago, when the Alcott girls went running down its stairs in costume to deliver their lines to the audience that waited on the other side of the sheet curtains. When you step inside the house you are very aware of entering the memory-filled home of these little women.

The Wayside: Home of Nathaniel Hawthorne

455 Lexington Road
Concord, MA 01742
(508) 369-6993; (508) 369-6975

Who: Park Headquarters

When: 10:00 A.M.–4:00 P.M. every day except Wednesday from mid-April through October. Last tour at 4:00 P.M.

How Much: $3

Senior Citizen Discount: $2 with Golden Age pass

Wheelchair Access: Limited to the barn

Directions: See brochure

What and Where: Concord, Massachusetts, was the final home of Nathaniel Hawthorne. He bought his house there, The Wayside, from the Alcott family, who lived next door.

After purchasing the home, he added a frame tower to it that could only be reached by a trapdoor. There, in total isolation, he did most of his later writing. Today The Wayside is a museum containing a collection of Hawthorne's possessions and memorabilia.

In the 1880s the house was bought by Margaret Sidney, author of the children's series *The Five Little Peppers,* and her husband. (They added the broad piazza to the house.) It was through the efforts and financial support of Margaret Sidney that Orchard House became a memorial to the Alcott family.

The Wayside. Photo by Chris Stein.

Hawthorne Inn

462 Lexington Road
Concord, MA 01742
(508) 369-5610
(508) 287-4949 Fax

Across the street from The Wayside, the home of Nathaniel Hawthorne, and Orchard House, the home of Louisa May Alcott, stands the Hawthorne Inn. The land the inn sits on has a remarkable history. It once belonged to Ralph Waldo Emerson and later Nathaniel Hawthorne. While it was in Emerson's possession, he kindly allowed Bronson Alcott to plant fruit trees on it and build a path on it to the Alcotts' bathhouse. When Hawthorne purchased the land, he bordered the path leading to his house with trees on either side. Remnants of these improvements still exist on the grounds of the inn.

When you walk into Hawthorne Inn, you know you're in a literary place. Books of the town's great writers are found in abundance in the Common Room, where a warm fire burns on chilly evenings. Each of the guest rooms has its own name: Emerson Room, Alcott Room, Musketquid Room, Walden Room, Sleepy Hollow Room, Punkatasset Room, and Concord Room. In each room the literature and furnishings create atmosphere.

Every morning at a common table guests are served a continental breakfast of homemade breads, fresh fruit, juices, and a selection of teas or freshly ground coffee. In season there are raspberries and grapes grown on the premises. Afternoon tea can be enjoyed in the garden.

If you have any questions about the area, don't hesitate to ask Gregory Burch, who owns the inn with Marilyn Mudry. He is an expert on the town and its inhabitants and can tell you little-known facts about Concord's literary greats.

Rates: $110–$215
Credit Cards Accepted: Visa, MC, AMEX, Discover
Number of Guest Rooms: 7
Number of Baths: 7
Wheelchair Access: No

Pets: No
Children: Yes
Smoking: No
Senior Citizen Discount: No
Directions: See brochure

Amerscot House

61 West Acton Road
Stow, MA 01775
(508) 897-0666
(508) 897-2585 Fax

If you'd like to spend a day in the New England countryside, you might consider the Amerscot House, a beautiful Early American farmhouse just minutes away from Concord. This bed and breakfast takes its name from the nationalities of its owners, Jerry and Doreen Gibson. Jerry is American and Doreen comes from Scotland, bringing with her not only tea and scones but also the warm hospitality of the Highlands.

The Amerscot House was built in 1734 and has retained the ambience of times long ago. Each of the three guest rooms has a fireplace and is furnished with antiques, handmade quilts, and freshly cut flowers.

Breakfast is served as you please, in the colonial dining room, the greenhouse, or the porch. A full breakfast includes dishes such as eggs Benedict or homemade quiche. (Homemade cookies are available any time you want them.)

Rates: $85–$100
Credit Cards Accepted: Visa, MC, AMEX, Discover
Number of Guest Rooms: 3
Number of Baths: 3
Wheelchair Access: Yes

Pets: No
Children: With restrictions
Smoking: No
Senior Citizen Discount: No
Directions: See brochure

Longfellow's Wayside Inn

Boston Post Road
Sudbury, MA 01776
(508) 443-1776
(508) 443-8041 Fax

One Autumn night, in Sudbury town,
Across the meadows bare and brown
The windows of the wayside inn
Gleamed red with firelight through the leaves
Of woodbine, hanging from the eaves
Their crimson curtains rent and thin.

So begins Henry Wadsworth Longfellow's *Tales of a Wayside Inn,* set in one of his favorite inns, the Red Horse Tavern on the Boston Post Road. There he spent many autumn evenings by the fireside, listening to the innkeeper, Lyman How, spin tales of his

grandfather's adventures during the American Revolution.

When Lyman How died in 1861, some friends encouraged Longfellow to write down the stories. In his retelling, Longfellow gave the tales to different characters—a poet, a musician, a theologian, a student, a Spanish Jew, and a Sicilian. But "Paul Revere's Ride" he left to the innkeeper to tell.

After Longfellow's book was published, the lodging house changed its name, fittingly enough, to the Wayside Inn. Today the Wayside Inn is America's oldest operating inn. It was opened in 1716 by David How, and it has offered hospitality to over ten generations of travelers along the Boston Post Road since.

In the main parlor stands the fireplace where the characters of *Tales of a Wayside Inn* took turns telling their stories. Upstairs is the Longfellow Chamber, decorated as it was when the poet stayed there. Also, there are several other guest rooms, including one in which Lafayette is supposed to have slept.

According to the early laws of the Massachusetts Bay Colony, an innkeeper had to provide for a man, his horses, and his cattle. Even today horses are accommodated in the barn across from the hostelry. The property of the Wayside Inn includes 106 acres of forest and cultivated fields that still produce much of the inn's seasonal produce. A grist mill 500 yards from the lodge grinds the wheat and corn that are harvested in the fields. (This reproduction of an early American mill was built in 1924 by none other than Henry Ford, who bought the inn in 1923, then donated it to a historic trust.)

This oldest-of-old bed and breakfasts has ten guest rooms, all with private baths. A full breakfast is included. Lunches and dinners are also available in the old dining room of the Wayside Inn.

Rates: $80–$130
Credit Cards Accepted: Visa, MC, AMEX, Discover
Number of Guest Rooms: 10
Number of Baths: 10
Wheelchair Access: No
Pets: With advance notice

Children: Yes
Smoking: No
Senior Citizen Discount: No
Directions: From Boston, take Massachusetts Turnpike (Route 90) west to Route 128 north. Take Exit 26 for Route 20 west for 11 miles. Turn right on Wayside Inn Road.

The Mount: Home of Edith Wharton

2 Plunkett Street (At the southern junction of Routes 7 and 7A)
Lenox, MA 01240
(413) 637-1899
(413) 637-0619 Fax

Who: Scot Marshall, deputy director

When: 9:00 A.M.–2:00 P.M. on weekends beginning in May; 9:00 A.M.–2:00 P.M. every day from Memorial Day through the end of October. Last tour at 2:00 P.M. Guided tours lasting about one hour focus on literary, historical, and biographical aspects of Wharton's life. The Edith Wharton Library sponsors the "Women of Achievement" lecture series, which takes place at 4:00 P.M. on Mondays

The Mount. Photo courtesy of The Mount.

during the months of July and August. These presentations are given by major women writers and scholars. The cost of each lecture is $15, which includes an afternoon tea.

How Much: $6 for adults; $4.50 for students ages 13 to 18; free for children under 12. Group rates for ten or more.

Senior Citizen Discount: $5.50

Wheelchair Access: Yes, with prior arrangement

Directions: Contact the office for a map

What and Where: If any house can be considered an autobiography, it is The Mount, the home of Edith Wharton. In 1897 Mrs. Wharton published her first book, a guide to classic architecture style. *The Decoration of Houses,* which she wrote with architect Ogden Codman, was a blatant rebellion against complicated Victorian style.

"What she wanted to do," says Scott Marshall, the deputy director of the Edith Wharton Restoration, "was to bring back the good taste and common sense of classical architecture." Three years after the book was published she built this house, a 35-room mansion set on a mount with terraces leading down to a pond. Her gardens were outdoor rooms with landscaping that both complimented the geometry of the house and blended into the natural land around the estate. "Decidedly," Wharton once wrote a friend, "I'm a better landscape gardener than a novelist and this place, every line of which is my work, far surpasses *The House of Mirth.*"

Wharton was born Edith Newbold Jones, a child of the privileged New York City upper class. Her family assumed she would take on the role of a proper society hostess, but instead she started writing. After her marriage to banker Edward Wharton, writing became a full-time pursuit. In the next 45 years she wrote and published 40 books. More often than not her subject was the stifling culture of the New York elite, a society that had no room for passion or self-expression. *The Age of Innocence,* for which she won the Pulitzer Prize in 1921, is about a woman who choses to return to a miserable marriage with an abusive husband rather than experience the scandal that would result from a divorce. Eventually Edith Wharton divorced her husband, who was subject to manic-depressive episodes. Although she never remarried, she had a long-term relationship with Morton Fullerton and was a close friend of Henry James, who encouraged and sustained her.

A good part of Mrs. Wharton's life was spent in France, where she is now buried. But each summer and fall between 1902 and 1911 she spent at The Mount. There she wrote *The House of Mirth,* a best-seller in America. Although most of her fiction was about New York society, her novel *Ethan Frome* is based on what she saw of the poor people living in the Berkshire countryside around The Mount.

Brook Farm Inn

15 Hawthorne Street
Lenox, MA 01240
(413) 637-3013; (800) 285-POET

"There is poetry here" is the first line of the Brook Farm Inn's brochure, and the inn is a bibliophile's dream come true.

If you're looking for a truly literary bed and breakfast in the town of Lenox, you might try Brook Farm Inn. In its library, which is furnished with wing chairs and Oriental rugs, there are over 1,500 volumes of prose and poetry, many of which are first editions. They were brought to the inn by its previous owner, Bob Jacob, who spent a good part of his life scouring the bookstores of New England for new and old volumes of poetry.

Brook Farm Inn takes its name from the original Brook Farm, the famous utopian community of the 1840s that attracted many writers, including Nathaniel Hawthorne. Joe and Anne Miller, the current owners of Brook Farm Inn, continue this tradition by bringing literature and music into the lives of their guests. The library is illuminated 24 hours a day for any guest who might want to slip down and do a little reading, or writing, on his own. Formal poetry readings take place every Saturday afternoon, followed by scones and tea.

And music? The flow of soft classical music in the background seems only natural in a place like this.

Brook Farm Inn has 12 guest rooms, all of which have private baths. If you're looking for elegance, you might try one of the Victorian rooms, which come complete with a working fireplace. If you like secret places tucked up and away from everything else, choose a room on the third story under the gables and close to the stars.

Breakfast—which includes granola, yogurt, fresh fruit, muffins, and a hot dish—is served in a chandeliered dining room overlooking garden and woods. Afternoon tea is served in the library with music.

During the summer, you can enjoy the heated swimming pool or the garden hammock while listening to the Boston Symphony Orchestra rehearsing at Tanglewood, on the other side of the woods.

Reach Brook Farm Inn by Stockbridge Road down a long, sloping hill to Hawthorne Street. It's the very hill Edith Wharton used as the setting for the final pages of *Ethan Frome*.

Rates: $70–$185

Credit Cards Accepted: Visa, MC, Discover

Number of Guest Rooms: 12

Number of Baths: 12

Wheelchair Access: No

Pets: No

Children: If older than 15

Smoking: No

Senior Citizen Discount: No

Directions: See brochure

Arrowhead: Home of Herman Melville

780 Holmes Road
Pittsfield, MA 01201
(413) 442-1793

Who: Stella Coolbroth

When: Memorial Day through Labor Day, 10:00 A.M.–5:00 P.M. every day; Labor Day through October 31, 10:00 A.M.–5:00 P.M. Friday through Monday. By appointment the rest of the year.

How Much: $5 for adults

Senior Citizen Discount: $4.50

Wheelchair Access: Yes

Directions: From the Massachusetts Turnpike, take Exit 3 (Lee exit). Go north on Route

20 (which merges with Route 7) into Lenox. Turn right at Holmes Road and proceed for approximately one mile to Arrowhead.

What and Where: When Herman Melville bought a farmhouse near Pittsfield, Massachusetts, his plan was to farm part-time, write part-time, and between the two make enough money to support his family. His family at that time included his wife, Elizabeth, two children, his mother, and four sisters. (Melville named his farm Arrowhead because of the arrowheads he found while plowing.) He had already achieved some literary success following the publication of five books. Two of them, *Typee* and *Omoo*, were stories based on his adventures while serving on whaling ships in the South Seas.

He took his responsibilities at Arrowhead very seriously. At dawn he'd rise to take care of his stock. After breakfast he'd climb the stairs to his study. Locking the door behind him, he'd kindle a fire and sit at his desk until midafternoon. From three o'clock on his wife and sisters rewrote his manuscripts, correcting misspellings and punctuation errors so the work was clean enough to send to publishers.

From the north window of Melville's study you can see Mount Greylock, a big, humpy mountain set against the distant blue hills. It's said that in October, when frost comes to the Berkshire countryside, the whole mountain glistens like a huge white whale set in a sea of blue hills. *Moby-Dick* was conceived while Melville sat at his desk, gazing out the window at Mount Greylock.

The book didn't have a promising beginning. The first draft was basically a documentary on whales. But Melville's friend and neighbor, Nathaniel Hawthorne, encouraged him to dig deeper with his writing. When the novel was rewritten, Captain Ahab's pursuit of the great white whale became man's struggle against the mysterious and complex forces of life. All of Melville's subsequent writing plunged more deeply into the complicated ambiguities of the universe.

Melville's popularity began to decline with the publication of his masterpiece, and he never again enjoyed the financial success of his earlier, lighter novels. Readers of the time couldn't accept the change in his style. After receiving poor reviews on three more books, Melville gave up writing, moved his family to New York City, and for the next 13 years worked as a deputy customs inspector, occasionally penning some poetry. It wasn't until the end of his life that he tried prose one more time. When he died in 1891 he left behind the completed manuscript of *Billy Budd*. Today this novel, along with *Moby-Dick*, secures for Herman Melville a place among the pantheon of great American writers.

When you visit Arrowhead, go into the kitchen to see the grand chimney, which Melville wrote about in "I and My Chimney." Take a stroll along the piazza on the north side of the house, where Melville paced back and forth, plotting the stories of *The Piazza Tales* in his mind. Climb the stairs to his study and take a few moments to stare out the north window at the distant mountains.

The Wainwright Inn

518 South Main Street
Great Barrington, MA 01230
(413) 528-2062
Website: http://www.wainwrightinn.com

Situated halfway between New York City and Boston, The Wainwright Inn provides the comfort and convenience travelers seek on the road. This Great Barrington local landmark home was built in 1766 by Captain Peter Ingersoll and known as the Tory Tavern and Inn. It is still possible to imagine colonists meeting in the living room. During the Revolution, the building served as a fort and armory. David Wainwright, statesman and state representative, purchased the home in 1790. It remained in his family until the turn of the twentieth century. Successive owners have added their own personal touches, maintaining the home with pride and using good sense in adding necessary amenities while keeping the original lines of the house intact. The many common areas welcome guests, as do the distinctive wraparound porches. The dining room is reserved for guests, and a fine place it is for breakfasts

The Wainwright Inn. Photo by Silver Ridge Photo.

that feature homemade breads, but it may also be reserved for private evening dining as well. All the historic and natural wonders of the beautiful Berkshires invite you from the doorstep of this special place.

Rates: $65–$150
Credit Cards Accepted: Visa, MC, AMEX
Number of Guest Rooms: 8
Number of Baths: 7
Wheelchair Access: Yes

Pets: Yes
Children: Yes
Smoking: No
Senior Citizen Discount: No
Directions: See brochure

Windflower Inn

684 South Egremont Road
Great Barrington, MA 01230
(413) 528-2720; (800) 992-1993

In an ever-changing world, the beauty of the Berkshires remains a constant, and driving through villages in the area we are reminded of days gone by. Today we can appreciate the same sights that attracted early settlers, authors, artists, and city-spent travelers a century or more ago.

Windflower Inn mirrors just this kind of beauty. All white clapboard siding, with huge maple trees outside and massive fireplaces within, this eighteenth-century beauty presides over a ten-acre domain. Thirteen bedrooms provide the perfect backdrop for antiques accumulated at country auctions. Many of the bathrooms contain nostalgic pedestal sinks and claw-foot tubs, but all pro-

The Windflower Inn. Photo courtesy of the Windflower Inn.

vide modern plumbing and conveniences. The Lieberts are affable hosts, and their daughter Claudia and her husband John are king and queen of the outstanding kitchen. It is a pleasure to become acquainted with an extended family (including grandchildren Jessica and Michael) that has found such a special delight in working and living together.

The double sofas in the living room are an invitation to relax until tea time. Or they might be a setting for an animated conver-sation, especially if you are talking with John about his extensive organic garden, which provides so much of the inn's splendid food. Be assured even before you begin a tour of The Mount or the Rockwell Museum that you will have experienced an encounter at Windflower with what so many of us have labeled the American Dream.

Rates: $100–$170
Credit Cards Accepted: AMEX
Number of Guest Rooms: 13
Number of Baths: 13
Wheelchair Access: Yes

Pets: No
Children: Yes
Smoking: Yes
Senior Citizen Discount: No
Directions: See brochure

The Emily Dickinson Homestead

280 Main Street
Amherst, MA 01002
(413) 542-8161

Who: Emily Dickinson Foundation; Cindy Dickinson, curator

When: March through mid-December, Wednesday through Saturday 1:30–4:30 P.M.; April through October, Wednesday through Saturday 1:30–4:30 P.M.; November and December, Wednesday and Saturday—tours in afternoon. Call for tour times.

How Much: $4 adults, $3 for students, $2 for juniors ages 6 to 11

Senior Citizen Discount: No

Wheelchair Access: No

Directions: From south I-91 take Exit 19; follow Route 9 to Amherst (approximately 6 miles). Turn left onto Main Street. From north I-91 take Exit 24; follow Route 116 south to Route 9, a mile out of Amherst. Proceed as above.

What and Where: Much has been written about Emily Dickinson, the white-clad recluse who constructed a universe of her own in the simple setting of the home and garden where she was born and died. Only seven of her poems were published during her lifetime. It may be that her sharp, intense images are better understood by contemporary readers than by those of her own time.

You get a sense of this fascinating poet when you visit her home, concealed behind layers of overgrown trees several blocks from the center of town. You might be surprised to learn that as a young woman the famous recluse was known as the "Belle of Amherst." In her early life Dickinson was a social butterfly who enjoyed rides into the countryside and who attended dances and teas and nurtured a number of intense friendships. The contrast with her later life is striking.

At the Dickinson Homestead you can imagine Emily writing her inventive poems as you stand in the room where she worked. The thin curtains that let the light of

Amherst through gave her a full view of "the world passing by." In the upstairs room of her little hermitage you can gaze at the world as she saw it. Examine the petite writing table and picture the nearly 2,000 poems her sister Lavinia discovered arranged in neatly tied bundles in Emily's desk after she died. A visit to the home of one of America's favorite poets is a truly mesmerizing experience.

The mystery of her life becomes even deeper when you notice the pictures surrounding her bed. One is of the Reverend Charles Wadsworth of Philadelphia, her father's best friend. Another is of Otis Lord, who may have asked for her hand in marriage. The third is of Thomas Wentworth Higginson, who served as her literary mentor for most of her adult life. You can learn more about this intriguing, enigmatic woman by reading some of the many Dickinson biographies.

You can obtain more insight into this eccentric poet by studying her engravings and daguerreotypes of Thomas Carlyle, Charlotte Brontë, and Elizabeth Barrett Browning, writers she admired. Other endearing artifacts are the little chair she used as a girl and one of the white dresses she wore, now hanging in her closet. I particularly liked the basket on a rope she used to lower cookies to children in the street.

It is obvious that the Dickinson spirit lives on in this house. The observant visitor can still envision Emily baking bread, cutting roses, wandering around the grounds in her famous white dresses, or retreating to her room when visitors arrived.

Allen House Victorian Inn

599 Main Street
Amherst, MA 01002
(413) 253-5000

Your hosts, Alan and Ann Zsieminski, who radiate warmth and energy as well as a deep respect for and knowledge of history, provide guests with hearty New England breakfasts. Conversation over Swedish pancakes, French toast, or eggs Benedict is often flavored with the English and German accents of guests who have studied the writings of one of America's foremost poets. The inn's setting offers easy access to the many colleges and universities in the area. Galleries, museums, theater, concerts, shops, and fine restaurants will surely enhance your visit to this most memorable inn.

The Allen House, in the heart of Amherst, is an award-winning Victorian bed and breakfast. Surrounded by tall shade trees, it is located just across the street from the Emily Dickinson house. With its many peaked roofs and rectangular windows, it is

The Allen House. Photo courtesy of the Allen House.

a fine example of Queen Anne Stick–style architecture.

This more than 100-year-old, 18-room architectural gem offers seven bedchambers with private baths, all rich in Victoriana. Wallpapers designed by Charles Eastlake, Walter Crane, and William Morris add to the charm of the building's interior. Hand-carved cherrywood mantels, original and lovingly restored woodwork, reflect the elegance of period ambience. The thoughtful hosts provide guests with a complimentary collection of selected poems of Emily Dickinson.

Rates: $45–$135
Credit Cards Accepted: Visa, MC, AMEX, Discover
Number of Guest Rooms: 7
Number of Baths: 7
Wheelchair Access: No

Pets: No
Children: If older than 8
Smoking: No
Senior Citizen Discount: No
Directions: See brochure

The House of Seven Gables

54 Turner Street
Salem, MA 01970-5698
(508) 744-0991

Who: Anne McCamy

When: From January 18 through March 31, 10:00 A.M.–4:30 P.M. Monday through Saturday, and 12:00 noon–4:30 P.M. on Sunday; from April 1 through June 30 and from November 1 through December 31, 10:00 A.M.–4:30 P.M. every day; July 1 through October 31, 9:00 A.M.–6:00 P.M. Closed January 1 to January 17.

How Much: $7, $4 for juniors ages 6 to 17

Senior Citizen Discount: No

Wheelchair Access: No

Directions: Call for directions

What and Where: If you want to know Nathaniel Hawthorne and the streets on which his characters walked, you must go to Salem, Massachusetts. It was in this little New England port town that 19 people were convicted of being witches and hung in the year 1692. Among the judges presiding over the trials was John Hathorne, an ancestor of Nathaniel Hawthorne. While walking toward the gallows, Rebecca Nurse, one of the convicted "witches," pronounced a curse on Hathorne and his posterity.

Four generations later, Nathaniel was born into the Hathorne family. His father, a sea captain, died when the boy was four, and his mother became a recluse. Growing up in this dismal household, Nathaniel apparently considered suicide at one point. As a young man he kept to himself, reading prodigiously, occasionally walking up to Gallows Hill to be by himself with his books.

After graduating from Bowdoin College, which he attended with Henry Wadsworth Longfellow and a future president, Franklin Pierce, Nathaniel altered his last name, adding a "w." Perhaps he also altered his perspective of Rebecca Nurse's curse that seemed, even yet, to haunt his family.

Nathaniel Hawthorne continually searched for an understanding of sin and how people are affected by their own misdeeds. He was haunted by his Puritan heritage and its rigid ethics that seem to run counter to man's broader, more humane instincts. Pride,

Hawthorne came to believe, was one of man's greatest sins, and with pride came an inheritance of guilt.

The House of Seven Gables, at 54 Turner Street in Salem, was owned by Hawthorne's maiden cousin, Susan Ingersoll. As a young man Hawthorne enjoyed visiting her. The house fascinated him, with its oddly pitched roof, its many rooms, and its secret chimney stairway leading to a chamber on the second level. The house had been built in 1668, shortly before the period of Salem's witch trials. At the time Hawthorne visited his cousin he was working at Salem's custom house, where he had access to family histories of those who had suffered from the trials. Slowly, a story began to fall into place in his mind.

It is the story of a curse placed on the family of Judge Pyncheon by Matthew Maule, a victim of the witch hunts. After the trial, the judge confiscated Maule's land, razed his hut, and built the grand House of Seven Gables where the hut once stood. In the years that follow, generations of Pyncheons inherit not only the house but also the vicious spiral of pride, greed, and guilt.

An author writing in the Puritan tradition would have ended the story here. Hawthorne, however, concludes with the marriage of Phoebe, a niece of the Pyncheon family, and Holgrave, the last of the Maules. This very situation is later reflected in Hawthorne's own life. The author's son chose as his wife a descendent of Philip English, a man his great-great-grandfather had persecuted.

Nathaniel Hawthorne left Salem only to return time and again. For a short period of time, he was part of the Brook Farm community. When he married Sophia Peabody, they moved to Concord, where he became close friends with Henry David Thoreau. After returning to Salem to serve in the custom house, Hawthorne moved his family to Lenox, Massachusetts, where he spent countless hours discussing writing and philosophy with Herman Melville. When Melville published *Moby-Dick,* he dedicated the book to Hawthorne.

In 1853, Hawthorne's college chum, Franklin Pierce, became president of the United States and in gratitude for the work Hawthorne had done in his campaign, Pierce gave him a consulship in Liverpool, England. On returning to the States, Hawthorne and family again settled in Concord, where he lived next door to the Alcotts.

Until the end of his life, Nathaniel Hawthorne's writings were fueled by his effort to understand the consequences of man's inhumanity to man and the possibility of redemption. Always, his thoughts returned to Salem and to his Puritan roots.

The pallbearers at Hawthorne's funeral were a literary Who's Who of the day and included Henry Wadsworth Longfellow, Bronson Alcott, Ralph Waldo Emerson, and Franklin Pierce.

Stephen Daniel House

1 Daniels Street
Salem, MA 01970
(508) 744-5709

Although many bed and breakfasts claim to be the oldest in town, Kay Gill of the Stephen Daniel House in Salem, Massachusetts, lays claim to being the oldest innkeeper—a regular relic of the town. She's one of those salt-of-the-earth characters who are as much a part of Salem as the mist coming in from the harbor. For 35 years she has welcomed guests to her 1667 home. The house is beautifully restored, with open hearth fireplaces, paneled walls, and antique furnishings.

If you're looking for a taste of Hawthorne, you couldn't be in a better place. The street where Hawthorne was born is just three blocks away, the customs house where he worked is around the corner, and his wife Sophia's childhood home is in the neighborhood. "That house has fallen into disrepair," said Mrs. Gill, "but the bootscrapers are still out front. I bet they're the same bootscrapers Hawthorne used when he came to call on Sophia."

Want to know more stories about Hawthorne? Ask Mrs. Gill. She'll be glad to tell you.

Rates: $95
Credit Cards Accepted: AMEX
Number of Guest Rooms: 3
Number of Baths: 3
Wheelchair Access: No
Pets: Yes
Children: Yes
Smoking: No

Senior Citizen Discount: Yes
Directions: Go down Derby Street until you reach the Pig's Eye Pub, then turn onto Daniels Street away from the waterfront. Stephen Daniel House is at the corner of Daniels and Essex Streets. Mrs. Gill will send a map to anyone who calls ahead.

MICHIGAN

—+—◣◆◢—+—

Ernest Hemingway in Northern Michigan

The spirit of Ernest Hemingway is very much alive in northern Michigan, and the sense of place noted in *The Nick Adams Stories* still exists there today. The little towns of Petoskey, Harbor Springs, and Horton's Bay that Hemingway so vividly documents are largely unchanged today. In "Ten Indians," Nick, looking from the top of the hill, "saw the lights of Petoskey and, off across Little Traverse Bay, the lights of Harbor Springs." If Hemingway or his alter ego, Nick Adams, were alive today, they would recognize many sights.

Petoskey, Michigan, is where Hemingway wrote his first fiction. Recuperating from wounds he received as a Red Cross ambulance driver in Italy in World War I, the 20-year-old told friends he went up north "to get away from my parents and do some serious writing." With that intent, Hemingway rented a room at Evva Potter's rooming house at 602 State Street and set up his typewriter in a upstairs room at the front window. There are no plaques on this tree-shaded frame house, but visitors, many coming from as far away as Japan, find it anyway. The present owner is good-natured about these interruptions and will let aficionados take photos and look around a bit.

From his boardinghouse, Hemingway used to walk down the street and pop into the Petoskey Public Library, where he would read the newspapers. The library probably looks very much as it did when Hemingway used it as his reading room, but gone are the days when the author's works were kept under lock and key in the basement because they were considered risqué. Today's shockproof Hemingway fans are shown the vertical files with hundreds of clippings about the author's Petoskey's days. There is also a collection of books by or about Hemingway.

At the library, a helpful librarian suggested I read *Torrents of Spring,* Hemingway's Petoskey novel, written in ten days. This book, which is very imitative of Henry Fielding's *Joseph Andrews,* is a must for Hemingway fans wanting to learn about his Petoskey days. One of my favorite parts was reading about Hemingway's character, Yogi, coming to the library where he could read maps or newspapers. Talk about art imitating life! I also poked around in the vertical files and discovered that in the always conservative Middle West, the staid founding mothers and fathers of Petoskey heartily disapproved of the way young Hemingway looked and dressed. With his old shoes and pants and a Mackinaw shirt, topped off with several days' growth of beard, the young author most assuredly did not look like a solid citizen. To make matters worse, he ran around with a wild gang and drank heavily during Prohibition.

His unkempt appearance and bad-boy demeanor must have made him terribly appealing to the ladies of the Northland. They turned out in droves to hear his speech about his war experiences. Picture, if you will, at this very library, the Petoskey Ladies Aid Society regaled by the handsome, unconventional war hero!

Next stop on the Hemingway tour of Petoskey is the Park Garden Cafe at 432 Lake Street. Local legends say that the young Ernest sat on the second stool at the bar when he wasn't in the corner writing. Other local Hemingway folklorists report that the author liked to hang out at the Park Garden's Billiard Hall. Mike Wilson, one of the organizers of the Hemingway Festival and a Hemingway lookalike, told me that "The Killers," a short story in *The Nick Adams Stories,* was set in this very bar. Whatever the true Hemingway Park Garden story is, the circa 1874 bar and cafe is a fun place for a drink or to sample the local favorite, Straits Area whitefish. The hand-carved Brunswick bar, made of black walnut, cherry, and hickory, is magnificent, and in the entryway you can get a Hemingway fix from the massive bookcases featuring books about and by the author, including many in Chinese and Japanese.

Another Hemingway haunt is said to be the Stafford Perry Hotel, where the aspiring writer is supposed to have stopped on a regular basis for bootleg whiskey laced with coffee. Audrey Collins-McMullen, the contact person for the annual Hemingway Festival, says that Hemingway actually stayed at the hotel. It seems only appropriate then that this beautiful old hotel should be the headquarters for the Michigan Hemingway Society's annual October Hemingway Weekend. Each year's activities are different, but they all honor the memory of the Nobel laureate whose first stories were set in northern Michigan. Some of the goals of the society are serious, such as encouraging the study of Hemingway's relationship to Michigan in his life and work. Others are just for fun, such as "Where I Fished During My Summer Vacation," a tongue-in-cheek parody writing contest in Hemingway style about one of Hemingway's favorite Michigan topics, fly fishing, or, purely in the interest of literary research, of course, regional bars frequented by the author!

To round out the Hemingway tour, you'll want to visit the Little Traverse Historical Museum, with its display of Hemingway memorabilia featuring autographed books, the young author's typewriter, and an old reading light from Windemere, the family cottage on nearby Walloon Lake. I particularly enjoyed the pictures of young Ernest fishing, the happy family portraits, and the first-edition books inscribed to his friend Edwin "Dutch" Pailthorp.

AUTHOR'S NOTE: There have been many delightful moments for me as I write this book; none more so than my visit with 97-year-old Irene Gordon. Irene is amazing, a former physical education teacher and entrepreneur who is an inspiration to all who meet her. For literary purposes, she is known, among her many other accomplishments, as a close friend of Ernest Hemingway. Many in Petoskey say Irene is the only woman the much-married Hemingway ever loved. Irene, who is a friend of my parents, Jane and Gene Guttman, invited us to her charming Petoskey home to tell us about her relationship with the famous author.

After graduating from Petoskey High School during World War I, Irene asserted her independence by leaving her family home for Lake Forest College, a small school in Illinois, where she pursued her dream of becoming a physical education teacher. After finishing college, she took her first job in Grand Island, Nebraska, where she taught physical expression and dance. One particularly snowy Christmas, she took the long, tedious train trip back to her beloved Petoskey. It was Christmas-party season, but the unusually heavy snowfall threatened to make the roads impassable. But her good friend, Dutch Pailthorp, told her rain, shine, snow, or hail, a party would be held at Dr. Ramsdell's cottage in Bay View. Only because Dr. Ramsdell was Irene's family physician did her family let her venture out with Dutch on that treacherous evening. Dutch had told Irene there was a particular man he wanted her to meet, one who was getting over a love affair with a nurse in Italy.

The handsome man with animated eyes and a lovely smile shared Irene's love of the outdoors, sports, and books. Ernest Hemingway invited Irene to have lunch with him in Chicago on her return trip to Grand Island. They had a pleasant lunch at a nearby Italian eatery where he told her of his excitement over having some newspaper columns accepted by an Arkansas newspaper. That winter the two new friends corresponded regularly. The next summer they met again in northern Michigan, when Irene was living in Petoskey. He was staying at his family's summer cottage in Walloon Lake, a short distance away. Soon they renewed their friendship on the tennis courts. In their first game she beat him in the first set and on the third and final set. A very competitive player, he was not pleased.

It seemed important to Hemingway that Irene admire his fishing prowess, and he would frequently stop by Irene's family store in downtown Petoskey to show her his latest catch. One time, she recalled, he offered to catch a meal for Irene and her Aunt Minnie and Uncle Alick. He arrived at the appointed hour with a large fish wrapped in a newspaper. The servants took it and prepared the family meal. Irene remembered with a twinkle in her eye that at that time fishmongers would hand their customers fish wrapped in newspaper. To this day she isn't certain whether Hemingway actually caught their dinner or bought it.

The two friends drifted apart after that summer. Hemingway married Hadley Richardson at nearby Horton Bay on September 3, 1921. The following year, Irene married Joe Gordon. It wasn't until July 1949 that the two saw each other again in Petoskey. Now divorced and the mother of two daughters, Irene was about to celebrate her fiftieth birthday and invited her friend, by then a famous writer, to join the festivities. Without any advance notice Hemingway showed up at the family store and literally swept her off her feet. Putting her down, he kissed her on the lips. He attended the party held at the Perry Hotel and later sent her a letter of admiration, which she has framed and hung on her wall. The letter, dated September 1, 1949, was sent from Cuba. I asked her how she responded to this letter, and Irene replied, "I never wrote him back. You don't think that's why he committed suicide, do you?"

If you don't have the good fortune to meet Irene in person as I did, you can make her acquaintance in the pages of *Harps upon the Willows*, a book of short stories by Patrick Posey Garrett.

Hemingway's Boarding House

(Now a private home)
602 State Street
Petoskey, MI 49770

Petoskey Public Library

451 East Mitchell
Petoskey, MI 49770
(616) 347-4211
(616) 347-3429 Fax

Who: Rex F. Miller, director

When: 10:00 A.M.–8:00 P.M. Monday through Wednesday, 10:00 A.M.–6:00 P.M. Thursday, 10:00 A.M.–5:00 P.M. Friday, 9:30 A.M.–3:00 P.M. Saturday, closed on Sunday.

How Much: Free

Senior Citizen Discount: NA

Wheelchair Access: Yes

Directions: Take U.S. 31 north to downtown Petoskey. Turn east on Mitchell Street. The library is on the north side of Mitchell at the east end of the business district.

Park Garden Cafe

(An Ernest Hemingway haunt)
432 East Lake Street
Petoskey, MI 49770
(616) 347-0101
Open every day at 11:30 A.M.

Stafford's Perry Hotel

(Headquarters of the Michigan Hemingway Society's October Weekend)
Bay and Lewis Streets
Petoskey, MI 49770
(616) 347-4000; (800) 456-1917

Hemingway Festival

Who: Audrey Collins-McMullen
(616) 348-8518; (616) 348-8518
Website: http://www.freeway.net/community/civic/hemingway

When: October

How Much: There is a fee, but amount varies from year to year.

Little Traverse Historical Society, Inc.

100 Depot Court (Waterfront)
Petoskey, MI 49770
(616) 347-2620

Who: Candace Eaton

When: 10:00 A.M.–4:00 P.M. Monday through Saturday from May 1 through November 1

How Much: $1; children under 12 free

Senior Citizen Discount: No

Wheelchair Access: Limited

Directions: Museum is located in the 1892 depot situated on the shores of Little Traverse Bay in front of the Petoskey Marina. It is directly opposite the Gaslight Shopping District.

Petoskey Regional Chamber of Commerce

401 East Mitchell Street
Petoskey, MI 49770
(616) 347-4150
(616) 348-1810 Fax

The Gingerbread House

1130 Bluff
P.O. Box 1273
Bay View, MI 49770
(616) 347-3538

The Gingerbread House lives up to its name. One of its guests even suggested that the inn "should be under a Christmas tree." The entire town of Bay View resembles a gingerbread village because it contains 400 Victorian cottages from the late nineteenth century. As a matter of fact, the town of Bay View, which has all the charm and grace of a simpler era, is a National Historic Landmark. It is little changed in appearance since Ernest Hemingway lived in this area.

Bay View has developed a tradition of hospitality, beginning with its early days as a Chautauqua. The community, which looks like yesterday's Main Street, continues to offer intellectual, cultural, and recreational events for its summer residents. A stroll through the peaceful streets is often accompanied by the sound of music as students practice under the guidance of skilled instructors. Music is heard more formally during the Bay View Music Festival concerts, which draw thousands over the course of the summer.

Mary Gruler, your hostess, has the perfect personality for an innkeeper—she's friendly, helpful, charming, and makes you feel right at home. "I love this job," she tells me as we rock on the white wicker rockers on the front porch. "I worked for years as a nurse and this job is so much more fun. The people that I see everyday in my inn are happy and healthy." After refilling our glasses of lemonade, she continued, "People arrive here so stressed, but by the time they leave, they are nice and relaxed. Which is why my job is filled with warm fuzzies and is so rewarding."

Mary and her sister, Margaret Perry, started the B&B as a retirement project in 1988. "We were both widows and needed something to do." When I pointed out that running a country inn is hardly retirement, Mary laughed and said, "Compared to nursing this is retirement. I love tending my flowers, cooking for my guests, and just making sure everyone has a good time."

Her flowers are lovely and her breakfasts of freshly baked breads or muffins, fresh fruit topped with yogurt and granola, juice and coffee are guaranteed to get your day off to a good start. An extra treat for guests is free concert or lecture tickets to the Bay View Association.

The guest rooms are gingerbready and comfortable. The Victoria Suite is a favorite choice for special occasions like honeymoons. An English rose garden adorns the walls of this spacious suite, and French doors invite you to enjoy the beauty of Little Traverse Bay from your own private balcony. Other features are a king-size bed, private entrance, and bath with shower.

Whether you decide to gaze at the famous Bay View sunsets or curl up with your favorite Ernest Hemingway novel, you will enjoy your stay at the Gingerbread House. If you forget to bring along Hemingway novels, head for Petoskey and the McLean and Eakin Booksellers, at 307 East Lake Street. It is a wonderful and well-stocked bookstore.

Rates: $80–$120
Credit Cards Accepted: Visa, MC
Number of Guest Rooms: 4
Number of Baths: 4
Wheelchair Access: No

Pets: No
Children: Yes
Smoking: No
Senior Citizen Discount: No
Directions: See brochure

Stafford's Bay View Inn

613 Woodland Avenue
Petoskey, MI 49770
(616) 347-2771; (800) 456-1917; (800) 258-1886

Stafford's Bay View Inn. Photo courtesy of Stafford's Bay View Inn.

Every year, no matter where my travels take me, I always spend part of my summer up north, and I never miss a visit to the Bay View Inn, usually for its famous Sunday brunch. It doesn't take insider status to know about this wonderful Sunday pastime. It is a tradition for cottage dwellers and tourists alike. *Michigan Living* voted the brunch a readers' favorite. What's so special about this brunch? Well, it could be the northern Michigan tomato pudding, the classic eggs Benedict, or the 30-some other tasty dishes offered at the buffet. Maybe it's the lavish table of inn-baked pastries or the beautiful linen, china, flowers, silver, or staff adorned in period costumes. Perhaps it is the way the chef pours the freshly stirred batter into the old-fashioned double waffle irons.

After brunch you might want to sit by the cozy fire in the lobby or enjoy a game of chess or skittles. Lawn croquet is available, or perhaps you would like to ride your bike through historic Bay View or go for a walk along the lakeshore. Take advantage of one of the country's few remaining active Chautauquas. Summer programs include travelogues, concerts, recitals, and theatrical productions.

Or you might want to just curl up in your room with Hemingway's *The Nick Adams Stories*—so many are set in the Petoskey and Harbor Springs area. The rooms still feature period furniture that you might have found in your great-grandmother's house, except you'll be glad to know the Bay View Inn has indoor plumbing and air conditioning. The newer suites feature whirlpool tubs and sitting rooms with fireplaces and incredible views of Little Traverse Bay.

My favorite thing to do in the North Country is nothing. I like to sit on the front-porch rocker and just let the rest of the world go by. The Bay View Inn, judged by Uncle Ben's Rice Company as one of the "Ten Best Inns" in the nation, knows how to help people relax. So kick back. Forget your fax, your e-mail, and throw your beeper in Lake Michigan.

Rates: $79–$218
Credit Cards Accepted: Visa, MC, AMEX
Number of Guest Rooms: 31
Number of Baths: 31
Wheelchair Access: Yes

Pets: No
Children: Yes
Smoking: No
Senior Citizen Discount: No
Directions: See brochure

Kimberly Country Estate

2287 Bester Road
Harbor Springs, MI 49740
(616) 526-7646; (616) 526-9502

It's obvious upon first entering Kimberly Country Estate that a skilled interior designer has been at work. Everything is beautifully appointed, and it's easy to see why this bed and breakfast was chosen as one of *Country Inns* magazine's top 12 inns of 1993. I was not surprised to discover that innkeeper Ron Serba is a well-known Michigan interior designer. This inn is certainly a good advertisement for his business.

The inn is named after Billie Serba's daughter, Kimberly. Now an adult and working as a forester, Kimberly has been the inspiration for many of the Serbas' businesses. Ron and Billie met in Detroit in the fifties, and their meeting almost seems like the plot from an old-fashioned Broadway play: Sweet ingenue from a small Michigan town goes to the big city, meets the man of her dreams at a department store. They marry, waltz into the sunset, and live happily ever after. Fade out.

They lived in Detroit, but every summer the Serba family would vacation in Harbor Springs. In 1982, after their second son, Kelly, finished high school, they decided "to run away up North." They opened a gift shop named—what else?—Kimberly's Nest and eventually decided to go into the innkeeping business.

The Serbas redecorated every room and the results are stunning. Each bedroom has its own special personality and design. Some have canopy beds; others have sitting areas and fireplaces. There is also a romantic suite with a Jacuzzi, canopy bed, and fireplace. A deluxe continental breakfast often features Michigan fruits and berries, and in the late afternoon you may join your hosts for wine and hors d'oeuvres.

Golf is king in the Midwest, and Michigan is no exception. This gracious home with veranda and terraces overlooks the Wequetonsing golf course. If swimming is more your sport, there is an inviting large pool in the backyard.

Kimberly Estates fits our literary theme perfectly, because each August the Serbas host the Gatsby Summer Affair, featuring champagne, cocktails, elegant appetizers, and roaring twenties jazz. This event, inspired by F. Scott Fitzgerald's classic novel, is a benefit for Holy Childhood Developmental Day Care.

Rates: $135–$225; ask about the rate reduction for three-night stays during January through May
Credit Cards Accepted: Visa, MC, AMEX
Number of Guest Rooms: 6
Number of Baths: 6

Wheelchair Access: No
Pets: No
Children: No
Smoking: No
Senior Citizen Discount: No
Directions: See brochure

MINNESOTA

―•―⋝◆⋜―•―

The Sinclair Lewis Foundation

Highway 71 and I-94 south
P.O. Box 222
Sauk Centre, MN 56378
(320) 352-5201

Who: Chamber of Commerce

When: Memorial Day through Labor Day, 8:30 A.M.–5:00 P.M. Monday through Friday, 9:00 A.M.–5:00 P.M. Saturday and Sunday; Labor Day through Memorial Day 8:30 A.M.–4:30 P.M. Monday through Friday

How Much: Donations gladly accepted

Senior Citizen Discount: NA

Wheelchair Access: Yes

Directions: Brochure includes maps for Sinclair's boyhood home and the Sinclair Lewis Foundation

What and Where: Harry Sinclair Lewis, America's first winner of the Nobel Prize in Literature, had a strange but strong attachment to his Sauk Centre, Minnesota, hometown. His novel *Main Street* offered a scathing indictment of the small-town life, yet he chose to permanently rest in his family's plot in the local Greenwood Cemetery. Following his lonely death in Rome in 1951, his ashes rest here.

Sauk Centre, a tiny prairie hamlet, displayed a similar attachment to its celebrated native son. After the 1920 publication of *Main Street,* which satirized Gopher Prairie, a thinly veiled Sauk Centre, residents were appalled at how Lewis had depicted them: "In all the town not one building save the Ionic bank which gave pleasure to Carol's eyes; not a dozen buildings which suggested that, in the fifty years of Gopher Prairie's existence, the citizens had realized that it was either desirable or possible to make this, their common home, amusing or attractive."

Today, however, Sauk Centre treasures Lewis, who is credited with introducing a new realism that swept American literature and art following the First World War. Not much has changed in the town that declared itself the country's butter capital in the 1940s, except that Lewis's influence crops up everywhere. There's a Main Street Theater and Main Street Cafe, a Main Street Drugs, which stocks Lewis paperbacks, a Sinclair Lewis Park, and a Sinclair Lewis Avenue.

The Sinclair Lewis Foundation operates the Sinclair Lewis Interpretative Center, which serves as a local history museum and a repository for Lewis's works and memorabilia. Lewis was born in 1885 in a house directly across the street from his boyhood home. The foundation owns his birthplace, which is not open to the public. In the early 1960s the foundation bought the house in which the author grew up and restored it to its original appearance during his occupancy there from 1889 to 1926. You can visit this home, which sits three and a half blocks west of the traffic signals at Sinclair Lewis Avenue. Half-hour guided tours of this turn-of-the-century gray clapboard house usher you into Lewis's unhappy life as the youngest of three sons of a stern and undemonstrative father, Dr. E. J. Lewis. "There was no dignity in it nor any hope of greatness," he once wrote. "It was not a place to live in, not possibly, not conceivably."

In its heyday, the cluttered house contained the newest household conveniences—steam heating and one of the earliest radios, a gift from Lewis to his father. The family's furnishings and clothing displayed here include the narrow wooden bed Lewis slept in as a boy and pictures of his mother, Emma, who died of tuberculosis when Lewis was six. The carriage house contains a small loft where Lewis often hid as a boy and later visited to write journal entries and short stories.

Lewis's boyhood home is on the National Register of Historic Places and is open from Memorial Day weekend through Labor Day from 9:30 A.M. to 5:00 P.M. Monday through Saturday, and from 10:30 A.M. to 5:00 P.M. Sunday. It's also open for weekends in September and by appointment from October through May.

At the Sinclair Lewis Museum, located in the Interpretative Center, at U.S. Highway 71 and I-94, you can see all sorts of photos and samples of Lewis's writing. There's a complete signed set of the 23 novels he wrote, as well as explanations of how the author structured his novels.

The Palmer House Hotel and Restaurant

228 Original Main Street
Sauk Centre, MN 56378
(320) 352-3431; (320) 352-5602

The Palmer House remains a first-class hotel that exhibits the beauty created by its original owner, Richard Palmer, who built the hotel in 1901. The 22 rooms retain an old-style charm with modern comforts, including Jacuzzis in some of the chambers. Each nonsmoking room has a private bathroom with shower. The hotel's spacious lobby provides a perfect place to sit and reacquaint yourself with Sinclair Lewis's classic novel *Main Street*, or to enjoy listening to music from the pianist at the baby grand. There's also an exercise room, a pub, and a full restaurant open seven days a week that serves breakfast, lunch, and dinner.

Lewis once worked as a night clerk at the Palmer House Hotel and Restaurant, which he called the Minniemashie House in *Main Street*. This stately hotel, listed on the National Historic Register, sits on the corner of Main Street and Sinclair Lewis Avenue. If you choose a room above Main Street, you can sit and imagine the life Sinclair witnessed on the streets below and documented with wit and insight in his work.

Rates: $59–$120
Credit Cards Accepted: Visa, MC, AMEX, Discover
Number of Guest Rooms: 22
Number of Baths: 22
Wheelchair Access: No

Pets: No
Children: Yes
Smoking: In designated areas
Senior Citizen Discount: No
Directions: The manager says, "If they can't find us at the only stop light in the town, then they're in real trouble."

MISSISSIPPI

—— ❧ ——

Rowan Oak: Home of William Faulkner

c/o University of Mississippi
Old Taylor Road
University, MS 38677
(601) 234-3284

Who: Cynthia Shearer, curator

When: 10:00 A.M.–12:00 noon and 2:00–4:00 P.M. Tuesday through Saturday, 2:00–4:00 P.M. Sunday, closed Monday and major holidays

How Much: Free

Senior Citizen Discount: NA

Wheelchair Access: Yes, call ahead

Directions: Stop at the information center on the Oxford Square for complete directions.

What and Where: William Faulkner's array of works steeped in folklore, mystery, and centuries of traditions capture the rich, tragic story of the South. A visit to Oxford, Mississippi—where Faulkner lived most of his life—is almost like entering the pages of one of his novels, which he often peopled with characters based on his neighbors. Yoknapatawpha County, the fictional setting of many of Faulkner's works, comes alive the moment you step into the thriving southern town of Oxford.

Start with a journey out Old Taylor Road to Rowan Oak, Faulkner's home from 1930 until his death in 1962. Shaded by tall cedar trees, this stately Greek Revival house predates the Civil War and has a history that fascinated Faulkner, who named it after the legend of the rowan tree from Sir James Frazer's *The Golden Bough:* Scottish peasants sought to keep away evil spirits and establish privacy and peace by placing a cross made of rowan wood over their doorways. Faulkner thought of his house as a sanctuary, especially after achieving enormous fame. He wrote many of his novels and stories here and, with his wife, Estelle, raised her two children and their own daughter, Jill.

Visit the library where Faulkner did much of his writing, with shelves of books arranged the way Faulkner left them. In 1950 he added an office that still contains the plot outline of *A Fable* that Faulkner wrote on the wall using a graphite pencil and a carpenter's red grease pencil. Most likely the storyboard method he picked up writing screenplays in Hollywood inspired him to work on his novels in the same fashion. His old Underwood portable typewriter still sits on a small table near the window, and a fold-top desk he made contains a bottle of horse liniment, a carpenter's pencil, and a bottle of ink.

Faulkner reportedly was in the kitchen when he answered the telephone in 1949 to hear that he'd received the Nobel Prize in literature. Across the hall is the parlor, where his daughter's wedding and his own funeral took place. But it's not hard to believe in Faulkner's presence in the house, for upstairs his bedroom still contains a pair of mud-caked boat shoes and folded clothes in drawers.

A stroll around the 32-acre grounds leads to the house's original garden, with a magnolia tree in its center, and to Faulkner's rose garden with its wisteria. The property also contains a cook's house and the original kitchen, which Faulkner converted into a smokehouse where he cured his own sausage, ham, and bacon.

Rowan Oak now belongs to the University of Mississippi, which maintains it as a literary landmark.

In Oxford's town square, stop by Jennie's Hallmark Shop at 102 South Lamar, originally the city hall and federal court building. Faulkner recast the building as a law office for the character Gavin Stevens in the novel *Intruder in the Dust*. The former site of the Lyric Theatre (1006 Van Buren Avenue) sits just down the street, where a film based on *Intruder in the Dust* premiered in 1949. The movie was filmed in Oxford and used local homes and businesses as settings.

Duvall's (103 Courthouse Square) is the former site of the First National Bank, founded in 1910 by Colonel J. W. T. Faulkner. William Faulkner briefly worked as a bookkeeper here and later dubbed the building the "Sartoris Bank" in the novels *Intruder in the Dust* and *The Unvanquished*.

Just a few blocks from Oxford's city hall lies St. Peter's Cemetery, where Faulkner's grave draws thousands of visitors annually.

Diehard Faulkner fans also come to Oxford each year for a week-long Faulkner Conference that is known throughout the world. They come to discuss such topics as "Faulkner and Gender" or "Faulkner and Cultural Context" with flocks of Faulkner scholars.

Faulkner has been studied more than any other author in the world, so it's appropriate that the library at the University of Mississippi houses an impressive collection of this author's works. Although Faulkner attended Ole Miss, he never graduated. (He never finished high school either, and most of his education came through extensive reading.) But he occasionally presented the library with his own books.

One of the library's greatest treasures is the "Rowan Oak Papers," an 1,800-page manuscript discovered in a broom closet in Faulkner's house. The papers contain written and typed drafts of poems, short stories, novels, and film scripts written between 1925 and 1939. Pages from the "Rowan Oak Papers" often are displayed in the exhibition room of the John Davis Williams Library.

The Faulkner Collection is housed in the John Davis Williams Library Archives and Special Collections at the University of Mississippi: (601) 232-7408. The collection is open when classes are in session from 8:30 A.M. to 5:00 P.M. Monday through Friday. It is closed weekends.

The Faulkner Conference, hosted by the University of Mississippi, is held during the first week of August each year. For information, contact the Center for Study of Southern Culture, University, MS 38677; (601) 232-5993.

Puddin Place Bed & Breakfast

1008 University Avenue
Oxford, MS 38655
(601) 234-1250

Puddin Place Bed and Breakfast. Photo courtesy of Puddin Place Bed and Breakfast.

Only in the South would we hear of an inn that was a sweet "puddin' of a place." And how accurate and complimentary a comment it is. This hundred-year-old sparkling white clapboard home, with its porch swing, dormer, and bay window, is a setting right out of Faulkner. The screen doors, rockers, and ceiling fans remind us of a more leisurely time. There's a lot to be said for modern plumbing and other amenities, however, as Puddin Place owner Ann Turbow is well aware. Both her accommodations are spacious suites with fireplaces, private baths, and antique furnishings. Breakfast is a movable feast, especially when it can be served on the screened-in back porch. For all its fame, the city of Oxford is still a town in which to ramble, and visitors to Puddin Place will find it equally convenient to historic sights and contemporary enterprises. Y'all come!

Rates: $85
Credit Cards Accepted: None
Number of Guest Rooms: 2
Number of Baths: 2
Wheelchair Access: No

Pets: No
Children: Yes
Smoking: No
Senior Citizen Discount: No
Directions: From Highway 6 take the Lamar-Downtown exit. Go left on Lamar to University Avenue. Take another left to 1008 University.

MISSOURI

—+ ⫸⫷ +—

Eugene Field House and Toy Museum

634 South Broadway
St. Louis, MO 63102
(314) 421-4689

Who: Frances Kerber Walrond

When: Open 10:00 A.M.–4:00 P.M. Wednesday–Saturday, 12:00 noon–4:00 P.M. Sunday. Closed Monday, Tuesday and national holidays. Open January and February by appointment only.

How Much: Adults $3, youths ages 12 to 18 $2; children under 12 $.50; special rates for groups by reservation

Senior Citizen Discount: No

Wheelchair Access: No

Directions: One and a half blocks from Bush Memorial Stadium at the corner of Cerre and Broadway. Free parking behind house.

What and Where: St. Louis schoolchildren broke their piggy banks to rescue the boyhood home of "The Children's Poet" from the wrecking ball. Although other houses in Walsh's Row were demolished in the 1930s, Eugene Field's birthplace was spared the ignominious fate of becoming a parking-lot site, thanks to the kids who loved him.

For most of his short life (1850–1895) Eugene Field earned his daily bread as a newspaperman. But he fed his soul on poetry. For more than a century, boys and girls have voyaged with Wynken, Blynken, and Nod in a wooden shoe, "on a river of crystal light into a sea of dew." They have giggled at the epic battle between the gingham dog and the calico cat (as told by the old Dutch clock and the Chinese plate). "And, oh! how the gingham and calico flew!"

The father of eight, Field would have been tickled to know his boyhood home is a museum of childhood. There is a large display of toys for children of all ages, including a large doll collection and Field's own toy collection. In imagination, the grown-up visitor is a child again, a cowboy on a wooden rocking horse, an engineer on a little tin train, or the hostess at a formal tea attended by china dolls in their Sunday best.

The Lemp Mansion, Restaurant, and Inn

3322 De Menil Place
St. Louis, MO 63118
(314) 664-8024; (314) 664-8027

In 1904, St. Louis proudly hosted both the Olympics and the World's Fair. Everybody was singing, "Meet me in St. Louie, Louie. Meet me at the Fair." That same year, beer baron William Lemp renovated his elegant home in South St. Louis from top to bottom—literally. Built during the 1860s, the three-story mansion boasted an elevator, an aviary, and underground caverns containing an auditorium, a ballroom, and a swimming pool!

John Adam Lemp, a German immigrant, originally sought his American fortune as a St. Louis grocer. But his store soon became known as the home of lager beer. Lemp had learned the art of brewing from his father in Eschwege, Germany, and the natural cave system under St. Louis provided the perfect temperature for aging beer. The rest, as they say, is brewing history. John Adam Lemp died a millionaire, and the brewery he bequeathed to his son was the largest in St. Louis. In 1897, two of the brewing industry's titans toasted each other when William Lemp's daughter, Hilda, married Gustav Pabst of the noted Milwaukee brewing family.

But Prohibition smashed the brewer's trade. The Lemp brewery, which was once worth $7,000,000, sold for a paltry half-million.

The brewer's house itself is haunted by tragedy. William Lemp's son died mysteriously in 1901, and Lemp shot himself three years later—the same year his magnificent house was finished. His daughter and two other sons were also victims of suicide. Surprisingly, the surviving son, heir to a house of bitter memories, died a natural death at the age of ninety. No wonder St. Louisians say the house is haunted!

But rest assured that only happy times await you at the Lemp Mansion today. The huge kitchen that once served the elite of St. Louis has been completely modernized and is ready to offer you lunch or dinner. The restaurant is open seven days a week. In keeping with midwestern tradition, beef is the *specialite de maison,* particularly prime rib and beef Wellington.

The mansion is conveniently located ten minutes from downtown St. Louis and only five minutes from the Eugene Field House. Every room in the mansion is decorated with period furniture reflecting the late Victorian era. In the sumptuous luxury of the Lavender Suite, you can feel like a St. Louis beer baron. The Lavender Suite is the master suite and includes not only a bedroom and a private bath but also a dining room. And the bathroom, by the way, features a marble and cast iron fireplace!

Reading all this brewery history may make you thirsty for a cold one. Alas, the Lemp Brewing Company is no more, but while you're in South St. Louis you can tour Anheuser-Busch, the world's largest brewery (I-55 and Arsenal Street, 314-577-2626). The tour includes free beer and a look at the stables that are home to the famous Clydesdale horses.

If you want a snack to go with the suds, stop by the Soulard Market, the country's oldest open-air market (Seventh Street exit off I-55, 314-781-7272). In 1850, when Eugene Field was a babe in arms, the market had already been in business for eight years.

There's plenty to see in St. Louis, but the most famous is the Gateway Arch, the country's tallest monument. You can ride the tram to the top of the arch for a bird's-eye view of the city from 1,630 feet above the mighty Mississippi. Visit the old downtown courthouse, a gem of the Classic Revival style, where Eugene Field's father argued unsuccessfully for Dred Scott's freedom in a case that helped to spark the Civil War.

Rates: $85–$157.50
Credit Cards Accepted: Visa, MC, AMEX, Discover, Diners Club, Carte Blanche
Number of Guest Rooms: 4
Number of Baths: 2
Wheelchair Access: No

Pets: No
Children: Yes
Smoking: No
Senior Citizen Discount: No
Directions: See brochure

Mark Twain Boyhood Home and Museum

208 Hill Street
Hannibal, MO 63401
(573) 221-9010

Who: Ila Woolen

When: November through February 10:00 A.M.–4:00 P.M. Monday through Saturday, noon–4:00 P.M. on Sunday; March 9:00 A.M.–4:00 P.M. Monday through Saturday, noon–4:00 P.M. on Sunday; April 9:00 A.M.–5:00 P.M. daily; May 8:00 A.M.–5:00 P.M. daily; June through August 8:00 A.M.–6:00 P.M. daily; September through October 8:00 A.M.–5:00 P.M. daily. Closed Thanksgiving, Christmas, and New Year's Day.

How Much: $5 for adults, $2 for juniors ages 6 to 12

Senior Citizen Discount: No

Wheelchair Access: Yes

Directions: See brochure

What and Where: "All that goes to make the me in me is a small Missouri village on the other side of the globe," Mark Twain once said while on a speaking tour in India.

That small Missouri village is Hannibal, a river town on the mighty Mississippi. When Mark Twain (Samuel Langhorne Clemens) wrote about the town of Tom Sawyer and Huckleberry Finn, he was writing about the town where he spent the impressionable years of his childhood. His home in Hannibal is a simple white-frame two-story house. The fence was surely the fence Twain thought of when he had Tom Sawyer convince the neighborhood boys that they should pay him for the privilege of whitewashing it.

Across the street, is the J. M. Clemens Law Office, where Mark Twain's father presided as the justice of the peace. Twain had the courtroom there clearly in his mind when he wrote about the trial of Muff Potter in Tom Sawyer.

On that same street, The Becky Thatcher House is really the home of Laura Hawkins. Laura was the sweetheart of young Sam Clemens. Years later, the memory of Laura helped create the character of Tom Sawyer's Becky Thatcher.

A few miles out of town is the Mark Twain Cave, where, in an intricate network of underground passageways, Tom and Becky had their run-in with Injun Joe.

Like Huckleberry Finn, Samuel Clemens left Hannibal, piloting riverboats between St. Louis and New Orleans for several years. He took his pen name, Mark Twain, from the river. "Mark Twain" is river slang meaning "two fathoms deep."

Fifth Street Mansion

213 South Fifth Street
Hannibal, MO 63401
(573) 221-0445; (800) 874-5661
(573) 221-3335 FAX

This house is a part of "Millionaire's Row," an impressive block of grand homes owned by some of Hannibal's wealthiest and most influential citizens. It was built in 1858 by

Brison Stilwell, three-term mayor of the city. After the Civil War the mansion became the townhouse of John and Helen Garth, schoolmates of young Sam Clemens, with whom they remained lifelong friends. Clemens, when famous as Mark Twain, dined here with his hosts and Laura Hawkins Frazer (Becky Thatcher) on his last visit to Hannibal in 1902. The Italianate architecture mimics country villas with its extended roof eaves, slender floor-to-ceiling windows to catch the summer breezes, and a rooftop cupola to provide a view of the town and the Mississippi River. A striking interior feature is the six-foot-by-eight-foot Tiffany window showcasing the front staircase landing. Eight fireplaces display imported ceramic tiles, and, happily, the original chandeliers and brass gasoliers are still in place. Two parlors, a library, and wraparound porches provide modern guests the space to converse with friends or to be alone. An added treat for many who stay here is a series of Mystery Weekends at the mansion, with a welcoming reception, two nights' lodging, candlelight dinners, and a murder to be solved!

Rates: $65–$95
Credit Cards Accepted: Visa, MC, AMEX, Discover
Number of Guest Rooms: 7
Number of Baths: 7
Wheelchair Access: No

Pets: No
Children: No
Smoking: No
Senior Citizen Discount: No
Directions: See brochure

Lula Belle's

111 Bird Street
Hannibal, MO 63401
(573) 221-6662; (800) 882-4890

Now this, for me, is a first. I have written about buildings with interesting former lives, such as barns, mansions, mills, and even summer kiddie camps, but never has a house built as a bordello crossed my experienced pen—until now. The house at 111 Bird Street was built in 1917 by Sarah Smith, an enterprising madam from Chicago. Her business flourished for over 20 years in the heyday of Prohibition, gambling, and freewheeling ambition. When Sarah died in 1932, Bessie Hoelscher continued the household tradition, redid the interior in a Spanish motif, and reportedly maintained strict privacy for the businessmen, railroaders, and riverboatmen who were her clientele. In the 1950s, police raids and church campaigners finally shut down the "establishment."

In its present reincarnation Lula Belle's is a staid and respectable inn and restaurant. The seven-room B&B features queen-size beds and a view of the Mississippi River. Heart-shaped whirlpool bathtubs and a dearth of closets may be the only hints to its original use. How could any traveler resist such a tempting look into the past!

Rates: $45–$80
Credit Cards Accepted: Visa, MC, AMEX, Discover
Number of Guest Rooms: 7
Number of Baths: 7
Wheelchair Access: No

Pets: Yes
Children: Yes
Smoking: Yes
Senior Citizen Discount: No
Directions: See brochure

Garth Woodside Mansion

RR 3, Box 578
Hannibal, MO 63401
(573) 221-2789
Website: http://hanmo.com/twanweb/garth/garth.html

"I spent many nights with John and Helen Garth in their spacious, beautiful home," Mark Twain wrote to his wife in an 1882 letter. "They were children with me, and schoolmates." Because of its many direct ties to America's favorite humorist, coupled with the stunning mansion on its 39 acres of manicured property, it is almost impossible to describe Garth Woodside Mansion in a thumbnail sketch. As did Twain in his short story, "His Grandfather's Old Ram," one is tempted to digress into gossip and bits of amusing history. Unlike many of the "grand old ladies," the provenance of this house is a happy one; it progressed from private home to museum to inn with barely a hitch, no ugly remodelings or modernization, and it survived the twentieth century with its furnishings as well as its famed "flying staircase" intact.

In 1987 Irv and Diana Feinberg purchased the property. With sensitivity and care, wallpapers, upholstery, and unglued furniture were restored; the result is an inn designated one of the ten best in the entire Midwest. Eight bedrooms are filled with pictures, period clothing, antimacassars, swags,

The Garth Woodside Mansion. Photo courtesy of the Garth Woodside Mansion.

canopies, and the general bric-a-brac characteristic of a Victorian home of wealth and reputation. Breakfast is a splendid repast in keeping with the elegant surroundings. Fruit cup with lemon cream sauce, quiche cups, caramel rolls—the menu reads more like an aria than a list of foodstuffs! Bedtime puts the finishing touches on the mood, when guests find old-fashioned nightshirts for their use spread at the feet of their beds. How could anyone have anything but sweet dreams in such a setting?

Rates: $65–$106
Credit Cards Accepted: Visa, MC
Number of Guest Rooms: 8
Number of Baths: 8
Wheelchair Access: No

Pets: No
Children: If older than 12
Smoking: On balcony or veranda
Senior Citizen Discount: No
Directions: See brochure

Laura Ingalls Wilder–Rose Wilder Lane Museum and Home

3068 Highway A
Mansfield, MO 65704
(417) 924-3626

Who: Front desk

When: March 1 to November 1, 9:00 A.M.–5:00 P.M. Monday through Saturday, 12:30 P.M.–5:30 P.M. on Sunday; October 16 to November 15, 9:00 A.M.–4:00 P.M. Monday through Saturday, 12:30–4:30 P.M. Sunday. Closed Easter.

How Much: $5 for adults, $3 for juniors ages 6 to 18; free for children under 6

Senior Citizen Discount: $4 for 65 and older

Wheelchair Access: Yes

Directions: 1.25 miles east of Town Square on Highway A

What and Where: Laura Ingalls Wilder's home is as she left it carefully preserved in 1957. Next to the historic Wilder home is the Laura Ingalls Wilder–Rose Wilder Lane Museum. The museum exhibits include artifacts spanning more than a century of the pioneering history described in the *Little House* books. The Little House Bookstore, next to the museum, features a full stock of Wilder books, souvenirs, gifts, and educational materials.

Other points of interest in Mansfield are the bronze bust of Laura on the Mansfield Square; the Laura Ingalls Wilder Public Library; and the Mansfield Cemetery, where Laura, Almanzo, and Rose are buried in the center section.

Mansfield's Laura Ingalls Wilder Festival is held the third weekend in September. The Ozark Mountain Players' "Little House Memories" outdoor pageant at Dogwood Valley Park on Highway A is held on the third and fourth weekend in August and the first and third weekends in September. Author's Day is held the Saturday closest to October 15.

AUTHOR'S NOTE: When I visited the home of the author of *Little House on the Prairie,* I suddenly was nine years old again, sitting in my little-girl bedroom reading about pioneer adventures. Though I am now grown, two wildly enthusiastic nine-year-old twins shared our tour of Laura Ingalls Wilder's house, and through them I relived the exciting days on the prairie.

The twins were oohing and aahing: "Look, this is where she sat. This is her real bed. This is where she wrote her books." As for me, I imagined her sitting at her desk in the writing room. I felt a sense of kinship with Wilder because, like me, she wrote at night. Unlike me, however, she had the luxury of a fainting couch next to her desk.

It was a thrill to see original manuscripts of *Little House in the Big Woods, Little House on the Prairie, On the Banks of Plum Creek,* and *By the Shores of Silver Lake.* Because of her excellent handwriting, the documents are easy to read. I was surprised to learn that Wilder didn't begin her writing career until she was in her sixties. When I visited the adjoining bookstore with shelf after shelf of her output, I was impressed with what a late bloomer she was. In reality, Wilder was only middle-aged at 60, because she lived to the ripe old age of 90. She died at her beloved Mansfield farm.

For *Little House* fans, the museum is a cornucopia of delights. Pa's fiddle, which was so important in the books, is prominently displayed. Other not-to-be-missed items include Laura's first school composition, her first teaching certificate, a gift book from Almanzo, who became Laura's husband, her sewing machine, and her trip diary. There are admiring letters from fans; sometimes Wilder received 50 fan letters a day. There are early pictures of Carrie, Mary, and Laura, the Ingalls girls who inspired the *Little House* series.

The museum features an entire section on Rose Wilder Lane, Laura's daughter, who, unbeknownst to me, was the second most highly paid writer of her day.

As we drove away from picturesque Mansfield, I thought of Wilder's description of her home in *On the Way Home* as the "Land of the Big Apple." In this diary of a trip from South Dakota to Mansfield, Wilder wrote, "Parts of Nebraska and Kansas are well enough but Missouri is simply glorious."

Walnut Street Inn

900 East Walnut
Springfield, MO 65806
(417) 864-6346
(417) 864-6184 Fax

Wake up to an Ozark breakfast of persimmon muffins and walnut bread with a piping hot beverage at the Walnut Street Inn. And wake up, too, to the beauty and history of the Springfield area, known as the Queen City of the Ozarks. Early settlers recognized the advantages of this location, among them grocery and wagon company owner Charles McCann. Prospering, McCann, built this home in 1894, and it is now one of the few remaining Victorian Gothic houses in the city. Twenty cast iron Corinthian columns surround the spacious inviting porch, and two of the original six fireplaces are still intact.

The 12 guest rooms, each with private bath, phone, and writing desk, are charmingly decorated and named for specific personalities—people who uniquely influenced the arts and the lifestyle of the community and of the nation. Almost all the owners of this stylish home have shared an interest in books, beginning with McCann, who was most influential in raising funds for the Springfield Public Library. It seems quite fitting, then, to include Missouri artists Rose

O'Neil and Thomas Hart Benton in the room names, and of course my favorite is the Wilder Room. Quaint and cozy with a queen-size bed, this room features handmade quilts, country flowers, a claw-foot tub, and a treetop balcony.

Gary, Nancy, and Karol Brown purchased the Walnut Street property in 1987, renovating extensively with the purpose in mind of opening a bed and breakfast, which, of course, means that guest service and accommodations are of primary importance. This attention to details shows in many ways, including the fact that, despite new plumbing and air conditioning, the rich history of the house is reflected in its style, spaciousness, and charm. This includes the renovated carriage house, which originally contained horse stalls and the carriage master's quarters. The three suites and rooms now boast four-poster feather beds, Jacuzzis, and fireplaces. Garden views and mature Missouri redbud trees are everywhere on this beautiful corner property, with rockers and a wicker swing to create for you the perfect picture of an Ozark holiday.

Rates: $84–$139
Credit Cards Accepted: Visa, MC, AMEX, Discover, Diners Club
Number of Guest Rooms: 12
Number of Baths: 12
Wheelchair Access: Yes

Pets: By prior arrangement
Children: Yes
Smoking: No
Senior Citizen Discount: No
Directions: See brochure

NEBRASKA

⸺ ⸱⸺ ⸱⸺

The Willa Cather State Historic Site

326 North Webster Street
Red Cloud, NE 68970
(402) 746-2653
(402) 746-2652 Fax

Who: Patricia K. Phillips, director

When: 8:00 A.M.–5:00 P.M. Monday through Saturday, 1:00–5:00 P.M. Sunday. Closed New Year's Day, Easter, Thanksgiving, and Christmas.

How Much: $1 for adults, $.25 for unaccompanied children

Senior Citizen Discount: No

Wheelchair Access: Some

Directions: From I-80, head south on Highway 281 (Hastings/Grand Island exit). Red Cloud is 60 miles south at the junction of Highways 136 and 281.

What and Where: In Red Cloud, Nebraska, sits a small, tree-shaded clapboard house that should be recognizable to fans of Pulitzer Prize–winning author Willa Cather. In 1884, at the age of nine, Cather moved here with her family from Virginia, and the wide open life of this prairie land figured greatly in her work.

Here's how she recalled her childhood home, at the corner of Third and Cedar Streets, in her poignant novel *The Song of the Lark*: "They turned into another street and saw before them lighted windows; a low story-and-a-half house, with a wing built on at the right and a kitchen addition at the back, everything a little on the slant— roofs, windows and doors."

Indeed, a visit to Red Cloud takes one completely into Cather's formative years, which shaped many of her novels and short stories. The little town is called Moonstone in *The Song of the Lark*, Black Hawk in *My Ántonia*, Hanover in *O Pioneers!*, and Frankfort in *One of Ours*, which won the Pulitzer Prize in 1922. Cather believed that one's early experiences leave the strongest imprints. It's no surprise, then, that many of her neighbors and friends from Red Cloud ended up in her books, as did the spirit of the vast Nebraska prairie.

Cather lived in Red Cloud only until 1890, when she left to attend the University of Nebraska in Lincoln and, finally, to settle back East. She died in New York in 1947, but the rich legacy she left in this tiny frontier town still resonates with the passion and admiration she felt for this land and its hard-working occupants.

Today, the Cather Childhood Home is a National Historic Landmark, part of a collection of buildings and archives overseen by the Willa Cather Historical Center and the Willa Cather Pioneer Memorial and Educational Foundation. Thanks to the efforts of these organizations, visitors can tour Red Cloud on foot or by car and take in the places that made up Cather's world.

Daily walking tours depart from the Cather Center, housed in the restored Farmers' and Merchants' Bank building (on Webster Street, two doors south of Fourth Avenue), which was built in 1889 by Silas Garber, former governor of Nebraska and the prototype for Captain Forrester in Cather's novel *A Lost Lady*. The building houses an impressive collection of more than 200 letters, nearly 2,000 photographs, and 400 books concerning Cather.

A visit to Cather's childhood is a highlight of the tour. Local guides read from Cather's descriptive writings that describe just about every room in the

Willa Cather. Photo courtesy of the WCPM Collection, Nebraska Sate Historical Society.

house she occupied along with her parents, six brothers and sisters, her maternal grandmother, and Marjorie Anderson, a domestic who came with the family from Virginia and inspired Mahailey in *One of Ours*.

The attic, which served as the children's dormitory, provides an intimate portrait of young Cather's life. As the oldest child, she had a separate room which still contains the red and brown rose-covered wallpaper she earned by working in Cook's Drugstore (on Webster Street, the second brick building from the corner of Webster and Fourth Avenue).

Other stops on this tour include sites relevant to Cather's life, especially those she recreated in *My Ántonia*, such as the restored nineteenth-century Burlington depot, one mile south of town on Seward Street, where Jim and the Shimerdas arrive. Across the street from Cather's house sits the Harling Home, which belonged to the J. L. Miner family. Miner served as the prototype for Mr. Harling in *My Ántonia*, and his family's house served as the model for the Harling's house, where Ántonia worked.

Other landmarks include the St. Juliana Catholic Church (on Third and Seward streets) where Ántonia was married, and the Grace Episcopal Church (Cedar Street and Sixth Avenue), which Cather joined in 1922.

You can hop in your car for the Catherland tour, a 50-mile route that covers many sites featured in Cather's writings. Included are visits to the Cloverton cemetery, where John and Anna Pavelka, the models for John Cuzak and Ántonia Shimerda, are buried. One mile south of the cemetery sits the Pavelka farmhouse, also featured in *My Ántonia*.

Five miles south of Red Cloud you'll find the Willa Cather Memorial Prairie, 610 acres of wilderness dedicated by The Nature Conservancy to Willa Cather. The wildflowers and shaggy grass show exactly what Cather meant when she described her beloved prairie as "the floor of the sky."

For serious scholars and casual readers alike, the Cather Foundation holds an annual conference the first weekend in May. Both the foundation and the Willa Cather

Historical Center also sponsor national seminars and workshops throughout the year.

Red Cloud still enjoys the church suppers, ballgames, Easter egg hunts, and fireman's ball that Cather knew as a girl. A visit to the town takes you into the heart of one of America's most beloved authors, who immortalized the courageous pioneers who settled on these plains.

The Willa Cather Memorial Foundation

326 North Webster Street
Red Cloud, NE 68970
(402) 746-2653
(406) 746-2652 Fax

Who: Patricia Phillips

When: The tours of the five restored buildings are given at 9:30 A.M., 11:00 A.M., 1:30 P.M., 2:45 P.M., and 4:00 P.M. The Foundation is open from 8:00 A.M.–5:00 P.M. Monday through Saturday and 1:00 P.M.–5:00 P.M. Sunday. Closed Christmas, New Year's Day, Easter, and Thanksgiving.

How Much: $1 per person for the tour, otherwise free

Senior Citizen Discount: No

Wheelchair Access: No

Directions: See brochure

The Kirschke House Bed and Breakfast

1124 West Third Street
Grand Island, NE 68801
(303) 381-6851; (800) 381-6951

Staying at the Kirschke House is like staying with a good friend or visiting your favorite neighbor. The owner, Lois Hank, is one of those friendly innkeepers who make you feel immediately at home. After breakfast we were chatting like old friends, and when she kissed me goodbye I felt as if I was leaving someone whom I had known for a very long time.

Lois loves being an innkeeper, and it shows. She likes to surprise her guests with special breakfasts; one of her favorite treats is the morning ice cream sundae. "Actually, it's frozen peach yogurt with fresh peaches,

but my guests all tell me it tastes like an ice cream sundae," Lois told me as we drank another cup of coffee on her pleasant porch in the early morning hours.

Opening her bed and breakfast has completely changed Lois's life. "When I opened a B&B, my whole life turned around. I thought I needed to travel to be happy. But I found instead that travelers came to me and that made me very happy indeed!"

The vine-covered two-story brick home features such architectural highlights as a windowed cupola, a turret, and stained glass windows over an open oak staircase. The vines and roses of the exterior are reflected in the guest rooms, which are accented with Victorian lace, period furnishings, and antique accessories. Masterfully blended into the Old World atmosphere of the house, the twentieth-century luxuries include a wooden hot tub in the lantern-lit brick washhouse.

David and I made the Roses Roses Room our home away from home after spending the day in Red Cloud at the Willa Cather house. With its cheerful wallpaper and pretty wicker furniture, it was a good choice. With both a canopy bed and a daybed, the room was perfect for sleeping, sitting, and reading. The romantic room seemed like the favorite little girl's room of my imagination. Even the shared bath proved no hardship.

The latest addition to the Kirschke House is the cottage guest house, a renovated carriage house located in the garden area behind the main house. With its private ve-randa off the loft bedroom, its claw-foot tub, fireplace, and queen four-poster bed, it's the perfect secluded hideway.

Whichever room you choose, save plenty of room for breakfast. Served on beautiful fine china, crystal, and silver, *petit déjeuner* is a treat. We were served French toast, ham, fresh peaches, juice, and coffee. If you give Lois some advance notice, you can make arrangments to have dinner or tea at Kirschke House.

Recently Lois took a partner and she couldn't have picked a better one, her own daughter, Kiffani Smith. Kiffani seems to have inheirited her mother's love of people and her zest for taking care of them. So, even though you have to drive at least an hour from Red Cloud to get here (the B&B in Red Cloud just closed!), it's worth the drive. The Kirschke House truly lives up to its motto, a quotation from Ralph Waldo Emerson: "The ornament of a house is the friends who frequent it."

Rates: $55–$155 (there is a discount for single occupancy)
Credit Cards Accepted: Visa, MC, AMEX, Discover
Number of Guest Rooms: 6
Number of Baths: 3
Wheelchair Access: Limited

Pets: No
Children: Yes
Smoking: No
Senior Citizen Discount: No
Directions: See brochure

New Hampshire

Robert Frost Farm National Historic Landmark

Route 28
P.O Box 1856
Concord, NH 03038
(603) 432-3091; (603) 271-3254

Who: Department of Recreation

When: The Robert Frost Farm is open from Memorial Day through Labor Day and there are three tours on each weekend day. Hours are subject to change, so call to determine what they are.

How Much: $2.50 adults, children under 18 free

Senior Citizen Discount: Free for New Hampshire residents older than 65

Wheelchair Access: Yes

Directions: Call for directions

What and Where: "Good fences make good neighbors," said Napoleon Guay. If you've never heard of farmer Guay, I know you have heard of his neighbor, Robert Frost. The little-known Guay was responsible for one of Frost's most famous poems. At spring mending time, Guay, who lived south of the Frost farm, always proposed a neighborly ritual of restoring the stone wall between his property and Frost's.

   The poet, his wife, Elinor, and daughter Lesley moved to the farm in Derry in 1900. Frost was a chicken farmer and teacher at nearby Pinkerton Academy (for the munificent sum of $200 a year), as well as a poet who wrote the "Mending Wall" and other favorites at home in the Granite State.

   But readers did not discover Frost until he sold the farm in 1911 and moved to England, where the collections *A Boy's Will* and *North of Boston* were published to loud huzzahs, none louder than Ezra Pound's. Pound championed the "Amur'kn" poet, thus assuring his success.

   Frost eventually returned to New Hampshire, but he never again lived at the Derry Farm. In his absence, the farmstead had become an unsightly auto graveyard. Lesley Frost Ballentine, the poet's daughter, later restored the farm to its turn-of-the-century condition. Furnishings that are not original were selected by Ms. Ballentine for being similar to those owned by the family. Several small paintings downstairs are the work of Mrs. Frost's sister, and the dishes in the dining room belonged to the Frost family.

   Today visitors can see the stone wall that the poet rebuilt with the help of farmer Guay, the remnants of an ancient orchard, and, south of the farm, Hyla Brook, its marsh brimming with cowslips, lady's slippers, and purple-fringed orchis.

"I must say the core of all my writing," Frost wrote, "was probably the five free years I had there on the farm down the road from Derry Village. The only thing we had plenty of was time and seclusion."

A delightful way to begin or end your sojourn to the Robert Frost Farm is to take a contemplative stroll on the half-mile Hyla Brook Nature/Poetry Trail, an old logging road that is directly related to elements in Frost's poetry, such as the mending wall and the brook itself. On this pleasant walk, you can get a sense of the naturalist poet, a man acutely sensitive to the delicate connection between humans and the land. The farm is the setting of 43 of Frost's poems, including "Bonfire" and "Ghost House." Walking around the grounds and the trail is a charming way to acquaint yourself with the poet's work while having a fling with nature yourself.

The Inn at Maplewood Farm

447 Center Road
P.O. Box 1478
Hillsborough, NH 03244
(604) 464-4242; (800) 644-6695

The Inn at Maplewood Farm. Photo by Arthur Boufford.

"Down the road" from Historic Hillsborough Center and less than an hour's drive from Derry, The Inn at Maplewood Farm is all a New England country inn should be and more. Built in 1794, the inn's white clapboard walls shelter a wide veranda where white wicker chairs invite the visitor to "sit a spell" before exploring the scenic Monadnock region of New Hampshire. Skiing, hiking up Mount Monadnock, and antiquing (the New Hampshire Antiques Show held every August in Manchester, is the state's largest) are only some of the many pleasures that have brought visitors to the Granite State since railroad excursions came into vogue at the turn of the century. And don't forget "leaf peeping" in the fall, when New England's emerald hills turn to topaz, gold, and ruby red.

But The Inn at Maplewood Farm is a destination in its own right. The innkeepers, Laura and Jayme Simoes, are fonts of knowledge about local history and are, in fact, the president and vice president of the local historical society. Laura, a lively, intelligent woman, told me that much of the history has a literary bent. "Last year David Watters, from the Department of English at the University of New Hampshire, spoke at the Hillsborough Historical Society Lecture Series and led a moving discussion of Frost's New Hampshire land poems."

As we were sipping wine one evening, Jayme, an amusing, professorial type, added to my literary knowledge of New Hampshire. "The Franklin Pierce Homestead is located here in Hillsborough, and Daniel Webster and Nathaniel Hawthorne were frequent visitors to this house." The Homestead is open for tours in the summer and fall.

"In addition," explained Jayme, adjusting his glasses, "Henry David Thoreau is well known in our area. Thoreau wrote a great deal about Mount Monadnock, just a half-hour south of us."

But literary history is just one of the passions of this young couple. Vintage radio shows are another interest the Simoeses happily share with their guests. And in no small way! It is the first bed and breakfast with its own radio station, where guests can regularly tune in to the sounds of the past. Radio Maplewood Farm offers regular evening pro-gramming of such shows as *Lights Out* and *The Lone Ranger*.

All this intense listening could work up an appetite, and you've come to the right place if you're hungry. Laura is an innovative chef and even gives cooking lectures around the state. Imagine these breakfast treats: poached pears, an assortment of fruit soups, vegetable strata with fresh salsa, Maplewood Farm corn pudding, and French toast with praline sauce.

Rates: $75–$115
Credit Cards Accepted: Visa, MC, AMEX, Discover
Number of Guest Rooms: 4
Number of Baths: 4
Wheelchair Access: No

Pets: No
Children: Yes
Smoking: No
Senior Citizen Discount: No
Directions: See brochure

New Jersey

—◦— ◄◆► —◦—

James Fenimore Cooper House

457 High Street
Burlington, NJ 08016
(609) 386-4773

Who: Burlington County Historical Society; front desk

When: 1:00–4:00 P.M. Monday through Thursday, 2:00–4:00 P.M. Sunday

How Much: $5

Senior Citizen Discount: No

Wheelchair Access: Yes, for the museum and the library

Directions: See brochure

What and Where: The historic city of Burlington, New Jersey is located on the Delaware River between Philadelphia and Trenton. It was here that John Fitch built the first steamboat some 21 years before Robert Fulton's commercially successful *Clermont*. Fitch, who inaugurated the first regularly scheduled steamboat service in the world in 1790, was a man ahead of his time. Fulton was later able to convince the world that steamboats were a practical mode of transportation; for this he received worldwide acclaim, whereas Fitch died penniless after suffering a long illness.

The legacy of water travel must have appealed to the citizenry of Burlington, for it was here that James Lawrence was born at 459 High Street in 1781. Commissioned in the U.S. Navy at the age of 21, he served in the war with Tripoli and in the War of 1812. As captain of the USS *Chesapeake,* he met the challenge of the British frigate *Shannon* on June 1, 1813. Although mortally wounded in the battle, he is famous for his command, "Don't give up the ship."

At 457 High Street in Burlington in 1789, James Fenimore Cooper was born to Quaker parents, William and Elizabeth Cooper. Although it is more commonly associated with the Otsego Lake region of New York state, the Cooper family's role in Burlington was significant. Cooper's father, and his partner, Robert Thomas, operated a store near the Friends' Meeting House on High Street in 1780 several years prior to James's birth. Following a four-year stay in Cooperstown in 1790, the family resettled in Burlington in 1794; shortly thereafter, William was elected to serve in the U.S. Congress.

As for James, his academic career was lackluster. He managed to get admitted to Yale but was expelled for disciplinary reasons two years later. Subsequently he joined the Navy and sailed aboard the USS *Wasp* with none other than Captain James Lawrence. This ocean experience obviously left its mark for, in addition to his *Leatherstocking*

Tales, Cooper wrote sea-adventure novels. Most noteworthy among these are *The Pilot, The Red Rover,* and *The Water-Witch.*

There are not many communities with populations of 10,000 or so that can boast such a rich heritage. When the Burlington County Historic Society was organized in 1915, its first major acquisition was the James Fenimore Cooper House in 1923. Although the Coopers never owned this 1780 building, they occupied it for several years. The four-room museum features Cooper memorabilia as well as objects belonging to another famous area resident, Joseph Bonaparte, eldest brother of the emperor Napoleon Bonaparte.

Next door to the Cooper House is the Captain James Lawrence House, which includes his personal possessions as well as War of 1812 artifacts. Just down the way at 453 High Street is the Bard-How House, built somewhere around 1743. This pre–Revolutionary War home is furnished with antiques and decorative arts of the area, including a magnificent Isaac Pearson tall case clock. Directly behind the Cooper House at 454 Lawrence Street is the Corson Poley Center, a recently opened facility that is the site of the Delia Biddle Pugh Library and the Aline Wolcott Museum. These two modern buildings house an ever-growing collection that reflects the life and times of Burlington County.

The Victorian Lady

301 West Main Street
Moorestown, NJ 08057
(609) 235-4988

The first thing that strikes many visitors in this fully restored B&B is the magnificent mansard roof. This unusual feature became popular in the later part of the last century, when local real estate taxes were based upon the number of windows a house contained. For some reason, windows in the roof weren't considered to be part of the house. So some clever folks built their homes to take advantage of this loophole, giving rise to the popularity of this unusual architectural style.

The ground floor of The Victorian Lady contains an antique shop stocked with glassware, Victorian furniture, and grandfather clocks. There are antiques throughout the house, highlighted by a splendid oak staircase leading to the second floor, where two bedrooms with private bathrooms are located. Both rooms are individually decorated with lace curtains and antique quilts. The feeling is one of warmth and comfort.

Breakfast in the elegant dining room typically features fresh fruit, homemade breads and muffins, and egg dishes. Before setting off for the James Fenimore Cooper House in Burlington a few miles away, you might want to stroll around Moorestown and visit some of the fine shops that grace this quaint community. Leisured travelers who are in the area for several days might also like to journey to the Jersey Coast or spend some time in Cape May, weather permitting. These and many other historic and scenic attractions are within a short drive of The Victorian Lady.

Rates: $85
Credit Cards Accepted: Visa, MC
Number of Guest Rooms: 3
Number of Baths: 3
Wheelchair Access: No

Pets: No
Children: No
Smoking: Yes
Senior Citizen Discount: Yes
Directions: See brochure

F. Scott Fitzgerald's Princeton

Although F. Scott Fitzgerald spent only a handful of his years studying at Princeton University, his Ivy League experience played a major role in his literary career.

Fitzgerald, who was born in St. Paul, Minnesota, in 1896, came to Princeton in 1913 after attending St. Paul Academy and the Newman School, a Catholic prep school in Hackensack, New Jersey. Already he'd embarked on a literary path, penning several plays and a detective story, which were published in St. Paul Academy's school newspaper when he was 13.

But the pretentiousness of Princeton proved challenging to Fitzgerald, who struggled to fit in. His family was proud of its Irish ancestry and ties to the Maryland aristocracy and named their son after a prominent distant relation—Francis Scott Key, author of "The Star-Spangled Banner." Fitzgerald's father, however, failed miserably as a businessman, leaving the family dependent on his wife's wealth. This humiliation set up lifelong conflicts in Fitzgerald and in his work.

At Princeton he sought acceptance into the most popular eating club—the university's equivalent of fraternities—and the literary world, to the neglect of his studies. As a member of the class of 1917, Fitzgerald spent more time writing scripts and lyrics for the annual Princeton Triangle Club musicals than he did studying in the gothic dorm rooms. His shows included *Fie! Fie! Fi-Fi!* in 1914, *The Evil Eye* in 1915, and *Safety First* in 1916. He also served as a contributor to the *Princeton Tiger* humor magazine and the *Nassau Literary* magazine. His college friends included writers Edmund Wilson and John Peale Bishop.

In December 1915, Fitzgerald left Princeton in the middle of his junior year because of ill health and poor grades. He returned in September 1916, only to drop out again and join the army as a second lieutenant the following year.

Fitzgerald once described Princeton as a "ring of silence" surrounded by "sordid Trenton" to the south and "the suburban slums of New York" 50 miles to the north. But his interlude in this picturesque colonial town was far from quiet. The years here introduced him to other literary figures and provided outlets for his writing talent. Princeton, in fact, is the setting of *This Side of Paradise*, which launched Fitzgerald into fame when it was published in 1920.

Strolling Princeton's tree-lined streets today, it's easy to imagine Fitzgerald here, dressed in the Brooks Brothers suits he purchased in New York, carrying stacks of scripts in progress to rehearsals, taking in all the details he would later recreate with painful accuracy in his novels and stories.

The Peacock Inn

20 Bayard Lane
Princeton, NJ 08540
(609) 924-1707; (609) 921-0050

George Washington may not have slept here, but F. Scott Fitzgerald did, and so did Bertrand Russell and Albert Einstein. The proximity of The Peacock Inn to the Princeton University campus is only one reason this handsome building is on the list of not-to-be-missed places. It is also one of Princeton's most historic residences, recorded on the tax rolls in 1775. Built as the home of John Deare, it was moved 100 years later to nearby Bayard Lane. It has been a public house since 1912, and during that time its various owners have upheld a tradition of convenient, comfortable lodging that, along with the building itself, has gained a rich patina through the years.

The house itself represents its era well: gambrel roof, gleaming white clapboard, high dormers, and a long porch and double-door entry that lend a dignity to the entrance of all guests. Eighteen rooms are available, each a bit different from the next and displaying the best in taste of France, England, and early America. The main floor houses an elegant French restaurant, Le Plumet Royal, referring to the glory of the peacock's feathers, and indeed, this newly redecorated area is pleasing to the eye as well as to the taste. Fireplaces and architectural touches have been carefully retained, but the addition of soft peach colors and the beauty of Queen Anne furniture lend a distinctive warmth and grace. The menu changes seasonally, taking full advantage of fresh garden fare and annual favorites. Special attention has been paid to the wine list, and all desserts—including the ice cream—are homemade. It's too bad George Washington never slept here. A little R and R here at The Peacock Inn seems just what was needed after a heavy day of fighting Hessians at Trenton!

Rates: $125–$135
Credit Cards Accepted: Visa, MC, AMEX
Number of Guest Rooms: 18
Number of Baths: 17
Wheelchair Access: No

Pets: Yes
Children: Yes
Smoking: No
Senior Citizen Discount: No
Directions: See brochure

Red Maple Farm

RR 4, Raymond Road
Princeton, NJ 08540
(908) 329-3821

Like the titles of books, the names of B&Bs are often descriptive and a major clue to what you can expect. Sometimes subtle, often humorous, but mostly straightforward and visual, these names seem to be chosen for easy recall or some kind of free association. Certain ones have a ring to them; others carry the distinction of a family name. I find it a fascinating subject and bring it up because I am impressed with the simplicity and imagery of the name, Red Maple Farm. Listed on the National Register of Historic Places, this sophisticated example of eighteenth-century pioneer farm architecture includes the large main structure, open space and ancient trees, a smokehouse, henhouse, and additional barn outbuildings. Several gardens please the eye, whether newly plowed, at summer ripeness, dormant with leaves crackling in a cool autumnal wind, or lying fallow under a blanket of snow. Organic vegetables, berries, and flowers flourish here, and the orchard is a spring glory, just as the red maples hold the stage in fall.

The farm is a family operation, and as might be expected, the rate includes a full country breakfast served on the patio or in front of a warming fire—all things here adapt to the changing seasons. Home-baked cookies, however, defy the weather and are always available. The room names, too, describe a simple elegance: Wild Strawberry (queen-size bed, fireplace), Blue Room (queen-size bed), and Flower Room (high-rise twin beds). All rooms share a bath with another room. Guests are given a taste of farm living, but without the chores (although another set of hands at picking time is always welcome). It is hard to believe that Princeton University is only four miles away or that Philadelphia or Trenton even exist. What's in a name? Come visualize the answer at Red Maple Farm.

Rates: $60–$85
Credit Cards Accepted: Visa, MC, AMEX, Discover
Number of Guest Rooms: 3
Number of Baths: 2
Wheelchair Access: No

Pets: No
Children: If older than 5
Smoking: No
Senior Citizen Discount: No
Directions: See brochure

New Mexico

Willa Cather's New Mexico

When Willa Cather published *Death Comes for the Archbishop* in 1927, she could hardly have guessed that her novel based on the life of New Mexico's first archbishop, Jean Baptiste Lamy, would become a classic. But Cather's fictionalized biography remains a best-seller to this day.

The Pulitzer Prize–winning novelist is best known for writing about the pioneer experience in the American West, and she made enough journeys to this region to know her subjects well. In 1915, she and her friend Edith Lewis went on a lengthy tour of the Southwest that included a month on horseback riding through Taos and nearby mountain villages. They returned in 1916 to see more, drawn by the landscape and the people.

Cather came back again and again to visit the majestic mountains and dramatic desert as well as writer friends who had settled in this region. She stayed with Mabel Dodge Luhan in Taos and Mary Austin in Santa Fe during her frequent visits. You can visit Luhan's house in Taos (the Mabel Dodge Luhan House, which operates as a bed and breakfast and conference center, is located at 240 Marada Lane, 505-751-9686 or 800-84-MABEL). Austin's Casa Querida (Spanish for "beloved house"), which now houses the Gerald Peters Gallery, is at 439 Camino del Monte Sol in Santa Fe.

In fact, Cather wrote portions of *Death Comes for the Archbishop* in Casa Querida. But the inspiration for her novel came while she was watching the sunset from the Cross of the Martyrs on the east side of Santa Fe. As the Sangre de Cristo Mountains turned red from the sun, Cather realized that, for her, the essential story of the Southwest lay in the story of its missionary priests and not the ancient Indian civilizations or Spanish conquerors other writers had focused on.

She immersed herself in the life of Lamy, a French missionary priest who came to Santa Fe in 1851 to oversee a new provisional diocese created by the Vatican after the end of the war between Mexico and the United States in 1848. One of Lamy's biggest legacies in Santa Fe is St. Francis Cathedral, a French Romanesque church that dominates the plaza. The cornerstone of the cathedral was laid in 1869 and the church was dedicated in 1886, just two years before Lamy's death from a lingering cold. Cather undoubtedly spent hours in the cathedral, contemplating the vision that inspired Lamy to build such a spectacular church in what was then such a remote and backward place.

But Lamy built a more personal sanctuary that Cather discovered and visited. His own version of a Camp David nestles in the foothills three miles from Santa Fe. He called it Villa Pintoresca (Italian for "picturesque villa") and used it as private retreat. Today the modest structure sits amid the buildings of the Bishop's Lodge resort. (Located on Bishop's Lodge Road, this resort offers stunning views from the Sangre de Cristo foothills. You can arrange to stay here by calling 505-983-6377 or 800-732-2240. The e-mail address is www.santafe.-org/bishop'slodge/.) The two rooms Lamy used for living quarters are closed to the public, but the one-room chapel remains open to visitors and still contains many of his personal items.

Cather visited Lamy's sanctuary while she was a guest at the Bishop's Lodge in 1928. At the time, the resort's owners had ordered a major restoration of the chapel's interior. She visited the chapel site to gain inspiration for her novel.

When Cather completed her classic, it came under attack from Mary Austin for its sympathetic stance toward the missionary movement. "She had given her allegiance to the French blood of the Archbishop; she had sympathized with his desire to build a French cathedral in a Spanish town," Austin wrote in *Earth Horizon*. "It was a calamity to the local culture. We have never got over it."

But Cather's book outlived such criticism. If you haven't yet read it, pick up a copy in one of the local bookshops: My favorites are Railyard Books at Guadalupe and Read Streets; the Collected Works Bookstore at 208-B West San Francisco Street; and Good Books at 1636 St. Michaels Drive. Trace the path of one of America's celebrated authors as she unraveled the compelling story of a priest determined to reshape centuries of tradition and cultural belief.

Lew Wallace in Santa Fe

The fourth floor of the unique capitol in Santa Fe features a chronologically ordered photo gallery of the governors of New Mexico from the territorial era to the present. One picture is of Lew Wallace as he looked during his gubernatorial tenure from 1878 to 1881. With his dark beard and piercing eyes he looks the very image of the lawyer, soldier, politician, and author he was.

Although he was born in Brookville, Indiana, and spent much of his life in Crawfordsville, Indiana, Wallace was something of a soldier of fortune and a romantic. While serving in the Mexican Civil Wars, he gained much of the inspiration and insight for his first novel, *The Fair God*. He had started writing *Ben-Hur: A Tale of the Christ* when President Rutherford B. Hayes appointed him governor of the territory of New Mexico. Life in the unruly Southwest did much to mold his outlook on life. In between suppressing Apache uprisings and dealing with outlaws such as the legendary Billy the Kid, he completed the manuscript of this highly successful novel in his residence at the Palace of the Governors on the Santa Fe plaza. People living in the capital city today can understand his frustrations with the frontier mentality of the Old West. He observed that "every calculation based on experience elsewhere fails in New Mexico."

Following his three-year stint in the territory of New Mexico, Wallace spent four years as a diplomat responsible for protecting U.S. citizens and looking after trade rights in Turkey. His literary failure, *The Prince of India*, a story of fifteenth-century intrigue, was based upon his experience living in Constantinople. In 1885 he returned to Crawfordsville, where he lived until his death in 1905. On the occasion of his funeral, the flag at the Indiana State House was flown at half-mast. James Whitcomb Riley honored the passing of his long-time friend with a poem. Such was Lew Wallace's reputation in the early part of this century that his statue was unveiled in Statuary Hall in the nation's Capitol. Of all the distinguished Americans so honored, Lew Wallace is the only novelist.

Palace of the Governors

105 West Palace
P.O. Box 2087
Santa Fe, NM 87504-2087
(505) 827-6487; (505) 827-6474

Who: Karen Gordon

When: 10:00 A.M.–5:00 P.M. Tuesday, Thursday, and Sunday; 5:00–8:00 P.M. Sunday. Closed Christmas, New Year's Day, and Easter.

How Much: $5 for adults (older than 17); children under 17 free. There is no admission charge on Friday.

Senior Citizen Discount: Yes

Wheelchair Access: Yes

Directions: Adjacent to the Plaza

What and Where: Built in 1610, this archaeology and history museum is the oldest public building in the United States. The museum depicts life in New Mexico from the time of the Spanish conquistadores to the present. For our literary purposes, it is a great place to learn more about Lew Wallace and Archbishop Lamy. The very helpful and knowledgeable docents at the Palace told me that although Lew Wallace enjoyed his duties as governor and writing his best-selling novel *Ben-Hur,* his wife, Susan, was counting the minutes until she could leave this Wild West outpost. Ask one of the docents to direct you to the Exploration and Settlement Room, which was once Lew Wallace's bedroom. It was in this room that he finished *Ben-Hur.* Next, ask to see the bust of Lew Wallace sculpted by Randolph Rogers, who served under General Wallace in the Civil War and created this bust as a tribute to his commander.

Switch gears to Willa Cather, and ask directions to the portrait of Bishop Jean B. Lamy, whom Cather immortalized in *Death Comes for the Archbishop.* Under his portrait the caption reads: "Bishop Jean B. Lamy of France came from Ohio in 1851 and tried to change the state's Roman Catholic Church to fit a more European form." As I mentioned earlier, Cather was not very popular with Santa Feans after the publication of *Death Comes for the Archbishop,* because they felt she glorified Lamy and vilified Padre Antonio Jose Martinez. For more information on this subject, pick up at a local bookstore (Railyard Books or Collected Works) a copy of *But Time and Chance* by Fray Angelico Chavez, a native New Mexican author and historian. Or better yet, step around the corner to 120 Washington and enter the newly opened Fray Angelico Chavez History Library to find out more about New Mexico's fascinating and controversial history, literary or otherwise.

Santa Fe Literary Walking Tour

Local writer and bibliophile Barbara Harrelson offers an interesting two-hour downtown walk that explores the legends, literature, and lore of Santa Fe and *el norte.* Besides discussing the literature of the Anasazi, Aztecs, and Spanish, she also includes contemporary regional authors whose works are representative of New Mexico's diverse peoples, including three noted authors of the Southwest who have died recently: Paul Horgan, Frank Waters, and Fray Angelico Chavez. Call (505) 989-4561 for details.

Alexander's Inn

529 East Palace Avenue
Santa Fe, NM 87501
(505) 986-1431
(505) 982-8572 Fax

There's something mildly decadent about staying at a bed and breakfast in your hometown. It's like playing hooky from school, and I love it. It's fun to watch the other guests at breakfast when you tell them where you live. At Alexander's Inn in downtown Santa Fe, after hearing about our other breakfast companions' hometowns of Ontario and Los Angeles, my husband and I confessed that we lived two miles away. They knew we weren't kidding when, after a delicious dinner at Babbo Ganzo, an Italian eatery downtown, we told the innkeepers and other guests we had to stop off at the house to feed our cats!

But I felt light years away from household responsibilities as we sat in the relaxing hot tub in the backyard of Alexander's Inn. We watched snow clouds build in the December sky and marvelled at the enormous Midwestern-looking trees in the yard. Next morning, awakening to sunlight streaming through the stained-glass windows of the elegant Lilac Room, I felt all vexing thoughts of chores fading away—I was so cozily ensconced in the four-poster bed with the snug down comforter. The smell of coffee and muffins, however, lured my husband from our room. Innkeeper Caroline Lee's homemade granola is itself worth a trip to Santa Fe. Normally I do not like granola, but Lee's version is so marvelously different that I asked for the recipe. The breakfast caters to the health-conscious but is so delicious you won't know it's good for you. The fresh fruit and yogurt, pumpkin muffins, and coffee got my day off to a good start.

There's a Midwestern wholesomeness about Alexander's Inn, from the inviting large porches to the bountiful gardens, from the quilts on the beds to the friendliness of Caroline Lee herself. While we enjoyed tea and homemade snickerdoodle cookies, Caroline told me that when she first came to Santa Fe she was a single mother with a nine-month-old baby to raise. "Not wanting to put him in a daycare while I worked outside the home, I decided to open a B&B so that I could care for my son while at work." The experiment was a success, because her son, Alexander (the inn's namesake), is now ten years old.

Lee has the ideal background for her chosen profession. As the daughter of a Foreign Service diplomat, she traveled extensively as a child. She has danced professionally, worked on Wall Street, and lived in Paris. As the oldest of five children, she learned the art of housekeeping at a very early age, a valuable asset for an innkeeper.

Personal touches at Alexander's include Caroline's list of suggested activities for her guests as well as files of local restaurant menus (complete with Caroline's personal recommendations). Even though the inn is close to the plaza, where you can explore the literary inspirations of Lew Wallace, Willa Cather, and Paul Horgan (Pulitzer Prize–winning author of *Lamy of Santa Fe*), you will feel far removed from the hustle-bustle of touristy Santa Fe.

Rates: $75–$150
Credit Cards Accepted: Visa, MC
Number of Guest Rooms: 9
Number of Baths: 9
Wheelchair Access: Yes

Pets: Yes
Children: Yes
Smoking: No
Senior Citizen Discount: No
Directions: See brochure

Water Street Inn

427 West Water Street
Santa Fe, NM 87501
(505) 984-1193

One of my occasional regrets is that I wasn't born in a more elegant era. My favorite fantasy is that I'm a pampered heroine in a Noel Coward play or, better yet, I'm Nora Charles of *Thin Man* fame. I indulged this role playing while enjoying breakfast in bed at the Water Street Inn. Picture, if you will, a tray discreetly placed at our bedroom door. My husband, emulating the gallant Nick Charles, brought said tray to our large four-poster bed, where we sat propped up by downy pillows, warmed by a roaring fire in the elegant bedside fireplace. To make matters even more romantic, it was literally a dark and stormy morning. A blizzard raged outside while we contentedly munched on our granola, fruit and yogurt, poppyseed muffins, tomato juice, and coffee. To enhance the experience of breaking the fast, we transported ourselves to another time and place as we watched the inn's video of *Sunset Boulevard.*

Later that evening we had an experience worthy of Nick and Nora. To be sure, we solved no crimes and drank no martinis, but we did enjoy the lovely happy hour provided by our congenial hosts at the Water Street. Tom Getgood, Kathy Whitman, and Harriet Mackie are every bit as sparkling as the characters in any Dashiell Hammett novel. We indulged in civilized conversation while partaking of New Mexico wines, homemade salsa, veggies and dip, and tamales. Fortunately, we managed to save room for the delicious dinner at Vanessie's, which is right next door. We split a half-order of onion rings, swordfish, salad, and baked potato, which turned out to be a wise decision. Make your dinner plans a little on the late side so you can hear the popular pianist Doug Montgomery performing in what *Esquire* magazine called "one of the ten best piano bars in the world."

When we returned to to our elegant room, our bed had been turned down and potato chip cookies had been placed on the bedside tray. We lit a fire, burrowed under the covers, and watched a video of *The Santa Fe Trail* for local color. Did we eat the cookies even though we were stuffed from dinner? You bet!

Even though the Water Street Inn is the ultimate in Southwestern luxury (the result of an award-winning adobe restoration), it is the staff that really makes this inn special. Bright, amusing, and helpful, they fully realize that people stay at inns for their hospitality. Tom frequently takes his guests to the ski basin or to the Shidoni sculpture gardens in nearby Tesuque. "I love it," he said. "Each guest gives me a fresh perspective on Santa Fe."

Rates: $125–$195
Credit Cards Accepted: Visa, MC, AMEX
Number of Guest Rooms: 11
Number of Baths: 11
Wheelchair Access: Yes

Pets: Yes
Children: Yes
Smoking: No
Senior Citizen Discount: No
Directions: See brochure

Inn of the Turquoise Bear

342 East Buena Vista Street
Santa Fe, NM 87501-4423
(505) 983-0798; (800) 396-4104
(505) 988-4225 Fax
E-mail: bluebear@roadrunner.com
Website: www.travelbase.com/destinations/santa-fe/turquoise-bear

Poet Witter Bynner, who lived in Santa Fe from 1922 until his death in 1968, may be better known in the Southwest than elsewhere in the country, where he seems to have slipped into obscurity. But that's about to change, thanks to Ralph Bolton and Robert Frost, the new owners of the Inn of the Turquoise Bear—an eclectic bed and breakfast housed in Bynner's former estate.

Bolton and Frost recently opened the doors of this rambling adobe house, which was built in the Spanish Pueblo Revival style from a core of rooms dating back to the mid-1800s. Their goal? To rekindle the creative and lively spirit Bynner established as one of the leading figures in the Santa Fe writers colony that flourished during the first half of this century. They've even placed a copy of the recent biography, *Who Is Witter Bynner?* in each bedroom for guests who want to know more about this eccentric intellectual.

Bynner, known as "Hal" to his friends, was a lyric poet who played a major role in the early-twentieth-century modern poetry movement in America. A 1902 graduate of Harvard University, he befriended Wallace Stevens, Mark Twain, Henry James, Ezra Pound, Willa Cather, and Edna St. Vincent Millay, to whom he was briefly betrothed before they both changed their minds.

Bynner came to Santa Fe in February 1922 to deliver a lecture on China. A bout with influenza, however, forced him to stay at a local sanitorium, where a number of celebrated artists and writers from around the country had come to recuperate. The spell of Santa Fe captivated him, and he decided to make the town his permanent home. "I have sent my roots of instinct into the earth," he confided to his friend, the poet Robinson Jeffers. "The beauty of the earth has made us beautiful too and has made us, if only for a moment, do beautiful things."

Once he was established in Santa Fe, many prominent people came to visit Bynner, including Pulitzer Prize–winning poet Robert Frost (who, incidentally, has no connection to the Robert Frost who co-owns the inn). Frost had been a Harvard classmate and friend—that is, until Bynner disagreed with something Frost said about poetry as the two shared a meal. In frustration, Bynner dumped a beer on Frost's head.

Despite such behavior, the arts community adored Bynner, who hosted legendary parties and scintillating salons in his 8,000-square-foot house. Guests included luminaries from Santa Fe as well as around the world: D. H. and Frieda Lawrence, Mabel Dodge Luhan, Thornton Wilder, Stephen Spender, Aldous Huxley, Georgia O'Keeffe, Ansel Adams, J. B. Priestley, Martha Graham, and even Errol Flynn and Rita Hayworth, who were in town for the 1940 world premiere of the film *Santa Fe Trail*. Everybody who counted in the arts circle back then was drawn to Bynner's infectious charm and his "roaring, rowdy laugh," which contrasted "so oddly with his Harvard accents," wrote Elizabeth Shipley Sargeant in a 1934 article on Santa Fe published in *The Saturday Review of Literature*.

Bynner cherished his rambling adobe home, which he purchased in 1925 when it contained just three small rooms. Bit by bit, he expanded the house, beginning with a two-story addition he dubbed the "O. Henry story," because he financed it with the sale of three O. Henry short stories the writer gave him to pay back a loan. Over the years he continued to add to and change his estate with the help of his partner, Robert Nichols Hunt, the son of a prominent southern California architect, Myron Hunt.

Also noted as an essayist and translator, Bynner was a passionate collector who filled his home with rich Chinese brocades and porcelain, American Indian blankets, and Persian rugs. He often strolled through town wearing so much Indian jewelry that he resembled a walking museum. Sometimes he'd host his salons swathed in a Chinese robe.

Bynner spent 47 years in this house and published more than 20 books. Three years after suffering a severe stroke, he died in his beloved home in 1968.

The owners of the Inn of the Turquoise Bear, who live on the premises, know their property belonged to an important literary figure. Naturally, they want the rest of the world to know this as well. They've planned readings of Bynner's work both inside the historical house as well as in the enchanting gardens, which are filled with lilacs, wild roses, and rock terraces and towering ponderosas.

Inside, they've furnished the house in a traditional Southwestern style that complements the adobe walls, kiva fireplaces, thick vigas, and uneven wooden floors. The 10 bedrooms include telephones, televisions, and VCRs, and guests can browse through video and book libraries for entertainment. The living and sitting rooms offer places for conversation, music, and pure relaxation.

Ralph and Robert serve an expanded continental breakfast that includes gourmet coffee from O'Hori's in Santa Fe and freshly made orange juice accompanied by a variety of cereals, fresh fruit, and delectable pastries such as cinnamon rolls, scones, and blueberry muffins prepared by the local Atalya Bakery.

Rates: $80–$160
Credit Cards Accepted: Visa, MC, AMEX, Discover
Number of Guest Rooms: 10
Number of Baths: 8

Wheelchair Access: 1 room has handicap accessibility
Pets: Yes
Children: Yes
Smoking: No
Senior Citizen Discount: 10%
Directions: See brochure

Grant Corner Inn

122 Grant Avenue
Santa Fe, NM 87501
(505) 983-6678

Garth Williams, noted illustrator of children's books, including *Charlotte's Web* and *Stuart Little,* did the sketches for the Grant Corner Inn brochure, and once inside, I'm sure that instead of "Some Pig!" he exclaimed, "Some Bunny!" This delightful property is chock-full of rabbits, a collection that ranges from chinaware and saltcellars to a life-size Mardi Gras costume that could be mistaken for just another eccentric guest!

After all, this *is* Santa Fe! Louise Stewart is so much a part of this special environment that to talk about her seems the best place to start. Here's a case of being to the manner, if not the manor, born, for she grew up at the noted Camelback Inn in Scottsdale, a venerable hostelry founded by her father. Louise herself was a decorator, and the liveliness, color, and contours of her inn are a remarkable tribute to her good taste.

And speaking of taste, let me add that brunch at Grant Corner is a well-kept town secret by the locals, who are welcome on weekends (with reservations). Menus include New Mexican souffle and eggs Florentine, always accompanied by my favorite, the milkshake-size fruit frappé. The special baked goods are as pleasing to the eye as to the palate. When served on the sweeping front porch, one can savor not only the finest food but also watch most of the town stroll by as well.

The house was originally built in the early 1900s for the Windsors, a ranching family, who no doubt appreciated the corner property. The inn's ideal location is only two short blocks from the historic plaza, the heart of Santa Fe for almost 400 years. Ten guest rooms of various arrangements are in the main house, and two additional rooms are available in the nearby hacienda. Vintage photographs from the Windsor album adorn the walls of the front hallway, fitting in perfectly with the eclectic decor, antiques from all over the world, and yes, that whole passle of bunnies!

Rates: $70–$155
Credit Cards Accepted: Visa, MC
Number of Guest Rooms: 12
Number of Baths: 10
Wheelchair Access: Yes

Pets: No
Children: Yes
Smoking: No
Senior Citizen Discount: No
Directions: See brochure

AUTHOR'S NOTE: Because I live in Santa Fe, I know how many excellent B&Bs there are in my hometown. Space doesn't allow for any more descriptions here, but I do want to mention that El Paradero on 220 West Manhattan 87501, (505) 988-1177, close to the plaza and featuring giant breakfasts, amusing hosts, and relaxing surroundings, is another fine choice. For the most romantic getaway in town, try the Don Gaspar Compound on 623 Don Gaspar, 87501; (505) 986-8664. The inn is renowned for its beautiful appointments and magnificent gardens.

D. H. Lawrence Ranch

P.O. Box 190
San Cristobal, NM 87564
(505) 776-2245

Who: Al Bearce, Manager

When: 8:00 A.M.–5:30 P.M. seven days a week. Call to verify that someone is there, because the drive from Taos is fairly long.

How Much: Free

Senior Citizen Discount: NA

Wheelchair Access: Limited

Directions: Take State Highway 522 North from Taos for approximately 15 miles. Look for the sign that reads D. H. Lawrence Ranch. Take the indicated dirt road that bears off to the right; the ranch is approximately five miles along this road.

The D. H. Lawrence Memorial, near Taos.
Photo by Don Laine.

What and Where: In the village of Taos, D. H. Lawrence, his aristocratic German wife, Frieda, and the legendary art patroness Mabel Dodge Luhan are still vital to the village's life. In fact, reminiscing about their lives has become a cottage industry in this beguiling town. Karen Young, the codirector of the Kit Carson Museums in Taos, is a delightful teller of early Taos tales. She tells her version of what happened during Taos's literary heyday: "What I have heard is that Frieda got the ashes from France and then somehow left them at a New York hotel. When the ashes finally made their way to Taos, Frieda once again absentmindedly left them at the home of her friend Tinka Fechin, the wife of the well-known Russian artist, Nicolai Fechin. The story goes that Tinka kept reminding Frieda to come pick up D. H.'s remains, but Frieda kept forgetting. Finally, the resourceful Tinka decided to create her own shrine, put the ashes on a table in her living room. and turned it into a memorial by surrounding the urn with candles."

You will get an inkling of the eccentricity of D. H. Lawrence by visiting his final resting place.

The extremely simple shrine contains yet more information about the famous ashes. Lawrence's death certificate from the City of Marseilles, written by the U.S. consul, declares: "I hereby certify this box bearing the seal of this consulate contains the urn which contains only the remains after cremation of David Herbert Lawrence, which are being taken to the U.S. on board the S.S. *Conte Di Savoia.*"

Georgia O'Keeffe was a visitor here and, as usual, left her individual mark. She painted a picture of the big pine tree that graces the front of the cabin and dubbed it "The Lawrence Tree." The bench on which she lay to paint remains at the base of the tree to this day.

La Fonda Hotel

P.O. Box 1447
Taos, NM 87571
(505) 758-2211

Who: Front desk

When: 8:00 A.M.–11:00 P.M. daily

How Much: $3

Senior Citizen Discount: No

Wheelchair Access: Some

Directions: See brochure

What and Where: For some more local color and D. H. Lawrence lore, head for La Fonda Hotel on the plaza to see Lawrence's famous, once-scandalous, erotic art. It is neither erotic nor art, but it is, nonetheless, historically interesting. You can't miss La Fonda, but just in case you think you're in the wrong spot, look for the sign on the hotel's entrance that reads: This is the only showing of the D. H. Lawrence controversial paintings since his exhibition was permanently banned by Scotland Yard when his show opened at the Warren Galleries, London, in 1929.

Touchstone

0110 Mabel Dodge Lane
P.O. Box 2896
Taos, NM 87571
(505) 758-0192; (800) 758-0192
(505) 758-3498 Fax
Website: http://www.taoswebb.com/touchstone

Breakfast at Touchstone was a study in serenity. Classical music played softly in the background; magpies flitted from one stately cottonwood tree to another while snow softly fell on Taos Mountain. The white winter exterior was a gentle contrast to the mélange of color inside the dining room. Bren Price, the owner of Touchstone and a painter of some renown, uses the breakfast area to exhibit her brightly hued artwork. Her paintings are accentuated by the many skylights that bring in the outside world.

Not surprisingly, the beautifully presented breakfast has an artist's touch. The Swiss quiche with fresh herbs, sliced grapes, kiwi, and Touchstone fruitcake arrived looking like a Cezanne still life. The attractively set table with its elegant white cloth and royal blue glasses added to the effect.

From a literary perspective, there is much to enjoy at Touchstone. One can almost picture Mabel Dodge Luhan, the colorful matron of the Taos art scene, holding salons in this elegant adobe hacienda. Mabel's husband, Tony Luhan, a Taos Indian, designed the fireplace in the common room. The names of the rooms—Lawrence Suite, Tony Room, Mabel Suite, O'Keeffe Suite, the Miriam Hapgood Library—evoke the feeling of an earlier era, when writers and artists held sway. Today at Touchstone, little of this artistic ambience has changed. In spring the grounds become a veritable bouquet of wild plums, lilacs, apple blossoms, tulips, and daffodils. Summer gives the feeling of a grand park with sunshine, shade, and wildflowers. The most glorious time of all is autumn, when the grandeur of the land gives way to the incredible honey color of Indian summer highlighted by the infinite blue of the sky and the indigo of the mountains.

All rooms have custom-designed private baths, phones, cable TV with VCR, cassette players, down comforters and pillows, Oriental rugs, rich textiles, fine art, and viga ceilings, and most have kiva fireplaces. A video collection and cassette library are available to guests, as is an outdoor hot tub.

Bren Price, who stayed in fine hotels all around the world when she was married to an oil executive, likes to pamper her guests and share the special spirit of the land with her hacienda visitors.

Plan to spend some time in Taos, because it is an interesting destination. Pick up some books by Taos authors at the excellent bookstores (Moby Dickens Book Shop, Brodsky Book Shop, and Taos Book Shop) and sample some of the fare at the town's first-rate restaurants. Three of my new personal favorites are the elegant Villa Fontana, (505) 758-5800, a world-class Italian restaurant; the lively Trading Post Cafe, (505) 758-5089, featuring Trading Post chicken noodle soup and delicious Creole pepper shrimp; and the Casa Fresen Bakery, (505) 776-2969, in nearby Arroyo Seco, with its incredible freshly baked breads and pastries and rich cappucinos.

Rates: $85–$150
Credit Cards Accepted: Visa, MC
Number of Guest Rooms: 8
Number of Baths: 8
Wheelchair Access: Yes

Pets: No
Children: If older than 12
Smoking: No
Senior Citizen Discount: Yes
Directions: See brochure

Hacienda del Sol

P.O. Box 177
Taos, NM 87571
(505) 758-0287
E-mail: sunhouse@taos.newmex.com
Website: http://taoswebb.com/hotel/haciendasol

A room at the Hacienda del Sol. Photo by Ken Gallard.

The Hacienda del Sol could qualify as a literary site in its own right. For many years the adobe was owned by legendary Taos art patroness, Mabel Dodge Luhan, and her fourth husband, Tony, from Taos Pueblo.

In those days when Taos was an artist colony without peer, the hacienda consisted of a four-room adobe, an apple orchard, and many acres of farmland and pastures. Mabel and Tony used the house as a temporary residence and a guest house for such notables as D. H. Lawrence, Georgia O'Keeffe, and Willa Cather. One of the Southwest's most revered authors, Frank Waters, lived here in 1939. It was during his stay that Frank wrote *The People of the Valley* and gathered the material for *The Man Who Killed the Deer* (which he dedicated to Mabel and Tony).

One of the fun things about visiting Taos is that practically every longtime resident has his favorite "Mabel story." D. H. Lawrence used to call Taos "Mabeltown"; years after her death, you can understand why. Marcine Landon, the gracious innkeeper of Hacienda del Sol, offers her own delightful Mabel anecdotes. After breakfast in late March, we sipped coffee in the dining room while watching snow falling on Taos Mountain. Marcine relates that it was in this very adobe that Mabel's houseguest, Georgia O'Keeffe, painted her first sunflower picture. I cozied up to the roaring fire in the fireplace while Marcine recounted that Ansel Adams was a favorite and frequent visitor to Mabel's famous salons. "Did you know that when Adams came to Taos he was a pianist? While in Taos he met photographers and decided to become a photographer." And the rest, as they say, is history.

I deserted the warmth of the fireplace somewhat reluctantly to take a tour of the old part of the house, but it was well worth the inconvenience. Marcine showed me

Tony's bedroom as she explained that Mabel bought this house in the mid-1920s for Tony. The entire house—particularly this bedroom—was a retreat for the reticent Taos Indian who knew no English when he met Mabel Dodge. I couldn't help but think what a change Tony must have been from Mabel's former lover, John Reed, the journalist, radical, and inspiration for the movie *Reds*.

There is plenty to like at Hacienda del Sol. The rooms are tastefully decorated with Taos-style handcrafted furniture, hand-woven baskets, Navajo rugs, patchwork quilts, snuggly down comforters, thick adobe walls, viga and latilla ceilings. What I especially liked in our room was the cassette player with what Marcine calls "our special selection of tapes," Native American–influenced music. It was quite relaxing sitting by our own private fireplace and listening to these soothing tapes while reading an autographed copy of Frank Waters's *People of the Valley*. One of the pleasant features of the Hacienda del Sol is its extensive library.

Because literary types do not live by books alone, I am glad to report that the breakfast of broiled grapefruit, French toast stuffed with fruit and cheese, orange juice, and coffee was delicious. John Landon, Marcine's husband and fellow innkeeper and breakfast purveyer, told us that he and Marcine "vowed when we turned fifty-five, we would retire early from our careers in sales management and education to pursue our dream of owning and operating a B&B. We saw an ad in *New Mexico Magazine*, came to Taos, and after just one look at the rambling adobe estate, we were hooked. Taos Mountain, looming majestically in the background of the Hacienda del Sol grounds, beckoned us to make the commitment."

"Look at that view," he said, pointing toward Taos Mountain. "This place has it all, the feel of an old historic adobe and location, location, location."

Rates: $70–$130
Credit Cards Accepted: Visa, MC
Number of Guest Rooms: 9
Number of Baths: 9
Wheelchair Access: Yes

Pets: No
Children: Yes
Smoking: No
Senior Citizen Discount: No
Directions: See brochure

Ernie Pyle Branch Library

900 Girard SE
Albuquerque, NM 87106
(505) 256-2065

Who: Front desk

When: 12:30 A.M.–9:00 P.M. Tuesday and Thursday, 9:00 A.M.–5:30 P.M. Wednesday, Friday, and Saturday. Hours are expected to change in February 1997.

How Much: Free

Senior Citizen Discount: NA

Wheelchair Access: Yes

Directions: From I-25, take the Central Street exit. Drive east on Central toward the Sandia Mountains. You will pass the University of New Mexico on your left. Turn right on Girard just after the campus ends. The library will be on your left at 900 Girard, just after the Lead/Coal intersection.

What and Where: Ernie Pyle's Albuquerque home, built in 1940, is now the Ernie Pyle Memorial Library. The property was given to the city of Albuquerque by the Pyle estate and in 1947 became the first branch of its public library system. When he was asked how he happened to pick Albuquerque as a place to build a home, Pyle responded as any self-respecting writer would do, by writing an article. In a piece for *New Mexico* magazine in May or June 1942, Pyle explained, "There are many little reasons. But probably the main thing is simply deep, unreasoning affection for the Southwest. ... So if we have only one house ... and that's all we want ... then it has to be in New Mexico and preferably right at the edge of Albuquerque where it is now."

Casas de Suenos

310 Rio Grande SW
Albuquerque, NM 87104
(505) 247-4560; (800) CHAT W/US
(505) 842-8493 Fax

If there's anything better than a Field of Dreams, it just might be a House of Dreams. Casas de Suenos has certainly been well named, for it is, literally and figuratively, an artist's "dream." J. R. Willis, controversial and colorful local artist and photographer, designed and built this garden compound. "Created" would be a better term, for the original plan included his home, studio, and 15 rental casitas. Willis planned an artists' colony, but he should have realized that his talented friends were just as eccentric and individual as he! A striking figure recognizable by his unfurled cape and outthrust cane, Willis often bartered paintings for construction materials and labor. Architect Bart Rice is responsible for the unique entranceway to this two-acre site bordering historic Old Town. A circular fantasia of tile and glowing color, the "Snail House" is an easily recognizable Albuquerque landmark.

Present owner Robert Hanna was quick to see the B&B potential in this extravagant setting. The guest casitas are primarily flat-roofed adobe style—some have fireplaces and kitchen facilities. The Territorial design of most of the interiors reflects a special period in New Mexico history, an eclectic blend of cultures as well as decorative tastes. The gardens, too, impart a dreamlike quality to the property, especially since many of the large trees and exotic plants are not indigenous to this high desert land of little rain.

What *is* expected here (and is quietly obvious) is the warmth of southwestern hospitality. The food, too, is to dream for, if not to die for, with a typical menu with three choices, such as chili and eggs, chili strata, or fresh fruits and homebaked goods—the latter specifically for those visitors who have not yet developed the need for what locals call a "regular chili fix." Hanna lives at the inn and practices law here out of his specially designed office. Future plans include a complete day spa and an unusual gallery to include artistic foods as well as paintings. In that great art gallery in the sky, Willis is probably wondering why he didn't think of that himself. Hanna calls Casas de Suenos a "Picasso Property," because being there is "like living in a work of art." Truly, this is what dreams are made of.

Rates: $85–$245
Credit Cards Accepted: None
Number of Guest Rooms: 19
Number of Baths: 19
Wheelchair Access: Yes

Pets: No
Children: Yes
Smoking: No
Senior Citizen Discount: No
Directions: Given on confirmation

NEW YORK

Elmira College: Mark Twain Study and Exhibit

1 Park Place
Elmira, NY 14901

Who: Gretchen Sharlow, Director

When: From mid-June through Labor Day, the hours are from 10:00 A.M.–5:00 P.M. Monday through Saturday and from 12:00 noon–5:00 P.M. Sunday. By appointment the rest of the year.

How Much: Free

Senior Citizen Discount: NA

Wheelchair Access: In the exhibit

Directions: Contact the director's office

What and Where: For most readers, Mark Twain is associated with the Mississippi River or the Far West or perhaps even Hartford, Connecticut. Elmira, New York, just doesn't conjure up the Huck Finn image for most of us. And yet it was here, on his family's Quarry Farm home, that Twain penned several of his masterpieces. As a matter of fact, Elmira played a very special role in Twain's life. He married Olivia Langdon, daughter of one of Elmira's established families, in 1870 and spent more than 20 of his summers in this area. The combination of the cool weather and privacy, along with the beauty of the Chemung River Valley, gave him the inspiration to work on *The Adventures of Tom Sawyer, The Adventures of Huckleberry Finn, A Connecticut Yankee in King Arthur's Court,* and many other stories.

Founded in 1788, Elmira is located in the south Finger Lakes region and just a few miles north of the Pennsylvania border. In the 1860s, Elmira was the site of a notorious Civil War prison camp where some 3,000 Confederate prisoners died. Along with Mark Twain, these soldiers are buried in Elmira's Woodlawn National Cemetery. Today, Elmira, with a population of roughly 35,000, is most noted as a manufacturing center for chemicals, office equipment, and sailplanes. The National Soaring Museum is in Elmira; associated with the museum is a national glider meet, held annually at nearby Harris Hill.

The 6.7-acre Quarry Farm home remained in the possession of the Langdon family for four generations, until 1982, when it was deeded to Elmira College by Jervis Langdon, Jr., Mark Twain's grand-nephew. Jarvis Langdon, Twain's father-in-law, had been prominent in the founding of Elmira College; his niece, Ida Langdon, served on the faculty as professor of English until her death in 1952.

Visitors in quest of Mark Twain lore are fortunate indeed that Elmira College has established the Center for Mark Twain Studies. The Victorian farmhouse provides lodging and inspiration for distinguished scholars. The center also hosts a range of activities, including school and community groups, lectures for the general public, Readers' Theater at Quarry Farm, and scholarly colloquia. The more casual visitor can enjoy the Mark Twain Exhibit and the Mark Twain Study. The historically inclined can view the remains of the foundation of his octagonal study as well as the exterior of the farmhouse, servants' cottage, and horse barn.

For those who would appreciate more information, contact the Center for Mark Twain Studies. The center's periodical, *Dear Friends*, will advise you of upcoming programs. It can also keep you informed about the *Quarry Farm Papers*, a series that features scholarly research on Mark Twain and several other nineteenth- and twentieth-century American authors.

The Blushing Rose

11 William Street
Hammondsport, NY 14840
(607) 569-3402; (800) 982-8818

Hammondsport, like so many villages in the Finger Lakes region of central New York, retains many turn-of-the-century characteristics. Highlighted by a bandstand on the village square and Keuka Lake Beach a short distance away, it conjures up images of hoop skirts, Sousa concerts, and swimming parties down by the shore.

Here, in the heart of New York's wine country, you feel that civic pride is in full flower. The houses are well maintained and the yards carefully manicured. One that stands out in particular is The Blushing Rose, a four-bedroom inn a stone's throw from Lake Keuka. The fact that Hammondsport is approximately 40 miles from Elmira is not a major drawback, considering the pleasant change of pace you'll experience. Innkeepers Ellen and Bucky Laufersweiler take great pride in their profession, as their relaxed style attests. The four rooms, dubbed Moonbeams, the Four Poster, the Magnificent Walnut, and the Burgundy Room, feature quilted comforters. Each room has a private bathroom. Whether you're in the area to enjoy the summer climate of the Finger Lakes region, to visit the Mark Twain Exhibit, or to bike along the shores of Lake Keuka, The Blushing Rose is an enjoyable getaway.

Ellen, who has served as president of the Finger Lakes Bed and Breakfast Association, is pleased to offer what she describes as a copious specialty breakfast. This is her way of getting her guests off on the proper footing. For those who are not sure whether they want to visit the glass museum in Corning (some 25 miles away) or tour the local wineries, she gladly provides suggestions. Airplane aficionados will also appreciate the Glenn Curtiss Museum, named after a Hammondsport native who did much to establish the aviation industry. For those who want a leisurely change of pace in the middle of the afternoon, Hammondsport has a vintage soda fountain that offers many of the beverages that were popular at a time when personal service was important.

Rates: $75–$85
Credit Cards Accepted: Call for specifics
Number of Guest Rooms: 4
Number of Baths: 4
Wheelchair Access: No

Pets: No
Children: If older than 12
Smoking: No
Senior Citizen Discount: No
Directions: See brochure

The Red House Country Inn

4586 Picnic Area Road
Burdett, NY 14818-9716
(607) 546-8566
(607) 546-4105 Fax
E-mail: redhsinn@aol.com

It's hard to imagine a more bucolic setting than the Red House Country Inn, located on Picnic Road within the 16,000-acre Finger Lakes National Forest along the eastern shore of Seneca Lake. Although this is no longer a working farm, the inn is home to five pet goats and a number of Samoyeds. You can enjoy the groomed lawns, pool, flower beds, and picnic areas. For hikers and naturalists, there are 28 miles of trail into the wooded hills of the forest; the trailheads are located on the inn property.

The Red House Country Inn. Photo courtesy of The Red House Country Inn.

The fully equipped guest country kitchen is available for preparing lunches, whether or not you are venturing out to hike. The restored farmhouse includes a public room, a large veranda, and five bedrooms sharing four bathrooms. The feeling of coziness is accentuated by turn-of-the century antiques throughout the house. In the morning, hosts Joan Martin and Sandy Schmanke offer a full country breakfast consisting of fresh fruit, eggs and sausage, and homemade breads and pastries.

For those who don't wish to spend all their waking hours on the hiking trails, the marvelous Glen Gorge in Watkins Glen is a short drive away. Somewhat closer to home are the swimming beaches and boat-launching facilities on Seneca Lake. The bibulous bibliophile will also be pleased to learn that there are numerous wineries in the immediate vicinity.

Rates: $45–$85
Credit Cards Accepted: Visa, MC, AMEX, Discover
Number of Guest Rooms: 5
Number of Baths: 4
Wheelchair Access: No

Pets: No
Children: If older than 12
Smoking: No
Senior Citizen Discount: Yes
Directions: See brochure

Rosewood Inn

134 East First Street
Corning, NY 14830
(607) 962-3253

At one time Corning was one of the major glass-producing cities in the world. The name of this community of 13,000 derives from Erastus Corning, an early tycoon and

New York State politician who, among other things, was active in promoting the New York Railroad Company around the middle of the nineteenth century. It was here that Margaret Sanger, pioneer in the birth-control movement, was born in 1879. Corning is now the home of the Rockwell Museum and the world-renowned Corning glass center, where Steuben glassmaking can still be observed. Because of the quiet ambience and residential atmosphere coupled with its cultural heritage, Corning is one of New York state's leading tourist attractions.

The Rosewood Inn is located a couple of blocks from historic Market Street in a quiet neighborhood. Built in 1855 as a Greek Revival home and modified in Tudor style six decades later, its Victorian decor gives it an eclectic atmosphere. The living room is highlighted by velvet swag curtains and a lace mantle drape. Suzanne and Stewart Sand-ers, who purchased the inn in 1992, brightened up the somber Victorian decor by adding cheery floral prints and white linens. At check-in time late in the afternoon, the hosts provide home-baked cookies and tea or lemonade.

The two suites and five double rooms at the Rosewood all have private baths or showers. Each is furnished with period antiques. The Carder Suite, named after the founder of the Steuben glass process, has bearded board paneling and a marble sink built into a rosewood bureau. The Gibson Room offers Eastlake furnishings and prints. Lace-covered French doors separate the living room from the elegant dining room, where breakfast is served every morning from 8:30 to 9:30. Stewart, who does most of the cooking, takes great pride in his work. The menu changes frequently but typically features fresh fruit salad, a variety of muffins, and French toast.

Rates: $100–$125 for the suites, $70–$105 for the five bedrooms. There is a surcharge of $20 for each extra person. On certain weekends during the summer and early fall, a two-day minimum stay may be required.

Credit Cards Accepted: MC, Visa, AMEX, Discover

Number of Guest Rooms: 5 bedrooms, 2 suites

Number of Baths: 7

Wheelchair Access: No

Pets: No; kennels nearby

Children: Over 11

Smoking: No

Directions: From Elmira, take Route 14 north to Watkins Glen (on the southern tip of Seneca Lake). From Franklin and Fourth Streets in Watkins Glen, go north on Route 414 for 8.7 miles to Schuyler County Road 2. Turn right and proceed 3.4 miles to the inn.

Walt Whitman Birthplace State Historic Site

246 Old Walt Whitman Road
Huntington Station, NY 11746-4148
(516) 427-5240
(516) 427-5247 Fax

Who: Barbara M. Bart, executive director

When: 1:00–4:00 P.M. Wednesday–Friday, 10 A.M.–4:00 P.M. Saturday and Sunday. Closed on holidays.

How Much: Free

Senior Citizen Discount: NA

Wheelchair Access: In the Visitor Interpretive Center

Directions: See brochure

What and Where: It is little wonder that *Leaves of Grass* was not well-received at first and, in fact, Whitman was unable to find a publisher for it. He seemed ahead of his time with his outspoken views and candid anatomical references,

The birthplace of Walt Whitman. Photo courtesy of Walt Whitman Birthplace Association.

which outraged many early readers. Whitman became a role model for many other writers by publishing and even typesetting his book himself. In the spring of 1855, Whitman employed his Brooklyn friends, the Rome brothers, to print his thin volume of poems. Although it was not a best-seller, *Leaves of Grass* was lauded by such intellectuals as Ralph Waldo Emerson and was accepted among progressively minded Americans.

The third of eight children, Walt Whitman was born on a small farm near Huntington, Long Island. Built sometime around 1820 by Walter Whitman, the poet's father, the house is a fine example of native Long Island craftsmanship. Built of hand-hewn beams that are held together by wooden pegs and laid on whole tree trunks supported by a foundation of small boulders, it is notable for several unusual architectural features. The spacious, twelve-over-eight pane windows provide air, light, and a rare note of elegance in this country farmhouse. The corbeled chimney and storage closets in the fireplace walls were innovative for their place and time.

Whitman's father built the house solidly, for the original glass in the windows, many hinges, and other hardware are still in good shape today. The dining area seems to be older than the rest of the house and might have been on the property before the larger main section was built. It is easy to imagine the young Whitman in this environment, because very few changes have been made to the house over the past century and a half. Only three other owners have lived here between 1832, when the Whitmans left it, and 1949, when the Walt Whitman Birthplace Association bought it.

Whitman had a long and rich Long Island history. He started teaching school here at the tender age of 17. In 1838–1939 he founded and edited a weekly newspaper, *The Long Islander,* which is still published today. Between 1841 and the summer of 1859, Whitman held editorial positions on seven different newspapers, four of them on Long Island. He was an outspoken advocate of social, economic, and political reform, and his political activism often cost him his job.

The Civil War greatly affected Whitman's life. In 1862 the poet left Brooklyn to search for his brother George, who was a prisoner of the Confederates. Moved by the plight of the wounded, Whitman got a Civil Service post and, in his spare time, made nearly 600 hospital visits. Characterizing this time as "the greatest privilege and satisfaction … and the most profound lesson of my life," he found these sickbed visits provided material for his poem, "The Wound Dresser." Heartsick over the assassination of his idol, Abraham Lincoln, Whitman wrote a poem, "O Captain! My Captain!" in honor of the slain president.

Although Whitman retired to Camden, New Jersey, he always considered himself a Long Islander. A lovely journal of the sounds and sights of the natural world of Long Island is recorded in *Specimen Days and Collect*. Today's visitors can take advantage of a guided tour of the house, the audiovisual presentation, Whitman's schoolmaster's desk, his voice on tape, the museum shop, poetry workshops and readings, concerts, lectures, and a poet-in-residence program.

Swan View Manor Bed and Breakfast Inn

45 Harbor Road
Cold Spring Harbor, NY 11724
(516) 367-2070
(516) 367-2085 Fax

Mary, Michelle, and Phil, your congenial hosts at Swan View Manor, have simply marvelous plans for your visit to their inn. And when you leave feeling relaxed and happy, they hope you will feel as pampered as if you were a favorite relative. Here's how they accomplish your perfect visit. It starts with your breakfast in the cheery dining room. Help yourself to the inviting buffet of fresh fruit and juices, choice of cereals, yogurt, assorted breads, bagels and muffins, preserves, coffee and specialty teas.

After your visit to Walt Whitman's home in nearby Huntington, return to the cozy sitting room, where you will be served a delightful afternoon tea. Before or after, perhaps you'll want to sit by the roaring fireplace and catch up on your Whitman reading, perhaps *Leaves of Grass* or *Specimen Days and Collect*. To add to your bookish pleasures, have a complimentary soft drink, tea, or coffee, which are available all day long.

Most of the newly refurbished guest rooms have views of the water, so you can gaze lazily at the scenic and historic fishing village of Cold Spring. The air-conditioned rooms are supplied with fresh flowers, floral comforters, and if you can't tear yourself away from the outside world, there are modern conveniences such as telephones and cable television.

Your hosts will happily point out the charms of Long Island and its interesting history. Theodore Roosevelt lived in nearby Sagamore Hill. In 1927 Charles Lindbergh took off from Roosevelt Field, Long Island, for his nonstop flight to Paris. Today, in spite of growth, the island manages to maintain its pristine beauty and has some of the nation's best beaches, wetlands, nature preserves, and parks.

Close to Swan View Manor are the Whaling Museum, the Vanderbilt Museum and Mansion, Old Westbury Gardens with its 100 acres of formal gardens, and Jones Beach.

Rates: $95–$160
Credit Cards Accepted: Visa, MC, AMEX, Discover
Number of Guest Rooms: 19
Number of Baths: 19
Wheelchair Access: No

Pets: No
Children: If older than 10
Smoking: No
Senior Citizen Discount: No
Directions: Brochure contains map

Literary New York City

Perhaps writers are attracted to New York because that's where most publishers are. And maybe writers like being in a town that is a story in itself. There are several guidebooks that highlight literary spots in New York City. A nice one to have on hand is *Literary Neighborhoods of New York* by Marcia Leisner.

- A good place to start your tour of literary New York is Greenwich Village. Before the Village took on the Bohemian flavor of the 1920s, it was an upscale neighborhood where many wealthy families resided. On the north side of Washington Square are a row of brownstone houses. Edith Wharton lived at number 7. Henry James, who lived nearby, used to visit his grandmother at number 19. Although he spent much of his adult life in Europe, one of his best-known books, *Washington Square*, is set in this neighborhood.

- On the other side of the park is Washington Square South. When the well-heeled families moved out, the buildings became boardinghouses occupied by lower income people, including a host of struggling writers. O. Henry, Eugene O'Neill, Stephen Crane, and Theodore Dreiser are but a few who lived on this side of the park. Edgar Allan Poe stayed just a block away, in the brick house at 85 West 3rd Street.

- Go west beyond the Village and you'll come to the old and deserted Gansevorst Street Pier. Here is where Herman Melville found work as a customs clerk after his reading audience turned away from him because of his unsettling novel *Moby-Dick*.

- Mark Twain, a man who lived in just about every corner of America, spent a year at 14 West 10th Street, just west of Fifth Avenue. He was 65 and at the peak of his fame, living and entertaining in grand style in this large brownstone building.

- Edna St. Vincent Millay lived many places in the Village, one being 75 Bedfort Street, a three-story building that is only nine and a half feet wide. Millay wrote short stories under the name of Nancy Boyd and acted with the Provincetown Players while trying to support herself as a poet. When the Village became too much of an "in" place to be, she moved to Paris, joining other famous literary expatriates.

- Willa Cather, a schoolteacher from rural Nebraska, came to New York at age 31 to become the editor of *McClure's Magazine*. Her home at 60 Washington Square South was a Bohemian studio that became the setting for the love story "Coming, Aphrodite." (It has since been replaced by the modern architecture of NYU's Law School.)

- Dylan Thomas loved to frequent the Irish bars of the Village during his tours of the States. His favorites were San Remo on MacDougal Street and White Horse on Hudson Street. He was wild, passionate, vulgar and profoundly a poet. At age 39, he died at Saint Vincent's Hospital in the Village.

- e. e. cummings spent the last 38 years of his life at 4 Patchin Place. Here he drew and painted and wrote the poetry known for its jazz beat and unpredictable format.

- Brooklyn Heights is an old aristocratic area of New York near the Brooklyn Bridge. Thomas Wolfe, who lived at 111 Columbia Heights, stood a respectable six foot four inches tall—so tall he used the top of his refrigerator as a writing table. Columbia Heights was the home of many other writers, including Katherine Anne Porter, Hart Crane, Truman Capote, and Tennessee Williams.

- On Orange Street in Brooklyn, between Hicks and Henry, is the Plymouth Church of the Pilgrims, whose pastor was Harriet Beecher Stowe's brother, Henry Ward Beecher. Charles Dickens once spoke from its pulpit.

- Across from the church, on Cranberry Street, Walt Whitman lived as a boy. From the time he was 12, Whitman worked for various papers, first as a printer's devil, then as a reporter, then as the editor of the *Brooklyn Eagle*. At the corner of Cranberry and Fulton, 170 Fulton Street, is the site of the print shop where *Leaves of Grass* was printed in 1855. Because no publisher would print it, Whitman published it himself. Throughout his life he reprinted *Leaves of Grass* several times, adding to it in each edition.
- After achieving literary success, O. Henry lived on Irving Place near Union Square in Manhattan. He loved New York, which he called "Baghdad on the Subway," and prowled the town, searching for new plots and characters in its neighborhoods. His favorite bar was Healy's (now Pete's) on 18th Street. Today there is a plaque above the booth where O. Henry sat and wrote his famous short story, "The Gift of the Magi."
- Stephen Crane lived in a studio apartment at 145 East 23rd Street. His first novel, *Maggie: A Girl of the Streets*, was about the rugged life in the Bowery. It was "too cruel" to be accepted by the publishers of the day, so he published it himself. His second book, *The Red Badge of Courage*, was completed by the time Crane was 24. He died five years later.
- A block beyond Stephen Crane's brownstone is the Hotel Chelsea (222 West 23rd Street, between Seventh and Eighth Avenues). This old Victorian hotel with wrought-iron balconies was a favorite residence of Dylan Thomas. Thomas Wolfe wrote *You Can't Go Home Again*, the last of his autobiographical novels, while living at the Chelsea. (In truth, he didn't go home, but lived out his life here.) Among the hotel's other noted guests were Mark Twain, O. Henry, Eugene O'Neill, and Edgar Lee Masters, who wrote the poem "The Hotel Chelsea."
- Edith Wharton's parents were among the established families who lived around Gramercy Park. In her Pulitzer Prize–winning novel, *The Age of Innocence*, Wharton tried to explain the tight restrictions and shallow morality of the turn-of-the-century New York City upper class.
- Not far away, Herman Melville lived with his family in a plain rowhouse on East 26th Street. At the end of his life he wrote *Billy Budd* while working in his bedroom here.
- The Players Club, at 16 Gramercy Park South, was founded by actor Edwin Booth. It became a gathering place for literary minds, including Mark Twain and Booth Tarkington.
- In midtown Manhattan you'll find the New York City Public Library, with its stone lions, Patience and Fortitude, guarding the steps. This huge building, which covers two city blocks (Fifth Avenue between 40th and 42nd Streets), houses millions of volumes of books and offers many special displays from its collections.
- The grand Algonquin Hotel, at 59 West 44th Street, is said to be the place where Harold Ross took the money he won in a card game to finance *The New Yorker* magazine. Dorothy Parker and Robert Benchley held their famous Roundtable at the Algonquin every noon during the twenties. Today the Roundtable, situated in the center of the main dining room, is still frequented by writers and publishers.
- The Biltmore Hotel (Madison Avenue and 43rd Street) is an elegant old hotel where Zelda and F. Scott Fitzgerald spent their honeymoon. The Plaza Hotel (Fifth Avenue and Central Park South) is the setting for the hotel scene in *The Great Gatsby*.
- While in midtown, you'll want to make a stop at the Gotham Book Mart at 41 West 47th Street, in the heart of the diamond district. Founded in 1920, this sprawling

bookstore, which specializes in poetry, twentieth-century novels, and books on theater and film, has always been a gathering place for writers.

- Turtle Bay Gardens are situated on 48th Street between Second and Third Avenues. Edgar Allan Poe lived at the Miller's farm in the 1840s. A little over a hundred years later John Steinbeck moved into a brownstone and kept a garden here.
- On the east side of Central Park, Willa Cather lived at 570 Park Avenue. Near there, Eugene O'Neill, playwright, Nobel laureate, and winner of four Pulitzer Prizes, lived in the penthouse at 35 East 84th Street. (Obviously he'd moved up in life since his Washington Square boardinghouse days.)
- On the Upper East Side, the New York Society Library, which prides itself as being the oldest library in New York, is located at 53 East 79th Street. Here is where Melville came to do research on *Moby-Dick,* and Edgar Lee Masters, Lillian Hellman, Norman Thomas, Clarence Day, and Eleanor Roosevelt came here to read and to write. The library requires membership to check out a book, but the public may use the reference sections, the reading room, and view the special displays.
- In Harlem you'll find the home turf of the Harlem Renaissance poets of the 1930s: Langston Hughes, James Weldon Johnson, and Zora Neale Hurston. Langston Hughes, whose poetry sings with African American jazz rhythm, lived at 20 East 120th Street. He first gained some fame when Vachel Lindsay noticed his talent and recited some of the young man's poetry in a Washington, D.C., hotel (see page 71).
- Also in Harlem is the Church of the Intercession, at 550 West 155th Street. While Dr. Clement Clarke Moore was a pastor there, he wrote "A Visit from St. Nicholas," which is better known as "The Night Before Christmas."
- In the Bronx, at 2640 Grand Concourse at Kingsbridge Road, you'll find Poe Cottage, where Edgar Allan Poe, his wife, Virginia, and his mother-in-law and aunt, Mrs. Clemm, lived in the late 1840s. It cost them $100 a year, which was a lot for the chronically ill and poverty-stricken poet. Here he wrote "Annabel Lee," "Ulalume," and "The Bells," and here his wife died. This dwelling has been restored and is open on weekends for a small charge.

The Inn at Irving Place

56 Irving Place
New York, NY 10003
(212) 533-4600; (800) 685-1447
(212) 533-4611 Fax

It may not quite bring to life the phrase "from the ridiculous to the sublime," but you'll have to admit that an inn offering in-room fax machines *and* tarot readings has something for everyone. And we also know that John Simoudis would not offer two such disparate services unless his guests appreciated them. This tells us much about the varied clientele of The Inn at Irving Place, and much, also, about the extremes to which this jewel of a hostelry will go for its guests. Two handsome Federal-style houses have been combined, offering 12 guest rooms, a grand staircase, and a five-course high tea every afternoon. From a book lover's perspective, this is a wonderful entry into a literary world of the past: This Gramercy Park area was home to many of the names on our favorite books. Edith Wharton lived nearby; Washington Irving lived in the neighborhood.

O. Henry wrote "The Gift of the Magi" in Pete's Tavern. All have rooms named after them, as do household names in New York such as Stanford White and Sarah Bernhardt. The front parlor reflects a society of 150 years ago, and perhaps this perfectly reconstructed atmosphere is one reason for the tarot readings.

Rates: $275–$350
Credit Cards Accepted: Visa, MC, AMEX, Diners Club
Number of Guest Rooms: 12
Number of Baths: 12
Wheelchair Access: No

Pets: No
Children: No
Smoking: Yes
Senior Citizen Discount: No
Directions: In lower east Manhattan between 17th and 18th Streets

... AAAH! B&B #1, Ltd.

P.O. Box 2093
New York, NY 10108
(212) 246-4000; (800) 362-8585
(212) 765-4229 Fax

The butler did it! No, this is not an Agatha Christie rewrite, it's a perfect lead-in to the ... AAAH! B&B #1, Ltd. concept, which was initiated by former butler William Salisbury. With locations in New York, London, and Paris, this reservation service is another example of savvy entrepreneurship: Salisbury has developed a reservation service that guarantees to match client, budget, and preferred location in cities that otherwise might be considered daunting to the uninitiated.

Rates: $40–$150
Credit Cards Accepted: None
Number of Guest Rooms: 50 apartments, B&Bs, and commercial properties located around the city
Number of Baths: Some private, some shared

Wheelchair Access: Yes
Pets: Yes
Children: Yes
Smoking: Yes
Senior Citizen Discount: Yes
Directions: When you make your reservation

B&B Network of New York

134 West 32nd Street, Suite 602
New York, NY 10001
(212) 645-8134; (800) 900-8134

A bite into the Big Apple can also mean a big bite into a visitor's pocketbook. This reservation service organization, B&B Network of New York, fills a real need in any large city, as Leslie Goldberg and her efficient staff prove daily while striving to provide a good match between guests and accommodations. The cost of visiting can be dramatically reduced by a stay in a private home, but the real advantage of this system may be in the knowledge pool of the "indigenous" hosts. Which form of transportation, where to find

real New York cheesecake or nearby clean-
ers, what's playing at the Garden tonight?—
all are questions easily answered. Specific
areas of the city are targeted according to the
visitor's interest: Greenwich Village, Wall
Street, the Upper West Side—take your pick!

Rates: $60–$300
Credit Cards Accepted: None
Number of Guest Rooms: Over 200
Number of Baths: Approximately half
  have private baths
Wheelchair Access: Limited

Pets: Some
Children: Some
Smoking: Some
Senior Citizen Discount: No
Directions: Given when making reser-
  vations are confirmed

Broadway Bed and Breakfast Inn

264 West 46th Street
New York, NY 10036
(212) 997-9200; (800) 826-6300
(212) 768-2807 Fax

Less is more, even if you're not visiting
MoMA. Certainly this truism can be applied
to the Broadway B&B, where sleekness and
simplicity apply to both the decor and the tar-
iff. A relative newcomer to the scene and located appropriately in the entertainment
district, this B&B reveals itself slowly, first with
a dignified entrance hall, then a glass-and-
chrome second-floor lobby, and thence to 40
guest rooms, all displaying the same moder-
nity with a color scheme of off-white, green,
and gray. The nineteenth-century building has
no elevator. A simple continental breakfast is
provided, much in keeping with the tone of
the place. For local color, a souvenir store and
an Irish pub are just downstairs.

Rates: $75–$150
Credit Cards Accepted: Visa, MC,
  AMEX, Discover, Diners
Number of Guest Rooms: 40
Number of Baths: 40
Wheelchair Access: No

Pets: No
Children: Yes
Smoking: Yes
Senior Citizen Discount: No
Directions: Between Broadway and 8th
  Avenue on 46th Street in the heart
  of the theater district

Chelsea Inn

46 West 17th Street
New York, NY 10011
(212) 645-8989; (800) 640-6469
(212) 645-1903 Fax

Don't confuse the Chelsea Inn with the
Chelsea Hotel (home to writers for half a
century), but the location is right and the
atmosphere is just as interesting. The handsome renovated brownstones are in the heart
of a New Yorker's New York. A choice of
suites or single rooms is available, with or
without private baths. This is not a conven-
tional B&B, so you're on your own for breakfast, but with all of New York's great delis,

who cares? Dylan Thomas found the area inspirational, as did Dorothy Parker, both of whom were residents of the Chelsea Hotel.

Who knows, your own muse may be ready to break out, given the right time and place—and this could be it!

Rates: $89–$179
Credit Cards Accepted: Visa, AMEX, Discover
Number of Guest Rooms: 17
Number of Baths: 10
Wheelchair Access: No

Pets: No
Children: Yes
Smoking: No
Senior Citizen Discount: No
Directions: In Manhattan on 23rd Street between Fifth Avenue and Sixth Avenue

Sunnyside: Home of Washington Irving

Historic Hudson Valley
West Sunnyside Lane
150 White Plains Road
Tarrytown, NY 10591
(914) 631-8200; (914) 591-8763
(914) 631-0089 Fax

Who: Front desk

When: Closed January and February. March through October 10:00 A.M.–5:00 P.M. Wednesday through Monday; November and December, 10:00 A.M.–4:00 P.M. Wednesday through Monday.

How Much: $7 for adults, $4 for juniors ages 6 to 17

Senior Citizen Discount: $6

Wheelchair Access: First floor

Directions: See brochure

What and Where: Sunnyside, as Washington Irving named his home, started out as a seventeenth-century two-room Dutch tenant farmhouse. He added rooms and passageways until, as magazine writer Suzanne Berne noted, it was "a picturesque hodgepodge of Dutch, Moorish, and Romanesque features, a tribute to Irving's love of anything romantic." Irving himself once confessed that it had "as many angles and corners as an old cocked hat."

The house is of the man: a traveler, a storyteller, a believer in all sorts of possibilities. At Sunnyside, Irving loved to entertain a motley collection of visitors. His literary friends, Oliver Wendell Holmes Sr. and William Cullen Bryant, passed the time with him. Millionaire businessman John Jacob Astor stopped by. The soon-to-be emperor, Napoleon III of France, paid a call. And of course the neighboring farmers were always welcome.

Irving chose the room by the front door as his study. From there he could easily answer the door for any guest who might happen by. Under a large leather chair by the door, in a lockable drawer, Irving stored his works-in-progress before greeting his guests.

When Irving's older brother, Ebenezer, became a widower, he and his five daughters moved into Sunnyside. With so many new inhabitants, not to mention the occasional overnight guest, Irving decided to move his own sleeping quarters to his study. In a small alcove to one side of the study he installed a couch. And there he slept for the next quarter of a century (that is, when he wasn't traveling to Europe or the American West, or living in Spain as the American ambassador). Eventually—a man does get tired of sleeping on a couch—he added an exotic three-story Moorish tower to his domain, which included bedrooms for his servants, for his visitors, and, yes, for himself. Or was it his books he wanted to house? He noted that "the books which were so long exiled to the garret have been brought down and arranged; and my library now makes a very respectable appearance."

Irving had a penchant for pen names as humorous as his writings. For satirical newspaper pieces, he was Jonathan Oldstyle. With his brothers and brother-in-law, he wrote "Whim-Whams and Opinions of Lancelot Longstaff, Esq." For his successful *History of New York*, he was Diedrich Knickerbocker. "The Legend of Sleepy Hollow" and "Rip Van Winkle" were first written under the name of Geoffrey Crayon.

In later years Irving turned to biography. At the end of his life, while attended by his friend, fellow writer, and doctor, Oliver Wendell Holmes Sr., Irving raced death to complete the biography of his namesake, George Washington.

North of town you'll find Irving's burial plot, among those of his family, in none other than Sleepy Hollow Cemetery. And just south of the cemetery is the Old Dutch Church, the legendary favorite haunt of Sleepy Hollow's Headless Horseman. Take a moment to imagine the thunder of goblin hooves and the crashing of a pumpkin as Ichabod Crane, astride old Gunpowder, races for the church bridge and safety on the other side.

Alexander Hamilton House

49 Van Wyck Street
Croton-on-Hudson, NY 10520
(914) 271-6737
(914) 271-3927 Fax

Set on a cliff overlooking the picturesque village of Croton-on-Hudson, the Alexander Hamilton House offers the spacious elegance of a well-appointed Victorian home. Since Barbara Notarius became owner of this manor she has added five bathrooms and four fireplaces and has redecorated each room in order to create a certain romantic ambience. "I realize people want something wonderful and magical," she says. The town itself is a bit magical. This is where Edna St. Vincent Millay married her husband, Eugen Boissevain.

The house is surrounded by gardens, and there's a view of the Hudson River from most every window. Twenty miles downriver is Washington Irving's house.

The backyard of the Alexander Hamilton House, enclosed by a patch of old forest, contains gardens and a 35-foot pool that is open from Memorial Day through Labor Day.

The private accommodations include two rooms, three suites, an apartment, and a third-floor bridal suite. All are spacious, well-lighted, and beautifully furnished.

Rates: $75–$250
Credit Cards Accepted: Visa, MC, AMEX, Discover, Diners
Number of Guest Rooms: 7
Number of Baths: 7
Wheelchair Access: No

Pets: No
Children: Yes
Smoking: No
Senior Citizen Discount: No
Directions: See brochure

Highland Flings and Hiking Tours

If you think you'd enjoy walking the same glens Rip Van Winkle wandered before his legendary nap in the Catskills, you might consider signing up for one of several hiking trips offered by Highland Flings. Owners John Murphy, Carol Clements, and Pat Murphy have developed a series of guided walking tours that allow hikers to spend days immersed in beautiful mountain scenery and nights enjoying the best bed and breakfasts in the northern Catskills.

The tours, lasting from three to seven days, include easy, moderate, and moderately difficult hikes. The season runs from May through the third week in October, and prices range from $350–$975. For more information, contact them at P.O. Box 1034, Kingston, NY 12402; (800) HLF-6665.

The Fenimore House Museum

Lake Road
P.O. Box 800
Cooperstown, NY 13326
(607) 547-1400
Website: http://www.cooperstown.net/mysha

Who: New York State Historical Museum; Mary Soule

When: The museum hours are seasonal, to say the least: From June to early September, 9:00 A.M.–5:00 P.M. daily. In May, the rest of September, and all of October, 10:00 A.M.–4:00 P.M. daily. In November and the last week of December, the hours are the same, but the museum is not open on Monday. From December 1 to 26 the hours are again the same, but only on Friday, Saturday, and Sunday. On the last few days of November, the museum is not open at all.

How Much: For those who are fortunate enough to have read the schedule correctly and who arrive when the museum is open, admission rates are $9 for adults and $4 for juniors ages 7 to 12. Be forewarned that the Farmer's Market and Baseball Hall of Fame cost extra.

Senior Citizen Discount: $1 off for 65 and older

Wheelchair Access: Yes

Directions: One mile north of Cooperstown on State Road 80

What and Where: Abner Doubleday was one of those people who are in the right spot when the time for assigning credits comes around. As a result, this military officer of Fort Sumpter fame is credited with the invention of the game of baseball. It is said that he did this while attending Green's Select School in Cooperstown, even though historians claim he never set foot in the town. In any event, the village of 2,500 on the shore of Lake Otsego came to be the home of the National Baseball Hall of Fame, albeit erroneously. Millions of people visit this shrine every year to pay tribute to the game and its alleged founder.

For literary buffs it is perhaps ironic that James Fenimore Cooper, whose father founded the village in 1790, commands nowhere near the adulation that Abner Doubleday receives. For although James was actually born in Burlington, New Jersey, his family moved to the Otsego Lake area when he was only one year old. Growing up in this remote region of New York State obviously made its impression, for it was his wilderness experience that inspired the five novels that make up *The Leatherstocking Tales: The Pioneers, The Last of the Mohicans, The Prairie, The Pathfinder,* and *The Deerslayer.* Lake Otsego itself was the basis for his Glimmerglass, which, in turn, gave its name to the critically acclaimed Opera Company that performs every summer at the Alice Busch Opera Theater.

Virtually nothing remains of James Fenimore Cooper's life in Cooperstown, although the Fenimore House Museum, built on the site of his boyhood home, contains portraits of the author's family as well as scenes from his novels and furnishings from his home. More important, perhaps, is the fact that this museum has captured much of the spirit of life in the time of James Fenimore Cooper. Paintings of the Hudson River School as well as American genre paintings are featured. The museum's Eugene and Clare Thaw Collection contains more than 600 Native American artifacts.

For those who want to be steeped in everyday life in Cooper's time, the Farmer's Museum just across Lake Road from the Fenimore House has served as a working farm since 1813. The multibuilding museum contains a printing office, a druggist's shop, a schoolhouse, and several other replicated buildings that depict agrarian life in the nineteenth century.

The Inn at Cooperstown

16 Chestnut Street
Cooperstown, NY 13326
(607) 547-5756

Visitors to the village of Cooperstown have a large number of exceptional B&Bs to choose from. My editor subtly recommended that I limit myself to one of them, so I chose The Inn at Cooperstown because it is located in the historic district. Because it is a short walk from the Baseball Hall of Fame it offers what I feel is a combination of convenience, atmosphere, and reasonable cost. A few of the other options include Litco Farms, (607) 547-2067; Thistlebrook, (607) 547-6093; and Brown-Williams House, (607) 547-5569.

The Inn at Cooperstown, which was constructed in 1874 as an annex to the luxurious Hotel Fenimore, was totally refurbished in 1985. Upon your arrival you might choose to relax in a rocking chair on the sweeping veranda of this Victorian inn or to read in one of the cozy sitting rooms. As for the accommodations, all 18 rooms have private baths. The furnishings are simple but tasteful. The walls are either white or painted a soft pastel color. Period reproductions and framed prints highlight the quality furnishings. In the morning, before exploring the Cooperstown area, enjoy a complimentary continental breakfast.

Rates: $75–$110
Credit Cards Accepted: Visa, MC, AMEX, Discover, Diners Club
Number of Guest Rooms: 18
Number of Baths: 18

Wheelchair Access: Yes
Pets: No
Children: Yes
Smoking: In designated rooms only
Senior Citizen Discount: No
Directions: See brochure

NORTH CAROLINA

——◆——

Carl Sandburg Home
National Historic Site

1928 Little River Road
Flat Rock, NC 28731
(704) 693-4178

Who: Connie Backlund, superintendent

When: 9:00 A.M.–5:00 P.M. every day except Christmas

How Much: $2 for adults, free for anyone younger than 16

Senior Citizen Discount: Golden Age Pass honored

Wheelchair Access: Yes

Directions: From I-26, take Exit 22. Follow signs to Carl Sandburg Home.

What and Where: Carl Sandburg, poet, author, lecturer, minstrel, and social thinker, spent the last 22 years of his life on a farm near Flat Rock, North Carolina. Connemara, as the farm was called, was homesteaded over a hundred years earlier by Christopher Gustavus Memminger, who later became the secretary of the treasury for the Confederate States of America. It is interesting that Sandburg, the great biographer of Abraham Lincoln, should be the home's last occupant.

When Sandburg and his wife moved to North Carolina, they brought with them their three daughters, two grandchildren, and over 10,000 volumes of prose and poetry they had collected over the years. Mrs. Sandburg went right to work on the farm tending her large prize-winning herd of goats.

Her husband, meanwhile, spent a good many hours in the cluttered upstairs workroom, where he often wrote late into the night. Mornings were meant for sleeping in. And early afternoons were meant for sitting on the front porch and looking out on the Blue Ridge Mountains while he read and answered letters. These years at Connemara were rich and productive years for Sandburg. During this time he wrote his autobiography, *Always the Young Strangers,* the novel *Remembrance Rock,* and several volumes of poetry, including *Complete Poems,* for which he was awarded the Pulitzer Prize in poetry in 1951.

When you visit Connemara, take time to walk the farm and to sit on the front porch where Sandburg sat gazing out at the North Carolina countryside.

The Waverly Inn

783 North Main Street
Hendersonville, NC 28792
(704) 693-9193; (800) 537-8195
(704) 692-1010 Fax

The Waverly Inn, Hendersonville's oldest inn, was chosen by *Innovations* magazine in 1993 as one of the top ten bed and breakfasts in the United States. When you walk into the foyer of the inn you're made to feel at home. The owners, John and Diana Sherry and Darla Olmstead, are known for their southern hospitality. They're also known for the huge breakfasts they cook to order for each of their guests: stone-ground grits, eggs, cinnamon French toast, huge pancakes, cereals, bacon, fruit, and homemade jam. (Fresh-baked cookies are available all day long.)

The 14 guest rooms of this three-story house are named after flowers, and each has its own unique decor, including canopy beds, brass beds, claw-foot tubs, and turn-of-the-century pedestal sinks.

The downstairs parlors and the rocking chairs on the front porch offer plenty of opportunity to relax and read. Or you might like to take a stroll around old Hendersonville. The Waverly Inn is on Main Street just two blocks from the historic district.

Rates: $79–$139
Credit Cards Accepted: Visa, MC, AMEX, Discover
Number of Guest Rooms: 14
Number of Baths: 14
Wheelchair Access: No
Pets: No

Children: Yes
Smoking: Limited
Senior Citizen Discount: No
Directions: The Waverly Inn is at the corner of North Main Street (US 25 North) and 8th Avenue in downtown Hendersonville across from the St. James Church.

Thomas Wolfe Memorial

52 North Market
P.O. Box 7143
Asheville, NC 28802
(704) 253-8304

Who: Steve Hill

When: The Thomas Wolfe Memorial is open April through October, Monday–Saturday, 9 A.M.–5 P.M., Sunday, 1–5 P.M.; November through March, the memorial is open Tuesday–Saturday, 10 A.M.–4 P.M., Sunday, 1–4 P.M. Closed Monday.

How Much: $1 for adults, $.50 for children

Senior Citizens Discount: No

Wheelchair Access: Visitors center

Directions: See brochure

What and Where: Thomas Wolfe was perhaps the most openly autobiographical of this country's major novelists. His childhood in the boardinghouse at 48 Spruce Street in Asheville colored his work and influenced the rest of his life. His remembrances were so realistic and honest that *Look Homeward, Angel* was banned from Asheville's public library for more than seven years. Fame and time have a way of dimming memories, and today Wolfe is celebrated as one of Asheville's most famous citizens. His boyhood home has become a part of the nation's literary history.

If you're a devotee of *Look Homeward, Angel,* you will know that you are visiting Dixieland, the boardinghouse run by Mrs. Eliza Gant in Wolfe's most autobiographical novel. However, here in Asheville, this white frame house (for its appearance, if nothing else) is known as the Old Kentucky Home. Not surprising to those in the know, this is indeed the very spot where Wolfe's mother, like Gant's in the novel, ran a boardinghouse on a tree-lined residential street. What you may not know is that Wolfe's mother, Julia Wolfe, is remembered in Asheville as a shrewd and uncompromising businesswoman who drove a hard bargain. Julia, a former teacher, had an obsession for the real estate market and used her profits to buy more property. Her husband, William Oliver Wolfe, could well afford to support his eight children with the earnings of the tombstone shop he owned and operated on Asheville's town square.

Thomas Wolfe remembered the house he moved into in 1906 as a "big cheaply constructed frame house of eighteen or twenty drafty, high-ceilinged rooms." In 1916 Wolfe's mother enlarged and modernized the house, adding electricity, additional indoor plumbing, and eleven rooms. Today the house of Thomas Wolfe's childhood and adolescence contains furnishings that symbolize the daily routine of life, in both fiction and fact. In his second novel, *Of Time and the River,* published 14 years before the Old Kentucky Home became a memorial to the author, Wolfe intuitively sensed the true significance of his childhood home: His mother's "old dilapidated house had now become a fit museum."

The house is preserved almost intact, with Wolfe's possessions arranged by family members very much the way they looked when the young author lived there. One room, in fact, is entirely furnished with items from his New York apartment, including an old brass lamp, a briefcase, one of his well-used suitcases, and his typewriter. Outside of the house is a playhouse that Wolfe played in as a lad. Shortly before his 38th birthday, Wolfe died of brain tuberculosis. His grave is in Riverside Cemetery in Asheville, which is also the burial site of O. Henry.

"And again, again the old house I feel beneath my tread the creak of the old stair, the worn rail, the whitewashed walls, the feel of darkness and the house asleep, and think, 'I was a child here.'"

Richmond Hill

87 Richmond Hill Drive
Asheville, NC 28806
(704) 252-7313
(704) 252-8726 Fax

What do F. Scott Fitzgerald, O. Henry, Thomas Wolfe, and Carl Sandburg have in common? Aside from being some of the most prominent names in American literature, they are all represented at Richmond Hill. Unfortunately, we cannot say they slept here, but this magnificent Queen Anne–style mansion has guest rooms named for each of them, as well as for other writers who were natives of Asheville or who spent time writing in the area. These third-floor guest rooms have sloped ceilings and skylights; a few have window seats. Each displays its namesake's portrait and biography and contains a collection of his works.

All twelve guest accommodations offer private baths and telephones. The second-floor rooms are named for historic figures associated with the Pearson family, including family friend Theodore Roosevelt. Richmond Pearson, congressman and U.S. ambassador, designed this gracious home, situated just three miles from downtown Asheville yet located in a wooded wonderland looking out on the French Broad River and the smoky blue mountains beyond. A century-old elegance is evident in this home, which contains an octagonal ballroom, double parlors, formal drawing room, and grand entrance hall with raised native oak paneling and exposed beams. Most impressive to me is the paneled library with its fine collection of western North Carolina authors that includes many first editions. This beautiful reading room also contains some 200 of the original 3,000 books from Richmond Pearson's personal collection.

In addition to the main house, Richmond Hill has other guest accommodations. The Croquet Cottages are situated around a manicured croquet courtyard and are charmingly named for trees indigenous to the area. Fireplaces, pencil-post beds, baths, ceiling fans (if only for southern atmosphere), and porches with requisite rocking chairs—who can resist this kind of place? The Garden Pavilion is Richmond Hill's newest addition and is designed in the grand tradition of the Victorian era. All 15 guest rooms overlook the mansion, the parterre garden, and the waterfall. A sophisticated kitchen provides restaurant meals—guests, of course, have a full breakfast, which is included in their room rate—and Sunday brunch is a specialty, as is the mood-setting piano at dinner. This is southern hospitality at its finest.

Rates: $135–$375
Credit Cards Accepted: Visa, MC, AMEX
Number of Guest Rooms: 36
Number of Baths: 36
Wheelchair Access: Yes

Pets: No
Children: Yes
Smoking: No
Senior Citizen Discount: No
Directions: See brochure

The Yellow House on Plott Creek Road

610 Plott Creek Road
Waynesville, NC 28786
(704) 452-0991; (800) 563-1236
(704) 452-1140 Fax

"We see our Future, and it is our Past," is a Haywood County motto, and one I can personally relate to. This put me in touch with innkeepers Ron and Sharon Smith, owners of The Yellow House, and big believers in the intrinsic qualities of bygone days. The six distinctive rooms and suites available for guests are beautifully appointed, and the entire century-old home reflects the casual elegance of a former time. Only a mile from town, but deep in an earlier era, the inn sits atop a grassy knoll surrounded by two and a half acres of lawn and garden, with a deck, footbridge, and lily pond. Shades of Monet!

The Yellow House on Plott Creek Road. Photo courtesy of the Yellow House.

He would have loved this place, not only for the flowers but for the cultivated European flavor and the colors of the interior rooms, borrowed from the Impressionists and the playful light and shadow of the French countryside. The E'staing and St. Paul de Vence suites capture memories of rural France.

All rooms have fireplaces, private baths, a wet bar or refrigerator, and splendid mountain views. Guests may enjoy breakfast in the dining room, on the front veranda, or bedside. The cost includes an evening hour of wine, hors d'oeuvres, and sparkling conversation. No cable TV. No pool or golf. Whatever will you do with your time? There are very few distractions here at The Yellow House, other than those you set your heart on. How about rereading some of your favorite Thomas Wolfe novels? This is the perfect place.

Rates: $115–$225
Credit Cards Accepted: Visa, MC
Number of Guest Rooms: 6
Number of Baths: 6
Wheelchair Access: No

Pets: No
Children: If older than 12
Smoking: No
Senior Citizen Discount: No
Directions: See brochure

The Lion and the Rose

276 Montford Avenue
Asheville, NC 28801
(704) 225-ROSE; (800) 546-6988

I like what innkeeper Lisa Yordy says about owning an old house: "Rice and I feel we are not really owners of this place, but rather caretakers for this beautiful southern lady." She also admits that restoration "is forever" and should be considered a process, not a result. With this in mind, The Lion and the Rose has been faithfully restored to its original elegance. All rooms are furnished with antiques, Oriental rugs, and period appointments. The high embossed ceilings and period leaded and stained glass windows are classic, in the finest sense of the word. The house was built in 1898 in an architectural style known as Simplified Queen Anne–Georgian, but simplicity has not robbed this three-story beauty of its wraparound porch, columns, and stone balustrades. The house is located in the Montford Historic District, listed in the National Register of Historic Places—we're talking the heart of Thomas Wolfe country here! The house is described in *Look Homeward, Angel,* as the home of a small boy named Richard. Wolfe himself is buried just around the corner in Riverside Cemetery, as is O. Henry.

Breakfast with the Yordys is a real treat, especially because it is served overlooking the parklike setting of flower gardens and century-old sugar maple trees. Popovers Romanov with fresh strawberries tastes as regal as it sounds, then there is herb souffle with mustard sauce, and a new twist on an old recipe, baked ambrosia. If there are such things as ghosts, I hope Thomas Wolfe gets to lean on the scalloped white picket fence and smell the wonderful kitchen smells emanating from the kitchen of The Lion and the Rose.

Rates: $115–$175
Credit Cards Accepted: Visa, MC, AMEX
Number of Guest Rooms: 5
Number of Baths: 5
Wheelchair Access: No

Pets: No
Children: If older than 12
Smoking: No
Senior Citizen Discount: No
Directions: See brochure

The Greensboro Historical Museum

130 Summit Avenue
Greensboro, NC 27410
(910) 373-2043

Who: Stephen Catlett, Gil Fripp, or Bill Moore

When: 10:00 A.M.–5:00 P.M. Tuesday through Saturday, 1:00–5:00 P.M. on Sunday

How Much: Free (donations are gladly accepted)

Senior Citizen Discount: NA

Wheelchair Access: Yes

Directions: See brochure

What and Where: The first European settlers in Guilford County, in the Piedmont region of North Carolina, arrived in 1749 seeking political and economic freedom. Some 60 years later the city of Greensboro was incorporated and named after Revolutionary War leader General Nathaniel Greene. The city's major growth, however, didn't take place until the middle of the nineteenth century, when the railroad connected it with the rest of the country.

William Sidney Porter (aka O. Henry) was born in Guilford County on September 11, 1862, when the Civil War was ravaging the nation. When he was only three years old, his mother, Mary Swaim Porter, and his little brother died of tuberculosis. Porter's father, a physician, took what remained of his family to live with his mother and sister, Lina. William grew up in their house in the 400 block of West Market Street.

In 1872 a fire devastated Greensboro, destroying virtually the entire city. Most of what we know about William Sidney Porter's 20 years in the area are to be found in the Greensboro Historical Museum, established in 1924. The second floor of the museum contains a reproduction of the village of 1880, featuring the drugstore where young William worked as a pharmacist just before leaving the area in 1882. There are also scale models of the doctor's office and Aunt Lina's one-room schoolhouse. For me, however, the raison d'être of the museum is a one-minute recording, made almost a century ago, in which Porter explains how simple it is to craft a short story.

A few blocks from the museum, the Greensboro Public Library has an extensive collection of O. Henry first editions, handwritten manuscripts, and cartoon drawings. Near the museum on Summit Street is a lifesize statue of O. Henry, commemorating Greensboro's most famous son.

Troy-Bumpas Inn

114 South Mendenhall Street
Greensboro, NC 27403
(910) 370-1660; (800) 370-9070
(910) 274-3939 Fax

In describing the literary connections of these B&Bs, I have come upon all sorts of wonderful parallels, allusions, personal references, and, yes, even a ghost, but the Troy-Bumpas Inn is unique: It actually contained a printing press on which, for more than 20 years, Frances Bumpas published Greensboro's *The Weekly Message*. Now this certainly places the building in the one-of-a-kind category! There are Civil War stories to tell as well, involving both the Blue and the Gray.

This handsome antebellum plantation–style home was built in 1847 by the Reverend Sidney Bumpas, and its gracious proportions have remained relatively intact. Following the Civil War, Captain Preston Troy married Duella Bumpas and the newlyweds eventually moved into the Bumpas home. The four spacious guest bedrooms contain antiques, and each room is named for one of the Troy sisters, known to Greensboro society for their wit and charm. Allah's room is carved cherry with elaborate Victorian stylings, and Lola's is all mahogany, *Gone with the Wind* lamps, and antebellum refinement. Nina inspired a setting of elegant green-and-purple bed curtains, a fireplace, and bay windows, whereas Miss Ethel, the youngest and last of the Troy-Bumpas family to live in the "old home," is remembered in terms of a hand-knotted bed canopy and four-poster bed. All rooms have private baths. The full southern breakfast is truly something to look forward to, and the complimentary prebreakfast beverage tray left outside the bedroom door is an inspiration. Remind yourself of that wonderful printing press once housed downstairs and enjoy the morning paper and a cup of good coffee in bed!

Rates: $75–$95
Credit Cards Accepted: Visa, MC, AMEX
Number of Guest Rooms: 4
Number of Baths: 4
Wheelchair Access: No

Pets: No
Children: Yes
Smoking: No
Senior Citizen Discount: No
Directions: See brochure

OHIO

——— ⚔ ———

Harriet Beecher Stowe House

2950 Gilbert Avenue
Cincinnati, OH 45206
(513) 632-5120

Who: Erma Cos, director

When: 10:00 A.M.–4:00 P.M. Tuesday through Thursday

How Much: Free, but donations are cheerfully accepted

Senior Citizen Discount: NA

Wheelchair Access: Yes

Directions: Call for directions

What and Where: Cincinnati had a huge influence on the life of Harriet Beecher Stowe. It was here that she wrote her first published works, married, had six of her seven children, and, probably most importantly for posterity, learned about the evils of slavery.

In 1832 Harriet moved with her father, the Reverend Lyman Beecher, to Cincinnati, where he had become the president of Lane Seminary. The young theologians who were faculty members at Lane were abolitionists and in 1834 offered African American students an education at a mission school. Needless to say, this was not a popular position.

The Beecher family was not your average American family. Harriet's sister, Catherine, believed strongly in female education and in her new Ohio home established the Western Female Institute. Harriet, one of nine children, was strongly influenced by her older sister and had served as a student teacher for Catherine's Hartford, Connecticut, Female Seminary. In Cincinnati, Harriet taught at Catherine's new school.

The energetic Harriet always seemed to find time for her writing. In 1834 her career took off when she won a prize for "A New England Sketch," published in *Western Monthly Magazine.* Her writing played second fiddle temporarily to marriage when, in 1836, she married Calvin E. Stowe, a professor of biblical literature at Lane Seminary. Her husband, who later became a distinguished biblical scholar, was in poor health, and their life in Cincinnati was difficult. They had seven children (six were born in Ohio) and little money. In spite of hardship and constant worry Harriet continued to write, and in 1834 wrote *The Mayflower,* a collection of sketches about New England life.

Cincinnati was pivotal in the development of Stowe's major work, *Uncle Tom's Cabin,* because it was an important stop on the Underground Railroad. Her beloved character Eliza was based on a real person, a slave who braved the thawing ice of the Ohio River in her escape from bondage. Stowe heard her inspiring story from the Reverend John Rankin, a local minister who helped fugitive slaves escape.

Because Cincinnati bordered a slave state, Kentucky, Harriet was able to visit a plantation across the river to see for herself the evils of slavery. *Uncle Tom's Cabin* was written in Brunswick, Maine, where the Stowes moved in 1850 when Calvin was appointed a professor at Bowdoin College.

The Harriet Beecher Stowe House. Photo courtesy of the Harriet Beecher Stowe House.

Today, her recently renovated Cincinnati home continues the early civil rights work Stowe began. The Harriet Beecher Stowe House serves as a cultural and educational resource center for youth and adults. The artifacts, pictures, guided tours, and informative lectures and seminars carry on the tradition of bringing about understanding between members of all ethnic groups.

The Victoria Inn

3567 Shaw Avenue
Cincinnati, OH 45208
(513) 321-3567
(513)321-3147 Fax

When Tom Possert and Debra Moore opened the Victoria Inn five years ago, they relied on their travel experiences to choose what was necessary for the comfort and convenience of their guests. High on the list were the private baths and phones, fax machines, and televisions, but also right up there for these two fitness buffs was a good scenic area in which to run! Your affable manager will even give you a running tour, which may be the ultimate way to appreciate the beauty of nearby Hyde Park. Guests can also enjoy a complimentary workout at the Cincinnati Sports Club.

Burning calories can bring on an appetite—a guest refrigerator just outside the rooms is stocked with complimentary soft drinks, yogurt, fruit, and snacks. Breakfast, too, is healthy and wholesome: try the breads and scones, with gourmet coffee for an eye-opener. The Victorian Suite has authentic 1880s furniture, a decorative fireplace, a whirlpool bath, and consists of a bedroom and adjoining sitting room. The Country Manor Room has the added pleasure of a private sleeping porch overlooking the pool, and the the turn-of-the-century English Garden Room offers a marvelous overstuffed chair and oversized claw-foot tub. Sky blue walls and white woodwork decorate the Wedgewood Room and accent the dark mahogany furnishings.

Rates: $79–$129
Credit Cards Accepted: Visa, MC, AMEX
Number of Guest Rooms: 4
Number of Baths: 4
Wheelchair Access: No

Pets: No
Children: If older than 14
Smoking: No
Senior Citizen Discount: No
Directions: See brochure

The Prospect Hill Bed and Breakfast

408 Boal Street
Cincinnati, OH 45210
(513) 421-4408

I love sitting in the past and admiring the future—something that can readily be done at the Prospect Hill. This elegantly restored 1867 Italianate townhouse has spectacular views of downtown Cincinnati, a city with an energy that can be felt and a skyline that redesigns itself overnight. The inn is located on a wooded hillside in the Prospect Hill National Historic District and is a superb example of the two-and-a-half-story brick homes that once were the hallmark of this section of the city. The rooms are large and decorated with period antiques, lawn furniture is arranged on back decks, and the garden is enjoyed by all. The hot tub is always a pleasant reminder of the creature comforts affordable to us today no matter how much we admire and often wish for simpler days, of which The Prospect Hill Bed and Breakfast is such a handsome reminder.

Rates: $89–$119
Credit Cards Accepted: Visa, MC, AMEX, Discover
Number of Guest Rooms: 3
Number of Baths: 2
Wheelchair Access: No

Pets: No
Children: Yes, with restrictions
Smoking: No
Senior Citizen Discount: No
Directions: See brochure

James Thurber House

77 Jefferson Avenue
Columbus, OH 43215
(614) 464-1032

Who: Erin Cody

When: 12:00 noon–4:00 P.M. every day except holidays

How Much: Admission is free; $.50 for brochure. Tours (on Sunday only) are $2 for adults, $1.50 for students.

Senior Citizen Discount: $1.50

Wheelchair Access: Yes, first floor only

Directions: When I-70 East or I-70 West merges with I-71 North, take the first exit, Broad Street. Go west (left) on Broad Street to the first street on the right, which is Jefferson Avenue.

What and Where: When James Thurber was awarded an honorary degree from his alma mater, Ohio State University, he declined to accept it. During the McCarthy era, it seems, campus speakers were required to submit their speeches for approval before they could be presented. As a vigorous opponent of censorship, Thurber considered the award to be no honor at all.

From my point of view, Thurber's decision to stand on principle was consistent with his personality and his view that human beings are victims of their frailties. Animals, he felt, would never stoop to such foolishness or arrogance. In his discussion of dogs, he notes that, "They demand very little of their heydey; a kind word is more to them than fame, a soup bone than gold; they are perfectly contented with a warm fire and a good book to chew (preferably an autographed first edition lent by a friend). ..."

His wry observations about animals and humans are most obvious in his whimsical *New Yorker* cartoons and stories. They carry over to his endearing character, Walter Mitty, who escapes the "real" world by living out his fantasies.

Whatever Thurber's inspiration, his life and personality are captured in the Thurber House. Unlike so many museums commemorating authors, there are no barriers here to prevent visitors from enjoying the ten rooms that make up the house. As in the Thurber Suite of the Algonquin Hotel in New York, we gain a feeling for the surroundings that created James Thurber and for the many people who molded his personality.

Located at 77 Jefferson Avenue in downtown Columbus, the house is on the site formerly occupied by the Central Ohio Lunatic Asylum. It is unlikely that this was lost on Thurber. In any event, after the asylum burned in 1868, the area was divided into three residential neighborhoods and also served temporarily as an exercising place for elephants when the circus came to town. The Thurber House itself was built in 1873 in the Victorian style that was the rage of the day. This is where James lived during his college days with his parents, two brothers, and a whimsical Airedale named Dakota.

Adjacent to the Thurber House are the Thurber Centennial Reading Garden (highlighted by five larger-than-life statues inspired by Thurber's dog cartoons) and the Thurber Center. These all serve as tribute to the man who described the house where "the alarms sound in the night, the electricity leaks, and the bed has been known to fall."

Harrison House Bed and Breakfast

313 West Fifth Avenue
Columbus, OH 43201
(614) 421-2202; (800) 827-4203

You don't have to be Walter Mitty to conjure up a convivial B&B conveniently located close to the Thurber House. Instead, simply choose the Harrison House, an elegant Queen Anne Victorian listed on the National Register of Historic Places. Step back to a more relaxed era and enjoy the magnificent woodwork, elegant lace curtains, and original cut-glass windows.

Congenial hosts Maryanne and Dick Olson offer four theme rooms that will catch your fancy. If you're a Victoriana buff, ask for the Victorian Room with its assortment of music boxes from all over the world, whose soothing melodies are guaranteed to lull you to sleep. Perhaps you're a "remember when" fan who would prefer the Memorabilia Room, filled with old wedding pictures and an Eastlake Victorian bed. Maybe you'd like to get back on track in the Railroad Room with its miniature engines, trains, railroad prints, and many railroad books. If you can never get enough of the yuletide spirit, try the Christmas Room, which features Maryanne's Santa collection, wall hangings, and needlework. Ho! Ho! Ho!

There is more year-round Christmas at One More Thing, the Olsons' gift shop, featuring Victorian mother and child prints by the award-winning artist Tina Mazzoni Solarz.

The Olsons report that their gourmet breakfasts are a hit with leisure and business travelers. If a conference is in your future, visit the third-floor cupola, which houses a fully equipped audiovisual conference room. Whether for business or pleasure, you'll enjoy the Harrison House, Victorian living in the heart of Columbus.

Rates: $79–$99
Credit Cards Accepted: Visa, MC, AMEX, Discover
Number of Guest Rooms: 4
Number of Baths: 4
Wheelchair Access: No

Pets: No
Children: Yes
Smoking: No
Senior Citizen Discount: No
Directions: See brochure

National Road/Zane Grey Museum

8850 East Pike
U.S. Route 40
Norwich, OH 43767
(614) 872-3143

Who: Alan P. King

When: March through November: Monday through Saturday, 9:30 A.M.–5:00 P.M. Sunday 12:00 noon–5:00 P.M.

How Much: $4 for adults, $1 for juniors ages 6 to 12

Senior Citizen Discount: Yes

Wheelchair Access: Yes

Directions: See brochure

What and Where: Zane Grey, father of the Western, was born and raised in Zanesville, Ohio. The city was named after the writer's great-grandfather, Ebenezer Zane, a pioneer who cut the first roads through central Ohio and helped lay the groundwork for the national highway system. During Ebenezer's lifetime Zanesville was a gateway to the Wild West, a place where civilization stopped. For Zane Grey, on the other hand, the West conjured up images of the high deserts and purple sage of Arizona, Utah, Colorado, and New Mexico. A retired buffalo hunter showed young Zane the wilds of the American Southwest. He in turn drew upon his knowledge of that spectacular land to bring the romance of the American cowboy into the lives of millions of readers. He wrote over 50 western novels, the most famous of which is *Riders of the Purple Sage*.

The National Road/Zane Grey Museum near Zanesville, Ohio, tells the story of the two Wests. A large section of the museum portrays the times in which the National Road was being built. The Zane Grey Wing contains an extensive collection of his trophies, manuscripts, and first editions of his novels.

Bogart's Bed & Breakfast

62 West Main Street
New Concord, OH 43762
(614) 826-7439; (614) 872-3514

It should come as no surprise that any bed and breakfast that serves an evening snack is my kind of place. Because I was raised in Indiana, homemade pies and cookies remind me of midwestern summers and state fairs. Bogart's B&B carries on this fine tradition by offering its guests a generous selection of home-baked goodies. If antiquing is your cup of tea, you've come to the right place. The B&B is furnished with antiques, all of which are for sale. For a perfect weekend of browsing, the New Concord area is an antiquer's paradise. Jack Bogart and his wife, Sharon, whose second business is their antique shop, are authorities when it comes to appreciating period pieces.

Perhaps what you'll really want after visiting the Zane Grey Museum is to sit in a cozy corner and read *Riders of the Purple Sage*.

Bogart's 70-foot wraparound screened porch offers the perfect spot for Zane Grey reading. Or perhaps you'd rather peruse your novels in the comfort of your well-appointed room.

Besides enjoying this 1830s landmark home and visiting the Zane Grey Museum, you are in the ideal location for visiting Muskingum College, Salt Fork State Park, and the Cambridge Glass Museum. Nature lovers will appreciate The Wilds, a 9,000-acre preserve dedicated to saving endangered animals. At Bogart's you'll be just a half hour's drive from the village of Dresden, home of the "world's largest basket." On the other hand, if you'd rather make a basket than gawk at the huge one listed in the *Guinness Book of World Records,* stop by the Longaberger "Make a Basket Shop" and learn how to weave your own masterpiece.

Rates: $65–$75
Credit Cards Accepted: Visa, MC, Discover
Number of Guest Rooms: 4
Number of Baths: 4
Wheelchair Access: No

Pets: No
Children: No
Smoking: No
Senior Citizen Discount: No
Directions: See brochure

OREGON

Oregon Shakespeare Festival

15 South Pioneer Street
P.O. Box 158
Ashland, OR 97520
(541) 482-4331
(541) 482-8045 Fax
Website: http://www.mind.net/osf/

Who: Box office

When: February 21 to November 2

How Much: $20–$45

Senior Citizen Discount: No

Wheelchair Access: Yes

Directions: Halfway between Portland and San Francisco on I-5 just minutes north of the Oregon-California border. The Medford–Rogue Valley International Airport is minutes away.

What and Where: Order tickets early because performances sell out quickly. You may fax, phone, or mail (orders are filled by postmark) your order. Book your backstage tour when placing your ticket order.

The Allen Pavilion of the Elizabethan Theatre seats 1,200. Here theatergoers enjoy the works of William Shakespeare and his contemporaries from June through September. The Festivals' two indoor theaters are open from February through October. Photo by Gregory Leiber.

Other events include unstaged readings of new plays, $5; spring and summer lectures, $4; Talks in the Park (informal talks with members of the acting company), free; The Feast of Will (a festive dinner with entertainment in Lithia Park celebrating the opening of the Elizabethan Theatre) $16; The Green Show (music and dance before every outdoor performance), free; The Exhibit Center (a museum of the Festival), open daily except Monday. Backstage Tour tickets separately or at the door are $2.

The Festival offers an embarrassment of riches. I highly recommend the free Green Show, which takes place at 7:00 P.M. before every outdoor performance. The Green is a lively Elizabethan musical revue, complete with beautiful period costumes and high-leaping dances.

Be sure to give yourself plenty of time to enjoy this magical village; in five days, we barely scratched the surface. Even if shopping usually makes you want to "get thee to a nunnery," the Tudor Guild Gift Shop is a *must*. It is a Shakespeare aficionado's dream; Shakespearean gifts are everywhere you look. Imagine Shakespeare tee-shirts, cocktail napkins, books entitled *Shakespeare for Lovers*, *Shakespeare Insults*, *Shakespeare on Management*, a game called "The Play's the Thing" and a Chaucer coloring book.

AUTHOR'S NOTE: An early act of the Festival's history could have been written by the bard himself. Convinced that Shakespearean productions would lose money, the city fathers asked Angus Bowmer, the theatre's founder, to allow them to hold boxing matches during the day. The proceeds from these matches would cover the Festival's losses. To the city fathers's surprise, Bowmer agreed, reasoning that if Shakespeare could put up with bull-and-bear baiting between shows, he could easily accept a less bloody sport. The amazing denouement to this first Fourth of July production was that Shakespeare fared better than boxing!

Chanticleer Bed and Breakfast Inn

120 Gresham Street
Ashland, OR 97520
(800) 898-1950

The Chanticleer Bed and Breakfast will immediately get you into a bookish mood. The very name of the inn comes from "Chanticleer and the Fox," a story related in Chaucer's *Canterbury Tales*. The inn feels cozy and snug—from the comfortable furniture, books, and fireplace in the living room to the inviting glasses of sherry. This popular bed and breakfast is one of the most romantic and desirable inns in Ashland. Shakespeare is only minutes away because the inn is within easy walking distance of the Festival.

The six guests rooms are all charming. The Rosette, with its queen-size antique wrought-iron bed and private entrance off the patio, is a favorite. Every room is furnished with antiques, fluffy goose-down comforters, fresh flowers, and crisp linens. Thoughtful touches are good reading lamps and imported soaps and lotions. Scripts of all the plays performed at the Shakespeare Festival highlight the appointments.

Measure for measure, the breakfasts are outstanding: shirred eggs with cream, Dutch babies, baked pears with orange sauce, blintzes, blueberry muffins, hot breads, fresh fruit, and excellent coffee and teas, not to mention the ultimate luxury, breakfast in bed. You can look forward to your delicious repast because the next day's breakfast menu is posted the night before.

Innkeeper Pebby Kuan offers a packet of excellent up-to-date information about Ashland in each of the guest rooms. One of her suggestions that I heartily endorse is dinner at a nearby restaurant, Monet. Here you're either surrounded by the beautiful Monet reproductions gracing the walls or seated in the Monet-inspired gardens. It's the food, however, that is worthy of a sonnet. I ordered the vegetable pâté appetizer, a creation of the chef and owner, Pierre, and an entree of salmon with spinach leaves.

Rates: $85–$160
Credit Cards Accepted: Visa, MC
Number of Guest Rooms: 6
Number of Baths: 6
Wheelchair Access: No
Pets: No
Children: No
Smoking: Outside only
Directions: Heading north on I-5, take Exit 14 (Ashland). Follow Siskiyou Boulevard; turn left on Union (Safeway on right in town); 2 blocks to Fairview Street; turn right, go 1 block, turn right on Gresham. From the north, take Ashland Exit 19 and follow the signs to downtown. Turn right on Gresham (library on right) and drive 2 blocks to Chanticleer on left.

Hersey House

451 North Main Street
Ashland, OR 97520
(541) 482-4563; (800) 482-4563

The Hersey House has been home to five generations of the family since 1904. When sisters Lynn Savage and Gail Orell converted it into an inn in 1983, they managed to keep the Victorian charm. The present-day Herseys felt the refurbishing was so authentic that they lent the inn family portraits of the first family members to live in the house. The Hersey House offers you a magnificent view of the Rogue Valley from the spacious front porch, and a lovely English garden. The innkeepers are always available to provide helpful advice. After a day of birding, bicycling, or barding, you'll be invited to partake of a social hour in the main parlor.

The four guest rooms are all charming. Each offers period furnishings, a queen-size bed, private bath, and central air conditioning. The Sunshine Terrace Room is a favorite, with a private balcony that overlooks the Cascade foothills. The Eastlake Room features an authentic Victorian bedstead along with a grand view of Mt. Ashland.

Breakfast is a civilized affair in which theater talk is sprinkled between courses of juice, fruit, and daily entrees such as eggs Hersey or gingerbread pancakes with lemon curd.

Save some time in your busy Ashland holiday for a trip to the new Pacific Northwest Museum of Natural History. It's one of the most exciting, hands-on, visually stimulating museums I've had the pleasure of visiting. The multisensory exhibits provide treats for all your senses. You'll feel a cool breeze wafting over you as you enter a lava tube. Inside, you'll see dioramas so lifelike that you'll be transported to the mountains or the coast. On a coastal wetlands boardwalk you can smell the outgoing tide and hear sea gulls mewing overhead. In the forest scene your feet will sink into the spongy pine forest floor. The whole experience is stunning.

Rates: $99–$130
Credit Cards Accepted: Visa, MC
Number of Guest Rooms: 5
Number of Baths: 5
Wheelchair Access: No

Pets: No
Children: If older than 12
Smoking: No
Senior Citizen Discount: No
Directions: See brochure

Morical House Garden Inn

668 North Main Street
Ashland, OR 97520
(541) 482-2254; (800) 208-0960

All that in this delightful garden grows,
Should happy be, and have immortal bliss.
—Edmund Spenser

If you want a treat for your senses, the expanded lush garden setting of the Morical House is the place to be. The garden is a veritable rainbow, and each season different-colored flowers take their turns delighting you. Birders will enjoy the bird sanctuary, with its variety of feeders, birdhouses, and plants.

The 1880s farmhouse is surrounded by an acre of rose gardens, rocks, lush lawns, and forest. Best of all, it has a splendid panoramic view of Bear Creek valley and the Cascade Mountains. The completely restored house offers twentieth-century comfort and nineteenth-century elegance: It features leaded and stained-glass windows, finely crafted woodwork, and antique furniture. Five of the guest rooms have mountain views, private baths with brass fixtures, air conditioning, and soundproofed walls. The two new garden rooms have vaulted wood ceilings, king-size beds, fireplaces, whirlpool tubs, cozy window seats, private entrances, and wet bars with refrigerators and microwaves. The carved wood mantels, stained-glass windows, and watercolors all represent the work of local artists.

Breakfast on the glassed-in sunporch is a treat. Partake of the smoothies and homemade baked goods; daily specials include such treats as Dutch pancakes and Oregon's own fruit basket of blueberries, raspberries, marionberries, and Red Haven peaches.

Between Shakespeare's theater and the inn's theater of the wild, you can play games in the parlor, enjoy a round of croquet, or watch quail families frolic in the ponds and waterfalls. Take part in some convivial banter with fellow guests and enjoy afternoon refreshments in the parlor or on the sunporch.

Innkeepers Gary and Sandye Moore will be pleased to give you private tours of their gardens. If you want to dig deeper into the Ashland garden scene, you'll enjoy the May Garden Tour, which features private and public gardens of Ashland, including Lithia Park and the Japanese Garden.

For a sensory delight of another type, guests who stay at the Morical for three nights, including the opening night of the Elizabethan Theater in mid-June, will get a free dinner at The Feast of Will. For other banquets on your own, I suggest the Plaza Cafe, a cheerful bistro featuring good food and a pleasant river setting; Alex's, where you can dine al fresco on delicious morsels; or Winchester Inn, which is also a B&B, where I recommend the smoked salmon appetizer and the rack of lamb.

Rates: $88–$160
Credit Cards Accepted: Visa, MC, AMEX, Discover
Number of Guest Rooms: 7
Number of Baths: 7
Wheelchair Access: Yes

Pets: No
Children: If older than 12
Smoking: No
Senior Citizen Discount: No
Directions: See brochure

Mt. Ashland Inn

550 Mt. Ashland Road
Ashland, OR 97520
(503) 482-8707; (800) 830-8707

If you are seeking a romantic adult summer camp that will pamper you, try the Mt. Ashland Inn. My husband and I spent three glorious days in mid-July roughing it in luxury. This magnificent cabin in the woods

was handcrafted from cedar logs cut on the surrounding property. Jerry and Elaine Shanafelt, the inn's former owners, are modern pioneers who designed and built this mountain hideaway. Jerry's woodworking skills and design sense are obvious throughout the inn, whether it be in the log archways, stained-glass windows, and log-slab circular staircase, or in the delightful hand-carved mountain scenes on the doors. Much of the furniture is his work as well.

Rock cliffs and forested slopes tower over one side of the road leading to the inn. On the other side, converging mountain ranges provide a breathtaking view. The Mt. Ashland Inn sits just two miles from the 7,500-foot summit of Mt. Ashland.

The Mt. Ashland Inn. Photo courtesy of the Mt. Ashland Inn.

This is an inn for all seasons. A path just outside the back door serves as a cross-country ski trail in the winter and the trailhead to a Pacific Crest Trail hike in the summer. Because it was July, David and I enjoyed a glorious stroll after breakfast. There is something satisfying about having a trailhead a few feet away from your bedroom door. Our walk in the picture-perfect setting was incredibly serene because we were virtually the only two-footed animals on the trail. Indoor sports enthusiasts, on the other hand, might prefer the selection of games or books in the inn's main room. Regardless, you can relax near the comfort of the large welcoming stone fireplace and enjoy some hot spiced cider.

Each of the guest rooms upstairs offers views of Mt. Shasta, Mt. McLoughlin, or some other part of the Cascades. Breakfast is a cozy affair, typically consisting of fresh juice and fruit followed by a hearty entree of puffy orange French toast and sausage or scrambled eggs with green chiles.

New innkeepers Chuck and Laurel Biegert continue the Shanafelts' fine tradition of spoiling their adult campers. Shakespeare Festival–goers are advised that the drive from Ashland to Mt. Ashland is time-consuming and somewhat inconvenient. But the Mt. Ashland Inn is not to be missed, so plan to stay here before or after you have seen the plays. There is a new outdoor spa and sauna where you can relax under beautiful Oregon skies and catch a view of Mt. McLoughlin. Another romantic treat is to stay at the new Skylakes Suite, complete with its own trickling waterfall and spectacular views of Mt. Shasta. Laurel says, "It has a sitting area with fireplace and a top-of-the-world atmosphere." If you want to get out in the mountains, you can borrow, free of charge, the inn's high-quality snowshoes or mountain bikes.

Rates: $76–$180
Credit Cards Accepted: Visa, MC, AMEX, Discover
Number of Guest Rooms: 5
Number of Baths: 5
Wheelchair Access: No

Pets: No
Children: If older than 10
Smoking: No
Senior Citizen Discount: No
Directions: See brochure

The Sylvia Beach Hotel

267 Northwest Cliff
Newport, OR 97365
(541) 265-5428

A hotel for bookaphiles and readaholics. Just think! We don't need to wait for the revolution, or next year in Marienbad, or until Godot shows up. We've finally been recognized as a bona fide subculture. Yes, the concept behind the Sylvia Beach Hotel excites me. The name is symbolic, a tribute to the admirable woman who owned the Shakespeare & Co. Bookstore in Paris in the 1920s and 1930s. We're talking about the Paris of that generation so poignantly and vividly described by Hemingway, Fitzgerald, and Stein, all of whom participated in that brief, shining artistic community. Sylvia Beach was a recognized patron of literature, and it is only fitting that her name live on in a hospitable establishment in another splendid setting. Owners Sally Ford and Goody Cable know she would approve!

This hotel for booklovers has 20 guest rooms that are furnished and named after some of our favorite authors. All rooms have private baths and are classified in three categories. The Classics rooms (oceanfront, fireplace, and deck) include Mark Twain, Colette, and Agatha Christie. The Novels rooms (nonocean, but still rooms with a view)

honor Robert Louis Stevenson, Willa Cather, Oscar Wilde, and Gertrude Stein. The Best-Sellers (ocean view) run a literary gamut bound to please in several categories: E. B. White, Alice Walker, Dr. Seuss, "Miss Emily" (Dickinson, that is), Tennessee Williams, Jane Austen, Herman Melville, F. Scott Fitzgerald, and Ernest Hemingway (inseparable, it seems), and Edgar Allan Poe.

Of course there is a library and a gift shop, well stocked with publications. Where else can you eat in a restaurant named Tables of Contents, where breakfast and dinner are served family-style? The sprawling beachhouse was built between 1910–1913 and under a number of previous noms de plume has always been a popular oceanside retreat. Four stories of distinctive dark green wood siding with a red roof, the hotel stands on a cliff above the surf of Nye Beach just outside Newport. Now recognized in the Register of Historic Landmarks, it seems as firmly ensconced in the annals of literature lovers as it is on the rugged Oregon coastline. My only suggestion to complement its perfection would be to have the rooms catalogued in the Dewey Decimal System.

Rates: $60–$139
Credit Cards Accepted: Visa, MC, AMEX
Number of Guest Rooms: 20
Number of Baths: 20
Wheelchair Access: Yes

Pets: No
Children: 5 and older
Smoking: No
Senior Citizen Discount: No
Directions: See brochure

Pennsylvania

⊷ ⊱⊰ ⊶

Green Hills Farm: Home of Pearl S. Buck

P.O. Box 181
Perkasie, PA 18944
(215) 249-0100

Who: The Pearl S. Buck Foundation; Joseph Ambrose, communications

When: The foundation is open all year except during the months of January and February. Tours at 10:30 A.M., 1:30 P.M., and 2:30 A.M. on Tuesday through Saturday, and 1:30 P.M. and 2:30 P.M. on Sunday. Closed Monday, holidays, January, and February.

How Much: $5 for adults, $4 for juniors

Senior Citizen Discount: $4

Wheelchair Access: Yes

Directions: See brochure

What and Where: "I decided on a region where the landscapes are varied, where farm and industry lived side by side, where sea was near at hand, mountains not far away, and city and countryside were not enemies." In her autobiography, *My Several Worlds,* Noble Prize–winner Pearl S. Buck so described her retreat, Green Hills Farm. Here on this beautiful 60-acre homestead you will feel inspired (at least I did) by this amazing humanitarian. Even if you are a dyed-in-the-wool cynic, you will still enjoy the wooded landscape and the lovely works of art.

The Green Hills Farm is a blend of the author's two worlds. In the spacious library, two Pennsylvania stoneware jugs serve as lamp bases upon the "Good Earth" desk, a beautifully handcarved Chinese hardwood piece, at which she wrote her award-winning novel. It is the perfect juxtaposition of East and West, which is symbolic of Pearl Buck's life.

The only American woman to win both the Pulitzer and Noble Prizes, Pearl Sydenstricker was born in Hillsboro, West Virginia, and raised in China as the daughter of missionary parents. Like many writers, the young Pearl was surrounded by storytellers. She had a Chinese nurse who told her magical stories. Pearl's father, whose missionary work took him to remote and dangerous parts of China, entertained her with his tales of adventure. Her mother regaled her for hours with stories of her own childhood in West Virginia. Her mother also served as her teacher and her first writing coach. As Pearl grew older, her mother started sending some of her daughter's short pieces to the *Shanghai Mercury,* an English-language newspaper that had a weekly edition for children. When she was 15, the young author left for boarding school in Shanghai, her first formal schooling, and at age 17 returned to the United States to enter

Randolph-Macon College. She wrote for the college paper and in her senior year won two literary prizes, one of which was for best short story.

When her mother became ill in China, Pearl went back to care for her. Pearl and her new husband, John Lossing Buck, an professor of agriculture, lived in a town in north China. The Bucks lived there for five years, and the sights and sounds and stories of those times were all recorded later in the novel *The Good Earth*. The marriage was not a happy one (he insisted she turn all her earnings from her writing over to him) and ended in divorce. They had one child, Carol, who was mentally retarded.

In January 1923, an article by Buck appeared in *Atlantic* magazine. She immediately became very much in demand by American magazines, and on April 10, 1930, her first book, which she wrote on a ship sailing to the United States, was published. It was an instant hit, and by the time *The Good Earth* came out ten months later, *East Wind, West Wind* was in its third printing.

After many trips to China and Europe, Pearl and her second husband, Richard J. Walsh, the president of the John Day Company (coincidentally the publishers of Pearl's books) moved to Green Hills and adopted five children. (After his death in 1960 she adopted four more.) She lived with her international family in the nineteenth-century Pennsylvania farmhouse for the next 38 years. She remarked that the stone walls of the 1835 farmhouse—now a National Historic Landmark—symbolized for her durability and strength.

You'll get a sense of this translator, gardener, and art fancier when you tour the ten furnished rooms at Green Hills Farm. Some highlights are the lovely Oriental antiques and the awards room displaying her many honors and awards, including the Nobel Prize. You are welcome to pay a visit to the humanitarian's grave, which is under a towering ash tree on the homestead, a place she called the "root place of my American life." Even though Pearl Buck died on March 6, 1973, at the age of 80, her vision is very much alive at Green Hills today. Through the efforts of The Pearl S. Buck Foundation, the nonprofit organization she founded in 1964 for the education and general welfare of the displaced children of the world, her spirit permeates the farm. She paid particular attention to children she called "Amerasians," the abandoned offspring of American service men and Asian women.

There are many tours, lunches, dinners, readings, and special events at the Pearl S. Buck Foundation. The grounds are also available for weddings and parties. Call for details.

Peace Valley Bed and Breakfast

75 Chapman Road
Doylestown, PA 18901
(215) 230-7711

A serene place to stay when you're visiting Pearl S. Buck's home is the Peace Valley B&B in nearby Doylestown. The tranquil country setting of this inn, far away from the hustle and bustle of everyday life, makes this renovated 200-year-old stone farmhouse a place where you will want to linger. On the grounds are lovely old trees overlooking a one-acre pond and private tennis courts. If you like the outdoors, you'll want to take advantage of the year-round bird-watching, biking, canoeing, and sailing. Bring your camera to capture on film the blue herons, waterfowl, and deer. If you're more indoorsy than outdoorsy, there are nearby antique shops, art galleries, and museums. Your hosts, Jane and Harry Beard, will be glad to suggest neighborhood restaurants.

Peace Valley offers four fully furnished guest rooms, all with private baths. There is also a two-bedroom suite available. A fresh continental breakfast will get your day off to a good start. After a day at the Pearl S. Buck Foundation and exploring beautiful Bucks County, relax in the living room with a good book or one of the Beards' many board games.

Rates: $90–$130
Credit Cards Accepted: Visa, MC, AMEX
Number of Guest Rooms: 4
Number of Baths: 4
Wheelchair Access: No

Pets: No
Children: With restrictions
Smoking: No
Senior Citizen Discount: No
Directions: See brochure

Edgar Allan Poe National Historic Site

313 Walnut Street
Philadelphia, PA 19106
(215) 597-8780

Who: Jim Heaney

When: 9:00 A.M.–5:00 P.M. Wednesday through Sunday from November through May and every day from June through October.

How Much: Free

Senior Citizen Discount: NA

Wheelchair Access: Yes, first floor only

Directions: See brochure

What and Where: Few cities in the United States are more imbued with American history than Philadelphia. Renowned as the home of the Constitutional Convention, Independence Hall, and the Liberty Bell, it served as the nation's capital for the last decade of the eighteenth century. During this period the city on the banks of the Schuylkill and Delaware Rivers witnessed many major events, such as President Washington's inauguration to a second term, the establishment of the U.S. Mint, and the formal adoption of the Bill of Rights. In the two centuries since the seat of government moved to its present site in Washington, D.C., Philadelphia has evolved into a major industrial and commercial center. In the process it has developed a strong cultural foundation as the home of the University of Pennsylvania, the Franklin Institute, the Philadelphia Orchestra, and the Philadelphia Museum of Art. There is a caveat for tourists, however, in that the mechanics of getting from here to there in the city is rarely simple; navigating the city's maze of streets is a daunting task that would tax the skills of Magellan. Therefore, if you are planning to visit the Independence National Historic Park and the nearby Edgar Allan Poe National Historic Site, I urge you to consider using Philadelphia's public transporation system.

There are not too many of us who associate the enigmatic Poe with Philadelphia, but he lived in the city from 1838 through 1844. It was here that he enjoyed his most successful years as an editor and critic. Here, also, he published some of his most famous tales, including "The Gold Bug," "The Fall of the House of Usher," "The Tell-Tale Heart," and "The Murders in the Rue Morgue." It was "Rue Morgue," incidentally, that gave rise to a new form of literature, the detective story, and that inspired such later writers as Sir Arthur Conan Doyle and Erle Stanley Gardner.

As for the Edgar Allan Poe National Historic Site, it consists of three buildings, including the small brick house at 530 North Seventh Street. This is where Poe lived for a year or so toward the end of his stay in Philadelphia, with his wife, Virginia, his mother-in-law, Maria Clemm, and their cat, Catterina. It is not known whether or not the rented house was furnished, but the original furniture there has disappeared. This unfortunate turn of events merely intensifies the mystery that shrouds the life of Edgar Allan Poe.

The Amsterdam Bed and Breakfast

P.O. Box 1139
Valley Forge, PA 19482-1139
(215) 983-9620; (800) 952-1580

Because of the name, it should come as no great surprise that Ino Vandersteur, one of the owners of the Amsterdam, is a chemical engineer from Holland. Pamela, his charming and hospitable wife, is a native Philadelphian who received her culinary training in the Netherlands. Her breakfasts reflect an Indonesian background. The Dutch East Indies eggs in curry sauce with a side of bacon were delicious and offered a refreshing change from standard bills of fare. A fruit compote made with brown sugar, butter, and amaretto rounded out the meal beautifully. With plenty of advance notice, Pam will produce her reknowned Indonesian rijsttafel. This dinner extravaganza consists of rice served with different sauces and other classic Indonesian foods.

The Amsterdam lives up to its name. The elegant living room is beautifully furnished with Dutch paintings and Dutch memorabilia. Our attractive second-floor bedroom was decorated with wooden shoes, Delft china, paintings of Dutch street scenes, and tulips.

Both Ino and Pam are blessed with a puckish sense of humor. Pam refers to my physicist husband and me as "Einstein and the literary lady." At breakfast, she will regale you with some of her more entertaining moments of innkeeping. B&Bs, after all, could provide a story line for many a situation comedy!

If you want to take the day off and indulge in some nonliterary activities, you can choose among Valley Forge National Park, the Lancaster County Amish country, the Reading and Lancaster factory outlets, or the Brandywine Valley Museum in Chadds Ford. Birders will enjoy the John Jay Audubon House, the only Audubon home remaining in this country. You can also relax in the Amsterdam's luxurious hot tub and follow it by a cozy evening of champagne sipping.

Rates: $65–$75
Credit Cards Accepted: Visa, MC
Number of Guest Rooms: 4
Number of Baths: 4
Wheelchair Access: No

Pets: Yes
Children: Yes
Smoking: In designated areas
Senior Citizen Discount: Yes
Directions: See brochure

The Thomas Bond House

129 South Second Street
Philadelphia, PA 19106
(215) 923-8523; (800) 845-BOND

If you consider Benjamin Franklin a literary figure, as I do, you'll enjoy the Thomas Bond House's linkage with Philadelphia's favorite Renaissance man. Dr. Thomas Bond and Benjamin Franklin founded Pennsylvania Hospital, the first public hospital in the United States, which was chartered in 1751. Eighteen years later, admittedly with no apparent help from Franklin, Bond built the original part of what we now know as the Thomas Bond House.

The Thomas Bond House is located in the heart of the historic district. It is tastefully furnished with period furniture and accessories. The bedrooms contain twin or queen-size beds. Two suites have queen-size beds and queen-size sofa beds, as well as whirlpool baths and working fireplaces. All rooms have a private bath, telephone, and television.

Before visiting the Edgar Allan Poe National Historic Site, relax with a continental breakfast on weekdays or a full breakfast on weekends. Spend an extra day in town and visit the Rodin Museum and the Barnes Foundation Museum in suburban Merion. Head back to the Thomas Bond House in the early evening for complimentary wine and cheese.

The innkeepers will give you suggestions for dinner choices at any one of Philadelphia's fine restaurants. You might want to resist dessert, because freshly baked cookies will await your return to the inn. On the other hand, if you feel that you can never have too many desserts, then go ahead and indulge!

Rates: $90–$160
Credit Cards Accepted: Visa, MC, AMEX, Discover, Diners Club
Number of Guest Rooms: 12
Number of Baths: 12
Wheelchair Access: No

Pets: No
Children: Yes
Smoking: No
Senior Citizen Discount: No
Directions: See brochure

SOUTH CAROLINA

— ᛜ◆ᛝ —

Fort Sumter National Monument

1214 Middle Street
Sullivans Island, SC 29482
(803) 883-3123

Who: Superintendent

When: 9:00 A.M.–5:00 P.M. every day except Christmas

How Much: Free

Senior Citizen Discount: NA

Wheelchair Access: Yes

Directions: From Charleston, take US 17N (business route) to Mount Pleasant; turn right on SC 703. At Sullivans Island, turn right on Middle Street; the fort is located 1.5 miles from this intersection.

What and Where: Fort Moultrie, a part of Fort Sumter National Monument, is interesting if you're a history buff because it spans the time period from the Revolutionary War to World War II. However, for our purposes, your visit here is mostly to envision the fort through the eyes of young Edgar Allan Poe. Under the alias Edgar A. Perry, Poe enlisted in the army and his unit was sent to Fort Moultrie. Poe was fascinated by Sullivans Island, which he immortalized in "The Gold Bug."

The Barksdale House Inn

27 George Street
Charleston, SC 29401
(803) 577-4800

Edgar Allan Poe never stayed in any place so elegant as the Barksdale House Inn—certainly not in the army! This inn is Charleston at its finest, from its historic atmosphere to its lovely formal gardens.

It's always good for your fantasy life to imagine yourself in a different era. How does living the life of a wealthy Charleston planter, a former member of the South Carolina House of Representatives, sound to you?

George Barksdale, if he were alive today, would be proud and happy to have you visit this restored and elegant inn that was once this Southern gentleman's townhouse. The Barksdale House's location in the heart of the historic district gives you easy access to historic Charleston.

This breathtakingly beautiful establishment reflects the great care that has gone into the creation of unique guest accommodations.

Guests may choose to stay in *chambres* whose motifs may be Oriental, French, Victorian, or Colonial. Each is a feast for the eyes and provides comforts galore.

Many quarters feature double baths, bay windows, king-size Rice beds, armoires, original arched fireplaces, crystal accessories, piecrust breakfast tables, dry bars, whirlpool baths with showers, and charming writing tables. All are furnished in decorator chosen colors and fabrics.

Begin your day with a complimentary continental breakfast complete with morning paper and fresh flowers. Breakfast is served in your room or in the courtyard.

Don't leave Charleston without taking a sight-seeing tour of this historic city. Afterward, and before heading out for some low-country cuisine, stop on the back porch or in the garden of the Barksdale House for afternoon tea or sherry.

Rates: $79–$180
Credit Cards Accepted: Visa, MC
Number of Guest Rooms: 14
Number of Baths: 14
Wheelchair Access: No

Pets: No
Children: If older than 7
Smoking: In designated areas
Senior Citizen Discount: For AARP members
Directions: Call for directions

John Rutledge House Inn

116 Broad Street
Charleston, SC 29401
(803) 723-7999; (800) 476-9741

I'm a sucker for breakfast delivered to my room—it seems so terribly civilized. So when a tray of fresh pastries, juice, and coffee arrived at the appointed hour at my room at the John Rutledge House, I felt like a southern lady of leisure. It was just the fortification I needed before heading out for my architectural walking tour of the city. This relaxing morning repast would also serve you well if you were planning on a tour of the beautiful Magnolia Plantation and Gardens or the Audubon Swamp Gardens.

If you would rather stay at home at the inn and revel in its history, here are some facts to get you started. George Washington did not sleep here, although he did breakfast here with the lady of the house in 1791. This fact alone would entitle the inn to its designation as a National Historic Landmark. But of course, the woman's husband, John Rutledge, earned his own special place in history. He was one of the signers of the

John Rutledge House Inn. Photo courtesy of John Rutledge House Inn.

Constitution and a chief justice of the U.S. Supreme Court.

The beautiful details of the building's eighteenth- and nineteenth-century architecture, such as the elaborately carved Italian marble fireplaces, the original plaster moldings, the inlaid floors, and the graceful ironwork, have all been authentically restored.

The inn has 19 rooms within a complex of three buildings. You can choose from the elegant rooms done in greens and pink, the spacious suites, or, for maximum seclusion, hideaways in the two carriage houses. All rooms have color TVs and private baths and refrigerators. In the afternoon and evening colonial Charleston is recreated in the inn's ballroom. Wine and sherry are offered in this opulent hall, where patriots, statesmen, and presidents have gathered. The city's finest restaurants, theaters, shops, and markets are all within a few minutes' walk. You can't leave town without trying some of Charleston's great seafood, especially the local favorite, she-crab soup.

Rates: $150–$260
Credit Cards Accepted: Visa, MC, AMEX, Discover, Diners Club
Number of Guest Rooms: 19
Number of Baths: 19
Wheelchair Access: Yes

Pets: No
Children: Yes
Smoking: Yes
Senior Citizen Discount: Yes
Directions: See brochure

Two Meeting Street Inn

2 Meeting Street
Charleston, SC 29401
(803) 723-7322

Charleston is a city of possibilities. There are wonderful beaches, interesting museums, and the world-famous Spoleto Festival. Take your pick. But to fully enjoy this city, which many have called a southern New York, stay at the elegant Two Meeting Street Inn.

To sit on the veranda of Two Meeting Street, a beautifully renovated 1892 Queen Anne mansion, is to enjoy the ambience of the Old South. In the quiet of a late afternoon, as you chat with new acquaintances, you will want to sip sherry and savor succulent hors d'oeuvres as you savor the scene. Here you have manicured lawns, bountiful blooming gardens, and ancient willows swaying in the breeze. In nearby Battery Park you might witness a wedding.

The mansion itself is filled with antiques, Oriental rugs, silver, and crystal. Tiffany stained-glass windows allow the sun to cast colorful shadows on the warm oak paneling.

Guest rooms are luxurious, with four-poster and canopied beds. Period pieces add charm to the delightful decor. Although the inn is known for its period elegance, it is not a please-do-not-touch kind of place. Manager Karen Spell, daughter of the owners and herself a permanent resident, will see to it that the highest-quality personal service is given. Small kitchens on each floor permit visitors to prepare coffee or cool wine. Continental breakfasts are served.

Later in the day, dine at Carolina's (try pea cakes, crayfish tasso pasta or pecan brittle fruit baskets) or Magnolia's (which does amazing things with grits and other southern specialities, uptown American cuisine with a down South flavor), two of Charleston's finest restaurants.

Rates: $135–$225
Credit Cards Accepted: None
Number of Guest Rooms: 9
Number of Baths: 9
Wheelchair Access: No
Pets: No
Children: If older than 12

Smoking: No
Senior Citizen Discount: No
Directions: Two Meeting Street Inn is 25 minutes from the airport. Take I-26 east to the last exit, Meeting Street downtown. The inn is the last house on Meeting Street.

SOUTH DAKOTA

—•— ≝◈≋ —•—

Laura Ingalls Wilder Memorial Society

105 Olivette
P.O. Box 344
De Smet, SD 57231-0344
(605) 854-3383

Who: Sherry Palmlund or Craig Munger

When: June through August 9:00 A.M.–7:00 P.M. daily; September 9:00 A.M.–4:00 P.M. Monday through Saturday, 12:00 noon–4:00 P.M. Sunday; October, April, and May 9:00 A.M.–4:00 P.M. Monday through Saturday; November through March 9:00 A.M.– 4:00 P.M. Monday through Friday

How Much: $5 for adults, $2 for juniors ages 5–12

Senior Citizen Discount: No

Wheelchair Access: No

Directions: Call for directions

What and Where: Is there a little girl alive who wasn't captivated by the adventures of Laura Ingalls Wilder in *Little House on the Prairie*? As a young reader, I felt every bump of the stagecoach, shared Laura's wide-eyed wonderment in discovering the Wild West, and enjoyed experiencing the intimacy of the close-knit Wilder family.

As a big kid, I was thrilled to visit the Laura Ingalls Wilder Memorial in De Smet, South Dakota. This was a chance to step back into the pages of six volumes of *Little House on the Prairie* and feel a kinship with the pioneer family and its early struggles. I enjoyed a wonderful tour of the town (sponsored by the Laura Ingalls Wilder Memorial Society), which pinpointed many of the sites that appear in the book. The tour begins at the restored Surveyor's House, the little frame structure where the Ingalls family spent their first fall and winter here (described so vividly in *By the Shores of Silver Lake*). The tour includes the sites of stores mentioned in the books and then continues to the Ingalls home, where the family lived from 1887 to 1928.

On Highway 14, just east of town, is the site of the Ingalls homestead, where the family occupied a claim shanty in 1889 before moving back to town to spend *The Long Winter*. If you will be visiting in late June or early July, be certain to get tickets for The Laura Ingalls Wilder Pageant.

These Happy Golden Years is the story of Laura after she married Almanzo Wilder. You can visit the site of this upbeat story just 1.5 miles north of town at the Wilder homestead. It was here that her daughter, Rose Wilder Lane, was born. Rose continued the literary tradition and wrote *Let the Hurricane Roar* and *Free Land*, the story of South Dakota pioneers in the 1870s and 1880s.

In order to appreciate De Smet and recapture the feeling of pioneer life, I recommend that you either read or reread *The First Four Years* and *On the Way Home,* two books set in De Smet, Wilder's adopted home.

The Prairie House Manor

209 Poinsett Avenue (SD 25)
DeSmet, SD 57231
(605) 854-9131; (800) 297-2146
(605) 854-9001 Fax

As a little girl I wished I could somehow materialize in the pages of Laura Ingalls Wilder's *Little House on the Prairie.* Somewhat older now, and I hope a bit more realistic, I was nonetheless thrilled to find that there really is a Prairie House Manor and that it is smack dab in the center of the Laura Ingalls Wilder homestead area. I loved being within walking distance of the homes and museum.

The Prairie House Manor has a variety of accommodations. In the newly restored home itself you can enjoy the gracious living of the past and all the luxury of the present. Four units, complete with private bath, color TV, table and chairs, and air conditioning, await your selection. You can pick My Rose Garden, featuring a queen-size four-poster bed in a stately room with a large bath, shower, and dressing room. This is a wonderful bridal or anniversary suite. How about Americana Medley, a large family room with three beds? Or Chantilly Lace, an exquisite room with a large bath, shower, and dressing area. This room is perfect for a quiet restful weekend in the heartland of America. Just curl up with some Laura Ingalls Wilder books and relive the pioneer woman's experience.

For larger literary groups, you might consider the Lodge or the Cottage. Innkeeper Connie Cheny is a good cook and no one goes away hungry. You'll be served a full breakfast, perhaps the house favorite, French toast. You also have a choice of pancakes, waffles, and farm-fresh eggs.

Rates: $45–$95
Credit Cards Accepted: None
Number of Guest Rooms: 6
Number of Baths: 6
Wheelchair Access: Yes

Pets: Yes
Children: Yes
Smoking: No
Senior Citizen Discount: Yes
Directions: See brochure

TEXAS

❈

Baylor University: Armstrong Browning Library

Eighth & Spreight Streets
P.O. Box 97152
Waco, TX 76798-7152
(817) 755-3566

Who: Paulette Smith

When: 8:00 A.M.–5:00 P.M. Monday through Friday, 9:00 A.M.–12:00 noon on Saturday

How Much: Free, donations gladly accepted

Senior Citizen Discount: NA

Wheelchair Access: Yes

Directions: From I-35, take the Fourth and Fifth Streets exit. Turn North toward Baylor (which will be to the right if you are coming from the south, left if from the north). Stay right on Fifth; at Dutton turn right and proceed to Eighth Street. Turn left on Eighth. The library is two blocks on the left.

What and Where: One man with a vision can be a powerful force. Dr. A. J. Armstrong, the re- markable man behind the Armstrong Brown- ing Library, had a dream: "If we can create a place where young people can meditate on great thoughts and by that means give the world another Dante, another Shakespeare, an-

Elizabeth Barrett Browning's writing desk. Photo courtesy of Armstrong Browning Library.

other Browning, we shall count the cost a bargain." As you can see from his portrait in the library, Dr. Armstrong was a man of steely determination. When I first looked at his likeness, I was struck by his resemblance to Clarence, the eccentric angel in Frank Capra's classic movie, *It's a Wonderful Life.* When I learned about Dr. Armstrong's life, I decided that the lookalikes were twins in many ways: in their creativity, resolve, and amazing ability to perform tasks people thought were undoable. In Armstrong's case, his goal was to give Waco a beautiful palace, a castle lasting 1,000 years, a legacy that would provide a sense of permanence.

One of the most popular teachers on campus, Armstrong had always been an avid collector of Browningiana. But he knew it took more than scholarship to realize his dream; he needed money. He facilitated the fund-raising effort in 1912 by establishing Armstrong Educational Tours. During the next 20 years Armstrong conducted summer tours of the world's major cultural centers for more than 4,000 people. In addition, he was the literary Sol Hurok of his day, bringing the likes of Robert Frost, William Butler Yeats, Carl Sandburg, Sinclair Lewis, and Amy Lowell to Baylor.

The Judge Baylor House

908 Spreight
Waco, TX 76706
(817) 756-0273; (888) JBAYLOR
(817) 756-0711 Fax
E-mail: jbaylor@iamerica.net

The Judge Baylor House is located just one and a half blocks from the incredible Armstrong Browning Library. You'll enjoy your stay at the Judge Baylor, a charming two-story red-brick home featuring four bedrooms and the Judge Baylor Suite, all with private baths and either king, queen, or twin beds. The innkeepers, Bruce and Dorothy Dyer, have kept their inn small enough that they are able to give time and attention to their guests. Their living quarters are located on the grounds of the Judge Baylor, so the Dyers are available whenever they are needed.

Ask your congenial hosts to tell you about the inn's namesake, Judge R.E.B. Baylor, the founder of Baylor University,

which was chartered by the Republic of Texas in 1845. The name is suitable, because the inn is adjacent to the university's campus.

The four bedrooms at the Judge Baylor House are named for the Dyer children, Anne, Aaron, Alan, and Amy. Identifying each room beside the door is a framed chalk profile drawing made on a trip to Disneyland in 1964.

You might enjoy playing the grand piano in the living room or relaxing in the swing that hangs from a large ash tree on the front lawn. Your literary destination, the Armstrong Browning Library, is minutes away, and if you want to pepper your visit with some more excitement, the Dr. Pepper Museum is also close at hand.

Rates: $69–$89
Credit Cards Accepted: Visa, MC
Number of Guest Rooms: 5
Number of Baths: 5
Wheelchair Access: Yes

Pets: No
Children: Yes
Smoking: No
Senior Citizen Discount: No
Directions: Directions on brochure

O. Henry's House: Lone Star Brewery

600 Lone Star Boulevard
San Antonio, TX 78204
(210) 270-9465

Who: Bill West

When: Open daily 9:00 A.M. to 5:00 P.M. Closed Christmas and New Year's Day.

How Much: Admission is $5 for adults, $1.75 for children ages 6 to 11; children under 6 admitted free. There is free parking and complimentary Lone Star beer and root beer.

Senior Citizen Discount: $4

Wheelchair Access: Yes

Directions: From I-10 East, take the Probandt exit left. Drive about 3 blocks and turn right on Lone Star Boulevard. The brewery is located about 2 blocks away. From I-10 West, turn right onto Probandt to Lone Star Boulevard.

What and Where: Only in the great state of Texas with its wild and woolly ways would the O. Henry House be sitting smack dab in the middle of a brewery. Lucky for short story fans, the Kush family, owners of the Lone Star Brewery, are preservationists, and when the house was in danger of falling under a wrecker's ball the Kushes moved the entire O. Henry home from South Presa Street to the brewery. It really is a happy and appropriate resting place for the colorful author's home: It seems that O. Henry was a frequent visitor to the Buckhorn Bar, which is also housed at the brewery. William Sydney Porter, known to literature as O. Henry, liked to belly up to the bar and sip a longneck while drawing on a wealth of Texas characters for his short stories. You can probably feel his ghost at the bar stool next to you as you sip your rootin' tootin' root beer or something stronger at the turn-of-the-century maple and cherrywood bar.

Besides O. Henry's House, you can mosey on over to the other exhibits; the brewery is an embarrassment of riches. You can see birds from around the world at the Buckhorn Hall of Feathers, wander through a weird and wild horn collection at the Buckhorn Hall of Horns, dive into the Buckhorn Hall of Fins and marvel at fish from the seven seas, or make friends with the Lone Star State's greatest heroes, immortalized in the Hall of Texas History Wax Museum.

Beckmann Inn and Carriage House

222 E. Guenther Street
San Antonio, TX 78204
(210) 229-1449; (800) 945-1449
(210) 229-1061 Fax
Website: http://saweb.com//beckbb

I admire people who pursue their roots; I am in equal admiration of those who lovingly and with great persistence seek out the history behind old homes. This is certainly the case with Betty Jo and Don Schwartz, who were able to trace their 1886 Historic Landmark house from its construction by Albert Beckmann (it was a present for his wife and built on the grounds of her family's flour mill, still a city landmark) through various owners and additions, including porches, new entryways, and even a new address less notorious than the original (the house faced on Madison Street, location of an infamous turn-of-the-century brothel). Fourteen-foot ceilings and tall classic windows lend stature to this single-story dwelling, the interior of which is much admired for its mosaic parquet floor shipped all the way from Paris. Victorian antiques of fine quality are comfortably arranged in every room and are pleasant reminders of the lifestyle of the early German bürgers.

The food, too, recalls a more leisurely time, when appetite and appreciation for a good meal went hand in glove. Dutch pancakes with spicy apples and sausage patties is a prime example, or stuffed cinnamon French toast with Canadian bacon. Served in the dining room or on wicker furniture on the very special sunporch, such meals are true delights. Both the Guenther and Madison Rooms have private entrances, beds with seven-foot walnut headboards, and other period pieces, such as a wardrobe and Victorian gentleman's chairs. The Library Room features a fireplace with a mantel of rare burl pine. Behind the main house is the carriage house, with two private suites, each with sitting room, bath, flower-filled window boxes, and brick patio or porch. Surrounding the entire property is a replica of the original cypress picket fence, which, I was told upon inquiring, would probably last "forever." I like that kind of forward thinking.

Rates: $90–$130
Credit Cards Accepted: Visa, MC, AMEX, Discover
Number of Guest Rooms: 5
Number of Baths: 5
Wheelchair Access: No

Pets: No
Children: If older than 12
Smoking: No
Senior Citizen Discount: Based on availability
Directions: See brochure

Adams House Bed and Breakfast

231 Adams Street
San Antonio, TX 78210
(210) 224-4791; (800) 666-4810
(210) 223-5125 Fax

While Scott Lancaster was traveling through Israel, Australia, and New Zealand and staying in bed and breakfasts, he decided to open one of his own. "I liked the people I encountered at B&Bs. Now, as an innkeeper, I enjoy my guests. It helps me relive my travels when I talk to my visitors, many of whom are European."

The genteel job of running a bed and breakfast is a far cry from Lancaster's former career as a theater arts teacher in an inner-city Dallas school. "It was a very stressful situation, to say the least," the bespectacled innkeeper told me as we sipped Earl Grey tea in his large kitchen. "I saw students and parents get beaten up. There were bomb threats almost every day and policemen patrolling in the hall."

The part of teaching Lancaster enjoyed, the theater, is evident in the Adams House. One guest room features theatrical posters and other theater memorabilia. Lancaster plans to implement murder mystery weekends, poetry readings, and other events for the literati. If you want to discuss Australian or Asian literature, he's your man—he studied both at the University of Hawaii.

Another subject near and dear to Lancaster's heart is family heirlooms, and the Adams House is full of beautiful ones, such as the family quilts his great-grandmother made. His grandfather's furniture fills the house, and it works nicely with the beautiful woodwork and banisters.

My favorite family treasures were Lancaster's mother's baby quilts and her doll collection, all in excellent condition. The old family pictures in the hallway are a nice touch.

When I first saw the Adams House, I had a flashback to Key West or New Orleans. The house evokes a charming, sleepy southern mood. My stepdaughter and I stayed in the sweet little cottage with its own bath, kitchen, and courtyard. The next morning we joined a jovial breakfast set for quiche with a side of salsa, French toast, bread (you can toast it yourself), coffee cake, juice, and coffee.

Although you are a short ride away from the O. Henry House in the Lone Star Brewery, you are already staying at a writer's house. Lancaster told me that he would like to emulate Harper Lee, author of *To Kill a Mockingbird*. While he scrubbed the dishes and I watched (travel writing does have its advantages), Lancaster explained that Harper Lee told her coterie of friends that she had a great novel in her. Her friends supported her during the year it took to write the novel. And the rest, as they say in the storybooks, is literary history.

Rates: $65–$125
Credit Cards Accepted: Visa, MC, AMEX, Discover
Number of Guest Rooms: 5
Number of Baths: 6
Wheelchair Access: No

Pets: No
Children: If older than 10
Smoking: No
Senior Citizen Discount: No
Directions: See brochure

A Yellow Rose B&B and Gallery

229 Madison
San Antonio, TX 78204
(800) 950-9903
(210) 229-1691 Fax

Located in the King William historic district yet only two blocks from the famous Riverwalk, the San Antonio Yellow Rose is a flowering beauty indeed. Charles Mueller built this brick home in 1878, making sure allowances were made for the grand staircase that rises 25 feet to the second-story ceiling. Triple-hung stenciled glass windows abound, and the parlor has ten-foot red pine pocket doors that lead into the Empire dining room. Trice heirlooms hinting of the family's eastern roots are a perfect match for this handsome period setting. Five bedrooms grace the household, reflecting the names of flowers and plants dear to the heart of Texans. The Yellow Rose Room offers a pencil-post bed set off by Pierre Duex fabrics and French-glazed yellow walls. Behind the main house is the original farmhouse, and just off the upstairs porch is the Blue Bonnet Room.

The antique bed has been adapted to accommodate queen-size bedding. Blue and white wallpaper recreates the ambience of the Victorian era. An elegantly grand suite is the Magnolia, with its centerpiece, a cinnabar and ebony four-poster rice bed. A sitting area contains a sofa, which allows the room to sleep four comfortably. As with all the rooms, there is a private bath. The Green Sage Room is spacious and simple yet contains a wing chair, writing desk, and mahogany four-poster. A time gone by is reflected in the furnishing of the Victorian Rose, with its rosewood sleigh bed, mahogany armoire, and antique rose wall coverings. Full gourmet breakfasts are served at the Yellow Rose, an invitation to sit in the formal dining room, on the front porch in front of the wrought-iron fence, or in any one of those beautiful bedrooms that you may not quite want to leave.

Rates: $90–$120
Credit Cards Accepted: Visa, MC, AMEX, Discover
Number of Guest Rooms: 5
Number of Baths: 5
Wheelchair Access: No

Pets: No
Children: If older than 12
Smoking: Yes
Senior Citizen Discount: No
Directions: Directions on brochure

Riverwalk Inn

329 Old Guilbeau
San Antonio, TX 78204
(210) 212-8300; (800) 254-4440
(210) 229-9422 Fax

Jan and Tracy Hammer, owners of the Riverwalk Inn, describe their hostelry as "a Texas tradition with a Tennessee flavor," and that sounds just about perfect to me. You can follow the old Mission Trail along the banks of the San Antonio River to the authenic nineteenth-century two-story log cabins that, combined, have become this award-winning showcase inn filled with primitive antiques, hooked rugs, and hand-sewn quilts. The five original homes were brought log by log from Tennessee, where they had been destined to become fence posts. It is the inn's mission to have guests relive the history of old San Antonio and remember Tennessee patriots such as Davy Crockett and James Bowie, who fought and died at the nearby Battle of the Alamo. All 11 rooms are named for the heroic men who fought here in the name of Texas independence. Each room has a fireplace, private bath, and phone, and most have access to the handsome 80-foot porch that extends the length of one of the two reconstructed buildings.

An "expanded" continental breakfast served by innkeeper Johnny Halpenny is apt to include kolaches, or peach-accented French toast, as well as fresh breads and a variety of morning drinks. Please beware, however, that after all this good food and friendly hospitality, you may have a hard time leaving the rocker on that wonderful front porch!

Rates: $89–$145
Credit Cards Accepted: Visa, MC, AMEX, Discover
Number of Guest Rooms: 11
Number of Baths: 11
Wheelchair Access: Yes

Pets: No
Children: No
Smoking: No
Senior Citizen Discount: Yes
Directions: See brochure

The University of Texas at Austin: Harry Ransom Humanities Research Center

Twenty-First Street and Guadalupe
P.O. Drawer 7219
Austin, TX 78705
(512) 471-9119
(512) 471-9646 Fax

Who: Front desk

When: 9:00 A.M.–5:00 P.M. Monday through Friday, 9:00 A.M.–noon Saturday

How Much: Free, but bring photo ID

Senior Citizen Discount: NA

Wheelchair Access: Yes

Directions: Call for directions

What and Where: The Humanities Research Center was established by Dr. Harry Huntt Ransom in 1957 for the purpose of acquiring primary research materials relating to modern English and American literature. When the center's present building opened in 1972, these research materials were combined with other literary and photographic special collections. By the mid-1970s, the center's holdings in modern British, American, and French literature, as well as in the history of photography, ranked among the finest in the world. The institution was renamed the Harry Ransom Humanities Research Center (HRHRC) in 1982. The Ransom Center now possesses some 36 million manuscripts, one million rare books, five million photographic images, and numerous works of art.

Authors who are particularly well represented at the Ransom Center include Graham Greene, Lillian Hellman, D. H. Lawrence, Carson McCullers, Arthur Miller, George Bernard Shaw, Anne Sexton, Dylan Thomas, Evelyn Waugh, and Tennessee Williams.

Book collections feature the libraries of James Joyce, Evelyn Waugh, the Vanderpoel Collection of Charles Dickens, and three Shakespeare first folios. The Ransom Center's single most valuable book is a Gutenberg Bible, which is housed in a special exhibition case in the Huntington Art Gallery on the first floor of the center.

The Ransom Center also maintains special exhibition rooms in the Flawn Academic Center and the Ransom Center. Among the Flawn Academic Center's permanent exhibition rooms are the J. Frank Dobie Room, which houses the noted folklorist's personal library, the Alfred A. and Blanche Knopf Library, and the reassembled work cabin of detective novelist Erle Stanley Gardner.

O. Henry Museum

409 East Fifth Street
Austin, TX 78701
(512) 472-1903

Who: Valerie Bennett

When: 12:00 noon–5:00 P.M. Wednesday through Sunday

How Much: Free; donations appreciated

Senior Citizen Discount: NA

Wheelchair Access: Yes

Directions: See brochure

What and Where: William Sydney Porter, better known to millions of readers as O. Henry, once made his home in this 1891 Queen Anne–style cottage. Short story master Porter and his family lived in the house between 1893 and 1895.

There is some question regarding the origin of Porter's pseudonym. Some claim he borrowed it from Orrin Henry, the captain of the prison guard during Porter's incarceration. Others prefer to think that the name derived from Etienne-Ossian Henry, a French pharmacist whose name was found in a reference work Porter was known to use in the prison pharmacy. Whatever the source, he employed twelve pseudonyms for his writing; several years elapsed before he settled upon O. Henry to the exclusion of the others.

You can "puntificate" if you attend the annual O. Henry Pun-off during the first weekend in May. Because of Porter's predilection for paronomasia, his tradition exists to this day. This popular and unique tournament of wordplay is "o-pun" to anyone. Contestants should contact the museum early in April to apply for registration.

Punsters as well as other visitors are requested to wear flat, soft-soled shoes to prevent damage to the original Bastrop pine floors. Advance reservations are requested for school or group tours.

Austin's Wildflower Inn

1200 West 22 $\frac{1}{2}$ Street
Austin, TX 78705
(512) 477-9639
(512) 474-4188 Fax
E-mail: kjackson@io.com
Website: http://wwwio.com/kjackson

Austin's Wildflower Inn has two owners, and one of them has four feet and a tail. Tiddle Tat, the innkeeper who just happens to be a black-and-white cat with the loudest, most engaging purr I've ever heard, is reason enough to visit this charming hostelry. If you need a cat fix, as I did, he will contentedly sit in your lap or sleep at the foot of your bed for no extra charge. In one of our many tête-à-têtes, Tiddle Tat related that he is quite the reader and, if encouraged, would read cat bedtime stories by the hour. Although he explained that he most admired the Cheshire Cat in *Alice in Wonderland,* his favorite tales are "The Cat That Walked by Himself" by Rudyard Kipling and "The King of the Cats" by Stephen Vincent Benét.

The two-legged co-owner, Kay Jackson, is a gracious third-generation Texan who enjoys "visiting with you," as they say in this great state. Tiddle Tat has delegated most of the chores to Kay—his job is to test the quilts in all the guest rooms. The two of them went about their duties while the guests feasted on Kay's delicious breakfast of croissants topped with hard-boiled eggs; avocado, tomato, and white sauce; fruit; hot cross buns; orange juice; and coffee.

We had a particularly lively bunch of companions the first morning and spent two hours exchanging Austin stories and just "visiting." During a break, Kay makes it a practice to sit down with her guests, which certainly adds to the fun. She is a descendant of David G. Burnet, erstwhile president of the Republic of Texas, so we had a rousing discussion about Texas politics. Because Wildflower is close to the University of Texas, site of the Harry Ransom Collection, Kay provides a home for international guests. A bulletin board near the stairs is crammed with thank-you letters from all over the world. A map with colored pins shows the homes of her foreign visitors.

The interior of the inn does justice to its name. There are beautiful arrangements throughout the house, and stencils of wildflowers grace the staircase. The large and comfortable Carolyn Pearl Walker Room, where I stayed, has lace curtains, a four-post oak bed, an antique oak rocker, stenciled blue walls, and a large bathroom.

Tiddle Tat is also in charge of innkeeping chores in the spacious backyard. He darts in and out among the large trees and thoughtfully points out the squirrels and, of course, the ever-present birds. He alerted me to a cardinal playing in the sprinkler and together we listened to the dulcet tones of a mockingbird serenading us. One of us was more attentive than the other.

Rates: $69–$89
Credit Cards Accepted: Visa, MC, AMEX
Number of Guest Rooms: 4
Number of Baths: 3
Wheelchair Access: No

Pets: No
Children: No
Smoking: No
Senior Citizen Discount: No
Directions: Directions on brochure

Woodburn House Bed and Breakfast

4401 Avenue D
Austin, TX 78751-3714
(512) 458-4335
(512) 458-4319 Fax
E-mail: woodburn@iamerica.net

Herb and Sandra Dickson, proprietors of the Woodburn House, know that God is in the details. They run their very professional inn accordingly. Unlike some innkeepers, the Dicksons recognize that running a B&B is not a hobby but a business. Guests will benefit as a result.

Herb, a traveling salesman for 25 years, knows what travelers need most—a comfortable, hospitable spot. The Woodburn House offers firm beds, luxurious linens, plenty of space for books and papers, computer tables, phones in the rooms, and accessible hosts to answer your questions. My favorite feature is the porches on both levels of the 1909 house. There I could read and write while pretending to live in a simpler era.

According to the Dicksons, many authors have encountered the muse on this porch and have felt the inspiration to begin writing their books here. Fellows from the nearby Harry Ransom Center often stay here. Hyde Park, the area in which the Woodburn House is located, is a neighborhood to inspire creativity, and many working authors live in the vicinity. Recognized as a National Historic Register neighborhood, Hyde Park was Austin's first suburb. Today it is a diverse neighborhood made up of grand old Victorian homes, farm-style Texas frame houses, and craftsman bungalows. Taking a stroll around this "yesterday's Main Street" is a rewarding experience. The first stop on the tour is the Avenue B Grocery, a century-old shopping spot complete with old Coke bottles. The charmingly eccentric owner delights in maintaining ties with the neighborhood's past. At the Elisabet Ney Museum on 304 East Forty-Fourth Street, you will discover the magnificent work of this German-born sculptor. Inspired by Henry David Thoreau, Ney originally came to the American West to pursue her art. Her artistry includes a lifelike statue of King Ludwig II of Bavaria, who allowed no other sculptor to create his likeness. Sarah Bernhardt, Enrico Caruso, and William Jennings Bryan frequently visited the free-spirited sculptress.

Don't buy too many sandwiches or candy bars at the Avenue B, because you'll want to save plenty of space for breakfast. Both the Dicksons are good cooks. When we were there, we had a delicious breakfast of bread pudding–French toast with peach sauce served with New Braunfels (a nearby German town) homemade sausage. One of the Dicksons always joins the guests for breakfast, adding zest to the lively discussions.

The amiable couple met on a blind date in Chicago, Sandra's hometown. "I liked Herb right away, but I couldn't understand a word he said. Even though he had been traveling for years, he never lost his heavy west Texas accent."

Eventually Herb was able to make himself understood enough to talk Sandra into leaving her beloved Chicago to move to Austin. She made her new husband promise her three things: that she could finally buy a B&B, that her mother could visit all the time, and that she could have her own sailboat. She now has everything but the sailboat. She missed the windy city at first, but Austin's friendliness won her over. "I could only remember two people who treated me rudely in an entire year in Austin, as opposed to three a day in Chicago."

Both Dicksons are involved in their neighborhood and in the process of turning their house into an inn. Their efforts have paid off, as the stately and elegant Woodburn House attests. The living room couch is so comfortable that once I had settled in, I never wanted to leave. The woodwork throughout the house is beautiful, especially highlighted by the old staircase banister.

Our room, with its rocking chair, family quilts, and hunter green sheets and towels, was extremely comfortable. The large windows offered a fine view of the giant trees in the yard. The best feature, however, was the cool ceiling fan, which enabled us to survive Austin's legendary humidity.

Many B&Bs have baskets filled with menus, but what I liked about the one at the Woodburn House is that it only contains menus the Dicksons personally approve. Five of the restaurants are in the Hyde Park neighborhood, which greatly simplified our decision-making.

Rates: $64–$89
Credit Cards Accepted: Visa, MC, AMEX
Number of Guest Rooms: 4
Number of Baths: 4
Wheelchair Access: No

Pets: No
Children: If older than 10
Smoking: No
Senior Citizen Discount: No
Directions: See brochure

Carrington's Bluff

1900 David Street
Austin, TX 78705
(512) 479-0638; (800) 871-8908

Governor's Inn

611 West Twenty-Second Street
Austin, TX 78705
(512) 477-0711; (800) 871-8901

Lisa Mugford is the proprietor of both Carrington's Bluff and the Governor's Inn. Her bustling energy serves her well, because running these two historic inns is indeed a full-time job. The Governor's Inn is named after famous Texas governors, and Carrington's Bluff has a British feel to it. Carrington's is known in Austin as the place for picture-perfect weddings in the lovely English gardens.

Mugford, a former screenwriter, could write her own screenplay about how she came to the bed-and-breakfast business. Like the majority of screenwriters, Mugford lived on promises and dreams but never saw anything produced on the silver screen. Her own story in the film industry made her decide that "cleaning toilets wasn't so bad after all." We drank tea on the spacious porch at Carrington's Bluff, and Mugford told me that she had always wanted to own a bed and breakfast. "I thought I was too young. I always assumed I'd have to wait until I was displaced from corporate America and had lots of financing to buy an inn."

After realizing she wasn't the lawyer type, Mugford dropped her plans to go to the University of Texas law school and joined the management track at the Four Seasons Hotel. Working as everything from a bus girl to a concierge was the ideal training for running a bed and breakfast.

She obviously learned well, because both inns are individual and tasteful. The first thing they have going for them is "location, location, location." Both are within walking distance of the Harry Ransom Center and minutes away from one of Austin's not-to-be-missed hike-and-bike trails. As a former Austinite, my favorite retreat is the magnificent Barton Springs. Although this immense spring-fed pool is threatened by developers, it still offers relief from Austin's hot, humid summers.

During our stay at the Governor's Inn, we relaxed on the inviting porch within view of the University of Texas's renowned tower. As for our room, it was an antique lover's delight, with a four-poster bed, antique armoire, claw-foot tub, and homemade quilt. Lace curtains, an essential ceiling fan, and beautiful wood floors complemented the room perfectly. A full breakfast of French toast, cereal, fruit, orange juice, and coffee was served buffet-style in the elegant dining room. If you're visiting the capital of Texas to combine business and pleasure, you'll be glad to know that the two inns are business-friendly, offering fax machines, answering machines, and of course, a good central location.

You might request the Writer's Cottage at Carrington's Bluff, which offers peace and quiet and, better yet, a place where you can be visited by your own private muse. Mugford recommends this retreat for writers, thinkers, or those wanting to get away from the rat race. Certainly that must include all of us!

After a day visiting the O. Henry House and the Harry Ransom Center, kick up your heels at one of Sixth's Streets many musical cafes. Austin is an internationally famous music capital.

Carrington's Bluff

Rates: $59–$99
Credit Cards Accepted: Visa, MC, AMEX, Discover, Diners Club
Number of Guest Rooms: 8
Number of Baths: 7
Wheelchair Access: No

Pets: Yes
Children: Yes
Smoking: No
Senior Citizen Discount: Upon request
Directions: Directions on confirmation letter

Governor's Inn

Rates: $59–$99
Credit Cards Accepted: Visa, MC, AMEX, Discover, Diners Club
Number of Guest Rooms: 10
Number of Baths: 10
Wheelchair Access: Yes

Pets: Yes
Children: Yes
Smoking: No
Senior Citizen Discount: Yes
Directions: See brochure

VERMONT

Naulakha:
Home of Rudyard Kipling

RR 1, Box 510
Brattleboro, VT 05301
(802) 254-6868
(802) 257-7783 Fax

Who: The Landmark Trust; Carol Barber

When: The public should be aware that this is not a museum and is not open to visitors. Instead, it is a house that is available for rent from the Landmark Trust.

How Much: $250 per night for a three-day winter weekend to about $2,125 per week in season

Senior Citizen Discount: No

Wheelchair Access: No

Directions: See brochure

What and Where: Rudyard Kipling became the ultimate chronicler of India and Africa, a man wearing khaki fatigues and elephant hat as he trekked the mountains and sweltering deserts in search of adventure. But in 1893, at the age of 28, he built a simple home for his American wife in Vermont's Connecticut River Valley.

Overlooking a meadow and the distant hills of neighboring New Hampshire, his house is comfortable and cozy. The warm, honey tones of natural wood highlight the dwelling that Kipling dubbed *Naulakha*, a Native American word meaning "great treasure." Built to resemble a ship cresting a mountainous wave, the house served as Kipling's residence for three years; during this time he wrote *The Jungle Book* and *Captains Courageous* and entertained such luminaries as Sir Arthur Conan Doyle.

The four-bedroom building has been meticulously restored by the Landmark Trust of Great Britain. Much of the original furniture is in place, and the gardens complement the views of the New England countryside. On a clear day you can even see majestic Mount Monadnock from the upstairs balcony.

Through the trust you can rent Naulakha for anywhere from three days to three weeks. Prices vary, depending on fluctuating exchange rates between the dollar and the pound, but should be approximately $250 per night for a three-day winter weekend and about $2,125 per week during the busy season.

VIRGINIA

---- ⚔ ----

Poe Museum

1914-16 East Main Street
Richmond, VA 23223
(804) 648-5523
(804) 648-8729 Fax

Who: Sean Daly for general information

When: March through October, 10:00 A.M.–4:00 P.M. Tuesday through Saturday, 12:00 noon–4:00 P.M. Sunday and Monday; November through February, 12:00 noon–4:00 P.M. Sunday through Friday, Saturday 10:00 A.M.–4:00 P.M.

How Much: $5 for adults, $3 for students

Senior Citizen Discount: $4

Wheelchair Access: Yes

Directions: The museum is located at the corner of East Main and 25th Streets in the historic Shockoe Bottom district.

What and Where: The Poe Museum provides a retreat to the early nineteenth-century Richmond of Edgar Allan Poe. The museum occupies five buildings; the center is Richmond's oldest structure, the Old Stone House, built around 1737. Behind the Old Stone House is the Enchanted Garden, with an array of flowers and other plants favored by Poe, as well as a shrine built from the bricks of the building that once housed his magazine, the *Southern Literary Messenger.*

AUTHOR'S NOTE: According to our tour guide, much of what we know about Poe was a lie created by his biographer, Lewis Griswald. We are informed today that Poe was not really an alcoholic nor a drug addict, but was sick probably with diabetes and also suffered from malnutrition due to poverty. Just recently findings linked his death with rabies!

The Henry Clay Inn

114 North Railroad Avenue
P.O. Box 135
Ashland, VA 23005
(804) 798-3100; (800) 343-4565

Fifteen miles from Richmond and the Poe Museum, the town of Ashland has an interesting history. It started as a railroad town and in 1854 was formally incorporated as

Ashland, named for the home of Henry Clay. Besides strolling around this historic burg, you could visit nearby Scotchtown, home of Patrick Henry, or take in some of the many Civil War sites.

However, you may just want to bring back the best of the Old South by rocking a spell on the grand front porch. Maybe have a mint julep or two. Or you could slip away from civilization (and its discontents) for a while in the suite, with its antique reproduction furniture, king-size canopy bed, and separate sitting room with a wet bar. Relax in the Jacuzzi tub or curl up in the balcony and re-read "Annabel Lee." If you can't unplug from the twentieth century, all 15 rooms are equipped with cable TV, computer-modem hook-ups, and telephones.

A civilized feature in the morning is coffee service prior to breakfast. Indulge in the buffet-style breakfast of hot and cold cereals, herbed cheese, and homemade bread and muffins rounded out with orange juice and tea and coffee. After *petit déjeuner*, browse through the on-site gift gallery specializing in train memorabilia and Virginia-made products. Take home a gift from the art gallery, where original works of local artists are shown. If all this shopping makes you hungry for your next meal, be advised that the inn has a nouvelle cuisine restaurant featuring Virginia wines and microbrews. After dinner, you could walk next door and take in the Randolph-Macon campus.

Rates: $80–$145
Credit Cards Accepted: Visa, MC, AMEX
Number of Guest Rooms: 15
Number of Baths: 15
Wheelchair Access: Yes

Pets: No
Children: Yes
Smoking: No
Senior Citizen Discount: Yes
Directions: See brochure

University of Virginia: Edgar Allan Poe's Room

Room 13 West Range
Charlottesville, VA 22901
(804) 924-6249

Who: Raymond Bice

When: Always open because it is viewed from outdoors

How Much: Free

Senior Citizen Discount: NA

Wheelchair Access: No

Directions: Information desk in Rotunda on McCormick Road

What and Where: You might be as surprised as I was to learn that Edgar Allan Poe, a man who died quite young and was always impoverished, was a man of many residences in many different cities. One of the places the fascinating Poe called home for a short time was the University of Virginia. He was there, as a matter of fact, a mere seven years after the university was founded in 1819 by Thomas Jefferson.

Edgar Allan Poe left his Richmond home and enrolled at the university on St. Valentine's Day 1826. He briefly lived elsewhere and later moved to this carefully preserved shrine on West Range. The room has been restored to its appearance when Poe lived here. The furniture is made up of inexpensive items that Poe might have been able to afford. There is a small table that is a replacement for the one Poe threw into his fireplace one icy winter night.

Poe was a good student and pursued courses in French, Italian, and Spanish as well as literature and ancient languages. Jefferson had an idealistic view of education: He felt he should abolish formal discipline and allow students to work on the honor system and conduct themselves in a gentlemanly fashion. Like all lofty ideals, this one didn't always work. In some of Poe's letters he describes in detail the gambling and fighting that took place, instead of education.

But whether he was studying or gambling, Poe always found time to write. His first published volume of poetry, *Tamerlane and Other Poems*, was written in this very room. He later wrote a story, "A Tale of the Ragged Mountains," about his life here. Unfortunately, Poe started hanging out with the wrong crowd, gambled heavily, and incurred debts. These expenses, on top of trying to keep up with the wealthy gentlemen in his class, were Poe's undoing. He had started university life with little money because his stingy foster father, John Allan, gave him a pittance to live on. By December 15, 1826, the strain became too much, and Poe left the university to return to Richmond. He returned "nevermore."

Guesthouses B&B, Inc. Reservation Service

P.O. Box 5737
Charlottesville, VA 22905
(804) 979-7264
(804) 292-7791 Fax

Some areas of the country have few choices for the traveler, whereas others abound with a richness of choice that leaves one stymied. Charlottesville, Virginia, is a case in point. Home to Thomas Jefferson and the University of Virginia, site of so many places historical, geographic, and literary that it boggles the mind—how can one even choose the right gas station in the midst of such abundance? Voilà! Enter Mary Hill Caperton and Guesthouses. This is a B&B reservation service nonpareil. Great attention is paid to setting, age (of house, that is, not guest), and specific interests. For instance, Mary reminded me that Jefferson himself was renowned in his day as a book collector and that he left his extensive collection as the nucleus for the Library of Congress. William Faulkner and Edgar Allan Poe had connections with this distinctive area. Mary specifically recommended Book Inn, located in Charlottesville's historic district, because it also houses an antiquarian book shop, and Riverside, in the Historic Woolen Mills district, because the host is a bibliographer who also practices bookbinding. Such attention to detail and need is to be commended—and recommended, which is exactly why I have included her service here.

Rates: $56–$200
Credit Cards Accepted: Visa, MC, AMEX
Number of Guest Rooms: Over 60
Number of Baths: Over 60
Wheelchair Access: No

Pets: No
Children: A few hosts will take children
Smoking: A few hosts will take smokers
Senior Citizen Discount: No
Directions: See brochure

Chief Seattle's Seattle

With humility, I include Chief Seattle as one of my revered authors. He was not a writer, to be sure, for Native Americans of the nineteenth century were orators, not writers. The words he spoke to the governor of the Washington Territory in 1854, however, indicate an eloquence and wisdom that are unsurpassed:

Every part of this soil is sacred in the estimation of my people. Every hillside, every valley, every plain and grove, has been hallowed by some sad or happy event in days long vanished. The very dust upon which you now stand responds more lovingly to their footsteps than to yours, because it is rich with the blood of our ancestors and our bare feet are conscious of the sympathetic touch.

We have an opportunity to experience the history of the Pacific Northwest Indians through the "Eyes of Chief Seattle" and his descendants at the Squamish Museum. Located a few miles from downtown Squamish, the museum is a short ferryboat ride from Seattle. Here you can get a glimpse of what life was like for the original inhabitants of Puget Sound before they were forced to live on the nearby reservation that has been their home for the past century and a half.

Squamish Museum

15838 Sandy Hook Road
Pulsbo, WA 98370
P.O. Box 498
Squamish, WA 98392
(360) 598-3311 Ext. 422

Who: Front Desk

When: May through September 10:00 A.M.–5:00 P.M. daily, October through April 11:00 A.M.–4:00 P.M.

How Much: $2.50 for adults, $1 for juniors ages 12 and younger

Senior Citizen Discount: $2

Wheelchair Access: Yes

Directions: See brochure

Beech Tree Manor

1405 Queen Anne Avenue NE
Seattle, WA 98109
(206) 281-7037
(206) 284-2350 Fax

The porcelain plates on the walls and the doily-covered mantel displaying turn-of-the-century bric-a-brac are but a few of the charming features that highlight the Beech Tree Manor. A stately copper beech tree welcomes visitors to the inn; a wicker rocker on the porch accents the feeling of casual elegance. Inside, the French doors and beamed ceiling provide a cosmopolitan aura. The ambience reflects the taste and personality of owner Virginia Lucero.

The Queen Anne Hill district is an eclectic, lively area on the outskirts of downtown Seattle. Beech Tree Manor is within walking distance of Seattle Center, former home of the World's Fair and now the cultural center of the city. Fine resaurants abound in this section of the city, which also offers concerts, sports events, and seasonal festivals. All are easily reached from the pleasant surroundings of the Beech Tree Manor.

Rates: $69–$105
Credit Cards Accepted: Visa, MC
Number of Guest Rooms: 7
Number of Baths: 5
Wheelchair Access: No

Pets: Yes
Children: If older than 5
Smoking: No
Senior Citizen Discount: No
Directions: See brochure

Chambered Nautilus Bed and Breakfast

5005 22nd Avenue NE
Seattle, WA 98105
(205) 522-2536; (800) 545-8459
(206) 528-0898 Fax

The porches, gabled windows, and columns of this classic three-story Georgian house reflect the characteristics of the pearly mollusk we know as the chambered nautilus. The green setting of the inn complements the connection with the sea. And yet the Nautilus, which is in the University District just minutes from downtown, also provides a breathtaking view of the Cascade Mountains. What a wonderful combination of big-city energy with natural beauty.

The living room is large enough to include a handsome grand piano; there is a mixture of English and American antiques throughout the house. Two fireplaces add their special ambience. Four of the comfortable guest rooms have private porches as well as private baths; two additional rooms share a bath. It should go without saying that the guest rooms include well-stocked bookcases.

Breakfast will typically include a choice of an award-winning apple quiche, homemade biscuits and muffins, fresh fruits and juices, cheese-baked eggs, or French toast served with a variety of homemade syrups.

Rates: $74–$105
Credit Cards Accepted: Visa, MC, AMEX
Number of Guest Rooms: 6
Number of Baths: 6
Wheelchair Access: No

Pets: No
Children: Over 12, by prior arrangement
Smoking: No
Senior Citizen Discount: No
Directions: See brochure

WISCONSIN

Canterbury Booksellers Coffeehouse and Inn

315 West Gorham
Madison, WI 53703
(608) 258-8899; (608) 258-9911 shop and coffeehouse

Chaucer fans, here's your chance. You've waited through eons of cocktail parties to deliver these memorable words, only to find that most people think you're practicing some exotic new language learned in Berlitz class:

> *Whan that Aprill with his shoures soote*
> *The droghte of March hath perced to the roote ...*
> *Thanne longen folk to goon on pilgrimages. ...*

Yes, at the Canterbury Inn you will finally get some respect. Geoffrey Chaucer is alive and well here and still delighting both the pious and the bawdy with his tales of a fourteenth-century pilgrimage. Happily, the bathroom amenities and kitchen facilities are quite modern. A long soak in a whirlpool bath, plus the promise of a homebaked breakfast, always restore the wanderer.

A medieval castle motif is evident but not overdone, and each of the six guest rooms features a mural of the particular tale with which it is associated: miller and nun, knight and wealthy widow—all ranks of early English society stride across the walls. On the nightstand is a copy of *The Canterbury Tales* (what, you expected a Gideon Bible?) in case you've forgotten who told that tale of the rewards of covetousness (it was the Pardoner), or where the Knight's noble tale of chivalry is set (an English version of ancient Greece). And better than any chocolates left on the pillow is the gift certificate for the bookstore below. Both the bookstore and coffeehouse provide lively entertainment, which includes folk music, readings, and signings.

I ask you, Pilgrims all, where else can we have all our most basic needs fulfilled at once? At the Canterbury Inn one may sleep, feed, and read—all under the same roof and practically at the same time! Chaucer himself would approve. And be sure to look around you; innkeeper Harry Bailey may be heading toward your table right now. And that worldly, deep-throated female laughter on the other side of the bookcase? Give way to your imagination, but check to see if, like the Wife of Bath, she's wearing red stockings!

Rates: $117–$290
Credit Cards Accepted: Visa, MC, AMEX
Number of Guest Rooms: 6
Number of Baths: 6
Wheelchair Access: Yes

Pets: No
Children: Yes
Smoking: No
Senior Citizen Discount: No
Directions: See brochure

SELECTED BIBLIOGRAPHY

Bellavance-Johnson, Marsha. *Mark Twain in the U.S.A.: A Guide*. Ketchum, Id.: The Computer Lab, 1991.

Bellavance-Johnson, Marsha, and Lee Bellavance-Johnson. *Ernest Hemingway in Idaho*, 2nd ed. Ketchum, Id.: The Computer Lab, 1989.

Bernal, Peggy Park. *The Huntington: Library, Art Collections, Botanical Gardens*. San Marino, Calif.: Huntington Library, 1992.

Bertsch, Werner J. *The Home and Museum of Ernest Hemingway*. Fort Lauderdale, Fla.: Pro Publishing, 1991.

Carpenter, Frederic I. *Eugene O'Neill*. Boston, Mass.: Twayne Publishers, 1964.

Cary, Pam. *Discover California*. Wheatley, England: Berlitz, 1993.

Cutler, David. *Literary Washington: A Complete Guide to the Literary Life in the Nation's Capital*, 2nd ed. Lanham, Md.: Madison Books, 1992.

Dale, Alzina Stone. *Mystery Reader's Walking Guide: New York*. Lincolnwood, Ill.: Passport Books, 1993.

Deedy, John. *Literary Places: A Guided Pilgrimage, New York and New England*. Kansas City: Sheed, Andrews and McMeel, 1978.

Denn, Wendy, and Jon Denn. *Professional Inn Guide: All Inspected and Approved*. Montvale, N.J.: Colburn Press, 1993.

Dyne, Larry van. "Passing Through." *Washingtonian*, January 1996.

Garrett, Patrick Posey. "The Way Ducks Fly." *Harps upon the Willows*. Ruston, La., 1995.

Gehres, Eleanor M., Sandra Dallas, Maxine Benson, and Stanley Cuba. *The Colorado Book*. Golden, Colo.: Fulcrum Publishing, 1993.

Gerber, Philip L. *Robert Frost*. Rev. ed. Boston, Mass.: Twayne Publishers, 1982.

Gurko, Miriam. *Restless Spirit: The Life of Edna St. Vincent Millay*. New York: Thomas Y. Crowell, 1962.

Harting, Emilie C. *A Literary Tour Guide to the United States: Northeast*. New York: William Morrow, 1978.

Hemp, Bill. *Taos: Landmarks and Legends*. Los Alamos, N. Mex.: Exceptional Books, 1996.

Herron, Don. *The Dashiell Hammett Tour*. San Francisco, Calif.: City Lights Books, 1991.

———. *The Literary World of San Francisco and Its Environs*. San Francisco, Calif.: City Lights Books, 1990.

Kaufelt, Lynn Mitsuko. *Key West Writers and Their Houses*. Sarasota, Fla.: Pineapple Press; Fort Lauderdale, Fla.: Omnigraphics, 1986.

Kennedy, Richard S. *Literary New Orleans: Essays and Meditations*. Southern Literary Studies, ed. Louis D. Rubin Jr. Baton Rouge: Louisiana State University Press, 1992.

Kinney, Kathryn, ed. *The Innkeepers' Register: Country Inns of North America*. Marshall, Mich.: Independent Innkeepers' Association, 1995.

Lane, Rose Wilder. Foreword and afterword to *On the Way Home: The Diary of a Trip from South Dakota to Mansfield, Missouri, in 1894*, by Laura Ingalls Wilder. New York: HarperCollins, 1990.

Leisner, Marcia. *Literary Neighborhoods of New York*. Washington, D.C.: Starrhill Press, 1989.

Machem, Meredith. "Home as Motivation and Metaphor in the Works of Willa Cather." Ph.D. diss., University of New Mexico, 1978.

McAleer, Edward C. *The Brownings of Casa Guidi.* New York: The Browning Institute, 1979.

McCarthy, Kevin M. *The Book Lover's Guide to Florida.* Sarasota, Fla.: Pineapple Press, 1992.

Miller, John, and Genevieve Anderson. *New Orleans Stories: Great Writers on the City.* San Francisco, Calif.: Chronicle Books, 1992.

Miller, Luree. *Literary Hills of San Francisco.* Washington, D.C.: Starrhill Press, 1992.

Morrow, Barbara Olenyik. *From Ben-Hur to Sister Carrie: Remembering the Lives and Works of Five Indiana Authors.* Indianapolis: Guild Press of Indiana, 1995.

O'Connor, Richard. *Jack London: A Biography.* Boston: Little, Brown, 1964.

O'Quinn, Trueman E., and Jenny Lind Porter. *Time to Write: How William Sidney Porter Became O. Henry.* Austin, Tex.: Eakin Press, 1986.

Poshek, Lucy, Naomi Black, Terry Berger, and Courtia Worth. *California: Southern California, Central Coast, San Francisco and the Bay Area, Gold Country, Wine Country, Northern California.* Frommer's Bed and Breakfast Guides. New York: Macmillan, 1996.

Sherman, John. *Taos: A Pictorial History.* Santa Fe, N. Mex.: William Gannon, 1990.

Soule, Sandra W. *America's Wonderful Little Hotels and Inns, 1996: U.S.A. and Canada.* New York: St. Martin's, 1995.

Stein, Rita. *A Literary Tour Guide to the United States: South and Southwest.* Americans Discover America Series. New York: William Morrow, 1979.

———. *A Literary Tour Guide to the United States: West and Midwest.* Americans Discover America Series. New York: William Morrow, 1979.

Thorpe, James. *Henry Edwards Huntington: A Brief Biography.* San Marino, Calif.: The Huntington Library, 1996.

Tomb, Eric. *California Authors.* Santa Barbara, Calif.: Bellerophon Books, 1992.

Weigle, Marta, and Kyle Fiore. *Santa Fe and Taos: The Writer's Era, 1916–1941.* Santa Fe, N. Mex.: Ancient City, 1994.

Williams, George III. *Mark Twain: Jackass Hill and the Jumping Frog.* Dayton, Nev.: Tree by the River, 1989.

Zandt, Roland van. *The Catskill Mountain House.* Hensonville, N.Y.: Black Dome, 1991.

INDEX

—•→ ☰✦☰ ←•—